The Princeton Review®

Reading and Writing Prep for the

SAT® & ACT®

The Staff of The Princeton Review

PrincetonReview.com

PENGUIN RANDOM HOUSE

The Princeton Review, Inc.
24 Prime Parkway, Suite 201
Natick MA 01760
Email: editorialsupport@review.com

Published in the United States by Random House LLC,
New York, and simultaneously in Canada by Random
House of Canada Limited, Toronto. A Penguin Random
House Company.

ISBN: 978-0-8041-2454-6

Editor: Alyssa Wolff
Production Editor: Michael Campbell
Production Coordinator: Deborah A. Silvestrini

Printed in the United States of America on partially
recycled paper.

10 9 8 7 6 5 4 3 2

First Edition

The material in this book was previously published as
English & Reading Workout for the ACT, 2nd Edition, a
trade paperback published by Random House, Inc. in
2013, and as *Reading and Writing Workout for the SAT,*
2nd Edition, a trade paperback published by Random
House, Inc. in 2011.

Editorial
Rob Franek, Senior VP, Publisher
Mary Beth Garrick, Director of Production
Selena Coppock, Senior Editor
Calvin Cato, Editor
Kristen O'Toole, Editor
Meave Shelton, Editor
Alyssa Wolff, Editorial Assistant

Random House Publishing Team
Tom Russell, Publisher
Nicole Benhabib, Publishing Manager
Ellen L. Reed, Production Manager
Alison Stoltzfus, Managing Editor

Acknowledgments

The Princeton Review would like to thank the following individuals for their help on this book:

Deborah Silvestrini, Michael Campbell, Mary Beth Garrick, Craig Patches, Melissa Hendrix, Geoff Martz, and Doug Pierce.

Contents

Part I
Orientation

Chapter 1
Introduction to the English, Reading, and Writing Tests

For more on admissions, see The Princeton Review's *The Best 378 Colleges* or visit our website, princetonreview.com

See The Princeton Review's companion book, *Math and Science Prep for the SAT & ACT.*

WELCOME

All schools that require a standardized test will take either the ACT or SAT. But which test are you going to take? For many students, the answer to this question has become, "Both!"

Since you bought this book, we assume you are already a part of this group. Maybe you're very happy with your scores on the Math and Science sections, but want to beef up your English, Reading or Writing scores. You have come to the right place. This book provides a strategic and efficient way to improve your scores specifically on English, Reading, and Writing for both the SAT and ACT exams. For a more thorough review of content and exhaustive practice, we recommend *Cracking the ACT* or *Cracking the SAT*.

THE ACT: AN OVERVIEW

Before we get started, here's a bit of background information about both of the exams, starting with the ACT. The ACT is nothing like the tests you take in school. In your English class, you may learn grammar, but do you have to fix underlined portions? You may have to read a lot, but do you write papers or take speed tests on comprehension?

All of the content review and strategies we teach in the following lessons are based on the specific structure and format of the ACT. Before you can beat a test, you have to know how it's built.

Structure

The ACT is made up of 4 multiple-choice tests and an optional Writing test.

The 5 tests are always given in the same order.

English	Math	Reading	Science	Writing
45 minutes	60 minutes	35 minutes	35 minutes	30 minutes
75 questions	60 questions	40 questions	40 questions	1 Essay

Scoring

When students and schools talk about ACT scores, they mean the composite score, a range of 1–36. The composite is an average of the 4 multiple choice tests, each scored on the same 1–36 scale. Neither the Writing test score nor the combined English plus Writing score affect the composite.

It's All About the Composite

Whether you look at your score online or wait to get it in the mail, the biggest number on the page is always the composite. While admissions' offices will certainly see the individual scores of all 5 tests (and their sub-scores), schools will use the composite to evaluate your application, and that's why in the end it's the only one that matters.

The composite is an average: let the full weight of that sink in. Do you need to bring up all 4 scores equally to raise your composite? Do you need to be a super star in all 4 tests? Should you focus more on your weaknesses than your strengths? No, no, and absolutely not. The best way to improve your composite is to shore up your weaknesses but exploit your strengths as much as possible.

> To improve your ACT score, use your strengths to lift the composite score as high as possible.

You don't need to be a rock star on all four tests. Identify two, maybe three tests, and focus on raising those scores as much as you can to raise your composite. Work on your weakest scores to keep them from pulling you down. Think of it this way: If you had only one hour to devote to practice the week before the ACT, put that hour to your best subjects.

English and Reading Scores

These two make a good pair. Every student is different, but many students begin with English as one of their higher scores and Reading as one of the lower. There is no content to review for Reading. Instead, it's entirely skill-based. If Reading ever had a child with Math, the result would be English. For the most part, English is rules-based, like Math. Review the right rules, and your score zooms. But English also requires comprehension and analysis, skills similar to those used for Reading.

Time

Time is your enemy on the ACT. You have less than a minute per question on either the English or Reading—and it's not as if there's extra time for reading the passages. The Princeton Review's strategies are all based on this time crunch. You can think of both the English and Reading tests as open-book tests, but you can neither waste all your time reading the whole book, nor skip it altogether.

STRATEGIES

You will raise your ACT score by working smarter, not harder, and a smart test-taker is a strategic test-taker. You will target specific content to review, you will apply an effective and efficient approach, and you will employ the common sense that frequently deserts many of us when we pick up a number 2 pencil.

Each test on the ACT demands a different approach, and even the most universal strategies vary in their applications. In the chapters that follow, we'll discuss these terms in greater detail customized to English and Reading.

Personal Order of Difficulty (POOD)

If time is going to run out, would you rather it run out on the hardest Reading passage or on the easiest? Of course you want it to run out on the points you are less likely to get right. On English, you can't afford to spend too long on questions you find the most time-consuming and never even get to a bunch of questions you'd nail. The trick is to know how to pick your order of passages and questions in Reading, and how to pace yourself in English to get to as many easy questions as you can.

We'll discuss in greater detail what these mean in the individual lessons, but for now, understand that you have to make smart decisions for good reasons quickly as you move through each test.

Now

Does a question look okay? Do you know how to do it? Do it *Now*.

The Best Way to Bubble In

Work a page at a time, circling your answers right on the booklet. Transfer a page worth of answers to the scantron at one time. It's better to stay focused on working questions rather than disrupt your concentration to find where you left off on the scantron. You'll be more accurate at both tasks. Do not wait to the end, however, to transfer all the answers of that test on your scantron. Go a page at a time.

Later

Will this question take a long time to work? Leave it and come back to it *Later*. Circle the question number for easy reference to return.

Never

Test-taker, know thyself. Know the topics that are your worst and learn the signs that flash danger. Don't waste time on questions you should *Never* do. Instead, use more time to answer the Now and Later questions accurately.

Letter of the Day (LOTD)

Just because you don't *work* a question doesn't mean you don't *answer* it. There is no penalty for wrong answers on the ACT, so you should never leave any blanks on your scantron. When you guess on Never questions, pick your favorite two-letter combo of answers and stick with it. For example, always choose A/F or C/H. If you're consistent, you're statistically more likely to pick up more points.

Process of Elimination (POE)

On English and Reading both, it's more important, and often easier, to know what's wrong and eliminate it rather than try to find out what's right. In fact, on English POE is so strong you may find few Never questions. It's worth the time to eliminate what's wrong and pick from what's left before you move on. On Reading, you may have absolutely no idea what you *have* read, but you'll likely know what you *haven't* and be able to eliminate a few wrong answers. Using POE to get rid of at least one or two wrong answers will substantially increase your odds of getting a question right.

Pacing

The ACT may be designed for you to run out of time, but you can't rush through it as fast as possible. All you'll do is make careless errors on easy questions you should get right and spend way too much time on difficult ones you're unlikely to get right.

To hit your target score, you have to know how many raw points you need. Your goals and strategies depend on the test and your own individual strengths.

On each test of the ACT, the number of correct answers converts to a scaled score 1–36. ACT works hard to adjust the scale of each test at each administration as necessary to make all scaled scores comparable, smoothing out any differences in level of difficulty across test dates. There is thus no truth to any one test date being "easier" than the others, but you can expect to see slight variations in the scale from test to test.

This is the scale from the free test ACT makes available on its website, act.org. We're going to use it to explain how to pick a target score and pace yourself.

English Pacing

Scale Score	Raw Score	Scale Score	Raw Score	Scale Score	Raw Score
36	75	27	62	18	41-42
35	73-74	26	60-61	17	39-40
34	71-72	25	58-59	16	36-38
33	70	24	56-57	15	33-35
32	69	23	54-55	14	30-32
31	67-68	22	52-53	13	28-29
30	66	21	49-51	12	26-27
29	65	20	46-48	11	24-25
28	63-64	19	43-45	10	22-23

For English, there is no order of difficulty of the passages or their questions. The most important thing is to finish, finding all the Now questions you can throughout the whole test.

Reading Pacing

Scale Score	Raw Score	Scale Score	Raw Score	Scale Score	Raw Score
36	40	27	30	18	18
35	39	26	29	17	16-17
34	38	25	27-28	16	15
33	37	24	26	15	14
32	36	23	24-25	14	12-13
31	35	22	23	13	11
30	34	21	22	12	9-10
29	32-33	20	20-21	11	8
28	31	19	19	10	6-7

When it comes to picking a pacing strategy for Reading, you have to practice extensively and figure out what works best for you.

Some students are slow but good readers. If you take 35 minutes to do fewer passages, you could get all of the questions right for each passage you do. Use your LOTD for the passages you don't work, and you should pick up a few additional points.

Other students could take hours to work each passage and never get all the questions right. But if you find all the questions you can do on many passages, using your LOTD on all those Never questions, you could hit your target score.

Which is better? There is no answer to that. True ACT score improvement will come with a willingness to experiment and analyze what works best for you.

Be Ruthless

The worst mistake a test-taker can make is to throw good time after bad. You read a question, don't understand it, so read it again. And again. If you stare at it really hard, you know you're going to just *see* it. And you can't move on, because really, after spending all that time it would be a waste not to keep at it, right? Actually, that way of thinking couldn't be more wrong.

You can't let one tough question drag you down. Instead, the best way to improve your ACT score is to follow our advice.

1. Use the techniques and strategies in the lessons to work efficiently and accurately through all your Now and Later questions.

2. Know your Never questions, and use your LOTD.

3. Know when to move on. Use POE, and guess from what's left.

Now move on to the lessons and learn the best way to approach the content.

Now if you're taking the SAT...

THE SAT: AN OVERVIEW

The SAT has nine scored sections, and the majority of them test your verbal skills. There are three sections of Critical Reading and a three-part Writing section, for a total of six sections that test some kind of verbal skills. This book will help you with what's tested in the Critical Reading and Writing sections, including sentence completions, critical reading, grammar, and essay writing.

The first thing you'll see on the SAT is the Writing section's essay, which will give you 25 minutes to write an essay. The Writing section also includes one 25-minute section and one 10-minute section, which test your grammar and writing skills by asking you to identify grammatical errors and improve sentences and paragraphs.

In the Critical Reading section, two 25-minute multiple-choice sections will test what ETS calls your "critical reading" abilities with sentence completions and short and long reading passages. An additional 20-minute section will have sentence completion and long reading passages, but no short reading.

Here's what the breakdown looks like:

1. One 25-minute Writing section made up of
   - 1 essay question
2. One 25-minute Writing section made up of
   - error identification questions
   - improving sentences questions
   - improving paragraphs questions
3. One 10-minute Writing section made up of only improving sentences
4. Two 25-minute Critical Reading sections made up of
   - sentence completion questions
   - short reading comprehension questions
   - long reading comprehension questions
5. One 20-minute Critical Reading section made up of
   - sentence completion questions
   - long reading comprehension questions

In this book, you will find two practice test sections: Reading Comprehension and Grammar. These practice sections are similar to what you will find on the SAT. Take them timed, just as you would on test day.

How the SAT Is Scored

There are a total of 67 Critical Reading questions on the SAT. Each correct answer earns you one "raw point." For each incorrect answer, ETS subtracts a quarter of a raw point. Your total raw score is then converted to a 200- to 800-point scale. Your Critical Reading SAT score (along with your Math and Writing SAT scores) will be sent to you (and the colleges to which you are applying) about five weeks after you take the test. These scores are reported in 10-point increments. In other words, you can get a 510 or a 520, but never a 514. The Writing sections of the test include 49 multiple-choice questions and one essay. The multiple-choice questions in the Writing section will be graded similarly to those in the Critical Reading section, with each correct answer earning you one raw point and each incorrect answer losing you a quarter of a raw point. Your essay will be scored by two separate graders for a combined raw score of 2–12 points. Through a magic conversion formula, the essay score will count for 30 percent of your score on the Writing section.

WHAT IS CONSIDERED A GOOD SCORE ON THE SAT?

The average Critical Reading SAT score is approximately 500. The average Writing score is a little lower, at 492 for the class of 2010. If you want to find out what scores are required at particular colleges, you should consult one of the college guides found in bookstores (we are partial to *The Princeton Review Guide to the Best 378 Colleges*). Bear in mind that the colleges report either average or median scores, which means that many students with SAT scores well below the published average or median scores are accepted by those colleges.

In addition, colleges consider several factors when making admissions decisions. Your SAT score is a big factor, but not the only one.

HOW YOU TRULY SCORE HIGHER ON THE SAT

The real way to improve your SAT Critical Reading and Writing scores is to answer more questions correctly. However, many students become frustrated on the Critical Reading and Writing portions of the SAT because they are not sure why the answer they pick isn't the "best" answer. This book will show you exactly how to find what ETS considers the best answer and thus help you increase the number of questions you answer correctly.

Part II
The ACT:
English

Chapter 2
The ACT
English Test

The English test is not a grammar test. It's also not a test of how well you write. In fact, it tests your editing skills: your ability to fix errors in grammar and punctuation and to improve the organization and style of five different passages. In this chapter, you'll learn the basic strategy of how to crack the passages and review three of the most heavily tested concepts—commas, apostrophes, and strategy questions.

FUN FACTS ABOUT THE ACT ENGLISH TEST

Before we dive into the details of the content and strategy, let's review what the English test looks like. Remember, the five tests on the ACT are always given in the same order and English is always first.

There are five prose passages on topics ranging from historical essays to personal narratives. Each passage is typically accompanied by 15 questions for a total of 75 questions that you must answer in 45 minutes. Portions of each passage are underlined, and you must decide if these are correct as written or if one of the other answers would fix or improve the selection. Other questions will ask you to add, cut, and re-order text, while still others will ask you to evaluate the passage as a whole.

WRITING

While the idea of English grammar makes most of us think of persnickety, picky rules long since outdated, English is actually a dynamic, adaptive language. We add new vocabulary all the time, and we let common usage influence and change many rules. Pick up a handful of style books and you'll find very few rules that everyone agrees upon. This is actually good news for studying for the ACT: You're unlikely to see questions testing the most obscure or most disputed rules. However, few of us follow ALL of even the most basic, universally accepted rules when we speak, much less when we email, text, or tweet.

The 4 C's: Complete, Consistent, Clear, and Concise

ACT test writers will never make you name a particular error. But with 75 questions, they can certainly test a lot of different rules—and yes, that's leaving out the obscure and debated rules. You would drive yourself crazy if you tried to learn, just for the ACT, all of the grammar you never knew in the first place. You're much better off with a common sense approach. That's where the 4 C's come in.

Good writing should be in *complete* sentences; everything should be *consistent*; the meaning should be *clear*. The best answer, free of any errors, will be the most *concise*.

Grammar Review

The 4 C's make sense of the rules you should specifically study. Focus your efforts on heavily tested topics that you can identify and know (or can learn) how to fix. In *Cracking the ACT 2014*, we focus on the use of punctuation and conjunctions to link complete and incomplete ideas, verbs, pronouns, apostrophes, and transitions. Can't identify what the question is testing? Apply the 4 C's.

In this book, we teach you how to crack two topics students find the trickiest: commas and apostrophes. We also teach you how to crack strategy questions, another heavily tested category.

But first, you need to know how crack the test and apply our 5-step Basic Approach.

HOW TO CRACK THE ACT ENGLISH TEST

The Passages

As always on the ACT, time is your enemy. With only 45 minutes to review five passages and answer 75 questions, you can't read a passage in its entirety and then go back to do the questions. For each passage, work the questions as you make your way through the passage. Read from the beginning until you get to an underlined selection, work that question, and then resume reading until the next underlined portion and the next question.

The Questions

Not all questions are created equal. In fact, ACT divides the questions on the English test into two categories: Usage and Mechanics, and Rhetorical Skills. These designations will mean very little to you when you're taking the test. All questions are worth the same amount of points, after all, and you'll crack most of the questions the same way, regardless of what ACT calls them. Many of the Rhetorical Skills questions, however, are those on organization and style, and some take longer to answer than other questions do. Since there is no order of difficulty of the passages or of the questions, all that matters is that you identify your *Now, Later, Never* questions and make sure you finish.

The Basic Approach

While some of the Rhetorical Skills questions come with actual questions, the majority of the 75 questions provide only 4 answer choices and little direction of what to do. So allow us to tell you *exactly* what to do.

Step 1: Identify the Topic

For each underlined portion, finish the sentence and then look at the answers. The answers are your clues to identifying what the question is testing. Let's start off with this first question.

For the first episode of its new radio

series, CBS decided to adapt H.G. Wells' *The*

War of the Worlds', the story of a Martian

invasion of Earth.

1. **A.** NO CHANGE
    B. Wells' *The War of the World's*,
    C. Wells' *The War of the Worlds*,
    D. Wells *The War of the Worlds*,

Do any of the words change? No. What is the only thing that does change? Apostrophes. So what must be the topic of the question? Apostrophes.

Always identify the topic of the question first. Pay attention to what changes versus what stays the same in the answers.

Step 2: Use POE

You may have chosen an answer for question 1 already. If you haven't, don't worry: we'll review all the rules of apostrophes later in the lesson. But let's use question 1 to learn the next step, POE. To go from good to great on the English test, you can't just fix a question in your head and then find an answer that matches. Instead, after you've identified what's wrong, eliminate all the choices that do not fix the error.

For question 1, no apostrophe is needed for *Worlds*. Cross off choices (A) and (B).

1. **A.** NO CHANGE
    B. Wells' *The War of the World's*,
    C. Wells' *The War of the Worlds*,
    D. Wells *The War of the Worlds*,

Now compare the two that remain, choices (C) and (D). Do you need the apostrophe for *Wells*? Yes, you do, so choice (C) is the correct answer. Here's where you could have messed up if you didn't use POE: if you fixed it in your head and looked for your answer, you could have missed the absence of the apostrophe in choice (D) and chosen incorrectly. POE on English isn't optional or a backup when you're stuck. You have to first eliminate wrong answers and then compare what's left.

Let's go onto the next step.

Step 3: Use the context

Even though you may struggle with time on the English test, you can't skip the non-underlined text in between questions in order to save yourself a few minutes. Take a look at this next question.

In order to tell the story in traditional
2

radio play format, however, the young

director Orson Welles decided to present it

as an unfolding news story and hired actors

to portray radio reporters "stunned" by the

horrific events unfolding before their eyes.

2. F. NO CHANGE
    G. Rather than
    H. Therefore, to
    J. Thus, to

Don't forget to apply the first two steps. The transition word is changing in the answers. Transitions test the correct direction to match the flow of the sentence. How do you know which direction to use? Read the entire sentence for the full context. The information that follows indicates Welles' direction would be a departure; the word *however* also helps. Eliminate all answers that are not *consistent* with the clues in the non-underlined portion and only choice (G) remains.

Always finish the sentence before attacking the question, and don't skip from question to question. The non-underlined text provides context you need.

Let's move on to the next step.

Step 4: Trust Your Ear, But Verify

Your ear can be pretty reliable at raising the alarm for outright errors and clunky, awkward phrasing.

You should, however, always verify what your ear signals by confirming the actual error. Steps 1 and 2 will help with that: use the answers to identify the topic, and use POE heavily.

But remember to be careful for errors your ear *won't* catch. Using the answers to identify the topic will save you there as well.

Let's try another question.

Any listener who tuned in after the
broadcast had started believed that the United
States faced an alien invasion in their skies.

3. **A.** NO CHANGE
   B. there skies.
   C. it's skies.
   D. its skies.

Need a Pronoun Refresher?
Check out the box
on page 24.

That sounded pretty good to us, how about you? But before we circle NO CHANGE and go on our merry way, look at the answers to identify the topic and confirm there is no error. Only the pronoun changes, so the question is testing pronouns. *Their* is a plural pronoun, but all countries take the singular verb and pronoun, including the *United States*. Cross off choices (A) and (B)—(B) isn't even the right type of pronoun, plural or not. Since we need a possessive pronoun, cross off choice (C) as well. Choice (D) is the correct answer.

Let's move on to our last step.

Step 5: Don't Fix What Isn't Broken
Read the next question.

In retrospect, it seems strange that so
many could have been fooled by what surely
could not have been all that convincing a
radio play.

4. **F.** NO CHANGE
   G. all that believable or credible a radio play.
   H. all convincing.
   J. considered convincing by most who listened to it.

Go to Step 1, and identify the topic. *Everything* seems to be changing in the answers for question 4: What the question is testing isn't obvious at all. You can't confirm what you can't identify, so leave "NO CHANGE," and apply the 4 C's.

Does one of the answers fix something you missed?

Does one of the answers make the sentence better by making it more concise?

If the answer to both questions is *No* for all three other answers, the correct answer choice is (F), or (A), NO CHANGE.

NO CHANGE *is* a legitimate answer choice. Don't make the mistake of assuming that all questions have an error that you just can't spot. If you use the five steps of our Basic Approach, you'll catch errors your ear would miss, and you'll confidently choose NO CHANGE when it's the correct answer.

THREE TO KNOW

We've chosen three types of questions to tackle in this book. Commas and apostrophes are heavily tested, and most students find them devilishly confusing. Strategy questions are among the most heavily tested Rhetorical Skills questions.

COMMAS

Find a reason to use a comma, not a reason to take it out. There are four reasons to use a comma on the ACT. If you can't justify a comma by one of these rules, it shouldn't be used. In other words, if a choice offers no commas, it's right unless you can name the reason to add a comma.

1. Stop Punctuation

ACT tests the correct way to link ideas in several ways. If two ideas are complete, that is they could each stand apart as a separate sentence, use Stop punctuation in between: a period, a semi-colon, a question mark, or an exclamation mark.

A comma on its own can never come in between two complete ideas. Coordinating conjunctions (*for, and, nor, but, or, yet, so*), or FANBOYS as we like to call them, can never come in between two complete ideas. But a comma paired with one of the FANBOYS becomes Stop punctuation.

Consider the following incorrect sentence:

Orson Welles wanted listeners to know the upcoming broadcast was a work of fiction he made sure that the program began with a disclaimer.

If you break this sentence in between *fiction* and *he*, you'll see that the two ideas could each be its own sentence. Two complete ideas have to be properly linked, and here are three ways to fix.

Orson Welles wanted listeners to know the upcoming broadcast was a work of fiction. He made sure that the program began with a disclaimer.

Orson Welles wanted listeners to know the upcoming broadcast was a work of fiction; he made sure that the program began with a disclaimer.

Orson Welles wanted listeners to know the upcoming broadcast was a work of fiction, and he made sure that the program began with a disclaimer.

On the ACT, any of these would be fine. In fact, ACT rarely makes you choose the nuanced difference among them. The particular FANBOYS word adds an element of direction that could affect the answer, but there is no structural difference among a period, a semi-colon, or a comma + FANBOYS. All are Stop punctuation, and all could work above.

2. Go Punctuation

An incomplete idea can't stand on its own. A comma is one way to link the incomplete idea to a complete idea to form one sentence.

Consider the following examples.

Once the broadcast began, listeners who tuned in late believed the Martian invasion to be real.

Many people reportedly tried to flee, desperate to escape certain destruction.

In the first example, *Once the broadcast began* is incomplete. In the second example, *desperate to escape certain destruction* is incomplete. In each case, a comma links the incomplete idea to the complete idea.

3. Lists

Use a comma to separate items on a list.

The chilling broadcast of War of the Worlds *was a long, tense hour for many listeners.*

Long and *tense* are both describing *hour*. If you would say *long and tense* then you can say *long, tense.*

Welles went on to direct such classics as Touch of Evil, The Magnificent Ambersons, *and* Citizen Kane.

Whenever you have three or more items on a list, always use a comma before the "and" preceding the final item. This is a rule that not everyone agrees on, but if you apply the 4 C's, the extra comma makes your meaning *Clear*. On the ACT, always use the comma before the "and."

4. Unnecessary Info

Use a pair of commas around unnecessary info.

It did not occur to Welles, however, that a great number of people would tune in after the broadcast had started.

If information is necessary to the sentence in either meaning or structure, don't use the commas. If the meaning would be exactly the same but less interesting, use a pair of commas—or a pair of dashes—around the information.

Try a few questions.

CBS hoped to draw on highbrow viewers who were more interested in serious literary [5] material, than in the songs and jokes that [5] dominated most radio programs.

5. **A.** NO CHANGE
   B. serious, literary material, than
   C. serious literary, material than
   D. serious literary material than

Here's How to Crack It

Step #1 identifies commas as the topic. Run through the 4 reasons to use a comma and see if any is in play, and use Step #2, POE. Choice (D) offers no commas at all, so find a reason to *not* pick it. There are no FANBOYS included, so it's not Stop punctuation. The two commas in choice (B) would make the information in between them unnecessary; the information is necessary, so eliminate (B). Compare choices (A) and (C). Each has one comma, but in a different placement. Is this a list? Is there a separate complete idea embedded in the sentence to link an incomplete idea to? No, and no. The correct choice is (D).

No other station reported the invasion, [6] but listeners still believed the program to be breaking news.

6. **F.** NO CHANGE
   G. invasion but listeners
   H. invasion, listeners
   J. invasion, but, listeners

Here's How to Crack It

Step #1 identifies commas as the topic. With the presence of *but*—one of our FANBOYS—decide first if the two ideas are complete on either side of , *but*. They are complete, so use Step #2, POE, to eliminate wrong answers. The correct choice is (F).

APOSTROPHES

Apostrophes make your writing more concise. They have two uses, possession and contraction.

Possession

To show possession with single nouns, add *'s*, and with plural nouns, add just the apostrophe. For tricky plurals that do not end in *s,* add *'s.*

Consider the following examples:

The career of Orson = Orson's career
The actions of the boys = the boys' actions.
The voices of the men = the men's voices.

To show possession with pronouns, never use apostrophes. Use the appropriate possessive pronoun.

His *direction.*
Their *fear.*
Its *legacy.*

Quick and Dirty Pronoun Lesson

Pronouns vary by number, gender, and case, that is, the function they perform in the sentence.

	1st person	2nd person	3rd person
Subject	I , we	you	she, he, it, they
Object	me, us	you	her, him, it, them
Possessive	my, mine, our, ours	your	her, hers, his, its, their, theirs

Contractions

Whenever you see a pronoun with an apostrophe, it's (it is) a contraction, which means the apostrophe takes the place of at least one letter.

Consider the following examples.

It is a classic. = **It's** *a classic.*
They are fans of the production. = **They're** *fans of the production.*
Who is the star of the play? = **Who's** *the star of the play?*

Because these particular contractions sound the same as some possessive pronouns, these questions can be very tricky on the ACT. You can't use your ear: you have to know the above rules.

Try a question.

While some suspect the reports were at best wildly overstated, the young <u>directors notoriety</u> soared.
₇

7. **A.** NO CHANGE
   B. director's notoriety,
   C. directors' notoriety,
   D. director's notoriety

Here's How to Crack It

Step #1 identifies apostrophes and commas as the topic. Use Step #2, POE, to eliminate wrong answers. *Director* is singular, so eliminate choice (C). The *notoriety* does belong to the *director*, so you need an apostrophe and can therefore eliminate choice (A). Between choices (B) and (D), decide if there is a reason to use a comma. In fact, the added comma would make *the young director's notoriety* unnecessary, which makes no sense. The correct choice is (D).

RHETORICAL SKILLS STRATEGY

Many Rhetorical Skills questions look just like the Usage and Mechanics questions, accompanied by four answer choices. But others feature a bona fide question. Of those, Strategy questions are among the most common and confusing.

Strategy questions come in many different forms, but they all revolve around the *purpose* of the text. Among the different types of Strategy questions, expect to see questions asking you to add and replace text, determine if text should be added or deleted, evaluate the impact on the passage if text is deleted, and judge the overall effect of the passage on the reader.

Try a question.

Many of them, assuming that what they were hearing was genuine on-the-scene coverage, panicked; <u>they were very frightened.</u>
₈

8. If all of the choices below are true, which of them best uses specific detail to convey the panic that the broadcast of *The War of the Worlds* caused?

   F. NO CHANGE.
   G. the highways were clogged with cars full of people seeking escape, and train stations were crowded with mobs willing to buy tickets to anywhere far away.
   H. many felt that they had never encountered anything as terrifying in their lives and fully believed that what they were hearing was the absolute truth.
   J. they did not stop to think that what they were hearing might be fiction; instead they leaped to the unlikely conclusion that an interplanetary invasion was indeed occurring.

Here's How to Crack It

Identify the purpose of the proposed text. According to the question, one of these choices *uses specific detail to convey the panic that the broadcast of* The War of the Worlds *caused*. We don't even need to go back into the passage: find an answer choice that fulfills the purpose. Answer choices (F), (H), and (J) all may be true, but they do not offer any *specific detail* conveying the panic. Only (G) does that, and it is our correct answer.

Try another.

In addition to directing the production, Orson Welles also acted as the narrator of The War of the Worlds. [9]

9. At this point, the writer is considering adding the following true statement:

> In the 1970s, Orson Welles made television commercials for a winery.

Should the writer add this sentence here?

  A. Yes, because it explains that Welles became famous outside of radio.

  B. Yes, because it explains why many people forgot he directed and narrated The War of the Worlds.

  C. No, because it doesn't explain why Welles stopped directing.

  D. No, because it distracts the reader from the main point of this paragraph.

Here's How to Crack It

Whenever the strategy question asks if you should add or delete new text, evaluate the reasons in the answer choices carefully. The reason should correctly explain the purpose of the selected text. Here, choice (D) is correct because there is no reason to add text that is irrelevant to the topic.

Try another.

In the 1930s, most American households
──────
10
owned a radio. After all, it seems likely that
──────
10
most people would have questioned why all of the other radio stations continued to play their regular programs if such a disaster of global proportions were underway.

10. Given that all choices are true, which one provides the best opening to this paragraph?

  F. NO CHANGE

  G. Soon the reports of panic were dismissed as overblown if not outright false.

  H. At the time of the broadcast, fears of a German invasion of Europe were growing.

  J. Today, many Americans believe in life on other planets.

Here's How to Crack It

In many strategy questions, the purpose is to add a sentence to open or close a paragraph, or tie two paragraphs together. Use the context of the paragraph, and read through to the end before deciding. Since the author provides a reason why most listeners would have doubted the story, choice (G) provides the best introduction to the paragraph.

Summary

Identify what the question is testing by changes in the answer choices.

Use POE heavily.

Don't skip the non-underlined text: use it for context.

Trust your ear, but verify by the rules.

NO CHANGE is a legitimate answer choice.

Good writing should be complete, consistent, clear, and concise.

There are only 4 reasons to use a comma. Name the reason to add a comma, and always be biased toward a choice with no commas.

Use an apostrophe with nouns to show possession. Use an apostrophe with pronouns to make a contraction. Be careful of your ear with contractions, since possessive pronouns will sound the same as a pronoun with a contraction.

Strategy questions always involve a purpose. Identify the purpose in the question, and pick an answer choice consistent with that purpose.

Chapter 3
English Practice
Drills for the ACT

DIRECTIONS: In the five passages that follow, certain words and phrases are underlined and numbered. In the right-hand column, you will find alternatives for each underlined part. In most cases, you are to choose the one that best expresses the idea, makes the statement appropriate for standard written English, or is worded most consistently with the style and tone of the passage as a whole. If you think the original version is best, choose "NO CHANGE." In some cases, you will find in the right-hand column a question about the underlined part. You are to choose the best answer to the question.

You will also find questions about a section of the passage or the passage as a whole. These questions do not refer to an underlined portion of the passage but rather are identified by a number or numbers in a box.

For each question, choose the alternative you consider best and blacken the corresponding oval on your answer document. Read each passage through once before you begin to answer the questions that accompany it. For many of the questions, you must read several sentences beyond the question to determine the answer. Be sure that you have read far enough ahead each time you choose an alternative.

PASSAGE I

What You See Isn't What You Get

Two freshmen stand, looking uncertainly at what appears to be a pleasant seating area just ahead. There are two tables: one is occupied by a young woman but the other is empty. Nevertheless, no one else seems to be considering walking in.
___1___

That's because the seating area is actually a life-size painting on the wall of one of the campus buildings.
___2___

A life-size seating area that's only a painting? That's John Pugh's specialty: large-scale public art that is available for anyone to see. He employs the trompe l'oeil, or "trick of the eye", style. His paintings are strikingly realistic, having carefully included shadows and reflections, making his paintings appear to be three-dimensional, as well as numerous details. The cafe scene includes not only the young woman and also a statute, a framed piece of art, and a small cat, peering around a corner. ☐6

1. Which of the following alternatives to the underlined portion would NOT be acceptable?
   A. However,
   B. Therefore,
   C. Even still,
   D. And yet,

2. F. NO CHANGE
   G. painting, on the wall,
   H. painting, on the wall
   J. painting; on the wall

3. A. NO CHANGE
   B. large-scale public art
   C. public art for everyone
   D. art that is public and freely available

4. F. NO CHANGE
   G. always including a variety of
   H. due to Pugh's inclusion of
   J. being careful to include

5. A. NO CHANGE
   B. nor
   C. or
   D. but

6. If the writer were to delete the question "A life-size painting that's only a painting?" from this paragraph, the essay would primarily lose:
   F. an acknowledgement that Pugh's work might seem unusual to some.
   G. a statement of the writer's central thesis for the remainder of the essay.
   H. an argumentative and persuasive tone.
   J. nothing, because the question simply confuses the main idea.

In another of his paintings, a wave looms across the entire front of a building. The painting is immense, the wave looks like it's about to crash, and three children appears to stand

directly in its path. Being life-size and incredibly life-like, a group of firefighters ran over to save the "children" shortly before the piece was completed. When the men got close enough to realize it was only a painting, they had a good laugh. No one seems to mind being fooled by Pugh's paintings. Most people, like the firefighters, are just impressed by Pugh's skill. 9

Pugh believes that by creating public art, he can communicate with a larger audience than if his art were in a gallery. Many of his pieces, including the café scene described above, use the existing architecture. One of his other pieces

created the illusion that part of a building's wall has collapsed, revealing an ancient Egyptian storeroom in the middle of Los Gatos, California. Like the café scene, the Egyptian scene includes a human figure. [A] In this case, however, the woman is not part of the scene. [B] Instead, she appears to be a passer-by, peering in to the revealed room. [C] Cities around the world have commissioned works from Pugh. [D] It is Pugh's ability to create an apparent mystery in the middle

7. A. NO CHANGE
   B. appeared
   C. appear
   D. was appearing

8. F. NO CHANGE
   G. Stopping their truck in the middle of traffic,
   H. Appearing young enough to be swept away,
   J. Like so many of Pugh's other works,

9. If the writer were to remove the quotation marks around the word "children," the paragraph would primarily lose:
   A. an explanation of why the firemen were so concerned about the wave.
   B. a rhetorical device that lessens the reader's fear.
   C. a way to distinguish between the painted wave and the real children.
   D. emphasis on the fact that the children were painted, not real.

10. Given that all the choices are true, which one best conveys the theory behind Pugh's method as discussed in the remainder of the paragraph?
    F. NO CHANGE
    G. Pugh prefers incorporating his work into the pre-existing environment to simply adding his art without regard for its surroundings.
    H. Drawing his inspiration from many different cultures, Pugh enjoys startling the viewer by placing objects in an unexpected context.
    J. The firefighters may not have been upset at Pugh's trick but they were certainly startled, just like so many other people who see Pugh's work.

11. A. NO CHANGE
    B. is creating
    C. creates
    D. creating

of everyday life that makes his work speak to so <u>much</u> people.
₁₂
After all, who doesn't appreciate being tricked once in a while?

12. F. NO CHANGE
    G. more
    H. most
    J. many

13. If the writer were to divide this paragraph into two, the most logical place to begin the new paragraph would be at Point:

    A. A.
    B. B.
    C. C.
    D. D.

Question 14 asks about the preceding passage as a whole.

14. Suppose the writer's goal had been to write a passage exploring some of the current trends in the art community. Would this essay accomplish that goal?

    F. Yes, because it looks at a variety of styles popular among muralists throughout the Los Angeles area.
    G. Yes, because is considers some of the reasons for Pugh's preference for large-scale public art.
    H. No, because it only explores Pugh's artistic vision without considering the broader context of the art world.
    J. No, because it details a number of incidents in which people have been confused by Pugh's artwork.

Leaving the Nest

My mother flew out with me and stayed for a few days, to make the transition easier for me. We went shopping and bought odds and ends for my dorm room—pillows, small decorative items, even a few pots and pans—to make it feel [15] more like home. It felt more like a vacation than anything else.

Then suddenly her brief stay was over. Her plane was leaving for San Juan, and I realized I wasn't going with her. She was going home, but I already was home. This strange new city was my home now. Sitting on my bed in the dorm room that remained half-empty, it hit me. [16] I had just turned eighteen. I was about to start college in a new place, with a new language, a new culture. I had just said my first real farewell to a mother whom I had never before been away from for more [17] than a weekend. I had to learn how to live on my own, with mi

familia so many miles away and me all by myself. [18]

During high school, I had fantasized about moving to the United States someday. I was born in a sleepy, rural village in southern Puerto Rico. My high school class had fifty people in it, and the small town where I grow up was a very close-knit [19] community. I had spent hours imagining what it would be like to be surrounded not by a few dozen people but by a few million.

Living in such a small town, I was used to knowing everyone and having everyone know me. [20] The very first

---

15. A. NO CHANGE
   B. pans; to make
   C. pans: to make
   D. pans. To make

16. F. NO CHANGE
   G. As I sat on the bed in my half-empty dorm room,
   H. Nervously looking around the half-empty dorm room,
   J. Looking around the half-empty dorm room from my bed,

17. Which of the following choices is most logically supported by the first part of the sentence?
   A. NO CHANGE
   B. who had always done my laundry, prepared my meals, and kissed me goodnight.
   C. whom I hoped was having a pleasant flight back to San Juan and then on to our village.
   D. who had herself spent some years living in the United States in her twenties, before I was born.

18. F. NO CHANGE
   G. and no one with me.
   H. not with me any more.
   J. DELETE the underlined portion and end the sentence with a period.

19. A. NO CHANGE
   B. grew
   C. grown
   D. growth

20. Given that all the choices are true, which provides the best transition to the topic discussed in the rest of the paragraph?
   F. NO CHANGE
   G. The idea of being surrounded by so many people, and being able to meet and talk with any of them seemed like a dream come true.
   H. When the time came to apply to colleges, I picked several, all in major metropolitan areas in the continental United States.
   J. I had considered applying to colleges in San Juan but decided that it was still too close to home, too familiar, too easy.

acceptance received by me was from this school, located in the
                    ___
                    21
middle of a city with millions of inhabitants. My parents

were so proud that I get this opportunity to see the world
                         ___
                         22
outside of our village. They had spent enough time outside

of Puerto Rico in the United States to know that the English
                   _____
                          23
language was not the only thing that was different. We
celebrated the weekend before I left, inviting all the neighbors

over to my parents home. We played music and ate and danced
           _____
              24

past midnight. ☐25

As the memory faded; I looked around my new room
                _____
                      26
again. Sure, it was small and a little bit dingy. True, I didn't
know anyone yet. None of that mattered, though. I had finally
made it. My new roommate would be arriving the next day.
Hopefully she would be a new friend and even if she wasn't,
my classes were starting in a few days. I had literally millions
of people to meet; surely a few of them would become my new
friends. I smiled, suddenly feeling nervous but excited, not
                                  _____
                                          27

21. A. NO CHANGE
    B. acceptance I received
    C. acceptance, I received,
    D. acceptance, receiving by me

22. F. NO CHANGE
    G. will get
    H. was getting
    J. had to get

23. The best placement for the underlined portion would be:
    A. where it is now.
    B. after the word time.
    C. after the word language.
    D. after the word different (and before the period).

24. F. NO CHANGE
    G. parents's
    H. parent's
    J. parents'

25. At this point, the writer is considering adding the following
    true statement:

    My favorite dance has always been la bomba.

    Should the writer make this addition here?
    A. Yes, because it adds a detail that helps explain the per-
       sonality of the narrator.
    B. Yes, because it provides a smooth transition to the fol-
       lowing paragraph.
    C. No, because it gives the false impression that the narrator
       will study dance in college.
    D. No, because it would be an unnecessary digression from
       the main point of the paragraph.

26. F. NO CHANGE
    G. faded, and I looked
    H. faded, I looked
    J. faded. I looked

27. Which of the following alternatives to the underlined portion
    would NOT be acceptable?

    A. excitement nervous
    B. nervously excited
    C. nervous excitement
    D. excitedly nervous

lonely any more. I was eighteen, in the city, and had to face
                                                           ___
                                                           28

the world. ☐29

28. Which choice most effectively expresses the narrator's confidence about her new life?

   F. NO CHANGE
   G. ready to take on
   H. all alone in
   J. about to enter

29. The writer is considered adding a concluding sentence here. Which of the following would be most logical and best express one of the main ideas of the essay?

   A. Still, I knew I would miss Puerto Rico and my friends I had left behind.
   B. Little did I know that my new roommate would become a lifelong friend.
   C. My dreams of living in the big city were finally going to become a reality.
   D. I hoped that my classes would be as exciting as my move had been.

NO TEST MATERIAL ON THIS PAGE.

Dual Personalities

[1]

When Lois Lane finds herself in serious danger, she looks
to Superman for help. When she needed help with an article,
_____
30
on the other hand, she calls on Clark Kent. Of course, as the
reader knows, the two men are actually the same person.

[2]

The tradition of giving superheroes alternate names and
characters, or "alter-egos" goes back as far as superhero stories
do. Today, when it's a commonplace writing technique.
_____
31
Batman fights crime by night, but he poses as millionaire Bruce

Wayne at day. Spider-Man protects the streets of New York—
_____
32

when he's not busy going to school as Peter Parker. [33]

[3]

Each of the superheroes have something in his (or her)
_____
34
back-story to explain the dual character. They all have a few
things in common too, though. Superheroes have a certain
image—the costume and the name, for example; that helps
_____
35

30. F. NO CHANGE
G. in need of
H. she was needing
J. needed

31. A. NO CHANGE
B. where
C. because
D. DELETE the underlined portion.

32. F. NO CHANGE
G. for
H. by
J. DELETE the underlined portion.

33. At this point, the writer is thinking about adding the following
true statement:

> Wonder Woman, on the other hand, is always herself,
> since she comes from a tribe of warrior women.

Should the writer make this addition here?

A. Yes, because it provides a balance for the previous examples of Batman and Spider-Man.
B. Yes, because it emphasizes the author's earlier claim that
the alter-ego is commonplace.
C. No, because it strays from the primary focus of the passage by providing irrelevant information.
D. No, because it poses the unnecessary hypothetical that
no superhero really needs an alternate identity.

34. F. NO CHANGE
G. has
H. is having
J. are having

35. A. NO CHANGE
B. for example,
C. for example.
D. for example—

them maintain their authority. If Batman didn't fight crime, he would probably do something else to deal with his past.
<u>36</u> Peter

Parker isn't a very awe-inspiring <u>name, but</u> Spider-Man is. At
<u>37</u>
the same time, the hero often has friends and family members

who are somehow completely unaware of their loved <u>ones'</u>
<u>38</u>
other identity. <u>Providing</u> the superheroes with everyday names
<u>39</u>

and jobs helps in <u>their</u> attempts to fit in with the people around
<u>40</u>
them.

[4]

Stan <u>Lee, creator of Spider-Man,</u> and dozens of other
<u>41</u>
superheroes, has often commented on what he believes makes

a true hero. His opinion is that in order for the reader to care

about the hero, the hero has to be flawed. <u>Do you agree with</u>
<u>42</u>
<u>him? According to Lee,</u> without some kind of flaw, the hero
<u>42</u>

wouldn't really seem human. Lee builds <u>tension, in his stories,</u>
<u>43</u>
by putting those human flaws and the hero's quest into conflict.

It is that tension, perhaps, that makes his storylines so gripping.

Even Superman, the least "normal" of all the heroes, has to

deal with the tension between his love for Lois Lane and her

36. Given that all the choices are true, which one provides the best support for the statement in the preceding sentence?
    F. NO CHANGE
    G. Batman, who lost his parents when he was young, were younger, he might have a harder time.
    H. Batman were just a regular-looking man, it would be harder for him to strike fear into the heart of criminals.
    J. Batman needed to, he could probably fight criminals without his gadgets since he knows several martial arts.

37. Which of the following alternatives to the underlined portion would NOT be acceptable?
    A. name; on the other hand,
    B. name, because
    C. name, although
    D. name; however,

38. **F.** NO CHANGE
    G. one's
    H. individuals
    J. individuals'

39. **A.** NO CHANGE
    B. Assuming
    C. Offering
    D. Allowing for

40. **F.** NO CHANGE
    G. it's
    H. his
    J. one's

41. **A.** NO CHANGE
    B. Lee creator of Spider-Man,
    C. Lee creator of Spider-Man
    D. Lee, creator of Spider-Man

42. Which choice provides the most logical and effective transition to the rest of this paragraph?
    F. NO CHANGE
    G. Why would anyone want a hero to be less than perfect?
    H. Are you familiar with Lee's various characters?
    J. What kind of flaw could a superhero have?

43. **A.** NO CHANGE
    B. tension in his stories
    C. tension in his stories,
    D. tension, in his stories

love for Superman, not Clark Kent. [44]

44. The writer is considering deleting the preceding sentence. Should this sentence be kept or deleted?

    F.   Kept, because it provides a specific example of the theory being discussed throughout the paragraph.

    G.   Kept, because it demonstrates that that the ultimate superhero will not seem human under any circumstances.

    H.   Deleted, because it takes away from the persuasiveness of the point made in the previous sentences.

    J.   Deleted, because it switches the focus from the more "human" superheroes to the "least" human of them.

Question 45 asks about the preceding passage as a whole.

---

45. While reviewing this essay, the writer thinks of some additional information and writes the following sentence:

> Even though many readers feel that Lane's ignorance is hard to believe, the Clark Kent persona provides a valuable, and time-honored, element to the Superhero story: the alter-ego.

If the writer were to include this sentence in the essay, the most logical place to add it would be after the last sentence in Paragraph:

    A.   1.
    B.   2.
    C.   3.
    D.   4.

NO TEST MATERIAL ON THIS PAGE.

Curly Hair: The circular trend

Curly hair: sometimes it's seen as a blessing, and sometimes as a curse. Passing trends, which can last a day or a decade, typically influence hairstyles, which can vary <u>dramatically; every</u> bit as much as clothing. Some segment
46
of the population will therefore always be fighting the natural tendency of their hair, unless the fashion becomes natural hair.

47 In the 1950s, curls were in, and the average American woman spent countless hours pinning, rolling, and curling her hair every week. Without blowdryers or curling irons, women were left with few options, maintaining properly stylish

hair-dos to <u>work hard and a great deal of time.</u> By the mid-
48
1960s, a lot of women started to wonder whether all that work was really necessary. Suddenly, natural hair was all the rage. Women began to grow <u>they're</u> hair out and allow it to remain in
49
its natural state, whether curly or straight. For a brief moment, it looked like women would be able to embrace their natural hair, whether straight or curly, light or dark, or <u>having length or</u>
50
<u>being short.</u>
50

The change was <u>short-lived, however, and</u> didn't last for
51
long, perhaps unsurprisingly. The desire to have long, natural hair somehow turned into the desire to have long, straight hair. During the 1970s, the movie and television <u>star Farrah Fawcett</u>
52   52
popularized a look that involved long hair that seemed naturally straight and feathered—cut into layers designed to frame the

46. F. NO CHANGE
   G. dramatically, being every
   H. dramatically, every
   J. dramatically. Every

47. Given that all of the following statements are true, which one, if added here, would most clearly and effectively introduce the main subject of this paragraph?
   A. Some people don't care for curly hair because it is considered more difficult to style than straight hair is.
   B. As far back as the Renaissance, people have faked having curly hair by wearing wigs and using curlers.
   C. Curly hair has bounced in and out of the American fashion scene for at least the last fifty years.
   D. Clothing styles also change frequently, and sometimes influence hairstyles in a direct, easily visible way.

48. F. NO CHANGE
   G. was hardly work
   H. with hard work
   J. by working hard

49. A. NO CHANGE
   B. their
   C. there
   D. her

50. F. NO CHANGE
   G. and regardless of length.
   H. which can be long or short.
   J. long or short.

51. A. NO CHANGE
   B. wasn't fated to continue, though, so it
   C. predictably enough failed to stick and
   D. DELETE the underlined portion.

52. F. NO CHANGE
   G. star, Farrah Fawcett
   H. star, Farrah Fawcett,
   J. star Farrah Fawcett,

face—yet slightly messy. [53] Women who had

naturally curly hair <u>were suddenly</u> the ones to suffer now, as
₅₄
they painstakingly ironed their hair to achieve that "natural"
look. The fashions of the 1980s, however, turned everything
around yet again. Big was in, and that went for hair as well as
clothes. Curly hair became incredibly popular, and <u>the main</u>
₅₅
<u>fashion goal was to make one's hair as curly and as big as</u>
₅₅
<u>possible.</u> Women who didn't have natural curls got "permanent
₅₅

waves," or "perms" to create the rampant curls <u>modeled by</u>
₅₆
their pop icons, such as Cyndi Lauper and Gloria Estefan.

[1] By the middle of the 1990s, however, the perm had
lost its appeal, and straight hair was back in fashion where it
remains today. [2] Some <u>commentator's</u> have recently claimed
₅₇
that curly hair is making a comeback, but only time will
tell. [3] Instead of using an iron, women can have their hair
chemically straightened in a sort of "reverse perm." [4] While
it's hard to know what the trend of tomorrow will be, one thing
seems certain: no style lasts forever. [58]

53. The writer is considering deleting the phrase "cut into layers designed to frame the face" from the preceding sentence (adjusting the punctuation as needed). Should this sentence be kept or deleted?

    A. Kept, because it contrasts the style popularized by Fawcett with earlier styles.

    B. Kept, because it defines the word used immediately before the phrase.

    C. Deleted, because it fails to adequately explain the term it is intended to modify.

    D. Deleted, because it digresses from the main point of the paragraph.

54. **F.** NO CHANGE
    G. suddenly we're
    H. sudden were
    J. sudden we're

55. **A.** NO CHANGE
    B. the curlier, the better.
    C. it.
    D. it didn't seem possible to have hair that was too curly, or too big to be fashionable.

56. Which of the following alternatives to the underlined portion would NOT be acceptable?

    F. worn
    G. displayed
    H. imitated
    J. popularized

57. **A.** NO CHANGE
    B. commentators
    C. commentators'
    D. commentators's

58. For the sake of the logic and coherence of this paragraph, Sentence 3 should be placed:

    F. where it is now.
    G. before Sentence 1.
    H. after Sentence 1.
    J. after Sentence 4.

Question 59 asks about the preceding passage as a whole.

59. Suppose the writer had been instructed to write an essay discussing modern attitudes towards curly hair. Would this essay meet that requirement?

    A. Yes, because it explains why some women prefer to wear their hair straight, regardless of current fashions.

    B. Yes, because it analyzes the reasons behind changes in fashion that affect the popularity of curly hair.

    C. No, because it focuses more on the changeability of fashions than the attitudes towards them.

    D. No, because it focuses primarily on the popularity of straight hair and the effort of style maintenance.

NO TEST MATERIAL ON THIS PAGE.

Marie Curie: Physicist, Chemist, and Woman

Marie Curie is famous today for two main reasons: her scientific discoveries and her defiance of gender stereotypes. She, along with her husband, identified two new elements, <u>polonium and radium.</u> She then coined the term "radioactive"
₆₀

60. The writer is considering deleting the underlined phrase and adjusting the punctuation accordingly. If the phrase were removed, the paragraph would primarily lose:

   F. a specific detail that provides information about the result of some of Curie's research.

   G. an explanation of how Curie was able to make such a variety of important scientific discoveries.

   H. information that identifies the reason Curie was awarded two Nobel prizes.

   J. a definition of radioactivity included by the writer and necessary to the paragraph as a whole.

and developed a theory to explain the phenomenon. <u>Curie first</u>
₆₁
<u>began to research radioactivity after noticing that the amount</u>
₆₁
<u>of radiation produced by a sample depended wholly on the</u>
₆₁
<u>quantity of uranium in the sample.</u>
₆₁

61. Given that all of the choices are true, which provides the most effective transition from this paragraph into the rest of the essay?

   A. NO CHANGE

   B. Due to her discoveries, she was both the first woman to receive a Nobel Prize and the first person to receive two Nobel Prizes, though her road to success was paved with difficulties.

   C. Although physics and chemistry are treated as separate fields, like so many other branches of science, the two are so interconnected in some areas that it can be difficult to tell them apart.

   D. Curie's husband, Pierre, was also a noted scientist who wrote several famous pieces on magnetism, including one that detailed the relationship between temperature and paramagnetism.

Curie was proficient in the fields of physics and chemistry, though her education was somewhat <u>unusual, which prevented</u>
₆₂
her from attending university due to a lack of money, Curie
₆₂
initially studied in a laboratory run by her cousin. Determined to pursue her love of science, Curie eventually enrolled at the University of Paris, <u>where she</u> later became the first female
₆₃
professor.

62. F. NO CHANGE

   G. unusual, prevented

   H. unusual. Prevented

   J. unusual prevented her

63. A. NO CHANGE

   B. like

   C. when

   D. DELETE the underlined portion.

While Curie is widely given recognition and credit for discovering radioactivity, this is not entirely accurate. Henri Becquerel, a French scientist, has that honor. When Curie made her discovery, Becquerel had already saw that rays, functioning much like X-rays but produced by uranium salt, existed; however, he did not identify the underlying process. Becquerel of radioactivity was performing

experimental involving photographic paper, and the discovery was accidental. He realized that something was exposing the photographic paper to rays even before he placed the paper in the sunlight. Nevertheless, further experiments revealed that the substance emitting rays was the fluorescent substance, potassium uranyl sulfate.

However, Becquerel didn't identify the underlying scientific principal, namely, that the rays were produced not by a molecular interaction but by the atom itself. Curie was

the first to make this discovery; it was she that isolated, and identified radium and polonium. The earliest scientist to realize that there was an element in the fluorescent substance more reactive than uranium, Curie dedicated the next twelve years to developing a method for isolating that substance,

which was not yet known but later came to be identified and is now called "radium."

64. **F.** NO CHANGE
G. credited and acknowledged as the person responsible for
H. generally credited with
J. appreciated often as deserving credit and recognition for

65. **A.** NO CHANGE
B. has already seen
C. had already seen
D. has already saw

66. The most logical placement of the underlined portion would be:

F. where it is now.
G. after the word performing.
H. after the word paper.
J. after the word discovery.

67. **A.** NO CHANGE
B. an experimental
C. experimentally
D. an experiment

68. **F.** NO CHANGE
G. Subsequently, further
H. Further
J. In contrast, further

69. **A.** NO CHANGE
B. principle namely,
C. principal namely,
D. principle: namely,

70. **F.** NO CHANGE
G. isolated
H. isolated it
J. isolated—

71. **A.** NO CHANGE
B. uranium;
C. uranium
D. uranium:

72. **F.** NO CHANGE
G. we now know as radium.
H. scientists and laypeople alike are familiar with today under the name "radium."
J. people in the present day refer to under the name of "radium."

Curie was progressive for a chemist; much less for a
₇₃

woman. Women in science would of often had a difficult
₇₄

time, and Curie was no exception. She was refused a position

at Krakow University due to her gender, and was ultimately

denied membership in the French Academy of Sciences.

However, the general consensus is that Curie was not bitter

about these rejections. Instead, she worked as hard as she
₇₅

could even when she wondered whether she would ever be
₇₅

recognized. She was a woman who knew her own worth, even
₇₅

when others did not: a trait as valuable today as during the

eighteenth century.

73. **A.** NO CHANGE
 B. chemist,
 C. chemist; moreover,
 D. chemist so

74. **F.** NO CHANGE
 G. might of
 H. have
 J. has

75. Given that all the choices are true, which one provides the most consistent description of Curie's personality as described in this paragraph?

 A. NO CHANGE
 B. became somewhat reclusive in her later years, preferring her work to society.
 C. spent many years in her eventually successful attempt to identify the source of Becquerel's mysterious rays.
 D. was generally described by those who knew her as persistent, friendly, and humble.

NO TEST MATERIAL ON THIS PAGE.

DIRECTIONS: In the five passages that follow, certain words and phrases are underlined and numbered. In the right-hand column, you will find alternatives for each underlined part. In most cases, you are to choose the one that best expresses the idea, makes the statement appropriate for standard written English, or is worded most consistently with the style and tone of the passage as a whole. If you think the original version is best, choose "NO CHANGE." In some cases, you will find in the right-hand column a question about the underlined part. You are to choose the best answer to the question.

You will also find questions about a section of the passage or the passage as a whole. These questions do not refer to an underlined portion of the passage but rather are identified by a number or numbers in a box.

For each question, choose the alternative you consider best and blacken the corresponding oval on your answer document. Read each passage through once before you begin to answer the questions that accompany it. For many of the questions, you must read several sentences beyond the question to determine the answer. Be sure that you have read far enough ahead each time you choose an alternative.

Passage I

A Day in the City

When I woke up this morning, I made myself a bowl of cereal and sat, listening to the traffic. Some of my friends ask
$\underline{}$
$_{1}$
me how I can stand living somewhere so noisy. It's true that

there's always some kind of noise in my neighborhood—taxi
$\underline{}$
$_{2}$
drivers honking their horns, kids playing their radios so loud
$\underline{}$
$_{2}$
that the bass makes my teeth vibrate, or people yelling in the
street. I know that some people wouldn't like it, but to me,
these are the sounds of life. $\boxed{3}$

It's Saturday, so this morning I decided to go to the park.
$\underline{}$
$_{4}$
The train is the fastest way to go but I took the bus instead.

When I ride the bus, you get to see so much more of the
$\underline{}$
$_{5}$
city. It can be kind of loud on the bus, with some people talking

1. Which of the following alternatives to the underlined portion would NOT be acceptable?

 A. cereal and sat while listening
 B. cereal, sat listening
 C. cereal, sat, and listened
 D. cereal before sitting and listening

2. F. NO CHANGE
 G. neighborhood, taxi drivers honking
 H. neighborhood; taxi drivers honking
 J. neighborhood taxi drivers honking

3. If the writer were to delete the preceding sentence, the essay would primarily lose:

 A. a contrast to the positive tone of the essay.
 B. an explanation for the narrator's trip to the park.
 C. information that shows the author's attitude toward the place she lives.
 D. nothing at all; this information is not relevant to the essay.

4. F. NO CHANGE
 G. Since today it is finally
 H. Allowing for it being
 J. The day of the week is

5. A. NO CHANGE
 B. one is riding
 C. you ride
 D. they are riding

on their phones, others chatting sociable with their friends, and
others playing music. Just like the traffic's sounds, though, the

noise on the bus represents people working, relaxing, and living.

      Once I get to the park, I pick a bench over near the play
area. The city added the bench so they could play while their
parents sit

nearby, obviously I like to sit there because there's a great big
oak tree for shade. I can see and hear almost

everything from there. I sit there watching, and listening to the
people around me. People-watching is one of my favorite

things to do, I like listening even better. The park is the best
place because you get to see and hear everything. The only
problem is that there's so much to see and hear!

      That's why people get so tired after a little while. That way,
I can pay more attention to the sounds and not get distracted by
what I see. With my eyes closed, I can pick out parts of

two old men's familiar conversation. One of them is telling the
other about something his grandson said. I can't hear the rest,
but whatever it was must have been hilarious because his

friends' laugh is so loud, it startles me.

      Later that night, after I've ridden the bus back home, I think
about those old men. When I'm old, I hope that I too will have
a friend who will sit in the park with me, and who will enjoy
listening to the sounds of the city as much as I do.

6. **F.** NO CHANGE
   G. sociably, with
   H. sociable with,
   J. sociably with

7. **A.** NO CHANGE
   B. people, working;
   C. people; working
   D. people, working,

8. **F.** NO CHANGE
   G. kids
   H. because they
   J. that it

9. **A.** NO CHANGE
   B. nearby.
   C. nearby,
   D. nearby, because

10. **F.** NO CHANGE
   G. there, watching, and listening,
   H. there, watching and listening
   J. there watching and listening,

11. **A.** NO CHANGE
   B. do, nevertheless,
   C. do, but
   D. do, however

12. Which choice most effectively introduces the idea discussed in this rest of the paragraph?

   F. NO CHANGE
   G. I close my eyes
   H. the park is interesting
   J. some people like quiet

13. Which choice would emphasize the narrator's curiosity and interest in the old men's conversation in the most logical and effective way?

   A. NO CHANGE
   B. noisy chatter.
   C. animated discussion.
   D. entertaining stories.

14. **F.** NO CHANGE
   G. friends's
   H. friends
   J. friend's

Question 15 asks about the preceding passage as a whole.

15. Suppose the writer's assignment was to write an essay analyzing one reason people might choose to live in a large city. Would this essay fit that description?

   A. Yes, because it discusses the convenience of public transportation.
   B. Yes, because it explains the narrator's enjoyment of one of the city's parks.
   C. No, because it focuses on one detail of city living that most people dislike.
   D. No, because it only discusses why the narrator prefers listening to watching.

NO TEST MATERIAL ON THIS PAGE.

Passage II

The Bridge They Said Couldn't Be Built

Visible in the fog as well as the sun, the Golden Gate Bridge is a symbol of San Francisco. The bridge was once famous for having the longest suspension span in the world; even today, its suspension span is the second longest in the United States. It is open to cars and pedestrians alike, and has only been shut down three times in that seventy-year history. The amount of concrete needed to anchor the bridge was enough to construct

a sidewalk five feet wide, all the way from San Francisco to New York City. Since the Golden Gate opened, almost two billion cars have crossed the bridge and it has been featured in countless movies.

The fame of the Golden Gate Bridge wasn't always assured. [A] When Joseph Strauss announced his intention of building the bridge, people flocked to support him. A combination of factors made building a bridge in that location difficult: cold, stormy seas below, foggy and damp weather, and winds that regularly reach speeds of 60 miles per hour.

[B] After two years of discussion, the voters approved a bond: which would raise $35 million, all dedicated to building the

bridge. Even then, there were many skeptics whom believed that it couldn't be done.

Strauss, a veteran bridge builder, refused to give up. Construction began in 1933 and ended in 1937, and lasted a

16. **F.** NO CHANGE
    G. their
    H. its
    J. DELETE the underlined portion.

17. **A.** NO CHANGE
    B. sidewalk five feet wide
    C. sidewalk—five feet wide
    D. sidewalk, five feet wide

18. Which choice provides the conclusion that relates to the rest of the paragraph in the most logical way?
    F. NO CHANGE
    G. many said it was impossible.
    H. some admired his vision.
    J. he had already built other bridges.

19. **A.** NO CHANGE
    B. bond, which
    C. bond; which
    D. bond which

20. **F.** NO CHANGE
    G. that
    H. who
    J. DELETE the underlined portion.

21. **A.** NO CHANGE
    B. being completed by 1937,
    C. ending four years later
    D. DELETE the underlined portion.

little more than four years. On May 28, 1937. The bridge, arching grandly over the water, opened to pedestrians. More than 200,000 people walked across the bridge that day to celebrate the grand achievement.

[C] By the time it was completed, the bridge had exceeded everyone's expectations. Not only was it built, it was also ahead of schedule and under budget. To top it off,

it was beautiful. Nevertheless, the Golden Gate Bridge is considered an artistic masterpiece, recognizable all around the world. At its highest point, the bridge rises 746 feet into the air— 191 feet taller than the Washington Monument.

The name "Golden Gate" refers not to the color of the bridge, which is actually orange, but to the stretch of water below, where the San Francisco Bay connects to the Pacific Ocean. [D] The color, called "International Orange," was chosen partly because it matched the natural surroundings and

partly because it would allow the bridge to remain visible on foggy days. ⟨27⟩

Today, the bridge is divided into six lanes for cars, and pedestrian lanes for people and bicycles. On sunny days, crowds of people flock to the bridge to enjoy the view. Rising out of the sea like a vision from a dream, the Golden Gate Bridge captures the imagination today, just as it did when

22. F. NO CHANGE
    G. On May 28, 1937; the bridge arching grandly
    H. On May 28, 1937, the bridge, arching grandly
    J. On May 28, 1937, the bridge, arching grandly,

23. A. NO CHANGE
    B. an achievement that was extremely impressive because it symbolized a significant victory over difficult circumstances.
    C. the successful completion of a project that was amazing both because of the obstacles that had been overcome and because of the magnitude of the product that was the result of the project.
    D. DELETE the underlined portion and end the sentence with a period.

24. F. NO CHANGE
    G. At the time,
    H. Regardless,
    J. Even today,

25. A. NO CHANGE
    B. air;
    C. air
    D. air, rising

26. F. NO CHANGE
    G. nature surrounding
    H. nature surrounded
    J. natural surrounds

27. The writer is considering deleting the phrase "on foggy days" from the preceding sentence in order to make the paragraph more concise. If the writer were to make this deletion, the sentence would primarily lose information that:

    A. explains why the color of the bridge is referred to as "International Orange."
    B. demonstrates the ways in which the bridge's color matches the environment.
    C. reveals the danger that the bridge can cause for some ships during bad weather, regardless of color.
    D. adds a detail that provides a specific situation in which the bridge's visibility is particularly important.

Strauss first envisioned it. ⟦28⟧

28. The writer is considering adding a sentence that demonstrates the wide variety of the bridge's uses today. Given that all the following statements are true, which one, if added here, would most clearly and effectively accomplish the writer's goal?

F. On weekdays, during the busiest times of day, the direction of certain lanes changes to accommodate rush hour commuters.

G. The weather is San Francisco is often foggy but when the sky is clear, the bright orange of the bridge stands out against its surroundings.

H. The bridge is 1.7 miles long, so some people walk across in one direction but hire a taxi or take the bus to return.

J. People use it to commute to work, to go on day trips to Marin or San Francisco, and even just to enjoy the beauty of the bridge itself.

Question 29 asks about the preceding passage as a whole.

---

29. Upon reviewing the essay, the writer realizes that some information has been omitted. The writer wants to incorporate that information and composes the following sentence:

The local community began to consider building a bridge to connect the San Francisco peninsula in 1928.

If the writer were to add this sentence to the essay, the most logical place to insert it would be at Point:

A. A
B. B
C. C
D. D

NO TEST MATERIAL ON THIS PAGE.

Father of a Language

The Italian language wasn't always the single, unified,
language that it is today. In fact, during the Middle Ages, Italy
wasn't a unified country. Even today, though Italy is politically
unified, each region speaks its own dialect. In some regions,
such as Tuscany, the dialect is virtually identical to the "official"
Italian language. In other regions, such as Venice, however, the
language is still distinct in many ways.

Dante Alighieri, more commonly known simply as Dante,
is sometimes called the "father of the Italian language." He
was born in Florence during the thirteenth century and was
a prolific writer. In approximately 1305, he published an
essay entitled "De Vulgari Eloquentia," or "In Defense of the
Vernacular." About three years later, Dante began work on his
masterpiece: *The Divine Comedy*. Today he is considered one

of the greatest writers of the Western world. [32] During his life,

however, his work was more controversial. Some of the main
reasons for this was his decision not to write in Latin, but in
"Italian."

30. **F.** NO CHANGE
    G. single yet unified,
    H. single, and unified,
    J. single unified

31. The writer is considering removing the underlined phrase. The primary effect of the deletion would be the loss of a detail that:
    A. provides context that is necessary to understanding the passage.
    B. creates confusion regarding the writer's point in this paragraph.
    C. interrupts the flow of the passage without adding any new information.
    D. provides a grammatically necessary connection.

32. The writer is considering adding the following phrase to the end of the preceding sentence (changing the period after "world" to a comma)

    alongside other recognized greats such as Homer, Shakespeare, and Sophocles.

    Should the writer make this addition?

    F. Yes, because it provides necessary context for the sentence's previous statement.
    G. Yes, because it explains the important role the creation of Italian played in Western literature.
    H. No, because it adds details that distract from the primary point of the sentence.
    J. No, the list of important writers does not include all important writers in the Western tradition.

33. **A.** NO CHANGE
    B. One
    C. Few
    D. Each

At that time, high literature was written not in the various local languages and in Latin. Dante believed that literature

should be available not only to the educated elite who had education but also to the common people. In order to make

this dream possible, Dante "created" a new language as he called "Italian." This new language wasn't really new at all; it consisted of bits and pieces from the different languages already spoken throughout Italy, and drew most heavily on Dante's native Tuscan dialect. Dante's creation laid the foundation for the unified language to be spoken in Italy today.

   The Divine Comedy is, in some ways, the beginning of national Italian literature. By writing it in the language spoken by the Italian people; Dante made *The Divine Comedy*

available to the people. Dante for his opinion that literature to anyone should be accessible drew criticism. However, the

movement that Dante helped begin led to diminished literacy among the Italian people, which, in turn, eventually led to the Renaissance.

   The title of *The Divine Comedy* confusing some people. At one time, the label of "comedy" was attached to any work not written in Latin. *The Divine Comedy* wasn't written in

Latin, but it was considered a comedy; however, today it is widely considered a masterpiece of serious literature. Dante's

34. **F.** NO CHANGE
    G. for
    H. as
    J. but

35. **A.** NO CHANGE
    B. who had been taught
    C. with a school background
    D. DELETE the underlined portion.

36. **F.** NO CHANGE
    G. and called
    H. that he called
    J. calling

37. **A.** NO CHANGE
    B. spoken
    C. if spoken
    D. to speak

38. **F.** NO CHANGE
    G. people, Dante
    H. people. Dante
    J. people: Dante

39. **A.** NO CHANGE
    B. Dante should be accessible for his opinion that literature to anyone drew criticism.
    C. Dante drew criticism for his opinion that literature should be accessible to anyone.
    D. Dante drew criticism to anyone for his opinion that literature should be accessible.

40. The writer wants to imply that prior to Dante's development of "Italian," illiteracy was common. Which choice best accomplishes that goal?

    F. NO CHANGE
    G. an increase in
    H. a passion for
    J. compulsory

41. **A.** NO CHANGE
    B. confusing
    C. confuses some
    D. that confuses

42. **F.** NO CHANGE
    G. since
    H. because
    J. so

brave decision, while, in defiance of the common beliefs of
his time, demonstrated that it was not necessary for a literary
masterpiece to be written in Latin, paved the way for future
writers and readers alike. Nevertheless, *The Divine Comedy*
remains a symbol of both literature and innovation today.

43. **A.** NO CHANGE
    B. and
    C. which,
    D. so that,

44. **F.** NO CHANGE
    G. In contrast,
    H. However,
    J. DELETE the underlined portion.

NO TEST MATERIAL ON THIS PAGE.

Baking Lessons

[1]

Both of my parents worked full-time when I was a little girl, so my grandmother would stay at our house during the day. We would sit in the living room on the couch at my family's house and watch game shows. Our favorite was

The Price is Right. We would call out their answers along with the contestants. When our answers were right, we would

scream with excitement, and when the contestants were wrong, we would moan with disappointment.

[2]

[1] When I got older and started going to school, we couldn't watch our game shows regular. [2] That was okay with me, though, because the one thing I liked better than watching game shows with my grandmother was helping her bake. [49] [3] Watching her in the kitchen was magical: she never seemed to need the recipes but everything she made tasted like heaven.

[3]

[1] As I got older, she let me help with the easy parts, such as sifting the flour and measuring the sugar. [2] At first I would

---

45. **A.** NO CHANGE
    B. on the couch in the living room at my family's house
    C. in the living room at my family's house on the couch
    D. at my family's house on the couch in the living room

46. **F.** NO CHANGE
    G. my
    H. our
    J. her

47. Which of the following alternatives to the underlined portion would NOT be acceptable?

    A. excitement, when
    B. excitement; when
    C. excitement. When
    D. excitement, or when

48. **F.** NO CHANGE
    G. as regular.
    H. but regularly.
    J. as regularly.

49. The writer is considering deleting the preceding sentence. If the sentence were removed, the essay would primarily lose:

    A. a transition from the narrator's discussion of watching game shows to the subject focused on in the remainder of the essay.
    B. unnecessary information that serves only to detract from the primary subject being discussed in the paragraph.
    C. details that are critical to understanding why the narrator took such pleasure in watching game shows with her grandmother.
    D. an insight into why the narrator would choose to spend her afternoons watching television with her grandmother.

50. Which of the following alternatives to the underlined portion would NOT be acceptable?

    F. during
    G. her with
    H. out with
    J. along

just sit on the kitchen stool and watch, even though I didn't understand what she was doing. [3] The day she let me separate
51
the eggs, I felt like I had reached the pinnacle of success. 52

[4]

Eventually, my parents decided that I could take care of myself, and my grandmother stopped coming over every day because I didn't need someone to keep an eye on me anymore.
53
The love of baking that she had inspired, however, stayed with me. I started baking by myself, and even if the cookies ended

up burned
54

sometimes, more often they turned out pretty well. I dropped
55
in new recipes, and whenever I got to a tricky part, I would call
55
my grandmother for advice. Sometimes I would call her just to talk, too. I felt like I could talk to her about anything.

[5]

Last week, I found a recipe book she made for me. It included her recipes for brownies, cookies, and my favorite, lemon meringue pie. As I flipped through the pages, I thought
56
for a moment I could hear her voice, although she's gone, I
57
know that in the way that matters most, she'll never really be

51. Which of the following would best express the narrator's respect for her grandmother's abilities in the kitchen, and the enjoyment the narrator feels at watching her grandmother bake?

A. NO CHANGE
B. or work on whatever homework I had for the next day.
C. awed by her skills and eager to taste whatever she was creating.
D. confused by all the different steps that went into each dish.

52. Which of the following is the most logical ordering of the sentence in Paragraph 3?

F. NO CHANGE
G. 3, 1, 2
H. 2, 3, 1
J. 2, 1, 3

53. A. NO CHANGE
B. since I was considered old enough to stay home by myself.
C. due to my parents' decision that I didn't need a babysitter.
D. DELETE the underlined portion and end the sentence with a period.

54. Which of the following alternatives to the underlined portion would NOT be acceptable?

F. spoiled
G. burnted
H. ruined
J. burnt

55. A. NO CHANGE
B. auditioned for
C. tried out
D. fell into

56. Which of the following alternatives to the underlined portion would NOT be acceptable?

F. leafed through
G. looked through
H. tossed out
J. read over

57. A. NO CHANGE
B. voice; but
C. voice. Although
D. voice although

gone at all. She was the one which taught me not just about
58

baking,

but about life. I imagine that I will enjoy baking for the rest of
59

my life.
59

58. F. NO CHANGE
  G. whom
  H. who
  J. whose

59. Given that all the choices are true, which one would provide a concluding sentence that best captures the main idea
of the essay?

  A. NO CHANGE
  B. To this day, I love watching game shows and baking delicious food for my family.
  C. Baking is a great way to relax, and it's often less expensive than buying cakes and pastries from a bakery.
  D. Every day, when I enter the kitchen, I remember my
grandmother and everything she taught me.

Question 60 asks about the passage as a whole.

---

60. After completing the essay, the writer realizes that she
forgot to include some information and composes the following sentence:

> My grandmother passed away ten years ago, but I still
> think of her every day.

This sentence would most logically be placed:

  F. at the end of Paragraph 1.
  G. after Sentence 1 in Paragraph 2.
  H. at the beginning of Paragraph 5.
  J. at the end of Paragraph 5.

NO TEST MATERIAL ON THIS PAGE.

Global Rat-titudes

The relationship between humans and animals have always
been complicated. Some cultures have developed entire
belief systems around favored animals. For example, cows
are treated with reverence in Hindu societies, in part because
some followers of the Hindu religion believe that any cow
could carry the spirits of one of their ancestors. Certain Native
American tribes believe that they're favored animal, the buffalo,
had a connection to the divine. The tribes still hunted the

buffalo, but carefully, according to such strict rules that the
hunt seemed more like a religious ritual. Even in cultures

with less formalized belief systems, regular interactions
between people and animals still lead to common opinions.

These stories usually develop around the animals that
interact with humans most frequently. Therefore, it should not
be surprising that so many stories surround the most common
of animals: rats. Rats live side-by-side with humans all over

the world, regularly interact with people. Human-rat

coexistence may be common all around the world, with
different cultures respond to that closeness in different ways.

In the United States and Europe, one typical attitude is that
the rat is a pest. This could be due to the common belief that

61. A. NO CHANGE
B. should of
C. had
D. has

62. F. NO CHANGE
G. their
H. theirs
J. there

63. A. NO CHANGE
B. so that
C. as to mean
D. because

64. Given that all of the choices are true, which of the following concludes this paragraph with the clearest allusion to the story of "The Pied Piper of Hamlin," which is discussed later in the essay?

F. NO CHANGE
G. it is well-known that other cultures hold religious beliefs about some animals.
H. people still tend to have beliefs, either individual or cultural, relating to animals.
J. folklore and stories relating to humans' relationship with animals abound.

65. Which of the following alternatives to the underlined portion would NOT be acceptable?

A. tales
B. legends
C. narrators
D. fables

66. F. NO CHANGE
G. world and regularly
H. world, regular
J. world, regularly,

67. A. NO CHANGE
B. world,
C. world, but with
D. world, but

68. F. NO CHANGE
G. pest, which is a common opinion.
H. pest, a belief many people share.
J. pest, moreover.

rats spread disease. They don't, at least not directly; but many people don't know that. "The Pied Piper of Hamlin," a well-known children's story, is one example of how rats have been portrayed in a different way in Western literature: in that story, rats cause such a problem that a town has to hire a piper to call them all away.

What's really wild is that in many Latin American countries, and some European countries as well, the rat is portrayed in a very different light. The tooth fairy legend is common all over the world, but in Latin America, the "fairy" is a rat! Rats do have very strong teeth, which could explain the association. Clearly, this shows another attitude toward rats that is much more positive.

[1] Yet another attitude toward the rat can be seen in the

Chinese *Zodiac*. [2] The Rat is one of the animals, of the zodiac along with the Sheep, the Rooster, the Boar, and eight others. [3] Like the other zodiac animals, the Rat is neither entirely good nor entirely bad. [4] It's described as clever and friendly, but also tricky and not entirely honest. [5] That may be the most accurate description of the rat so far. [6] Whether you like rats or not, it's hard to deny their reputation for cleverness. [7] As many people are discovering these days, rats can even make excellent pets, so long as you remember to latch the cage carefully! 75

69. **A.** NO CHANGE
 B. don't, at least not directly,
 C. don't: at least not directly,
 D. don't, at least not directly

70. Given that all the choices are true, which one states a detail that most clearly relates to the information conveyed at the end of this sentence?
 F. NO CHANGE
 G. mystical
 H. negative
 J. juvenile

71. **A.** NO CHANGE
 B. In
 C. Dig this: in the minds of those born and raised in
 D. You'll be shocked to discover that in

72. Given that all the choices are true, which one provides a physical detail about rats that relates most clearly to the preceding sentence?
 F. NO CHANGE
 G. particularly curious natures,
 H. a reputation for excessive chewing,
 J. long and somewhat unusual tails,

73. **A.** NO CHANGE
 B. China's
 C. Chinese mysticism's
 D. Their

74. **F.** NO CHANGE
 G. is one of the animals, of the zodiac,
 H. is one of the animals of the zodiac,
 J. is one, of the animals of the zodiac

75. The writer wants to create a concluding paragraph that focuses on one characteristic of rats outside of any specific cultural frame of reference by dividing the preceding paragraph in two. The best place the begin the new paragraph would be at the beginning of Sentence:
 A. 4.
 B. 5.
 C. 6.
 D. 7.

Chapter 4
English Practice
Drills for the
ACT Answers and
Explanations

ACT ENGLISH DRILL 1 ANSWERS

1.	B	47.	C
2.	F	48.	H
3.	B	49.	B
4.	H	50.	J
5.	D	51.	D
6.	F	52.	F
7.	C	53.	B
8.	G	54.	F
9.	D	55.	B
10.	G	56.	H
11.	C	57.	B
12.	J	58.	H
13.	C	59.	C
14.	H	60.	F
15.	A	61.	B
16.	G	62.	H
17.	A	63.	A
18.	J	64.	H
19.	B	65.	C
20.	H	66.	J
21.	B	67.	D
22.	H	68.	H
23.	D	69.	D
24.	G	70.	G
25.	D	71.	A
26.	H	72.	G
27.	A	73.	B
28.	G	74.	H
29.	C	75.	D
30.	G		
31.	D		
32.	H		
33.	C		
34.	G		
35.	B		
36.	H		
37.	B		
38.	G		
39.	A		
40.	F		
41.	D		
42.	G		
43.	B		
44.	F		
45.	A		
46.	H		

ACT ENGLISH DRILL 1 EXPLANATIONS

Passage I

1. **B** The question asks you to find the answer choice that is NOT acceptable as a replacement for the underlined portion—remember, that means the passage is correct as written. Look at the answer choices—they are all transition words, so you need to find the one that can't be used to connect the two ideas. The original word, *Nevertheless*, is used to connect two different ideas. Choices (A), (C), and (D) are all used in the same way. Choice (B), *Therefore*, is used to connect two similar ideas, so it can't be used to replace *Nevertheless*.

2. **F** When you see answer choices "stacked" like this, using all (or mostly all) the same words with Stop and Go punctuation changing in the same spot, check for Complete/Incomplete on either side of that spot. In this case, *That's because the seating area is actually a life-size painting* is a complete idea, and *painting on the wall of one of the campus buildings* is incomplete. Since Stop punctuation can only separate complete ideas, eliminate (J). There's not a good reason to insert a comma either after *painting* or *wall*, so the best answer choice is (F).

3. **B** The answer choices here all say the same thing in slightly different ways, but none contains an obvious grammatical error. Remember your fourth "C," concise! *Public* denotes the same idea as *for anyone/everyone* and *freely available*, so there's no need to say both—eliminate (A), (C), and (D).

4. **H** Here you have three answer choices with different "-ing" forms of verbs, and one without. Whenever you see a 3/1 split in the answer choices, take a look at the one that is different. We know ACT doesn't like the "-ing" form—it's not concise—and (H) has no grammatical errors; therefore, it's the best answer.

5. **D** The answer choices are all transition words, but this time ACT is testing idioms—specifically the "*not only, ___ also*" construction. The proper word to use is *but*, answer choice (D).

6. **F** To identify what the essay would lose by deleting the sentence, you must first determine the purpose of that sentence. In this case, the author asks, "A life-size painting that's just a painting?" rhetorically, anticipating the reader's possible surprise at such a notion. (F) is the only answer choice that expresses that purpose.

7. **C** You need to find the correct form of the verb here. Eliminate (A) and (D)—they are singular forms and don't agree with the plural subject, *children*. (B) is the correct plural form, but the wrong tense—the correct answer choice has to be consistent with the other present-tense verbs in the passage: *looms*, *is*, and *looks*—that is choice (C).

8. **G**   Here again you see a 3/1 split with three "-ing" verbs and one without, so check the one without. Unfortunately, (J) actually creates an error, because in this question, the answer choices are all modifying phrases, and ACT wants a modifying phrase to be right next to the thing that it describes. That means you need to find the phrase that describes a *group of firefighters*. (F) describes the image of the wave, (H) describes the children, and (J) describes the painting itself, leaving (G) as the only possible choice.

9. **D**   The author is using the quotation marks to emphasize the fact that there weren't really any children there to rescue, so if you take out the quotation marks, you will lose that emphasis—choice (D). Choice (A) might seem tempting, but the firefighters' concern was for the "children," not the wave, and in any case, the quotations don't explain anything.

10. **G**   The remainder of the paragraph talks about how Pugh uses his art to transform the appearance of an existing building, which agrees with (G). There is no comparison with gallery displays as in (F), nor is there discussion of multi-cultural influence on his work, as in (H). Choice (J) refers to the preceding paragraph.

11. **C**   The correct form of the verb needs to be consistent with the preceding sentence: *use* is present-tense, so eliminate (A). Remember, ACT doesn't like "-ing" verbs, so you should only choose one if you have eliminated every other answer choice. In this case, even though (B) and (D) are both present-tense, (C) is as well, and it isn't an "-ing" verb, making it the best answer.

12. **J**   There is no comparison being made here, so eliminate (G) and (H). The author is trying to express a large number of people, so you have to use *many*—answer choice (J).

13. **C**   A good place to begin a new paragraph is a point where there is a shift in focus or topic. Prior to point C the author is describing one of Pugh's works; after point C the discussion turns to the high demand for his work and his worldwide popularity. (A), (B), and (D) all separate sentences that belong together.

14. **H**   The question asks about "trends" in the plural, and only one artist and one style was discussed in the essay—eliminate (F) and (G). (J) is incorrect because although the essay does talk about people being confused by Pugh's art, that's not the reason the essay doesn't accomplish the stated goal—it's a problem of scope, as outlined in (H).

Passage II

15. **A**   On the ACT, a semicolon is used in exactly the same way as a period, so you can eliminate (B) and (D)—they can't both be correct! *Besides, to make it feel more like home* is an incomplete idea, and Stop punctuation can only be used to separate two complete ideas. The colon in (C) comes after a complete idea, which is correct, but saying *to make it feel more like home* after it is awkward. You'll need a dash to be consistent with the rest of the sentence and set off the unnecessary *pillows, …pots and pans* from the rest of the sentence—answer choice (A).

16. **G**   The answer choices here all say the same thing in slightly different ways, but none contains an obvious grammatical error. Remember your fourth "C"—concise! (G) is the only answer choice that doesn't use an "-ing" form of the verb (which ACT doesn't like), and has no grammatical errors, so it's the best choice.

17. **A**   You need to find an answer choice that agrees with *I had just said my first real farewell to a mother.* The sentence as written accomplishes this by explaining that she had never been away from her mother *for more than a weekend.* Choices (B), (C), and (D) all introduce new and off-topic information.

18. **J**   When you see DELETE or OMIT as an answer choice, do that first. If you can take out the underlined portion without creating an error, chances are you've found your answer. In this case, deleting *and me all by myself* doesn't create an error, and leaving it in would be redundant—the narrator has already described herself as *on my own*—so eliminate (F). Choices (G) and (H) are redundant for the same reason.

19. **B**   The correct tense of the verb here needs to be consistent with the non-underlined portion of the passage. The narrator is talking about her life before coming to college, so you must use the past tense, *grew*, to be consistent with the other verbs in the sentence, *had* and *was*. (A), *grow*, is present tense, and (D), *growth*, isn't a verb, so eliminate them. (C), *grown* could be past tense, but needs to be paired with a helping verb.

20. **H**   The task here is to transition from a discussion of the narrator's life in high school to her acceptance at a major university in the United States. (H) begins with her in high school—*when the time came to apply to colleges*—and ends with her applying to several in the United States. (F) and (G) don't talk about applying to college at all, and (J) only talks about applying to college in Puerto Rico.

21. **B**   There are a couple of things changing in the answer choices here—commas and pronouns—work with one first and then the other. Remember that unless you have a reason to use a comma, no punctuation is preferable. Here, we have no reason to use a comma after *acceptance*, so eliminate (C) and (D). Now it's a matter of comparing *acceptance received by me* or *acceptance I received.* They both say the same thing, but the latter is more concise—choose (B).

22. **H**   The answer choices are forms of the verb "to get." To choose the correct one, look at the non-underlined portion of the sentence. The narrator says her parents *were* proud, so you need a past-tense verb to agree with that—eliminate (F) and (G). (J) changes the meaning of the sentence, so the only answer choice left is (H), even though it uses the "-ing" form of the verb.

23. **D**   The difference being talked about here is between Puerto Rico and the United States, so *in the United States* needs to be placed in the spot that will make that most clear. (A) makes it sound like Puerto Rico is in the United States—eliminate it. Neither (B) nor (C) make it clear that the United States is where things are different—only (D) does.

24. **J**   Apostrophes are used to show either possession or contraction. The word after *parents* is *house*, so you want to show possession. The narrator is referring to the house that belongs to both of her parents, and with a plural noun that ends in "s," all you need to do is add an apostrophe—choice (J).

25. **D**   Remember that on the ACT, less is more, so you should have a really compelling reason to add something. In an essay discussing the narrator's feelings about being away from her home and family for the first time, it's not really important to know what is her favorite dance—eliminate (A) and (B). The reason it's not important isn't because of any false impression created, so (D) is the best answer choice.

26. **H**   Here you see nicely "stacked" answer choices with Stop and Go punctuation changing in the same spot. Check for Complete/Incomplete on either side: *As the memory faded* is Incomplete, so no matter what, you're not going to be able to use Stop punctuation—that can only connect two complete ideas. Eliminate (F), (G), and (J), and you're done.

27. **A**   You're looking for the answer choice that can NOT be used in place of the underlined portion—remember, that means the sentence is correct as written. Choices (B), (C), and (D) all express either how the narrator was feeling or what she was feeling; (A) is the only choice that makes no sense—you wouldn't feel "excitement nervous"—and is therefore the one to choose.

28. **G**   The assignment here is to *emphasize the narrator's confidence*, so the correct answer choice must do exactly that. (G), *ready to take on*, does that much more effectively than *had to face*, *all alone in*, or *about to enter*.

29. **C**   Make sure to read the question carefully—the goal here is to not only pick a logical concluding sentence but also the one that *best expresses one of the main ideas of the essay*. A main idea is one that recurs throughout the essay, so you can eliminate (B) and (D). While Puerto Rico is certainly mentioned throughout the essay, it wouldn't be logical for the narrator to express her regret at leaving home—the preceding sentence has an upbeat and confident tone, which (C) continues while including another main idea—her dream of living in a large city.

Passage III

30. **G** Three of the answer choices offer a form of the verb "to need," and one offers no verb at all—that's a 3/1 split, and on the English test, you always want to check the "1" first. That makes the sentence read *When in need of help with an article, she calls on Clark Kent*, which is a present-tense sentence that is consistent with the first: *When Lois Lane finds herself in serious danger, she looks to Superman for help.* The verbs in (F), (H), and (J) are all past-tense, so (G) is the best answer.

31. **D** DELETE is an answer choice, so do that first—if you don't create an error by taking out the underlined portion, it's probably the correct choice. In this case, taking out the question word *when* leaves *Today it's a commonplace writing technique*—a perfectly good, complete sentence. Leaving *when*, *where*, or *because* in there would make the sentence incomplete, so you shouldn't choose (A), (B), or (C).

32. **H** You've got DELETE as an option, so try it. This time, it creates an error: *...he poses as millionaire Bruce Wayne day* doesn't make sense, so eliminate (J). Now your choices are all prepositions, which means ACT is testing idioms. To express the notion that something occurs during the day, you need to say *by day*—answer choice (H).

33. **C** To decide whether to make the addition here, take a look at the main theme of the passage—Dual Personalities—and what's going on in the paragraph. The author is talking about the *tradition of giving superheroes alternate names and characters*, so adding a sentence about a superhero that doesn't need an alter-ego would be a bad idea—eliminate (A) and (B). (D) is incorrect because the sentence poses no hypothetical situation.

34. **G** The correct verb here needs to agree in number with the subject, *Each*. Careful—*of the superheroes* is a prepositional phrase, so it's not the subject, but it can make the wrong verb sound correct. To avoid confusion, you should cross out prepositional phrases you find inserted between a verb and its subject, one of ACT's favorite tricks. Now you know the subject is *Each*, a singular noun, so it needs a singular verb—eliminate (F) and (J). (G) and (H) are both singular and present-tense, but beware the "-ing" form! They both say the same thing, but (G) is more concise, making it the better answer choice.

35. **B** ACT is testing comma usage here, specifically the use of commas to separate unnecessary information. In this case, *for example* is unnecessary to the sentence, so it needs to have commas on either side, as in (B). If you chose (D), you may have remembered that dashes can separate unnecessary information—and so they can—but it must be a pair of dashes or a pair of commas, not one of each.

36. **H** You need to provide support for the preceding sentence, which states that impressive costumes and names help superheroes maintain their authority. Only (H) addresses anything to do with this theme by stating that it would be more difficult for Batman to fight crime if he lacked those things.

37. **B** You need to find the answer choice that can NOT be used to replace the underlined portion in the passage. A quick glance at the answer choices might give you the impression that Stop/Go punctuation is being tested here, but look closer; the words changing after the punctuation are all transition words, and that typically means ACT is testing direction. Remember, when NO CHANGE is not an answer choice, the sentence in the passage is correct as written, and that gives you an important clue: the transition word used is *but*, an opposite-direction transition—that means a suitable replacement will also have to use one. *On the other hand, although,* and *however* in (A), (C), and (D) are all opposite-direction transitions, but *because* in (B) is same-direction, and so can NOT be used—making (B) the correct answer.

38. **G** There are two things changing here: apostrophes showing possession and word choice between *one* and *individual*. In the sentence, the *loved one/individual* with the *other identity* refers back to *the hero*, so you know you need to choose a singular noun, and to show possession, you need to add an "'s." Choice (G), *one's*, is the only one that offers that construction.

39. **A** The superheroes are given these alter-egos by their creators in order to help the characters fit into a societal context. *Providing* best communicates this meaning; there is no assumption being made as in (B), and (C) and (D) make it seem as if the fictional characters had a choice in the matter.

40. **F** This is a pronoun question, so find the noun that's being replaced. In this case, it's the superheroes who are making the attempts, and *superheroes* is plural. That helps a lot, since, apostrophes or not, you can eliminate (G), (H), and (J)—they're all singular pronouns and can't be used to replace a plural noun.

41. **D** This is a comma question, so keep your comma rules in mind. There is unnecessary information in this sentence: *creator of Spider-Man and dozens of other superheroes*. This needs to be set off with commas—one after *Lee* (eliminate (B) and (C)) and one after *superheroes*. The only answer choice that offers this without adding additional, unnecessary commas is (D).

42. **G** The rest of the paragraph discusses the reasons Stan Lee gives his superheroes human flaws, so if you're going to introduce that sort of discussion with a rhetorical question, the natural choice for that question would be one that asks, "Why?" Choice (G) is the only one that asks that question.

43. **B** This question is testing comma usage, but none of the situational rules seem to apply—there's no introductory idea, list, or unnecessary information. Therefore, the issue is whether there is a definite need to pause at any point in *Lee builds tension in his stories by putting those human flaws and the hero's quest into conflict.* If it helps, you can take an exaggerated pause at the spots ACT suggests putting commas. If the pause creates a little tension, you probably need the comma; if the pause just seems irritating or awkward, you don't. This sentence is a little on the long side, but it doesn't need the commas—answer choice (B).

44. **F** The sentence should be kept, since it's giving an example of what the entire previous paragraph is talking about—eliminate (H) and (J). (G) is the direct opposite of what's happening in the sentence: the ultimate superhero does in fact have human feelings.

45. **A** This sentence fits best with the discussion in the first paragraph about Lois Lane's misconception that Superman and Clark Kent are two different individuals. It also introduces the concept of the alter-ego, the subject of the second paragraph, so it functions nicely as a transition sentence as well.

Passage IV

46. **H**   Here you have nicely "stacked" answer choices with Stop and Go punctuation changing in the same spot—check for Complete/Incomplete on either side. *Passing trends… vary dramatically* is Complete, and *every bit as much as clothing* is Incomplete. You'll need Go punctuation to connect these two—eliminate (F) and (J). (G) uses the less-concise "-ing" form of the verb, making (H) the best answer.

47. **C**   The assigned task is to introduce the main subject of the paragraph, which begins by talking about curly hair being the fashion in the 1950s and the progression towards "natural" hair by the mid-1960s. (A) is addressed in the paragraph, but it's not a main subject. The Renaissance is never mentioned, so eliminate (B), and (D) introduces a new topic—clothing styles—so the best answer is (C).

48. **H**   The answer choices here are all very similar and don't contain any obvious errors. You'll need to check the non-underlined portion on either side and make sure the answer is consistent with both. To the left you have *maintaining properly stylish hair-dos*, and to the left you have *and a great deal of time*. (F) and (J) aren't consistent with both, and (G) is not only inconsistent, but it also contradicts the preceding sentence—these hairdos took a lot of work.

49. **B**   There are pronouns changing in the answer choices, and an apostrophe in the sentence as written. If you're in doubt about whether you need the contraction or a pronoun, expand out the contraction: in this case, *they're* becomes "they are," which doesn't make sense—eliminate (A). The noun being replaced here is *Women*, which is plural, so you need a plural pronoun—eliminate (D). (B) is the possessive, plural pronoun you're looking for, but watch out for its sound-alike, *there*, in (C).

50. **J**   All the answer choices basically say the same thing, and none creates a grammatical error, so pick the one that says what they all do in the most concise way. That's (J)—*long or short*.

51. **D**   DELETE is an answer choice, so try that first. Taking out the underlined portion leaves *The change didn't last long, perhaps unsurprisingly*. That is a complete sentence, and the meaning hasn't changed, so it's the best answer.

52. **F**   This question is testing comma usage, so keep your comma rules in mind. It might be tempting to think of *Farrah Fawcett* as unnecessary information, but if you remove it from the sentence, it is no longer clear who *the movie and television star* is. Because it's necessary, no commas are needed, which corresponds with answer choice (F), NO CHANGE.

53. **B**   Be careful—the question is asking whether the phrase inside the dashes *should* be deleted, not whether it *can* be. In this case, the author is using the phrase inside the dashes to define a term with which the reader may not be familiar, and you know ACT likes things to be clear. Therefore, the phrase should be kept—eliminate (C) and (D). (A) is incorrect because there is no contrast made to an earlier style.

54. **F**   There are two things changing here: apostrophes showing contraction and word choice between *sudden* and *suddenly*. You need the adverb *suddenly*, so eliminate (H) and (J). (G) is incorrect because we're is a contraction of "we are," which wouldn't make sense in the sentence.

55. **B**   Three of the answer choices say the same thing in slightly different ways, while one just says *it*. While you may be tempted to read *it* in the slang sense of "something really popular," remember there's no slang on the ACT—eliminate (C). Now you're left with the three answer choices that don't contain errors, but all say the same thing—pick the one that's most concise, (B).

56. **H**   You need to find the answer choice that can NOT replace the underlined portion in the sentence, and since NO CHANGE isn't an option, you know the sentence in the passage is correct. The option here is to find an alternate word for *modeled*, so this is just a vocabulary question. (F), (G), and (J) all work as replacements in the context of the sentence, so select (H), the one that does NOT. If this question tricked you, you may have picked *imitated*, since the sentence talks about women imitating the pop icons, but the pop icons are the ones doing the modeling.

57. **B**   If you're unsure about whether an apostrophe is showing possession or expansion, expand it out. In this case, "commentator is" wouldn't make sense, so if you need an apostrophe at all, it would be to show possession. However, look at the word after the underlined portion: *have*. Only nouns can be possessed, and *have* is not a noun; therefore, you can't use an apostrophe here at all—eliminate (A), (C), and (D).

58. **H**   Sentence 3 talks about how women can now have their hair chemically straightened. Both sentence 2 and sentence 4 talk about curly hair, so eliminate (F) and (J). Sentence 3 would naturally follow sentence 1, which transitions from the previous paragraph and introduces the idea of straight hair being the fashion now, so (H) is a better answer choice than (G).

59. **C**   The essay mentions the "modern" preference for straight hair, but that's a long way from *discussing modern attitudes toward curly hair*—eliminate (A) and (B). (D) is incorrect because for the same reason: the primary focus is not on the popularity of straight hair.

Passage V

60. **F**   The phrase *polonium and radium* names the *two new elements* discovered by the Curies. It doesn't provide an explanation as (G) claims, nor does it offer the reason Marie Curie won the Nobel Prize, as in (H). (J) is incorrect because the phrase does not define radioactivity—it simply lists two radioactive elements—leaving (F) as the best answer choice.

61. **B**   The assigned task is to *provide the most effective transition* to the rest of the essay. The next paragraph talks about some of the problems Curie encountered in her academic and professional career, so an *effective transition* will need to incorporate that theme, as (B) does. (A) only provides a specific detail about Curie's research, (C) doesn't mention Curie at all, and (D) talks only about Curie's husband, Pierre.

62. **H**   Here you see nicely "stacked" answer choices with Stop and Go punctuation changing in the same spot, but before checking for Complete/Incomplete on either side to see which kind of punctuation you need, notice you have one answer choice with *which* in it, and three without. Whenever you see a 3/1 split like that on the English test, check the "1" first. In (F), the idea after the comma would be *which prevented her from attending university due to a lack of money, Curie initially studied in a laboratory run by her cousin*, which doesn't make sense—eliminate (F). The remaining three answer choices all have *prevented* as the first word in the second idea, but (J) has *prevented her*, which creates another error—eliminate (J). Now it's down to a choice between a period and a comma. The ideas on either side are both complete (make sure to read the entire sentence!), so you need Stop punctuation—answer choice (H).

63. **A**   You're given the option to DELETE the underlined portion, so try that first. Taking out *where* in this case leaves you with a comma joining two complete ideas, so eliminate (D). *Like* doesn't make sense, so eliminate (B). Both *when* and *where* might seem to work, but keep in mind that the two things happening in the sentence are Curie enrolling at the University of Paris and becoming the first woman professor there. Those two things didn't happen simultaneously, so you can't use *when* to connect them—choose (A).

64. **H**   All the answer choices here say basically the same thing, and none creates a grammatical error, so pick the one that says what they all do in the most concise way. That's (H)—*generally credited with*.

65. **C**   There are two things changing in the answer choices: we have *seen* vs. *saw* and *has* vs. *had*. Start with whichever seems easier, and eliminate answer choices that don't agree. The correct form of the verb (regardless of whether you use *has* or *have*) is *has/have seen*, so delete (A) and (D). To figure out which tense you need, check the non-underlined rest of the passage for context. In the same sentence, you have past-tense verbs: *made, existed, did*—(C) is past-tense and therefore consistent with the rest of the sentence.

66. **J** Here it's really just a matter of inserting the underlined portion, *of radioactivity*, in each of the places in the answer choices; the only place it makes any sense at all is after *discovery*, answer choice (J).

67. **D** This question is basically just testing word choice. If you happen to notice that there's a 3/1 split in the answers—one noun and three modifiers—then you could probably save a step or two, but from the context of the (now altered) passage, you know that *Bequerel was performing* [something] *involving photographic paper*, not *performing* [in some manner] involving photographic paper. If you need a thing, you need a noun, and the only choice you have is (D).

68. **H** There are transition words changing in the answer choices, which can often be an indication that ACT is testing direction, but notice the 3/1 split—three answer choices with transitions and one without. If you try the one without, you're left with *Further experiments revealed... potassium uranyl sulfate*, which is a perfectly good sentence, and more concise than the other three. There's no real need for a transition at all here, so (H) is the best answer.

69. **D** This is another word choice question with some punctuation thrown in to confuse the issue—start easy! *Principal* means something that is highest in rank or value; *principle* means a fundamental assumption. In the context of the sentence, you need to use *principle*—eliminate (A) and (C). Using a colon after *principle* might seem obviously preferable to the comma after *namely*, which seems awkward, but remember that ACT mandates that a colon must follow a complete idea, and must itself be followed by a list, definition, expansion, or explanation of that complete idea; make sure to check that. *However, Bequerel... principle* is a complete idea, and the idea after the colon is a definition (as evidenced by the introductory word *namely*)—pick (D).

70. **G** You have a 3/1 split of sorts here: all the answer choices have *isolated* by itself with some kind of punctuation, and one that adds *it*—that's probably a good place to start. Adding the pronoun *it* here, though, creates an error: the pronoun is not replacing any noun—eliminate (H). The action in the idea after the semicolon is *she* (Curie) *isolated and identified* the two elements, so there's no need for any punctuation in between the two verbs—choose (G).

71. **A** The answer choices have Stop and Go punctuation changing in the same spot and all use the same word, so check for Complete/Incomplete on either side: before the punctuation you have *The earliest scientist to realize that there was an element in the fluorescent substance more reactive than uranium*—an incomplete idea, and afterward you have *Curie dedicated the next twelve years to developing a method for isolating that substance, which was not yet known but later came to be identified and is now called "radium"*, which is a complete idea, so you need Go punctuation to separate them—eliminate (B) and (D), which has a colon, which you know has to follow a complete idea. You definitely need to pause after the incomplete idea, so leave the comma where it is—answer choice (A).

72. **G** You know ACT is testing Concise when all the answer choices here say basically the same thing, and none creates a grammatical error. That's what's happening here, so pick the one that says what they all do in the most concise way. That's (G)—*we now know as radium*.

73. **B**   Here you see Stop and Go punctuation changing in the same spot and nicely "stacked" answer choices, so check for Complete/Incomplete on either side: before the punctuation you have *Curie was progressive for a chemist*—a complete idea, and afterward you have *much less for a woman*, which is an incomplete idea, so you need Go punctuation to separate them—eliminate (A) and (C). (D) is awkward and doesn't really make sense—choose (B).

74. **H**   There are two things changing in the answer choices here: word choice and helping verbs. It's incorrect to say *would of* or *might of*—it's "would have" and "might have." Eliminate (F) and (G). Helping verbs need to agree with the subject in number, just like regular verbs. In this case, the subject is *Women*, which is plural, so choose (H), *have*.

75. **D**   The correct answer choice will provide *the most consistent description of Curie's personality as described in this paragraph*. There is no mention in the paragraph of her seeking recognition as in (A), and likewise in (B), no proof that she became reclusive. (C) doesn't talk about her personality at all, leaving (D) as the best answer choice.

ACT ENGLISH DRILL 2 ANSWERS

1.	B		47.	A
2.	F		48.	J
3.	C		49.	A
4.	F		50.	J
5.	C		51.	C
6.	J		52.	J
7.	A		53.	D
8.	G		54.	G
9.	B		55.	C
10.	H		56.	H
11.	C		57.	C
12.	G		58.	H
13.	D		59.	D
14.	J		60.	H
15.	B		61.	D
16.	H		62.	G
17.	B		63.	A
18.	G		64.	J
19.	D		65.	C
20.	H		66.	G
21.	D		67.	D
22.	H		68.	F
23.	A		69.	B
24.	J		70.	H
25.	A		71.	B
26.	F		72.	F
27.	D		73.	A
28.	J		74.	H
29.	A		75.	C
30.	J			
31.	A			
32.	H			
33.	B			
34.	J			
35.	D			
36.	H			
37.	B			
38.	G			
39.	C			
40.	G			
41.	C			
42.	J			
43.	C			
44.	J			
45.	B			
46.	H			

ACT ENGLISH DRILL 2 EXPLANATIONS

Passage I

1. **B** The question asks you to find the answer choice that is NOT acceptable as a replacement for the underlined portion—remember, that means the passage is correct as written. Look at the answer choices—some change words, some change punctuation. In a case like this, you'll need to check each answer choice. (A), (C), and (D) can all be inserted in place of the underlined portion without creating an error, but (B) makes the sentence *When I woke up this morning, I made myself a bowl of cereal, sat listening to the traffic* which doesn't make sense and therefore can NOT be used.

2. **F** When you see answer choices "stacked" like this, using all the same words with Stop and Go punctuation changing in the same spot, check for Complete/Incomplete on either side of that spot. In this case, *It's true that there's always some kind of noise in my neighborhood* is complete, and *taxi drivers honking their horns, kids playing their radios so loud that the bass makes my teeth vibrate, or people yelling in the street* is incomplete. Since Stop punctuation can only separate two complete ideas, eliminate (H). You definitely need some kind of pause after *neighborhood*, so (J) can be eliminated. Now you must choose between a comma and a dash. Using a comma would make it seem like the sentence is giving a list of things that are true, when the intention is to list the kinds of noises in the neighborhood. Remember a single dash is the same thing as a colon—it must follow a complete idea and must itself be followed by a list, definition or explanation of the first complete idea. That's what the sentence has as written, so choose (F).

3. **C** The preceding sentence is *I know that some people wouldn't like it, but to me, these are the sounds of life.* This is almost the exact opposite of what (A) says—the narrator is putting a positive spin on what many would find an annoyance. There is no trip to the park mentioned as in (B), and (D) is incorrect because this sentence is very much relevant to the essay—choose (C).

4. **F** None of the answer choices contains a grammatical error, and they all say roughly the same thing, so pick the one that says it with the fewest words—*It's*.

5. **C** Careful—all of these answer choices may seem fit to use, but on the ACT, there is always a reason to choose the best answer choice. In this case the entire sentence reads *When I ride the bus, you get to see so much more of the city.* The underlined portion you select must have a pronoun that is consistent with the non-underlined *you get*, which is (C), *you ride*.

6. **J** Here you need to choose between *sociable* and *sociably*, but there's punctuation changing as well—start easy! You need the adverb *sociably* because it's describing how the people are chatting—eliminate (F) and (H). (G) is incorrect because there's no need for a pause after *sociably*, so no comma is needed.

7. **A** The answer choices have "stacked" words with Stop and Go punctuation changing in one spot, so check for Complete/Incomplete on either side of that spot. *Just like the traffic's sounds, though, the noise on the bus represents people* is complete (but awkward), and *working, relaxing, and living* is incomplete, so you need Go punctuation—eliminate (B) and (C). (D) is incorrect because you don't need a comma after *people*—you only need commas to separate the items in the list of things the people are doing.

8. **G** Here you have a 3/1 split with three answer choices using pronouns and one that uses the noun *kids*, so check that one first. *Kids* makes sense in the context of the sentence and is consistent with the non-underlined *their parents*.

9. **B** In the answer choices you see Stop and Go punctuation changing after the word *nearby*, so check for Complete/Incomplete on either side of the punctuation. *The city added the bench so kids could play while their parents sit nearby* is complete, and, regardless of whether it begins with *obviously,* or not, *I like to sit there because there's a great big oak tree for shade* is also complete. Two complete ideas must be connected with Stop punctuation—eliminate (A) and (C). While adding the word *because* in (D) makes the second idea incomplete and might make you think it's OK to use a comma, it's still incorrect: to use the word *because*, you need a causal relationship between the ideas, and there is none in this case.

10. **H** This question is testing proper comma placement. You don't need a comma after either *watching* or *listening*, since the idea being expressed is *watching and listening to the people around me*—eliminate (F), (G), and (J).

11. **C** In the answer choices you see Stop and Go punctuation changing after the word *do*, so check for Complete/Incomplete on either side of the punctuation. *People-watching is one of my favorite things to do* is complete, and *I like listening even better* is complete as well. Two complete ideas must be connected with Stop punctuation—eliminate (A). You can also eliminate (B) and (D), because even though they respectively add *nevertheless* and *however* after the punctuation change, both of those are transition words that only indicate direction—they don't make a complete idea incomplete. (C), which uses a comma + FANBOYS (but), is the only choice that gives you the Stop punctuation you're looking for.

12. **G** The following sentence says *That way, I can pay more attention to the sounds and not get distracted by what I see*, so the most logical introduction would be one that has the narrator closing her eyes—(G).

13. **D** You need to emphasize the narrator's curiosity and interest in the old men's conversation, so the correct answer choice needs to incorporate the narrator's point of view. Choices (A), (B), and (C) are all objective descriptions of the conversation itself or the old men. (D) characterizes the stories as entertaining, meaning *entertaining* to the narrator, and so is the best answer.

14. **J**   Here apostrophes are being used to show possession. You know there are two old men having the conversation, so the laugh that comes in response to the story one of them is telling must come from his *friend*, not his *friends*. To show possession for a singular noun, all you have to do is add "'s"—answer choice (J).

15. **B**   This essay is definitely pro-city living, and really only explores one aspect of what the narrator likes about the city, so you can eliminate (C) and (D). (A) is incorrect, because although public transportation is mentioned, it isn't the convenience the narrator enjoys—it's the sounds and sights of the city.

Passage II

16. **H**   When you see DELETE as an answer choice, try that first. In this case, taking out *that* causes a syntax error—you wouldn't say *…three times in seventy-year history*. You need to find the correct pronoun, so the first step is to identify the noun that the pronoun replaces—it's *bridge*. Since *bridge* is a singular noun, eliminate (G); you can't replace a singular noun with a plural pronoun. The pronoun *that* in the sentence as written is incorrect; you can't use it because there is no prior reference to the seventy-year history.

17. **B**   The sentence is saying the amount of concrete was *enough to construct a sidewalk five feet wide all the way from San Francisco to New York City*. There isn't a reason to use commas here, so eliminate (A) and (D). (C) has a dash (which is the same as a colon) after *sidewalk*, which creates an awkward and unclear construction afterwards.

18. **G**   The sentence immediately following details the various reasons San Francisco Bay is a bad spot for bridge-building, so a logical introduction will introduce this theme. Neither (F), (G), nor (J) do this as well as (G).

19. **D**   Here you see Stop and Go Punctuation changing after the word *bond* in each answer choice, so check for Complete/Incomplete on either side of the punctuation. *After two years of discussion, the voters approved a bond* is complete, and *which would raise $35 million, all dedicated to building the bridge* is incomplete, so eliminate (C). (A) has a colon after a complete idea, but the incomplete idea after it is awkward and unclear. (B) is incorrect because the phrase *which would raise $35 million* is necessary, and thus there is no need for a comma here, much less two.

20. **H**   You have the option to DELETE the underlined portion, so try that first. That leaves *Even then, there were many skeptics believed that it couldn't be done*, which is a bad sentence—eliminate (J). Now you have to choose the correct pronoun, so identify the noun that's being replaced—it's *skeptics*. You can't use *that* to replace skeptics: it's singular and *that* can't be used to refer to people, so eliminate (G). If you have trouble deciding between *who* and *whom*, try substituting a different pronoun: there are multiple skeptics, so you can use "they" and "them." You would use the subject-case "they believed it couldn't be done," not the object-case "them believed it couldn't be done." That means you need to use the subject-case *who*—answer choice (H).

21. **D**   When DELETE is an option, you should always check that first—you know ACT likes things concise. Taking out the underlined portion leaves *Construction began in 1933 and lasted a little more than four years*. That's a perfectly good sentence, and you're not adding any new information with (A), (B), or (C)—(D) is the best (most concise) answer.

22. **H** The answer choices have "stacked" words with Stop and Go punctuation changing after *1937*, so check for Complete/Incomplete on either side of that spot. *On May 28, 1937* is an incomplete idea, so you know you can't use Stop punctuation—that's only for connecting two complete ideas—eliminate (F) and (G). (H) and (J) both give you the comma you need after *1937*, but (J) goes a little too far by adding another that you don't need after *grandly*.

23. **A** DELETE the underlined portion first, since that's an option. That leaves *More than 200,000 people walked across the bridge that day to celebrate*, which is a complete idea, but is not as clear as it could be (celebrate what?) The better option is (A)—it's a little less concise, but much more clear. (B) and (C) are much too wordy; neither says anything that (A) doesn't.

24. **J** The answer choices are all transition words, which is usually a sign that the question is testing direction. The two sentences on either side are *To top it off, it was beautiful* and *the Golden Gate Bridge is considered an artistic masterpiece*—two similar ideas (although note the shift in tense between the two from past to present.) You can eliminate the two opposite-direction transitions, (F) and (H), and eliminate (G) because it's still past-tense; you want a transition that will make the change to present tense, as *Even today* does.

25. **A** The answer choices all have Stop and Go punctuation (and a dash) changing after the word *air*, so check for Complete/Incomplete before and after the punctuation. Before the punctuation is *At its highest point, the bridge rises 746 feet into the air*, which is complete, and afterward is *191 feet taller than the Washington Monument*, an incomplete idea. Eliminate (B)—you can't use Stop punctuation here. (C) and (D) both create an awkward construction: you wouldn't say a building "rises taller" than another—you would say it "rises higher." That leaves (A) as the best answer choice.

26. **F** The answer choices are all different word combinations—you just have to pick the correct one. The idiomatic expression for "environment" is *natural surroundings*—answer choice (F). If you're not sure here, you can try substituting each answer choice into the sentence; you should at least be able to eliminate one or two answer choices. Always keep in mind that NO CHANGE is going to be correct about 25 percent of the time it appears, so don't be afraid to pick it—especially if you can't identify an error in the sentence as it's written.

27. **D** The whole sentence says *The color, called "International Orange," was chosen partly because it matched the natural surroundings and partly because it would allow the bridge to remain visible on foggy days.* Saying *on foggy days* provides a detail about when the bridge might be hard to see, so if you take out that portion, you would lose that detail. That most closely matches (D).

28. **J** You need to emphasize the *wide variety of the bridge's uses* here, so the correct answer choice must do that. (F) only talks about commuter traffic, (G) describes the bridge itself, not how it is used, and (H) talks about how some people cross the bridge—none of which describe *a wide variety of uses*. (J) talks about the bridge's multiple uses for commuters, travelers, and as a tourist destination in its own right, and so is the best answer choice.

29. **A**   The added sentence talks about the original idea for building the bridge, so it belongs somewhere very early in the discussion of its construction—eliminate (C) and (D). Between (A) and (B), the more logical choice for the placement of the original idea for the bridge would be (A), just before the decision to actually build it.

Passage III

30. **J**   Here you have nicely "stacked" answer choices with Stop (comma + FANBOYS) and Go punctuation changing after *single*—check for Complete/Incomplete on either side. *The Italian language wasn't always the single* is incomplete, as is *unified, language that it is today*. You'll need Go punctuation to connect these two—eliminate (H). Remember your comma rules; there's no reason to use a comma after *unified*—eliminate (F) and (G), leaving (J) as the best answer choice.

31. **A**   The phrase *during the thirteenth century* introduces the time period the passage will be talking about, so that's what you lose if you take it out—there's no confusion created as in (B), no interruption as in (C), and it's not grammatically necessary as (D) claims; (A) is the best answer.

32. **H**   Remember that less is more on the ACT; any time you have the option to add anything, make sure you have a compelling reason to do so. In this case, the sentence (not to mention the passage as a whole) is talking about Dante Alighieri, so adding a list of other writers doesn't add anything necessary to the essay. If you're still unsure, you can check the reasons given in the answer choices and eliminate those that don't agree with the passage: you can eliminate (F) as previously stated, there's no discussion of the creation of Italian as (G) states, and the reason you aren't adding the list isn't because it's not exhaustive, as (J) claims—it's because it's unnecessary.

33. **B**   At first glance this may look like a pronoun question, but your task is actually to pick the subject of the sentence. Any of these could function as a subject, but recall that the subject and main verb in a sentence must agree in number. The main verb here is *was*, which is singular; therefore you need to match it with a singular subject—only (B) fits that description.

34. **J**   The meaning of the sentence is not to say that literature was not written in the local languages and also not in Latin; the idea is that high literature was written in Latin instead of the local languages. To express that, you need to say *literature was written not in the various local languages but in Latin*—answer choice (J).

35. **D**   DELETE is an answer choice, so try that first. Taking out the underlined portion leaves *Dante believed that literature should be available not only to the educated elite but also to the common people*. That is a complete sentence, and the meaning hasn't changed, so (D) is the best answer.

36. **H**   Three of the answer choices use *called* and one uses *calling*, so you should check that one first, but remember ACT doesn't really like the "-ing" form of verbs, and you should only pick it when all the other answer choices have an actual error. In this case, however, it doesn't make sense in the sentence—Dante was not literally calling out the word "Italian"—you can eliminate (J), and also (F) and (G), which make the sentence read the same way.

37. **B** Three of the answer choices use *spoken* and one uses *speak*, so you should check that one first. However, *to speak* doesn't make sense in the context of the sentence, so eliminate (D). There's no need to include *to be* or *if* as in (A) and (C); (B) makes the most sense—and it's the most concise—so it's the best answer choice.

38. **G** The answer choices all have Stop and Go punctuation (plus a colon) changing after the word *people*, so check for Complete/Incomplete on either side to see which you need. In this case, *By writing it in the language spoken by the Italian people* is incomplete, and since Stop punctuation can only connect two complete ideas, you can now eliminate (F) and (H). You can also eliminate (J), since a colon can only follow a complete idea. That leaves (G) as the only possible choice.

39. **C** All of the answer choices use the exact same words, just in different orders—you'll need to select the one that is most clear. Dante thought literature should be available to everyone, and was criticized for that opinion. The answer choice that expresses that idea in the most clear fashion is (C).

40. **G** Remember when ACT gives you a task to accomplish with an answer choice, you must read very literally—an answer choice that does the thing you want is a better choice than one that "could" do the thing you want. In this case, we need an answer choice that will imply that illiteracy changed from more common to less common. Be careful! If you just look at the words in the answer choices, *diminished* might seem the perfect candidate, but the passage is talking about *literacy*, not illiteracy. Therefore, you want the answer choice that says that literacy became more common, which would *imply* that illiteracy became less common—answer choice (G). Both (H) and (J) might conceivably accompany an increase in literacy, neither state that as clearly as (G) does.

41. **C** A good place to start here is to decide which verb form you need—always keeping in mind ACT's opinion of the "-ing" form. *Confuses* agrees with the subject, *title*, so eliminate (A) and (B). The use of *that* in (D) makes the sentence an incomplete idea, so the best answer choice is (C).

42. **J** There are transition words changing in the answer choices, but not punctuation, which will typically mean ACT is testing direction. Make sure you read enough to get the proper context! The two ideas we have to connect are *The Divine Comedy wasn't written in Latin* and *it was considered a comedy*. The sentence prior to this says *the label of "comedy" was attached to any work not written in Latin*, so you're going to need a same-direction transition—eliminate (F). (G), (H), and (J) are all same-direction transitions, but (G) and (H) have the relationship wrong—*The Divine Comedy* wasn't written in Latin as a result of being considered a comedy; it was the other way around. Note that in this case, (G) and (H) are "same" answer choices: *since* and *because* mean the exact same thing in this context, which means one cannot be more correct than the other; therefore, you cannot select either one.

43. **C** The answer choices all feature different transition words, but there's some punctuation changing as well. In fact, three of the answer choices use a comma and one doesn't—start there. In this instance, *and* causes an error, so eliminate (B). All the other answer choices end in a comma, which means the phrase *in defiance of the common beliefs of his time* is unnecessary since it's set off by a pair of commas— it may help to cross it out or simply ignore it to help answer the question. Without the unnecessary phrase (and its commas), the sentence now reads *Dante's brave decision, while demonstrated that it was not necessary for a literary masterpiece to be written in Latin, paved the way for future writers and readers alike.* That's not correct, so eliminate (A), and substituting *so that* for *while* doesn't help either— eliminate (D). That leaves answer choice (C), *which* as the correct answer.

44. **J** You have the option to DELETE the underlined portion, so try that first. You're left with a complete sentence, so it's at least possible to take out that word without creating an error. However, notice that the other choices are all transition words, so it may be a good idea to assess whether a transition is needed here. The prior sentence (now) reads *Dante's brave decision, which, in defiance of the common beliefs of his time, demonstrated that it was not necessary for a literary masterpiece to be written in Latin, paved the way for future writers and readers alike,* and then you have *The Divine Comedy remains a symbol of both literature and innovation today.* No transition is really needed here, and even if one were, it wouldn't be an opposite-direction one, as are (F), (G), and (H).

Passage IV

45. **B**   The answer choices are all different arrangements of the same three modifying phrases. On the ACT, (and in good writing in general), a modifying phrase must be placed next to the thing it's modifying. In this case, the words right before the underlined portion are *We would sit*, and the phrase that most directly modifies that is *on the couch*, so the correct answer choice must start with that phrase. Only (B) matches that description.

46. **H**   You have possessive pronouns changing in the answer choices, so to choose the correct one, you'll need to find the context in the non-underlined part of the passage. The answers being called out belong to the narrator and her grandmother, and since the passage is written in the first person, you need to use *our*, answer choice (H). If you're still unsure, notice that using *our* is consistent with the following sentence: *When our answers were right…*

47. **A**   You need to find the answer choice that is NOT a suitable replacement for the correctly-written underlined portion in the passage. The answer choices all have Stop and Go punctuation changing after the word *excitement*, so you should check for Complete/Incomplete on either side. Notice the sentence as written uses Stop punctuation (comma + FANBOYS), so you know the two ideas are complete. (B) and (C) both use different forms of Stop punctuation, and so can be used as replacements, and (D), even though it uses Go punctuation, inserts the word *or* into the second idea, making it incomplete, and so is also correct. What can NOT be used as a replacement is (A), which uses a comma to separate two complete ideas.

48. **J**   The first decision to make here is whether you need *regular* or *regularly*. The verb *watch* is being modified, so you need the adverb *regularly*—eliminate (F) and (G). (H) is incorrect because it uses the correct adverb but the wrong conjunction—the narrator and her grandmother don't watch the shows *as regularly* as they did prior to school starting.

49. **A**   The sentence *That was okay with me, though, because the one thing I liked better than watching game shows with my grandmother was helping her bake* introduces the main idea of the essay, and so serves as a transition between the discussion of the two activities the narrator enjoys with her grandmother. That's not unnecessary or detracting information as in (B), and (C) and (D) can be eliminated because they only talk about watching television.

50. **J**   You need to find the answer choice that is NOT a suitable replacement for the correctly-written underlined portion in the passage. (F), (G), and (H) all keep the original meaning of the sentence, but *help along* has a different meaning, and *help along the easy parts* doesn't really make sense; therefore (J) is NOT a suitable replacement.

51. **C** (C) describes the narrator as *awed* and *eager to taste*, which accomplishes both tasks: expressing both respect and enjoyment. (A) and (D) express lack of understanding and confusion, and (B) talks about homework.

52. **J** The three sentences describe a progression in the amount of help the narrator was allowed to give her grandmother in the kitchen: *At first* she only sat and watched (sentence 2). *As* [she] *got older*, she helped with the easier tasks (sentence 1). Finally, she reaches *the pinnacle of success* when she gets to separate the eggs (sentence 3).

53. **D** Whenever DELETE is an option, you should try that first. In this case, taking out *because I didn't need someone to keep an eye on me anymore* does not create an error or change the meaning; in fact, it gets rid of redundancy because the narrator has already said *my parents decided that I could take care of myself.* (B) and (C) are both redundant and wordy as well—pick (D).

54. **G** You need to find the answer choice that is NOT a suitable replacement for the correctly-written underlined portion in the passage. (F), (H), and (J) can all be used in place of *burned* in this context, but (G), *burnted*, far from being a replacement, can NOT be used—it's not even a word.

55. **C** The answer choices all have different pairs of words; notice the second word in each is a preposition. When you see prepositions changing, that's a good sign that ACT may be testing idioms. In this case, in order to express the idea of "attempted something for the first time," you need to use *tried out*, answer choice (C)

56. **H** You need to find the answer choice that is NOT a suitable replacement for the correctly-written underlined portion in the passage. Notice the answer choices all have different pairs of words, and the second word in each is a preposition: that's a good sign that ACT is testing idioms. In the context of the sentence, *flipped through* means, "quickly read the contents of a book." (F), (G), and (J) all convey that same meaning, but *tossed out* in (H) would imply she threw the book away, and so can NOT be used as a replacement.

57. **C** The answer choices all have Stop and Go punctuation changing after the same word: *voice*. Check for Complete/Incomplete on both sides. *As I flipped through the pages, I thought for a moment I could hear her voice* is complete, as is *although she's gone, I know that in the way that matters most, she'll never really be gone at all*. You need to use Stop punctuation to separate two complete ideas—eliminate (A) and (D). (B) is incorrect because the transition word makes the second idea incomplete, so you can't use it with a semicolon.

58. **H** When you see pronouns changing in the answer choice, find the noun that's being replaced: *She* (referring to the narrator's grandmother). Eliminate (F) because you can't use *which* to refer a person. (J) is the possessive pronoun *whose*, so look at the word that follows it; only nouns can be possessed. You can't possess *taught*, so eliminate (J). In this case, the pronoun is the subject of the verb *taught*, so you need *who*—answer choice (H).

59. **D** The main focus of the passage isn't baking; it's the relationship between the narrator and her grandmother—eliminate (A). (B) and (C) have the same problem. (D) is the only answer choice that mentions the narrator's grandmother.

60. **H** This sentence doesn't fit in the narrative of either paragraph 1 or 2, so eliminate (F) and (G). It should also come before the narrator says *Although she's gone* so that it's clear to the reader that her grandmother has passed away—(H) is the better answer choice for that reason.

Passage V

61. **D**   You have helping verbs changing in the answer choices, and recall the helping verbs need to agree with the subject, just like regular verbs. In this case, the subject of the sentence is *relationship*, which is singular, so eliminate (A), which is plural. (B) is an incorrect construction: It's "should have," not "should of." (C) makes the sentence seem to imply that the relationship was only complicated in the past, and isn't anymore, but there's no support for the latter in the passage. (D) is the best answer choice: The relationship *has always been complicated*.

62. **G**   The answer choices are all similar-sounding, so your ear isn't going to help much on this question. Expand out (F)—it means "they are," which doesn't make sense here. You need a word that shows the buffalo was the favored animal of the tribes, and in this context, that's the possessive pronoun *their*, answer choice (G).

63. **A**   The passage says the hunts were carried out *according to such strict rules... the hunt seemed more like a religious ritual*. When you use the word *such* in this context, you have to pair it with *that*, answer choice (A). If you chose (D), you may have misunderstood the relationship; the rules weren't strict as a result of the hunts seeming like a religious ritual—it's the other way around.

64. **J**   You need to choose an answer choice that makes a *clear allusion* to a story later in the essay. The only answer choice that even mentions a story is (J): *folklore and stories relating to humans' relationship with animals*.

65. **C**   You need to find the answer choice that is NOT a suitable replacement for the correctly-written underlined portion in the passage. (A), (B), and (D) all mean the same thing as the underlined word, *stories*. *Narrator* does NOT mean the same thing—it refers to someone who tells stories—so (C) is the correct choice.

66. **G**   You have three answer choices with *regularly* and one with *regular*, so check that one first. You need an adverb to modify the verb *interact*, so eliminate (H). In both (A) and (C), the verb *interact* has no subject, so eliminate them—(G), which joins the two verbs *live* and *interact* with *and*, giving them both a subject, is correct.

67. **D**   The answer choices all have Stop (comma + FANBOYS) and Go punctuation changing after the same word: *world*, so check for Complete/Incomplete on either side. *Human-rat coexistence may be common all around the world* is complete, and so is the part after the underlined portion: *different cultures respond to that closeness in different ways*. (A) has Go punctuation and adds *with*, which makes the second idea incomplete, but also doesn't make sense. (B) joins two complete ideas with a comma—eliminate it. (C) has the FANBOYS conjunction you're looking for, but like (A), adds *with*, which makes no sense. (D) is the best answer choice—it uses Stop punctuation to separate the two complete ideas.

68. **F** All four answer choices say the same thing in slightly different ways, and none contains a grammatical error. Therefore, pick the one that is the most concise: (F), NO CHANGE.

69. **B** The answer choices mostly have commas changing around, but one uses a colon, so start there. The colon follows a complete idea, *They don't*, which is proper, but what follows the colon is not a list, definition, or expansion of that idea (not to mention it's an extremely awkward construction), so eliminate (B). To choose the correct comma placement, remember your comma rules: *at least not directly* is unnecessary information, so you need to set it off with commas—the only answer choice that does that is (B).

70. **H** In the end of the sentence you have the statement *rats cause such a problem that a town has to hire a piper to call them all away* and you need to find the word to describe how rats have been portrayed that agrees with that most closely. (H), *negative*, agrees with the notion of the rats being a *problem* better than *different, mystical,* or *juvenile*.

71. **B** Aside from being the most concise, (B) avoids the problems found in the other choices. Remember, there's no slang on the ACT! (A) and (C) are too informal, besides being far too wordy. (D) might be tempting, but it's a bit too strong, and not very concise; remember the author has already told you different cultures respond to that [human-rat] closeness in different ways, so an example of one of those ways shouldn't really shock you.

72. **F** The correct answer choice has to provide a physical detail about rats, so (G) and (H) can be eliminated—neither of those is a physical detail. (J) certainly is a physical characteristic, but probably has less to do with the rat's association with teeth than a description of the rat's *very strong* teeth.

73. **A** The underlined portion introduces a new paragraph and the sentence *attitude toward the rat can be seen in the Chinese zodiac.* (B) and (C) cause redundancy in the sentence: the phrase *Chinese zodiac* already tells you you're talking about mysticism in China. (D) is temptingly concise, but the pronoun *their* has no noun to refer to, so you can't use it. (A) is the best answer since it both makes sense in the sentence and acts as an effective transition to the new paragraph after the discussion of a different example of people's attitude toward rats in the previous paragraph.

74. **H** Remember your comma rules here: This isn't a list, introductory idea, or unnecessary information, so there's really no reason to use a comma between any of the underlined words—eliminate (F), (G), and (J); the only choice you have is (H).

75. **C** If you want to divide the last paragraph into two based on a non-cultural frame of reference, you'll need to begin after the rat's description based on the Chinese zodiac—eliminate (A) and (B). The most logical place to begin the new paragraph, then, is (C), which begins talking about the rat's *cleverness*.

Part III
The ACT:
Reading

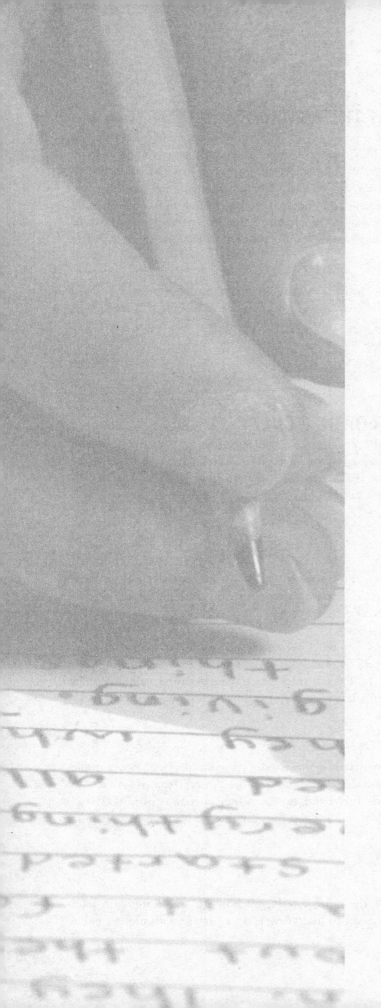

Chapter 5
The ACT
Reading Test

Even students with superior reading skills find this test to be tough. To crack the Reading test, you have to learn a strategic approach of *how* to work the passages in an order that makes sense for you. In this chapter, you'll learn how to order the passages and apply a basic approach.

FUN FACTS ABOUT THE ACT READING TEST

The Reading test consists of 4 passages, 10 questions each, for a total of 40 questions that you must answer in 35 minutes. There are many factors about the structure of this test that make it difficult. For one thing, the particular passages will obviously vary from test to test, so you can't predict whether you'll like the topic or find the passage more readable than not. Moreover, the questions are in neither order of difficulty nor chronological order. And while line references in the questions can make finding answers easier, it's not unusual to have passages with few line reference questions.

There are, however, several consistent factors on each test. The passages are all roughly the same length, and they always come in the same order: Prose Fiction, Social Science, Humanities, and Natural Science. But just because that's ACT's order doesn't mean it has to be yours.

PERSONAL ORDER OF DIFFICULTY (POOD)

To get your best score on the Reading test, you have to pick your own order of the passages, and on each passage, your own order of the questions. When time is your enemy, as it is on the ACT, find and work up front what's easier for you. Leave for last, or never, what's difficult for you.

The Passages

You can't risk doing the passages in the order ACT provides *just* because they're in that order. What if the Natural Science passage turned out to be the easiest and you ran out of time before you could get to it?

Every time you take the ACT, for practice and for real, pick the order of the passages that makes sense for you. There are four issues to consider when picking your order. In practice, you may build up a track record to determine a typical order. But pay attention to the particulars of each test and be willing to adapt your order.

1. Your POOD

Use your own POOD to identify the genres and topics you like best. For example, do you rarely read fiction outside of school? Then the Prose Fiction is unlikely to be a smart choice to do first. The topics, however, may change your mind. Read the blurbs to see if that day's Social Science, for example, is a topic you know more about than, say, the topic of the Humanities.

2. Paragraphs

The passages are all roughly the same length, but how they're arranged in paragraphs will differ. It's much easier to find answers on a passage with more, smaller paragraphs than on a passage with just a few huge paragraphs. Look for passages with 6–8 decent-sized paragraphs.

3. Questions

ACT can be pretty cheap with line references, so the more questions with line references the better. Glance at the questions: do you see many with numbers? That's a great sign.

4. Answers

Difficult questions tend to need longer answers. So look for many questions with short answers. Just like with line references, the more the better.

Be Flexible and Ruthless

Picking your order isn't a long, deliberative process. Use the practice passages in Chapter 6 to determine a typical order, but always be prepared to adapt. Take 10 seconds at the start of every ACT to look at the topics, paragraphs, questions, and answers to confirm or adapt your order.

Need More Practice?
1,296 ACT Practice Questions provides 6 tests' worth of Reading passages. That's 24 passages and 240 questions.

The Questions

Same song, different verse. You can't do the questions in the order ACT provides. They're not in order of difficulty, and they're not in chronological order. Instead, think of *Now, Later, Never*. Do Now any question that is either easy to answer OR for which the answer is easy to *find*. Do Later, or perhaps Never, questions that are both difficult to answer AND for which the answers are difficult to find.

1. Easy to Answer

ACT describes the questions in two categories: those that ask you to *refer* to what is directly stated, and those that require you to *reason* an implied meaning. In other words, reference questions ask what does the author *say*, while the reasoning questions ask what does the author *mean*. It's easier to answer "what does the author say?" than to answer "what is the author *really* saying?"

2. Easy to Find the Answer

A question easy to answer may do you no good if you can't find the answer in the passage. On the other hand, a reasoning question with a line reference tells you exactly where you can find the answer. Even if it's a tougher question to answer, do it Now if you know where to find the answer.

In a perfect world, we'd give you an exact order to follow every time. The ACT is not a perfect world. Instead, you have to consider the particulars of each test and know how to make an order that works on that test.

PACING

With just 35 minutes to do 4 passages and 40 questions, you don't have even 9 minutes for every passage. But should you do all 4 passages? Think about the pacing chart we discussed in Chapter 1. You may hit your scoring goals if you take more time and if you do fewer passages. On the other hand, you may decide that you can't get all of the questions right no matter how much time you spend. In that case, you're better off getting to as many Now questions as you can.

35 ÷ 4 ≠ 36

Whichever pacing strategy works for you, don't treat all the passages you work equally. That is, even if you work all 4, you shouldn't spend 8.75 minutes on each. Spend more time on your best passages and spend less on your worst. For example, spend 12 minutes on your first passage, 10 minutes on your second, 8 minutes on your third, and 5 minutes on your last. This is just an example: practice, practice, and practice to figure out a pacing strategy that will reach your target score.

POE

Many students destroy their pacing with one particular bad habit on the Reading test: they keep rereading and rereading part of the passage, trying to understand the answer to a tough question. But you're ignoring the one advantage of a multiple-choice test: the correct answer is right on the page. Use POE to eliminate three wrong answers to find the correct answer. It's not always easy to answer these questions, but you will likely be able to spot at least one wrong answer. In fact, using POE is a crucial step of our 4-step Basic Approach.

Now that you know how to pick your order of the passages, it's time to learn the Basic Approach.

THE BASIC APPROACH

The Reading test is an open-book test. You wouldn't read a whole book and answer all the questions from memory, so you shouldn't do that on the ACT. Instead, you need a smart, effective strategy.

Step 1: Preview
This step involves two parts.

First, check the blurb to see if there is additional information other than the title, author, and copyright. There usually isn't, but occasionally there is. You have to check each time to see if this one time is the exception.

> **HUMANITIES:** This passage is taken from The Century by Peter Jennings (© 1998 by ABC Television Network Group).

Second, map the questions. Put a star next to each line or paragraph reference, and underline the lead words. By lead words we mean words you'll actually find in the passage. Don't underline generic words like "main idea" or "how the author would characterize."

Here are ten mapped questions.

21. One of the main points the author formulates is that:

☆ 22. The author mentions a "photographic motion study" (line 36) in order to emphasize what quality of Duchamp's _Nude_?

☆ 23. The first paragraph states that certain early critics of modern art:

☆ 24. It can be inferred from the author's reference to "an explosion" and "an earthquake" (lines 38–40) that Duchamp's _Nude_:

☆ 25. As it is used in line 42, the word _abhorrent_ most nearly means:

26. It can be reasonably concluded from the passage that the most important characteristic of "modern" art was that it was:

27. Which of the following best describes Roosevelt's reaction to modern art?

☆ 28. It can reasonably be inferred that the use of the words "Ellis Island" (line 17) indicated that:

☆ 29. It can be inferred from the last paragraph that the organizers of the Armory Show:

30. Which of the following is NOT answered by the passage?

Spend no more than 30 seconds mapping the questions. Do not read the questions thoroughly for comprehension at this stage. Just spot the line and paragraph references to star and the lead words to underline.

Do look at the lead words you've underlined, however. They telegraph the main idea before you've read one word of the passage: this passage is about modern art.

Step 2: Work the Passage

In this next step, spend no more than 3 minutes on the passage. Look for and underline your lead words. If you struggle with time, read only the first sentence of each paragraph. You'll read what you need to answer specific questions.

Here are the first sentences of each paragraph to our passage, with the lead words from some questions found and underlined.

> The show was grandly titled "The International Exhibition of <u>Modern Art</u>," but the dynamite, as *The New Yorker* later commented, was in the word <u>"modern."</u>
>
> The star image of the exhibition was most certainly <u>Duchamp's *Nude Descending a Staircase*</u> (or, as <u>Roosevelt</u> called it, "a naked man going downstairs"), a painting so abstract it defied its own title, which, of course, was the point.
>
> <u>Roosevelt said Duchamp's *Nude*</u> reminded him of a Navaho rug he stood upon while shaving each morning in his bathroom.
>
> Anticipating a reluctant audience, the <u>organizers of the Armory Show</u> had included an editorial in the exhibition catalog urging viewers to greet the new art with an open mind.

Between the stars and the lead words you found in the first sentences of the paragraphs, you have a lot of questions whose answers are easy to find, and you're ready to move on to the next step.

Step 3: Work the Questions

Work the questions in an order that makes sense: do the Now questions that are easy to answer or whose answers are easy to find. Look at all the stars on questions 22, 23, 24, 25, 28, and 29. You know where to read to find those answers. But when you worked the passage, you found the locations for questions 26 and 27.

Do Later, or Never, questions that are both difficult to answer and whose answers are difficult to find. Questions 21 and 30 are both good Later/Never questions.

As you make your way through the Now questions, read a window of 5–10 lines to find the answer.

Here's an example.

> **22.** The author mentions a "photographic motion study" (line 36) in order to emphasize what quality of Duchamp's *Nude*?

Now read lines 27–37 to find the answer.

> The star image of the exhibition was most certainly Duchamp's <u>*Nude Descending a Staircase*</u> (or, as <u>Roosevelt</u> called it, "a naked man going downstairs"), a painting so
> 30 abstract it defied its own title, which, of course, was the point. As critic Robert Hughes has pointed out, the nude had a long and distinguished history with painting, where she (and, more rarely, he) was usually portrayed in a blissful state of recline; by contrast, <u>Duchamp's *Nude*</u>, to the degree that it looked at
> 35 all like what it was supposed to be, was a nude on the move (indeed, the painting had the quality of a photographic motion study), a metaphor for the change that it heralded.

You may feel you've spotted the exact line with the answer, but don't worry if you haven't. Move to the last step, and Work the Answers with POE.

Step 4: Work the Answers

If you can answer the question in your own words, go through the answers and look for a match. If you can't answer it, don't worry. Review each answer, and eliminate the ones you're confident are wrong.

> **F.** The different interpretations of the painting
> **G.** The painting's photographic realism
> **H.** The painting's inappropriate subject matter
> **J.** The movement implied in the painting

Here's How to Crack It

Lines 35–37 describe the painting as *a nude on the move*, which choice (J) paraphrases well. Alternatively, use POE to get rid of choice (F), because there is only one interpretation of the painting, and choice (H), because there is no proof that the author disapproves of the subject matter. Choice (G) may tempt you because of *to the degree that it looked at all like what it was supposed to be* in lines 34–35, but those lines actually argue against photographic realism.

Never answer specific questions from memory. Always read a window of 5–10 lines to find the answer to each question, using the line references and lead words as a guide.

Step 4

Repeat

Steps 3 and 4 repeat: make your way through the rest of the questions, reading what you need for each. Use POE to find the answers. Continue to make smart choices about the order of your questions, doing every Now question that is easy to answer or whose answer is easy to find.

Save for Last

The toughest reasoning questions should be done last (if at all—your pacing strategy may mark them as Never). After you've worked all the specific questions on the passage, you understand the main theme better. Questions 21 and 30 for this passage are both smart choices to do last.

Now move to chapter 6 to practice picking your order and applying the Basic Approach.

Summary

Pick your order of the passages.

Use your POOD to identify the genres and topics you like best.

Pay attention to your track record in practice.

Examine the particulars of each test and be prepared to confirm or change your order each time.

Look for passages with many, small paragraphs.

Look for passages with many line reference questions.

Look for passages with many short answers.

Use the 4-step Basic Approach.

1. Preview
2. Work the Passage
3. Work the Questions
4. Work the Answers

Chapter 6
Reading Practice
Drills for the ACT

READING TEST

35 Minutes—40 Questions

DIRECTIONS: There are four passages in this test. Each passage is followed by several questions. After reading each passage, choose the best answer to each question and blacken the corresponding oval on your answer document. You may refer to the passages as often as necessary.

Passage I

PROSE FICTION: The following passage is adapted from the short story "Between Two Homes" by Herbert Malloy (© 1993 by Herbert Malloy).

The fact that air travel allows me to fall asleep on the west coast and wake up on the east coast is bittersweet magic. On a red-eye flight, the continent passes stealthily underneath like an ugly secret we prefer not to acknowledge. Passengers drift
5 in and out of an unsteady slumber, reluctantly awakening to the realization that they are still stuck on an airplane. Sometimes I open my eyes wide enough to gaze out the window at the twinkling lights of the towns and cities below.

I try to decipher which city glimmers below from the size
10 of its grid of light, as well as my perception of how long I have been flying. Could that be Denver? Have I already napped a third of the flight? I look around the cabin to see how many other people are having trouble sleeping and become instantly jealous of the families and couples who have the luxury of
15 leaning on each other.

The aura of cool sunlight begins to infiltrate the cabin as we near Dulles, Virginia. We see flocks of birds sharing the sky with us. By the time we arrive, we will have flown through three time zones, compressing a normal night by removing three of
20 its sacred hours. We are not only cheating space by crossing a continent in the course of a long nap, but also cheating time by turning back our watches and rushing prematurely toward the sunrise.

25 My hometown is still a car ride away, but the vicinity of the airport is close enough to be a tonic to my nostalgic yearnings. As soon as I see the dense stands of oak and hickory blanketing the hills, I know I am back home. There's no trace of palm trees, no unrelenting flat stretches of compacted and
30 perpendicular city streets. Left behind in our plane's exhaust, Southern California is still fast asleep.

*   *   *   *   *   *

My dad has driven to the airport to pick me up, but I very nearly miss him—I'd forgotten he now drives a different car. I'm sure I've heard him speak of his new blue Toyota, but I
35 always expect him to be driving the brown Lexus he owned when I moved away. Happily, the smell inside the car remains the same: stretched leather, cologne, and the faint hint of a cigarette that was meant to go undetected. I covertly scan the side of his face while he drives, hoping to see the same face I
40 remember. Instead I see new wrinkles, new spots on his face, new folds of skin on his neck.

We pass by familiar landmarks as we near our house, as well as some not-so-familiar ones. The performance stage in the town center that was merely a proposal when I left is now
45 up-and-running, according to the marquee listing its upcoming shows. The Olde Towne Tavern is apparently now called Summit Station. The old dance studio above the apartment buildings on West Deer Park seems to have finally closed – I always wondered how it stayed in business. The cluster of shops that
50 famously burned to the ground near the high school has open doors and cars gliding in and out of the parking lot.

We've arrived at the house, and as soon as I walk through the door, I am flooded with further reminders of my absence – trinkets on the wall I don't recognize, rearranged furniture in
55 the kitchen and living room, sugary cereals and snacks strangely absent from the top of the fridge. What was once my home has become someone else's house – my parents' house.

I suddenly see the mundane routines of my parents cast in a tragic light: my mother's agitation at the grackles that scare
60 the goldfinches away from the bird-feeders, my father's habit of pretending to read the newspaper on the porch (just an opportunity to keep an eye on the neighborhood), the uninspired television they watch at night, often in separate rooms, and, most depressingly, the way they often fall asleep in front of
65 the television, mouths gaping.

*   *   *   *   *   *

The in-flight movie on the way back to California portrays the story of a physicist who awakens after spending ten years in a coma. His initial joy gradually subsides and ultimately leads to confusion and sadness as he attempts to reintegrate into a
70 world that has moved on without him. Even science, that rock of immutable truths, has changed in his absence. He finds the entire body of research he had been working on prior to his coma now obsolete—years of advances in his field had furnished the answers he was pursuing.

75 As a physicist, he knew that time is a relative phenomenon, a concept that only has meaning in relation to an individual's succession of experiences and ordering of memories. Clearly, though, his world, like mine, had continued to age, changing despite his lack of participation in it. Years are passing whether
80 you're there to observe them or not.

1. It can reasonably be inferred from the passage that the narrator thinks air travel is:

   A. the most enjoyable way to travel.
   B. an ordinary part of the world.
   C. more uncomfortable than convenient.
   D. somewhat unnatural in what it makes possible.

2. The first three paragraphs (lines 1–24) establish all of the following about the narrator EXCEPT that he is:

   F. onboard an airplane
   G. traveling east.
   H. departing from Denver.
   J. noticing sights below.

3. The point of view from which the passage is told is best described as that of:

   A. a young adult returning from a vacation to Southern California.
   B. an adult relating his reactions to visiting to his hometown.
   C. a young adult awakening from a long coma.
   D. an adult who prefers Southern California to his new home.

4. According to the narrator, which of the following things is relatively new to his parents' house?

   F. Certain trinkets on the wall.
   G. The fridge.
   H. His father's brown Lexus.
   J. The bird-feeders.

5. The passage contains recurring references to all of the following EXCEPT:

   A. difficulty sleeping.
   B. birds.
   C. grids of light.
   D. dancing.

6. The narrator indicates that the most upsetting habit of his parents is:

   F. buying new cars.
   G. how and where they fall asleep.
   H. what they watch on television.
   J. how many trinkets they buy.

7. According to the passage, the coma victim has a sense of time as a relative phenomenon because:

   A. ten years had gone by quickly.
   B. he was a physicist.
   C. it was a side effect of his medical treatments.
   D. it was the focus of his research before his coma.

8. Based on the narrator's account, all of the following are part of the present, rather than the past, in his hometown EXCEPT:

   F. the closed dance studio.
   G. the upcoming show marquee.
   H. Summit Station.
   J. the burnt remains of a shopping center.

9. Details in the passage most strongly suggest that one characteristic of the narrator's hometown is:

   A. flat stretches.
   B. palm trees.
   C. oak trees.
   D. perpendicular streets.

10. When the narrator refers to science as "that rock of immutable truths" (lines 70–71), he is most likely directly referring to:

   F. the unchanging nature believed to be characteristic of scientific knowledge.
   G. the physicist's inability to understand the recent advances in science.
   H. the body of research conducted in the physicist's field during his coma.
   J. the ten years' worth of scientific advances that the narrator had missed.

SOCIAL SCIENCE: The following passage is adapted from the 2002 article "Indigenous Goes Global" by Sally Mayfield.

MayaWorks is a nonprofit organization that attempts to promote fair trade practices with Mayan artisans who would otherwise have little commercial outlet for their talents. In a broader sense, the organization aims to help traditionally
5 marginalized Guatemalan women attain the literacy, advanced skills, business acumen, and confidence they need to contribute to the economic well-being of their families.

"Buried deep in the Guatemalan mountains are these amazing pockets of Mayan communities," begins Dennis Ho-
10 gan, a chief program administrator for Berhorst Partners for Development. Communities such as Agua Caliente, Xetonox, and Tzanjuyu are often as small as 50-100 people. They speak their own ancient Mayan dialects and rarely interact with the Spanish-speaking majority of Guatemala. "They have a rich
15 lineage of religious, linguistic, and artistic traditions that get passed down from generation to generation. However, they are deeply threatened by extreme poverty and lack of potable water. We want to find a way for these women to grow with the times, despite rigidly-defined gender roles that relegate women to food
20 preparation and child care, but also to help them utilize and preserve the cultural traditions that make them so irreplaceable."

When representatives from MayaWorks first reached out to women in Agua Caliente in 1994, the men of the village were deeply suspicious. The women were extremely shy, avoiding
25 almost all eye contact with the strangers. Ultimately, though, the women of the village agreed to the idea of forming a weaving cooperative and came up with an initial product order they felt they could fill. Each of eight women was to weave a dozen brightly colored wall hangings that spelled the word "peace"
30 in a number of languages. Weeks later, with great pride, the women delivered their order, using local material for the hanging rods and the finest yarn they could find, dyed and then washed to prevent staining.

"When we returned to pick up the finished products and
35 pay them, there was a remarkable change in the way we were received by the villagers," Hogan reflects with deep satisfaction. "The women were beaming with self-confidence, and the children even thanked us in their native tongue for helping give their mothers work."

40 The variety of wares created by MayaWorks artisans has greatly expanded over time. Corn husks are used to make decorative angels. Yarn is woven into brightly-colored placemats, napkins, pouches, Beanies, and footbags. Some groups even make religious items, such as stoles for Christian priests
45 and yarmulkes, or kippahs, for Jewish observers. Making the kippahs was initially an engineering challenge for the villagers, as the small head-coverings frequently came out either too flat or too round. Given a mannequin, however, the villagers were soon able to master the correct shape. Once told that the kippah

50 was a symbol for the wearer's reverence to God, the villagers became even more devoted and loving in their craft.

The capacity of these artisans for learning, adapting, and innovating has delighted the founders of MayaWorks. As relationships develop between MayaWorks and individual groups of
55 artisans, new equipment and training is introduced to broaden their design capacity. 36-inch treadle-foot looms now allow members of Xetonox to create fabrics that can be sold by the yard side-by-side with mass-manufactured textiles.

In addition to broadening the range of products these vil-
60 lagers can create, MayaWorks hopes to expand the knowledge base of the women and help provide infrastructure to enable a better life for them and future generations. Leslie Buchanan heads up the Literacy Initiative for MayaWorks and explains, "Part of the challenge these communities face is their cultural
65 isolation from other Guatemalans. They avoid going to marketplaces in nearby cities because they don't speak Spanish. That makes it difficult for them to navigate the buses and other transportation. And it makes it hard to negotiate with Spanish-speaking merchants. In an economy where the first price you
70 hear is never supposed to be the final price, the inability to haggle makes you unfit to make purchases."

Although literacy programs provided by outsiders are typically met with resistance by Mayan communities, MayaWorks has achieved considerable success in motivating Mayan villag-
75 ers to learn Spanish. This success where others have failed has more to do with the economic initiatives of MayaWorks than its literacy campaigns: once the villagers have the opportunity and means to expand their economic base, the desire to learn Spanish comes naturally, from within, as a tool to help them
80 achieve even greater success. Rather than appearing as a threat to their traditions, the Spanish language now appears as a means of preserving the well-being of their traditional communities.

Another component of MayaWorks is coordinating and encouraging the financing of microcredit loans, small loans
85 offered to impoverished people who have no collateral or credit history (and thus could never qualify for a traditional banking loan). By providing these Mayan villagers with much-needed capital, MayaWorks helps them to upgrade their weaving equipment, install water pumps (which greatly reduces the
90 health problems associated with meager and contaminated water sources), and buy crops such as blackberries, potatoes, and strawberries. These measures both increase the sustainability of the community and encourage entrepreneurship. So far, MayaWorks reports, 100% of their microcredit loans have
95 been paid back in full and on time.

11. In the context of the passage, the statement "the men of the village were deeply suspicious" (lines 23–24) most nearly suggests that Mayan men:

A. felt uneasy about the potential interest in employing their village's women.
B. didn't believe that MayaWorks representatives were who they said they were.
C. rarely were visited by people who could speak Spanish.
D. were skeptical that the women of the village had artistic talents.

12. The main purpose of the second paragraph (lines 8–21) is to:

F. lend support to the notion that women in Guatemala deserve stronger legal rights.
G. point out the small number of people who live in Amazon villages.
H. establish the value that programs such as MayaWorks could provide.
J. explain how Berhorst Partners for Development became based in Guatemala.

13. The passage indicates all of the following as problems initially faced by the fledgling Mayan artisans EXCEPT that:

A. they lacked a mannequin to facilitate designing headwear.
B. they could not communicate well in Spanish-speaking marketplaces.
C. they did not have looms capable of making yard-width fabrics.
D. they were unable to find material for the hanging rods in their wall hangings.

14. It can most reasonably be inferred from the passage that regarding MayaWorks, the author feels:

F. appreciative of the organization's methods and intentions.
G. convinced that mountain villagers in other countries will join MayaWorks.
H. doubtful about the quality of the artisans' wares.
J. confused by the organization's conflicting priorities.

15. Which of the following assumptions would be most critical for a reader to accept in order to agree with the author's claims in the passage?

A. Mayan communities should fully assimilate into their surrounding Spanish-speaking communities.
B. One's self-esteem can be improved by performing productive work in exchange for money.
C. Mayan artisans have much difficulty in adapting to design specifications of items that are not traditionally Mayan.
D. Most major banks would consider the Mayan artist co-operatives to be appealing candidates for loans.

16. The passage indicates that approximately how many wall hangings were part of the initial order filled by the Agua Caliente village?

F. Eight
G. A Dozen
H. One hundred
J. One thousand

17. According to the passage, when villagers were told of the religious function of a kippah, they became even more:

A. confused about its shape.
B. appreciative of their mannequin.
C. intrigued about Judaism.
D. dedicated to their work.

18. The passage states that each of the following is among the products made by MayaWorks artists EXCEPT:

F. yarmulkes.
G. wall hangings.
H. mass-manufactured textiles.
J. placemats.

19. The main function of the last paragraph (lines 83–95) is to:

A. discuss the specific terms and requirements of several types of loans.
B. describe some important ways that outside investment has helped strengthen Mayan communities.
C. itemize some of the ways Mayan artisans have reinvested their earnings.
D. demonstrate that Mayan villagers are as trustworthy in business as they are skilled in art.

20. The passage indicates that the efforts of MayaWorks to increase the Spanish literacy of the Mayan community may succeed because they:

F. have instilled in the Mayan women an economic incentive to learn Spanish.
G. have familiarized Mayan women with the bartering rules of Guatemalan marketplaces.
H. convinced Mayan women that their traditions will be better preserved in Spanish.
J. designed a more innovative and thoughtful literacy campaign than had previous initiatives.

Passage III

HUMANITIES: This passage is adapted from the article "Life in the Pits" by Bob Gullberg (© 2003 by Hennen Press).

Mozart and Handel refer to Wolfgang Amadeus Mozart (1756-91), Classical-era composer, and George Frideric Handel (1685-1759), Baroque-era composer.

Looking back over a twenty-year career of playing, composing, and now conducting orchestra music, I often feel a sense of wonder—not at what I have accomplished, but how someone with my agrarian, rather workaday upbringing should
5 have chosen such a path at all. It would have been easy for me to stay on the family farm, eventually to become part-owner, as my brother did quite successfully. However, rewarding as this existence was, it was somehow unfulfilling; my youthful imagination, much to my parents' dismay, often cast about for
10 other, greater pursuits to occupy it. Still, growing up as I did in a household where the radio dispensed milk prices instead of Mozart and hog futures instead of Handel, the thought of embarking on a career in classical music went beyond even my wildest imagination.

15 Perhaps what started me down this unforeseen path was my fascination with other languages. At church services I would hear snippets of Latin and Greek; I was learning Spanish at school; I was instantly drawn to the German, Italian, and Yiddish words and phrases I heard in movies and on T.V.
20 Surrounded as I was by the fairly common language of farm and field, these "glamorous" expressions seemed to fill a void in me, and I collected them with the energy of a lepidopterist netting butterflies. As my interest in other languages grew, so did my awareness that music is itself a language, just as capable
25 of expressing and inspiring emotion or thought as the spoken word—sometimes even more so. Take The Tempest, the piece I'm currently rehearsing with my orchestra. It begins in a major key, with just the stringed instruments playing lightly, evoking a sense of peace and contentment—a calm, sunny summer's
30 day. In the second movement, the key diminishes; the mood darkens—clouds and apprehension are building. As the piece progresses, wind instruments, as if blown by the storm, begin to howl, horns blare and shout, overwhelming the senses, thrilling and frightening at once. As the "storm" reaches its height,
35 timpani-roll thunder echoes, and cymbal-clash lightning bolts crash relentlessly, until, when it becomes almost unbearable, the music eases, hope and reason are restored, and soothing notes help the listener forget the chaos and fear he or she felt only moments ago. I've read many accounts of severe weather,
40 even seen them in movies and on TV, but few of them, if any, have been able to replicate not only the sensory experience of a thunderstorm, but also the emotional one the way this piece of music can.

I believe it was music's emotive influence—particularly
45 powerful in my impressionable youth—that ultimately led me to pursue a career in music. Once I began to experience music on an emotional level, I remember having the feeling that others just didn't "get it" like I did, as if somehow music were meant just for musicians. It was only later that I became
50 aware of music's true value—it is a universal language, able to speak to all people, regardless of the linguistic differences that may exist between them. Eventually, of course, music began to eclipse the numerous other "passions" I had throughout my adolescence. Years before I began to pursue music in earnest,
55 I had developed quite an interest in all things motorized. I've always had a mechanical bent (which has served me well in later life, allowing me to turn my hand to almost any musical instrument), and being around farm equipment from an early age certainly gave me an outlet to exercise my abilities. How-
60 ever, my real focus was on cars—I virtually never set down *Automobile Monthly*, a magazine for auto enthusiasts, and I eagerly devoured articles describing which models had the highest horsepower or quickest times in the quarter-mile, and effortlessly committing that information to memory. Eventu-
65 ally, though, like my previous infatuations with archery, and before that dinosaurs, my fixation on cars was to take a "back seat" to a new, greater, and this time lasting, passion for music.

So what made the difference? What made my passion for music continue to burn where other passions had fizzled out?
70 Maturity, perhaps—I know I'd like to think that's the case—or maybe it was just a process of compare-and-contrast; trying different things until I found the one that "fit." If I'm honest with myself, however, I'm forced to admit the answer isn't a "what" or "when", but a "who." For me, like many who find
75 themselves adrift on a sea of uncertainty, it took a mentor to help me find my way to dry land. In my case, that mentor was the conductor of my high-school orchestra, Ms. Fenchurch. A woman of boundless energy and enthusiasm, and with an all-consuming love for music, it was she who first taught me the
80 joy of composition and creation, and helped me to realize that making music is more than just playing notes in a particular order, no matter how well it's done—it's about expression, and perhaps more important, communication. Just like a language.

21. The author mentions *Automobile Monthly* and his mechanical bent primarily to suggest that his:

A. infatuation with cars was at one time as intense as his passion for music.

B. interest in and love of all things motorized has remained unchanged throughout his life.

C. experience with motorized things accounts for his mechanical style of playing music.

D. obsession with automotive knowledge distracted him from focusing on music.

22. In the first paragraph, the author most nearly characterizes his upbringing as:

    F. easy and usually spent working with his brother.

    G. frustrating yet able to translate easily into music.

    H. somewhat satisfying yet ultimately unable to captivate.

    J. unfulfilling and invariably resulting in his parents' approval.

23. Based on the passage, which of the following was most likely the first to engage the author's passionate interest?

    A. Automobiles

    B. Archery

    C. Dinosaurs

    D. Music

24. Viewed in the context of the passage, the statement in lines 39–43 is most likely intended to suggest that:

    F. music more vividly conveys some experiences than do visual or written accounts.

    G. movies can provide a misleading experience of what a thunderstorm is like.

    H. news reports should more accurately reflect emotional experiences.

    J. thunderstorms are among the hardest experiences to accurately replicate.

25. The passage suggests that the lepidopterist netting butterflies represents:

    A. the author as a child, relishing learning foreign expressions.

    B. the author presently, enjoying his most recent passion.

    C. Ms. Fenchurch, with her boundless energy.

    D. the opening movement of The Tempest.

26. In the context of the passage, lines 34–39 are best described as presenting images of:

    F. jealously, mercy, and resentment.

    G. hate, fear, and disbelief.

    H. conflict, optimism, and love.

    J. chaos, resolution, and relaxation.

27. The author discusses "playing notes in a particular order" (lines 81–82) as part of Ms. Fenchurch's argument that:

    A. the order of notes matters less than the speed at which they are played.

    B. all music consists of the same parts but rearranged in creative ways.

    C. while one aims to be skilled at performing notes, one should also aim to convey their meaning.

    D. although communication is important, there is more joy to be found in composition itself.

28. Which of the following does NOT reasonably describe a transition presented by the author in lines 27–34?

    F. Lightness to darkness

    G. Calm to thrilling

    H. Apprehension to fright

    J. Overwhelmed to peaceful

29. The main purpose of the last paragraph is to:

    A. describe the lasting influence of Ms. Fenchurch's encouragement.

    B. present an anecdote that conveys Ms. Fenchurch's unique conducting style.

    C. provide detailed background information about Ms. Fenchurch.

    D. illustrate the effect music has on teachers such as Ms. Fenchurch.

30. The passage is best described as being told from the point of view of a musician who is:

    F. telling a linear story that connects momentous events from the beginning of his career to some from the end.

    G. describing how modern works of music such as The Tempest have advanced the vision of classical composers such as Mozart and Handel.

    H. suggesting that people who have an interest in universal languages would be well served in studying music.

    J. marveling at his eventual choice of career and considering the people and interests that contributed to it.

Passage IV

NATURAL SCIENCE: This passage is adapted from the article "Debunking the Seahorse" by Clark Millingham (© 2002 by Halcyon Press).

Scientists and laymen alike have long been fascinated by fish known colloquially as seahorses, due to the species' remarkable appearance, unusual mating habits, and incredibly rare reversal of male and female parental roles. The scientific name for the
5   genus is Hippocampus, which combines the Greek word for "horse," *hippos*, with the Greek word for "sea monster," *kampos*. Its distinctive equine head and tapered body shape are a great disadvantage when it comes to the seahorse's swimming ability. It manages to maneuver about by fluttering its dorsal fin up to
10   35 times a second, but it lacks the caudal, or "tail" fin, which provides the powerful forward thrust for most fish. Instead of swimming to find food, the seahorse coils its signature prehensile tail around stationary objects while using its long snout like a straw to suck in vast numbers of tiny larvae, plankton, and
15   algae. Because the seahorse lacks teeth and a stomach, food passes quickly through its digestive tract, resulting in the need for nearly incessant consumption of food (a typical seahorse can ingest more than 3,000 brine shrimp per day).

The peculiar physical features of the seahorse are intriguing,
20   but its mating and reproductive habits are most often the subject of scientists' fascination and debate. Seahorses' courtship rituals often involve a male and a female coordinating their movements, swimming side by side with tails intertwined or coiling around the same strand of sea grass and spinning around it together.
25   They even "dress up" for these rituals, turning a whole array of vivid colors—a sharp contrast to the dull browns and grays with which they typically camouflage themselves among the sea grasses. Courtship typically lasts about two weeks, during which the female and her potential mate will meet once a day,
30   while other males continue to compete for the female's attention, snapping their heads at each other and tail-wrestling.

By the end of the courtship, the female has become engorged with a clutch of around 1,000 eggs, equivalent in mass to one-third her body weight. It is the male, however, who possesses
35   the incubating organ for the eggs, a brood pouch located on his ventral (front) side. The male forces sea water through the pouch to open it up, signifying his readiness to receive the eggs. Uncoiling their tail-grips, the two attach to each other and begin a spiraling ascent towards the surface. The female inserts her
40   ovipositor, a specialized biological apparatus for conducting the eggs into the male's pouch, and the eggs are transferred over the course of eight or nine hours. After that, the male stays put while the female ventures off, only to check in briefly once a day for the next few weeks.

45   Inside the male's brood pouch, the eggs are fertilized and receive prolactin, the same hormone mammals use for milk production. The pouch delivers oxygen to the eggs via a network of capillaries and regulates a low-salinity environment. As the gestation continues, the eggs hatch and the pouch becomes
50   increasingly saline to help acclimate the young seahorses to the salt-water that is waiting outside. The male typically gives birth at night, expelling anywhere from 100 to 1,500 live fry from its pouch. By morning, he once again has an empty pouch to offer his partner if she is ready to mate again.

55   Because male parenting is such a rarity in the animal kingdom, and male gestation almost unheard-of, scientists often speculate on why male seahorses assume birthing duties. Since giving birth is so energy-intensive and physically limiting, it greatly increases one's risk of death and therefore needs an
60   explanation in terms of evolutionary cost. Bateman's principle holds that whichever sex expends less energy in the reproductive process should be the sex that spends more energy competing for a mate. Only with seahorses do we see the males both compete for mates and give birth. A study conducted by Pierre
65   Robinson at the University of Tallahassee argued that, contrary to appearances, the total energy investment of the mother in growing the clutch of eggs inside of her still outweighed the energy investment of the male in the incubation and birthing process. Male oxygen intake rates go up by 33% during their
70   parental involvement, while the female spends twice as much energy when generating eggs.

In addition to male pregnancy, seahorses also have the distinction of being one of a very small number of monoga-mous species. Scientists believe this is due to the tremendous
75   investment of time and energy that goes into each clutch of eggs a female produces. If her eggs are ready to be incubated and the female does not have a trustworthy male partner ready to receive them, they will be expelled into the ocean and months will have been lost. Additionally, by transferring incubation
80   and birthing duties to the male, a stable monogamous couple can develop an efficient birthing cycle in which he incubates one clutch of eggs while the female begins generating the next.

31. The passage notes that the courtship rituals of seahorses include:

A. males snapping their heads at females.
B. camouflaging their body coloring.
C. allowing sea water to open the brood pouch.
D. daily meetings for two weeks.

32. The passage states that the seahorse's swimming ability is hindered by its:

F. tapered body shape.
G. weak caudal fin.
H. fluttering dorsal fin.
J. lack of teeth.

33. Which of the following pieces of information does the most to resolve scientists' confusion as to why male seahorses both compete for mates and give birth?

A. The fact that the female seahorse possesses an ovipositor.
B. Pierre Robinson's research on the total energy investment of each sex.
C. The habit of seahorses to mate with only one partner.
D. The length of time male seahorses devote to courtship rituals.

34. One of the main ideas established by the passage is that:

F. seahorses are actually quite capable swimmers, despite their unusual appearance.
G. scientists cannot come up with any coherent explanation for why male seahorses have the evolutionary burden of gestation.
H. the brood pouch of the male is located on its ventral side.
J. it is not customary in the animal kingdom for animals to keep the same mating partner for life.

35. As it is used in line 13, the word *signature* most nearly means:

A. distinctive-looking.
B. very useful.
C. autograph.
D. legally obligated.

36. The main purpose of the fourth paragraph (lines 46–55) is to describe the:

F. process linking fertilization to hatching.
G. intricacies of the seahorse's capillary network.
H. quantity of fry to which males give birth.
J. amount of salinity seahorse eggs can tolerate.

37. The passage most strongly emphasizes that the monogamy of seahorse mates is most advantageous for the transition from:

A. low-salinity to high-salinity.
B. one birthing cycle to the next.
C. fertilization to incubation.
D. courtship to mating.

38. As it is used in line 80, the word *lost* most nearly means:

F. mislaid.
G. disoriented.
H. squandered.
J. defeated.

39. According to the passage, which of the following aspects of a male seahorse's pregnancy provides the best evidence that the seahorse species conforms to the idea behind Bateman's Principle?

A. Brood pouch
B. Ovipositor
C. Prolactin
D. Oxygen intake

40. The passage indicates that the brood pouch becomes increasingly saline because seahorse eggs:

F. would otherwise run the risk of prematurely hatching.
G. begin gestation in a low salinity environment but ultimately get released into the surrounding water.
H. have salt extracted from them by the capillary network that delivers oxygen to the brood pouch.
J. receive the hormone prolactin but do not have the exposure to salt that other mammals do.

READING TEST
35 Minutes—40 Questions

DIRECTIONS: There are four passages in this test. Each passage is followed by several questions. After reading each passage, choose the best answer to each question and blacken the corresponding oval on your answer document. You may refer to the passages as often as necessary.

Passage I

PROSE FICTION: This passage is adapted from the novel *The Smell of Fresh Muffins* by Woody Jessup (©1985 by Woody Jessup).

The narrator is going to help his grandfather paint a room in the narrator's house. Garth is a friend of the narrator's grandfather.

Garth should be here any minute. I'm kind of glad, actually, that Grandpa sent his buddy to pick us up. Daddy always runs late because he tries to squeeze in one extra thing at the last minute, and Grandpa tends to misjudge how slowly he drives
5 nowadays. Garth has only picked us up a couple times before, but each time he was here at 2:17 on the nose.

Garth seems to see his schedule as various-sized blocks of activities that must be inserted into the correct-sized slot of time. Grandpa says that since Garth's wife died, Garth has
10 married his schedule. He says people use a routine to distract themselves from their life. Grandpa seems to know human nature pretty well, so I believe him.

We see Garth's tan Oldsmobile pull slowly into the parking lot. His car is a good match for his personality: boring but reli-
15 able. Garth doesn't joke too much with people besides Grandpa. He was in the Marines for many years in the fifties. His posture and his way of speaking to people are both perfectly upright.

"Hey, kids. How was school?" Garth asks as we start pil-ing into the back seat. "You know, one of you can sit up front."

20 Sis and I exchange a look with each other, hiding our feel-ings of reluctance. I remind her, with my eyes, that last time I rode up front, and she silently accepts her fate.

We start to drive off towards our house, where my Grandpa is currently re-painting our living room.

25 "You two ever done any painting?" Garth asks. We shake our heads. "It's like icing a cupcake. Does your mom ever let you do that? I mean, did she?"

"Sometimes." Clara chimes in. "She normally gave us one or two to play with, but she knew we couldn't make 'em as
30 pretty as she could, with that little swirl thing on top."

"Ah, of course." Garth grins. "Well, that swirl is what paint-ing is all about. If you start with too little icing, you smear it

out thin to cover the whole top of the cupcake, but you can still see the cake peeking through, right?"

35 We nod. He continues, "But if you start with a good dollop, more than you really need, you can swoosh it around with one clever twist of your wrist. The extra stuff just comes off onto your knife ... or your paintbrush if you're painting."

"Maybe I need smarter wrists," Clara sighs skeptically.

40 We park a block down from our house so that Daddy won't see Garth's car when he gets home from work. Grandpa wanted the painted room to be a surprise.

As soon as we step in our kitchen door, we can smell the paint from the living room. Grandpa is wearing paint-covered
45 overalls, but the paint stains are dry, and none of them are the bright sky color that Clara picked for the living room.

"Hey, Sam. Hey, Clara. Grab yourself a brush and a smock before I steal all the good spots for myself!" Grandpa chuckles. We assume he will not let us up on a ladder, so he must be
50 counting on us to work on the bottom three feet of the wall.

Sis and I grab two new brushes that Grandpa must have just bought at the store. It seems a crime to dip them into the paint the first time and forever ruin their purity.

"Don't be afraid to give it some elbow grease, now." Grandpa
55 encourages, letting us watch him as he applies thick strokes of paint to the wall.

We begin working in our own areas, creating splotchy islands of blue.

Grandpa pauses from his work to watch our technique. He
60 grins. "Fun, isn't it?"

"What if Daddy's disappointed he didn't get to do this himself?" I ask.

"Disappointed I did him a favor? If I know Arthur, he'll be happy to have avoided the manual labor. He'll just be dis-
65 appointed he didn't get to see his kids finally covering up the awful beige wall that came with the house."

Grandpa resumes painting and adds, "Maybe when we're done, we can cover up the awful beige on Garth's car." He starts laughing.

70 Garth seems not to mind or notice. He is concentrating on painting the corner without getting any stray streaks on the ceiling.

Grandpa notices Garth's serious expression and says, "He even paints like a Marine." Another chuckle. Garth does not
75 look away from his corner but adds, "and your Grandpa likes talking more than working—just like a civilian." Sis and I are accustomed to their jovial back-and-forth.

I feel sad to hear Grandpa say we will cover up the wall that came with the house. That is the color we grew up with.
80 That is the color of the living room with Mom still in it. I don't want to cover up our memories, even though they make us sad now. But covering up is different from removing. We will put a layer of sky blue on the surface so that we feel invigorated, but we will know that Mom's layer is always protected underneath.

1. Which of the following statements regarding the idea for painting the room is best supported by the passage?

   A. While Clara was reluctant to do it, Grandpa ultimately convinced her it was okay.
   B. Garth suggested the idea to Grandpa, who then told the narrator and her sister.
   C. Clara envisioned the idea, and Garth helped provide some of the supplies.
   D. Although Grandpa planned the activity, Clara was involved in the decision making.

2. As presented in the passage, the exchange between the narrator and his sister when Garth comes to pick them up can best be described as:

   F. an expression of frustration due to the curiosity the narrator and his sister felt regarding Garth's unusual tardiness.
   G. a situation that is initially confusing to the narrator until his sister reminds him about the project to repaint the living room.
   H. a favorite game that the narrator plays with his sister to determine which person gets the honor of sitting in front.
   J. a nonverbal conversation that allows the narrator and his sister to determine which of them receives an unfavorable consequence.

3. Based on the passage, Garth and Grandpa can be reasonably said to share all of the following characteristics EXCEPT:

   A. painting experience.
   B. good posture.
   C. the ability to drive.
   D. willingness to poke fun.

4. Clara's reference to having smarter wrists (line 39) primarily serves to suggest her:

   F. remaining doubt about equaling her mother's skills.
   G. growing excitement regarding learning how to paint.
   H. deepening confusion about how painting relates to cupcakes.
   J. increasing concern that people see her as intelligent.

5. Viewed in the context of the passage, Grandpa's grin (lines 59–60) most nearly reflects a feeling of:

   A. irony.
   B. intense relaxation.
   C. mild satisfaction.
   D. harsh disapproval.

6. The narrator's statement "His car is a good match for his personality" (line 14), most nearly means that in the narrator's opinion, Garth is:

   F. too conservative in his choice of cars.
   G. highly dependable, but not very flashy.
   H. more upright than many Oldsmobile drivers.
   J. too concerned with how others see him.

7. Garth clearly recommends that the children apply both paint and icing in which of the following ways?

   A. Gently
   B. Respectfully
   C. Conservatively
   D. Confidently

8. In the second paragraph, the main conclusion the narrator reaches is that:

   F. Garth considers tardiness a character flaw.
   G. Garth is extremely talented at organizing his schedule.
   H. people can use a routine to avoid focusing on something painful.
   J. Grandpa is a very keen observer of human behavior.

9. In terms of the development of the narrator as a character, the last paragraph primarily serves to:

   A. add to the reader's understanding of his guilt.
   B. explain his relationship to his mother.
   C. describe his underlying emotional conflict
   D. portray the strained relationship he has with Grandpa.

10. It can most reasonably be inferred that Arthur is the name of:

    F. Garth and Grandpa's friend.
    G. the narrator.
    H. the narrator's father.
    J. the neighbor who lent them the ladder.

Passage II

SOCIAL SCIENCE: The following is an excerpt from the article "Electric Cars Face Power Outage" by Justin Sabo (© 2010 by Justin Sabo).

Many people look forward to the day when an American automobile company will mass-produce an emissions-free vehicle. Those people may be surprised to learn that day actually came to pass almost fifteen years ago.

5 So why are there hardly any purely electric vehicles on the road today? In 1996, General Motors released the EV1, the first fully electric vehicle designed and released by a major auto manufacturer. GM entered this unfamiliar territory bravely but reluctantly, motivated by emissions-control legislation enacted
10 by the California Air Resources Board (CARB). CARB felt automakers were dragging their feet in developing lower emissions vehicles, so it mandated that American car companies make a certain percentage of their cars available for sale in California to be electric vehicles.

15 This could not possibly have been good news for American automakers. Many believed that electric vehicles were not commercially viable. It would be very expensive to research, develop, and market a new type of car, and with consumer demand for such cars a big unknown, the companies feared stiff
20 economic losses would result from the new regulations. GM was pessimistic its EV1 could be a viable commodity, but it felt that the best way to force CARB to undo the mandate was to play ball: they would bring an electric car to the market and let everyone watch it fail.

25 Previous electric vehicle prototypes from major automakers had consisted of converting existing gasoline models, a process neither elegant nor inexpensive. The EV1, however, was designed from the start as an electric car, and lightness and efficiency were incorporated throughout the design. Engineers
30 selected aluminum for the EV's body, which, unlike the steel typically used in car frames, is a relatively light metal. The wheels were made with a magnesium alloy, which was another lightweight but sturdy replacement. The EV1's unusual, futuristic body shape is a consequence of aiming for a low drag
35 coefficient and reference area.

Early versions of the EV1 used a lead-acid based battery, replaced by nickel metal hydride in second generation models. Owners could charge their cars in their garages overnight or at power stations situated around the cities where they were
40 leased. A full charge would last 70 to 100 miles. The cars were only available to be leased, because GM wanted to be able to reclaim them if necessary. This also allowed GM to avoid having to comply with a law that requires car companies to maintain service and repair infrastructure for fifteen years following the
45 sale of any model of car (something GM thought would surely become a moot point since they didn't expect production of EV1's to get past the initial trial stage).

The public reaction to the EV1 is a source of ongoing debate to this day. The initial fleet of 288 EV1's that GM released was
50 not enough to meet consumer demand, as waiting lists began growing with customers who wanted their chance to lease an EV1. At a suggested retail price of $34,000, the cars were leased at a rate between $400–550/month. This high monthly payment skewed demand toward a more affluent customer
55 base, which included many famous and wealthy celebrities, politicians, and executives. However, the auto industry used the lessees' fame to portray the car as something beyond the limits of the average consumer (despite the fact that GM had hand-picked the lessees).

60 Ultimately, GM reclaimed all the EV1's it had leased, intending to destroy them. EV1 owners were livid that their prized possessions were going to become scrap metal. They offered GM "no-risk" purchasing terms, essentially begging GM to let them buy the car while exempting GM from being accountable
65 for any future maintenance or repair issues. They were denied.

Why? Skepticism brewed regarding GM's deeper motives for canceling the EV1 program. Alleged pressure from the oil industry helped coax CARB into repealing their electric-car mandate. Others pointed to the fiscal losses GM would suffer
70 if electric cars became popular: GM was currently making billions per year in the spare parts market, selling the types of mufflers, brake pads, air filters, and the like that would no longer be required with electric car technology.

While the passion and protest surrounding the recall of
75 the EV1 suggest a burning desire for electric vehicles, other researchers portrayed a different story. Dr. Kenneth Train of UC Berkeley presented a study which claimed Americans would only be interested in buying an electric car if it were priced at least $28,000 less than a comparable gasoline-fueled car.
80 This study was frequently touted by automakers who hoped to prove that the electric car was not a financially viable product. Meanwhile, similar studies conducted by the California Electric Transportation Coalition (CETC) disagreed, finding that consumer demand for electric vehicles would represent
85 12–18% of the market for light-duty new cars.

Whether the electric car can transcend consumers' distrust of the unfamiliar and the auto and oil industries' reluctance to change is unknown. What is certain is the fact that a new technology poses challenges that go well beyond mechanical
90 engineering. Technological hurdles can often come in the form of political, economic, and social obstacles.

11. The author implies that for an electric car to be more appealing to most car buyers, the most important factor would be changing which of the following?

A. Body shape
B. Distance per charge
C. Aluminum frame
D. Price

12. The statement in lines 16–17 most likely represents the view of all of the following groups EXCEPT:

F. the executives at GM who commissioned the design of the EV1.
G. the members of the California Air Resources Board who issued the mandate.
H. the other American automakers at the time the CARB mandate was issued.
J. Dr. Kenneth Train and his research team at UC Berkeley.

13. According to the passage, the number of drivers who first leased an EV1 was around:

A. 70–100
B. 288
C. 400–550
D. 12–18% of the light duty market

14. The author most nearly portrays the efforts of GM to design an electric car as:

F. resulting from overconfidence in estimating consumer enthusiasm for electric vehicles.
G. directed more at perfecting the marketing than at perfecting the science.
H. intended to showcase GM's superiority over its competitors.
J. motivated in part by a desire to fail.

15. According to information presented in the fourth paragraph (lines 25–35), which of the following comparisons between previous electric vehicle prototypes and the EV1 would the author make?

A. The EV1s were more deliberately and insightfully designed.
B. The EV1s were just converted from previous gasoline prototypes.
C. The previous electric prototypes were basically the same as the EV1.
D. The previous electric prototypes were made out of cheaper, lighter materials.

16. Based on information presented in the sixth paragraph (lines 48–59), it can reasonably be inferred that which of the following determinations would have the biggest effect on the potential marketability of electric vehicles?

F. The strength of affiliation that most car buyers have for environmental organizations
G. Whether most car buyers would consider buying an automobile that costs over $25,000
H. How many other states might enact regulations similar to that of CARB's in California
J. The extent to which most car buyers identify with wealthy politicians and celebrities

17. According to the passage, aluminum's role in the EV1 was:

A. a lightweight wheel.
B. to lower drag coefficient.
C. an alternative to steel.
D. magnesium alloy substitute.

18. The author most likely intends his answer to the question posed in line 67 to be:

F. definitive; he believes the real reasons are plain to see.
G. incomplete; he is convinced that CARB had some unknown involvement.
H. genuine; he is unsure about GM's motives for the denial.
J. speculative; he thinks that plausible explanations have been put forth.

19. The author indicates that one cause behind GM reclaiming EV1's from their owners may have been:

A. the unwillingness of owners to renew their leases.
B. CARB's decision to change the terms of its original low-emissions mandate.
C. a financial disincentive GM would face should the EV1 become popular.
D. customers' shock at the $28,000 price tag.

20. It can reasonably be inferred from the last paragraph that the author thinks that any forthcoming electric vehicle will:

F. have to solve non-technological problems.
G. be embraced by most automakers.
H. overcome the skepticism of consumers.
J. succeed if sold at a lower price.

SOCIAL SCIENCE: The following passage is adapted from the essay "The Torres Revolution" by Greg Spearman (©2001 by Greg Spearman).

The question of who invented the guitar may forever remain a mystery. However, the father of the modern classical guitar is generally regarded as Antonio Torres Jurado, a carpenter from Sevilla, Spain, who began making guitars as a hobby in
5 the 1850's and ultimately created the design that practically all classical guitar makers use to the present day. By refining the craft of guitar-making, Torres expanded the dynamic and tonal range of the instrument, allowing the guitar to go beyond its traditional, supporting role and into the spotlight as a featured
10 concert solo instrument.

Early guitars had four pairs of strings—the word "guitar" itself being a translation from a Persian word meaning "four strings." During the Renaissance, instruments resembling the modern guitar had begun to appear throughout Europe. One
15 of these, the lute, became the standard stringed instrument across most of Europe, but in Spain there was more variation in developing forms of the guitar. A plucked version called the *vihuela* was popular in aristocratic society, while a strummed instrument referred to as the *guitarra latina* was used by com-
20 moners. Once a fifth string was ultimately added to the latter, the *guitarra latina* became the national preference and rendered the *vihuela* obsolete.

As the 17th century progressed, Spanish guitars, widely
25 adored by monarchs, noblemen, and common folk alike, spread throughout the rest of Europe and began to displace the once-popular lute. Along the way a sixth string was added to the design. The 18th century saw the more "prestigious" music of harpsichords, pianos, and violins come to the fore, while the
30 guitar was relegated back to the informal gatherings of common folk. Eventually, however, the virtuosity of such Spanish guitarists as Ferdinand Sor rekindled the public's respect and admiration for guitar music. Esteemed composers such as Haydn and Schubert began writing guitar music, but while the
35 performances of the Spanish guitar masters were wildly popular, the acoustic and structural limitations of the guitar continued to present a problem when playing in large concert halls—a problem that Andres Torres meant to solve.

40 One of the guitar's chief limitations that Andres Torres tackled was its feeble sound output. Torres enlarged the body of the guitar, particularly the "bouts" (rounded parts) in the soundbox, significantly increasing its volume and giving the guitar its familiar hourglass shape. Because the guitar also
45 had to compete with the impressive polyphony (the number of notes that can be played at one time) of the piano, Torres also reduced the width of the fretboard, making it easier for guitar-ists to reach many notes at once and allowing them to perform music with a complexity comparable to that of pieces played
50 on keyboard instruments.

The genius of Torres's design, however, was the way he re-engineered the internal structure of the instrument. Because the strings on a guitar must be wound tightly to produce enough tension to vibrate at the correct pitch, they constantly pull on
55 the neck of the guitar, essentially trying to snap it in two. The arch of the neck counters some of this force, but the majority is absorbed by wooden braces inside the instrument. Torres did not invent the idea of fan-bracing, which refers to pieces of wood laid out diagonally inside the body to distribute both
60 tension and sound waves, but he did perfect it. He increased the number of braces from three to seven, and organized them in a symmetric pattern allowing the vibrations of the guitar to be evenly distributed within the soundbox.

The effectiveness and elegance of Torres's design was
65 immediately apparent in the improved tone and volume of the instrument, and ultimately revealed by the fact that his design has remained virtually unchanged in over 150 years. Torres guitars were extremely rare and highly-sought by musicians in the 19th century. One aspiring guitarist of the time, Francisco
70 Tarrega, traveled to Sevilla in the hopes of buying one of Torres's famous guitars. Although Torres initially intended to sell Tarrega one of the stock guitars he had available, he reconsidered once he heard Tarrega play. Deeply impressed, Torres instead gave Tarrega a guitar he had made for himself several years before.

75 Just as Torres revolutionized the design of classical guitars, so would Tarrega eventually become recognized as the singular authority on classical guitar playing techniques. Tarrega had grown up playing both guitar and piano, the latter being rec-ognized as the more useful compositional tool, while the guitar
80 was regarded as merely a functional accompaniment to a singer or a larger ensemble. Once Tarrega beheld the beauty and range of expression of the Torres guitar, he committed himself fully to exploring its compositional palette.

Tarrega, who studied at the Madrid Conservatory, rose
85 to great prominence, not only playing original pieces but also translating the great piano works of such composers as Beethoven and Chopin for guitar. He became a global ambassador for the guitar, introducing and refining many of the techniques that classical guitarists worldwide now consider essential, including
90 how to position the guitar on one's knee and optimal fingering and plucking techniques for the left and right hand.

21. Based on the passage, the author would most likely agree that both Torres and Tarrega were:

A. not fully appreciated for their musical genius until after their deaths.
B. local sensations whose reputation never reached the global fame of other composers.
C. extremely influential contributors to the evolution of classical guitar playing.
D. very talented instrument makers who gained much fame for their talents.

22. As it is used in lines 51–52, the phrase *the genius of Torres's design* most nearly refers to the:

F. innovative idea that classical guitars could be the center-piece of a performance, rather than merely an accompaniment.
G. improved tonal quality and volume resulting from the number and positioning of wooden braces within the soundbox.
H. invention of an arched neck, which counters the effects of the tension caused by the tightly wound strings.
J. expansion of the width of the guitar, in order to accommodate a sixth string and allow for more polyphony.

23. Which of the following statements best describes how the second paragraph (lines 11–23) relates to the first paragraph?

A. It provides supporting details concerning Torres's innovative idea to use a fifth string.
B. It compares the modern guitar to its earlier relatives, such as the lute and *vihuela*.
C. It moves the discussion to a period that predates the innovator described in the first paragraph.
D. It counterbalances the argument in the first paragraph by providing details that suggest early guitars were superior in many ways to later guitars.

24. As it is used in line 83, the phrase *compositional palette* most nearly means:

F. artistic potential.
G. colorful components.
H. volume output.
J. physical features.

25. For purposes of the passage, the significance of Spanish guitarists such as Ferdinand Sor is that they:

A. were reluctant to accept modifications to the traditional design of the guitar.
B. gave Torres suggestions about his design.
C. were among the most talented lute players in Europe at the time.
D. helped develop and sustain interest in the guitar as a reputable instrument.

26. Which of the following questions is NOT answered by the passage?

F. What is the meaning of an instrument's polyphony?
G. When was the beginning and the ending of the Renaissance?
H. Who is the father of the modern guitar?
J. What were some of the earlier forms of the guitar?

27. According to the passage, the *vihuela* was a Renaissance version of the guitar that:

A. was ultimately overtaken in national popularity by another type of guitar.
B. became the Spanish aristocrats' version of the lute.
C. initially came to fame through the notoriety of Ferdinand Sor.
D. one of Torres's earlier models before he perfected his fan-bracing design.

28. According to the passage, the Torres guitar was better suited than previous versions of the guitar to:

F. Beethoven's works.
G. being a featured instrument.
H. five strings.
J. folk music.

29. According to the passage, the popularity of Spanish-style guitars during the 18th century was:

A. increasing due to the simultaneous decline in popularity of the lute.
B. aided by the growing popularity of other instruments that complemented the guitar's sound.
C. hindered by common folk's inability to master fingering and plucking techniques.
D. diminished by the perception that it was not as refined as other contemporary instruments.

30. It can most reasonably be inferred that which of the following was a direct expression of respect for Tarrega's playing abilities?

F. The manner in which Torres determined which guitar he would sell to Tarrega.
G. The translation of Beethoven's and Chopin's works from piano to guitar.
H. The eventual end to the popularity of the *guitarra latina*.
J. The way Haydn and Schubert began composing music specifically for guitar.

Passage IV

NATURAL SCIENCE: The following passage is adapted from the article "Heavyweights of the Sea" by Carmen Grandola (©2001 by Carmen Grandola).

The earth's oceans possess an incredible variety of life, ranging from nearly microscopic plankton to the blue whale, the largest animal on the planet. In the world of fish, the mola sunfish and the whale shark are the two biggest varieties. The
5 mola is the biggest bony fish, whereas the whale shark, which is a cartilaginous fish, is simply the biggest fish there is. While most ocean-dwellers spend their days balancing their position on the food chain as both predators and prey, these titanic swimmers have little to worry about from predators. Instead, they must
10 focus on finding enough food to sustain the massive amounts of nutrients needed to support their bulky bodies.

Truly one of the most unusual-looking products of evolution's creative hand, the mola sunfish resembles a giant fish head with a tail. Most fish have long bodies, with fins in the
15 middle roughly dividing their length in two. Rather than having a caudal (tail) fin, like most fish, the mola looks like a fish that has been chopped just past the halfway point, with a rounded clavus joining its dorsal (top) and anal (bottom) fins. The mola uses its clavus to steer its rather awkwardly-shaped body
20 through the water. Its body has a very narrow cross-section—it is basically a flattened oval with a head at the front, and very high dorsal and anal fins at the back. In fact, the mola's height is often equal to its length, which is unusual in fish, which are typically elongated. Mola means "millstone" in Latin, and these
25 fish live up to their name, growing to 10–20 ft. in length and height and weighing in at an average of 2,000 lbs.

The mola's diet is extremely varied but nutrient-poor, consisting mainly of jellyfish, but also comb jellies, squid, and eel grasses. In order to consume enough daily nutrients, the mola
30 must be a voracious eater and be willing to travel through a wide range of oceanic depths—from surface to floor in some areas—in search of their food. After ascending from cooler waters, the mola will float on its side at the ocean's surface in order to warm itself through solar energy. Molas have a beaked
35 mouth that does not totally close, so they chew their food in several stages, breaking down each mouthful into smaller chunks before spitting them out and then going to work on the more bite-sized pieces.

The whale shark, another giant of the sea, grows to sizes
40 that dwarf the maximum size of a bony fish. Some have been measured at over 40 ft. in length and over 75,000 lbs. in weight. This leviathan, like the mola, mostly frequents tropical and warm-temperate waters. The whale shark possesses over 300 rows of teeth, but it does not use them in the same manner as
45 most other sharks. The whale shark is one of only a handful of filter-feeding sharks. This means rather than using powerful teeth and jaws to rip apart large prey, the whale shark eats tiny, nearly microscopic food such as zooplankton, krill, and macro-algae. The whale shark "hunts" by opening its mouth

50 and sucking in a huge mouthful of ocean water. It then closes its mouth and expels the water through its gills, at which point gill rakers act as sieves, separating the tiny, sometimes millimeter-wide, life forms from the water. Once all the water is expelled, the food is swallowed.

55 When you're one of the biggest species in your neighborhood, you probably don't have to worry about getting picked on much. This is certainly true of the whale shark, which has no natural predators and can easily live 70–100 years in the ocean. Its biggest health risk comes through exposure to humans.
60 The whale shark does much of its feeding near the surface of the water, where it has been known to accidentally bump into boats. Both animal and vessel can end up severely damaged in these exchanges. The other hazard humans create for whale sharks is pollution in the water. As the whale shark filter feeds,
65 it sometimes takes in garbage and nautical debris such as oars.

The mola, on the other hand, has a few challenges. Its thick skin is covered in a dense layer of mucus, which is host to a vast array of parasites. To try and rid itself of these uninvited guests, the mola will often float on its side near the surface of
70 the water, inviting gulls and other birds to feast on the parasites. Similarly, the mola will sometimes launch its considerable bulk up to ten feet out of the water before crashing back down in an effort to dislodge some of the parasites. With its habit of floating near the surface, the mola, like the whale shark, often
75 runs the risk of being hit by boats. Finally, smaller molas are sometimes subject to attack by sea lions.

31. The author's attitude regarding molas and whale sharks can best be described as one of:

A. conviction that human interference will ultimately jeopardize each species.
B. resentment towards their need to eat so much other marine life on a daily basis.
C. impartiality in considering the perils of their environment compared to other fish.
D. interest in how their grandiose size affects their habits and survival.

32. It can reasonably be concluded from the passage that the mola temporarily expels its food when eating due to the fact that it:

F. is a bony fish rather than a cartilaginous one.
G. possesses a mouth that cannot completely close.
H. hunts on the ocean floor but eats at the surface.
J. it is normally floating on its side near the surface.

33. According to the passage, the most significant difference between the predatory threats facing the whale shark and the mola is that the whale shark:

  A. does not compete for the same food as its predators do, while the mola competes for the same food its predators do.

  B. is unaffected by its proximity to humans while the mola is sometimes endangered by humans.

  C. faces few genuine environmental threats but must contend with the nuisance of parasites.

  D. is less likely to be attacked by another ocean-dwelling species than is the mola.

34. It can most reasonably be inferred from the passage that nautical vessels pose a threat to both the mola and the whale shark primarily because these vessels:

  F. can sometimes unsuspectingly collide with fish.

  G. stir up a violent wake that disrupts the ocean currents.

  H. jettison large debris overboard which can land on fish.

  J. deplete the fish's supply of prey through over-fishing.

35. The passage indicates that the quantity of food a fish must eat is primarily determined by the:

  A. mass of the fish's body.

  B. depth at which the fish hunts.

  C. type of gill rakers it has.

  D. number of its teeth and size of its mouth.

36. The passage supports the idea that all of the following are included in the diet of the mola EXCEPT:

  F. comb jellies.

  G. zooplankton.

  H. eel grasses.

  J. squid.

37. The main purpose of the last two paragraphs is to:

  A. provide additional support for the earlier claim that the mola and the whale shark are two of the biggest creatures inhabiting the ocean.

  B. convey to the reader to the ironic fact that such large species of fish can be vulnerable to miniature threats such as parasites.

  C. summarize the types of threats, or lack thereof, present in the environments of the mola and whale shark.

  D. demonstrate the fact that even the biggest fish in the sea have to worry about being preyed upon by something.

38. According to the passage, the gill rakers a whale shark has are primarily intended to:

  F. spit out partially chewed food.

  G. rip apart the whale shark's large prey.

  H. bridge together its 300 rows of teeth.

  J. filter out food from a mouthful of water.

39. According to the passage, the Latin-derived name for the mola refers to the:

  A. atypical rounded clavus of the mola.

  B. mola's distinctive half-fish shape.

  C. voracious eating the mola's diet requires.

  D. mola's enormous size and weight.

40. The main purpose of the passage is to:

  F. offer support for the notion that the mola is pound-for-pound a better hunter than is the whale shark.

  G. provide a general overview of the habitats, eating habits, and survival challenges relating to two of the biggest species of fish.

  H. increase awareness for the fragile status of mola and whale shark populations and encourage conservationists to intervene.

  J. suggest that the unlikely traits possessed by the mola and the whale shark do not have clear evolutionary answers.

READING TEST

35 Minutes—40 Questions

DIRECTIONS: There are four passages in this test. Each passage is followed by several questions. After reading each passage, choose the best answer to each question and blacken the corresponding oval on your answer document. You may refer to the passages as often as necessary.

Passage I

PROSE FICTION: This passage is an excerpt from the short story "Whimpering Wanderlust" by Gretchen Mueller (© 1955 by Gretchen Mueller).

Jacob Mathinson accepted, almost too early in his life, that he would never be a world-famous architect. His grandmother had instilled an indelible streak of humility in Jacob as a boy, telling him that he was special to her, but that the rest of the world
5 was under no obligation to feel the same way. He attended Mount St. Mary's College, not because it had a renowned architectural program, but because he was able to get a partial scholarship by playing on the school's tennis team. Jacob did not want to admit it, especially years later, but his decision may have also
10 been swayed by his desire to follow Erin Crawford, his high school crush, wherever she decided to go. Architecture was not his first calling, and, hence, his ambition towards ascending in the field extended only so far as his desire to walk through the streets of, say, Prague one day, a fetching girl on his arm,
15 commenting on the array of Baroque, Renaissance, and even Cubist masterpieces along the Old Town Square.

Growing up in Gettysburg, Pennsylvania, Jacob, an average though not exceptional student, was not exactly exposed to a climate of forward thinking. The local economy was a traditional,
20 if unimaginative, one. Most of the infrastructure had been built during the Reconstruction to support the railroad industry. In the summer of 1919, when Jacob was born, the town seemed frozen in the late 19th century, with bootblack, locksmith, and apothecary shops that seemed more at home in pre-industrial
25 times. This lack of innovation deepened Jacob's disinterest in personal or academic enterprise. His impression was that there was little of interest to be discovered outside of Gettysburg, save a patchwork of towns as predictable as the repeating pattern of black and white tiles on a checkerboard.

30 During his junior year in high school, Jacob worked as a tour guide on one of the double-decker buses that shuttled tourists, Civil War enthusiasts mostly, around the perimeter of Gettysburg. Fancying himself as cutting quite a figure in his clean, pressed uniform, it was his great hope that one day Erin
35 Crawford might take the tour and see him in action. He even went so far as to give her a voucher for a free ride, but as each tour began, he would heave a lonesome sigh, crestfallen that she with her sweet lilac fragrance had not whisked past him as the customers loaded on to the bus.

40 Nonetheless, Jacob enjoyed the job, partly because it was easy—it consisted of reading a script of noteworthy details about the Gettysburg Battlefield—but mostly because it allowed for personal embellishment, since the tour included some of the area's historic buildings as well. Jacob spent months explain-
45 ing to his customers that the sloping roof on the Dobbin House Tavern is a pristine example of Celtic style architecture, and that the Shriver House Museum is one of the oldest standing pre-colonial buildings in America. Although for months he described these buildings of architectural interest, it wasn't
50 until he left that job that he actually began to think about them, notice them, and allow the buildings to "speak" to him in an aesthetic conversation.

The following summer, Jacob worked with his uncle, a residential plumber. Jacob enjoyed seeing homes in the in-
55 termediate stages of construction, half-naked, their internal structure exposed. Jacob found great satisfaction in the task of finding the most efficient and cohesive way to intertwine the circulatory system of plumbing into the skeletal structure of each house's wooden framework. Again, he found a way to
60 incorporate visions of Erin into his work, imagining that Erin's parents would get a flooded basement, and he and his uncle would arrive heroically, save the day, and leave her parents thinking, "that Jacob is a great boy." (Jacob's fascination with the science and art of building blossomed in his freshman
65 year at Mount St. Mary's, as did his fascination with the many young women also attending the school. Perhaps their attentions provided much-needed distraction from the difficulties he was having in his pursuit of Erin.)

He had not accounted for Mount St. Mary's size relative
70 to his high school and the difficulty of "accidentally" running into someone in the halls. Throughout the first semester, Erin might as well have been a ghost to Jacob, who tried his very best to make her acquaintance, but to no avail. Many years later, already married to Martha, a seamstress from Gettysburg, Jacob
75 would daydream about the single time he and Erin had some-thing resembling a date. With a resigned sigh, he remembered his hands trembling, even while jammed into the pockets of his pressed Ogilvy's slacks; and the curious nature of her fragrance that seemed floral from a distance but minty up close; and the
80 musical sound her shoes made on the cobblestone road leading to the assembly hall; and the way she seemed to be fearlessly striding toward an unknown future while he was just trying to acclimate to the present.

1. The passage supports all of the following statements about Jacob's job as a tour guide EXCEPT that:

   A. he observed many buildings with their skeletal structure exposed.
   B. there were some prepared remarks that Jacob was to read.
   C. the tour catered to certain people with a common interest.
   D. he wore what he considered to be a flattering uniform.

2. One of the main ideas of the second paragraph (lines 17–23) is that:

   F. due to the nature of Gettysburg, Jacob did not have much desire to travel elsewhere.
   G. Jacob imagined a better architectural plan for the town's older buildings.
   H. it was hard for Jacob to find a job with mainly pre-industrial types of merchants.
   J. Jacob lacked motivation for his studies because he planned to work for the railroad.

3. The events in the passage are described primarily from the point of view of a narrator who presents the:

   A. actions and thoughts of both Jacob and Erin.
   B. the inner emotions and thoughts of only Jacob.
   C. actions and thoughts of all the characters discussed.
   D. dialogue of all the characters, which suggests their thoughts.

4. According to the passage, all of the following were aspects of Jacob's job with his uncle EXCEPT:

   F. seeing unfinished construction.
   G. impressing Erin's parents.
   H. daydreaming while he worked.
   J. finding efficient paths for plumbing.

5. According to the passage, Jacob's ambition toward becoming an architect included a desire to:

   A. point out interesting architecture to a girl.
   B. find a new way to utilize plumbing.
   C. redesign the Dobbin House roof.
   D. enroll at a renowned architectural school.

6. Which of the following questions is NOT answered by the passage?

   F. What factors influenced Jacob's choice to go to Mount St. Mary's College?
   G. Did Erin ever use her voucher for a free tour with Jacob?
   H. How many people went to Jacob's high school?
   J. What effect did the old infrastructure of Gettysburg have on Jacob?

7. The passage indicates that compared to when Jacob worked as a tour guide, after he stopped working there he found the buildings of Gettysburg:

   A. less fascinating.
   B. more fascinating.
   C. less historically noteworthy.
   D. more historically noteworthy.

8. The passage indicates that Jacob's primary response to the events described in the last paragraph is:

   F. remorse that he and Erin were largely disconnected.
   G. anger concerning the excessive size of Mount St. Mary's.
   H. gratitude for ultimately meeting and marrying Martha.
   J. contentment regarding the fact that he got to date Erin.

9. That Jacob had an indelible streak of humility was:

   A. a quality shared by most people who grew up in a working class community like that of Gettysburg.
   B. a consequence of accepting that he would probably never be a world-famous architect.
   C. an effect of Jacob's grandmother's words of caution regarding the unbiased impressions of the rest of the world.
   D. a character trait that evolved through years of pursuing but never obtaining Erin's affection.

10. In the passage, the statement that Erin was fearlessly striding toward an unknown future (lines 81–82) is best described as the opinion of:

   F. the author of the passage, but not the opinion of Jacob.
   G. Jacob as he struggled to "accidentally" run in to Erin at Mount St. Mary's.
   H. Erin, who has little interest in Jacob because he has no urge to leave Gettysburg.
   J. Jacob as he reflects on the one date he had with Erin.

Passage II

SOCIAL SCIENCE: This passage is excerpted from the article "The Irresistible Force" by Angela Suspak. (© 2008 by Luminary)

The author is reviewing the biographical book *The Long Walk Home* by Grace Jergensen.

During the summer of 1892, a reputable black store owner was lynched in Memphis, Tennessee. This outraged many local citizens, but Ida B. Wells felt compelled to take action and write a letter decrying the horrific act in the local press. However, as a
5 black woman, her race and identity posed formidable obstacles. The volatility of her message, combined with the pervasive chauvinism of the times, made her "a hushed voice in the race debate", according to Grace Jergensen, who writes a biography of Wells, entitled *The Long Walk Home*. Wells, taking matters
10 into her own hands, joined a fledgling black newspaper called "The Free Speech and Headlight" as co-owner and editor.

Writing under the pseudonym of "Iola," Wells lashed out against the intolerance and brutality of racially-motivated lynchings. She vilified the perpetrators of the crime, while also
15 chastising the white community at large for virtually condoning these actions by its inaction. With her incendiary rhetoric, Wells became a hero in the civil rights community and a potential target for violence. Jergensen details the difficulties Wells underwent shortly after her article was published. While at an
20 editing convention in New York, Wells learned that she had become a despised figure in Memphis, and the target of death threats. Considering the imminent danger she would face if she returned home, "Wells had to decide whether she would rather be a nomad or a martyr."

25 Wells was not used to backing down from a challenge, though. She was born just months before the Emancipation Proclamation put a legal end to slavery. She grew up with the mindset of equal rights for all, despite being exposed to the deeply ingrained and intractable racial divisions in the South.
30 Her parents perished when she was only 18 during a bout of yellow fever that plagued her hometown of Holly Springs, Mississippi. Wells, the oldest of eight siblings, was thrust into the role of caretaker. Wells's Aunt Georgine recalls that "Ida saw herself now as the grown-up and wanted to be strong. She
35 did all her crying in private so the little ones wouldn't see her." Jergensen reflects that Wells learned early on "that she was in charge of protecting her brothers and sisters, and that feeling extended later in life to her figurative brothers and sisters in the struggle for racial and gender equality."

40 Wells went to Rust College to become a teacher, and her ability to mold the thought processes of others made her a persuasive orator and writer. Jergensen compares Wells's debating style to that of Socrates, who used shrewdly-worded questions and statements to lead his opponent from his original
45 sense of certainty into a state of doubt about the correctness of his convictions. Similarly, Wells frequently started her essays and speeches with general questions about morality, fairness, and human rights, baiting her opposition into admitting certain core principles before challenging them to reconcile these
50 fundamental rights with the unfair and discriminatory laws and practices they endorsed.

After a public speaking tour of England, Wells made a home for herself in Chicago, where she met the man who would eventually become her husband, Ferdinand Barnett. Together, they
55 raised two sons and two daughters, though later in life, Wells would bemoan the fact that she felt as though the responsibility of raising and supporting the four children became her primary concern, while her husband became engrossed in a political bid to become a Circuit Court judge.

60 Domestic life didn't spell the end of Wells's struggle against inequality, however—during her time in Chicago, she founded the nation's first civic organization for black women. It was initially called the Women's Era Club, though it would later be renamed the Ida B. Wells Club. In 1895, her book
65 *A Red Record* was published, documenting the history of racially-motivated lynchings in America. Although the book succeeded in motivating an audience of progressive thinkers, race-related riots and violence continued virtually unabated into the early 20th century.

70 Jergensen conveys a clear appreciation for the deep reserves of patience on which Wells was repeatedly forced to draw in order to maintain her devotion to both family and society, despite often being castigated or ignored by both. By retracing Wells's "long walk home" from the grueling aftermath of her parents' death,
75 through her exile from Memphis, to her eventual involvement in creating the NAACP (National Association for the Advancement of Colored People), Jergensen leaves the reader feeling exhausted, expending such vast amounts of sympathy for the injustices Wells faces. As portrayed by Jergensen, Wells is a
80 protagonist who nobly walks a self-chosen path of monumental toil, with rewards few and far between. One such reward must have been the passage of women's suffrage in 1920 with the 19th Amendment which Wells, then a grandmother, was finally able to see first-hand.

11. In the statement in lines 22–24 Jergensen most strongly stresses:

A. a consistent propensity Wells had to take care of those in need of help.

B. the way Wells's family persuaded her to take part in the civil rights struggle.

C. the lessons of equality that Wells learned by acting like a parent to her siblings.

D. a powerful metaphor Wells would later use in many of her incendiary speeches.

12. As portrayed in the passage, the reaction of Wells to her parents dying from a bout a yellow fever is best described as:

    F. sad and frightened.
    G. mournful but resilient.
    H. relieved and emboldened.
    J. brave but hopeless.

13. The passage's author most strongly implies that Wells's relationship with her husband:

    A. began a decline in her activism as she turned her focus to starting a family.
    B. was the most lasting consequence of her public speaking tour in England.
    C. did not diminish the efforts she expended in the struggle for equality.
    D. was the main reason behind her starting the Ida B. Wells Club.

14. Lines 6–9 most nearly mean that Wells:

    F. faced the problem of audiences reluctant to hear what she had to say.
    G. spoke too softly for many people to take her ideas seriouly.
    H. did not believe that people would discredit her because of her race or gender.
    J. had to create a pen name in order to have her newspaper articles be read by the mainstream.

15. According to the passage, who disapproved of the ideas described in lines 12–16?

    A. Wells herself
    B. Jergensen
    C. Some people in Memphis
    D. The civil rights community

16. Another reviewer of Jergensen's book sums up Wells in this way:

    > A tireless and outspoken advocate of equality, Ida B. Wells did not shy away from making controversial demands of her audience ... sometimes jeopardizing her own safety, always reminding her listeners that equality was in accord with their fundamental sense of fairness.

    How does this account of Wells compare to that of the passage's author?

    F. This account portrays Wells's demands as fair, whereas the passage's author remains less convinced.
    G. This account emphasizes the danger Wells put herself in, whereas the passage's author does not mention this.
    H. Both provide a comparably unflattering portrayal of Wells's goals and tactics.
    J. Both provide a comparably flattering portrayal of Wells's goals and tactics.

17. For the passage's author, lines 81–84 mainly support her earlier point that:

    A. Wells did manage to see some of her goals realized in her lifetime.
    B. family was an essential factor in motivating Wells's struggle.
    C. significant changes happen in society with each new generation.
    D. Wells became much wiser and more thankful in her old age.

18. According to the passage, Jergensen believes that Wells'had a style of debating similar to that of Socrates because Wells:

    F. had a strong sense of certainty about her philosophical convictions.
    G. did not advance her own agenda but only wanted to understand her opponent.
    H. understood that clever oration can only do so much to further a cause.
    J. used points of agreement to show her opponents problems with their points of view.

19. The passage's author characterizes the book *A Red Record* most nearly as:

    A. a good effort that was troubled by philosophical inconsistencies.
    B. unusually radical compared to other books from the same era.
    C. impressively broad in the scope of social issues it tackled.
    D. mainly effective at inspiring its like-minded readers .

20. The passage most strongly suggests that Wells approached her life as a:

    F. bleak marathon.
    G. determined struggle.
    H. confusing journey.
    J. constant triumph.

Passage III

HUMANITIES: This passage is adapted from the novel *Southern Charmed Life* by Robert Anderson (© 1978 by Robert Anderson).

B.B. King has been a popular singer and blues guitarist since the 1950s.

In the summer of 1953, Uncle Randy was particularly excited for our visit. Sis and I got to spend a couple weeks with him each summer, to escape the heat of our home in Thibadeux, Louisiana. He was choir director at St. Peter's church in Des
5 Moines, Iowa. Sometimes we went with him to visit the homes of the older parishioners, helping him clean up their yards, grocery shopping for them, or cleaning their gutters.

Uncle Randy told us his friend from Mississippi was coming through town, a man named Riley King, although people
10 called him 'B.B'. He spoke in hushed awe of his friend B.B., who was "King of the Blues." "I don't much like the Blues," Sis would say. "You can't dance to it."

Before we left for B.B.'s hotel, to take him over to Sunday mass, Uncle Randy cleaned his Chevrolet Deluxe like an infantry
15 man would his rifle. It was a humble man's car, but we got it shining like the President's limousine.

As we pulled into the parking lot of the Majestic Hotel, I saw a man waiting near the front doors, looking off into the distance. His guitar case stood vertically, parallel with his up-
20 right posture, his hands folded serenely on the top of the case, slightly rocking back and forth on his heels.

"Hey! Somebody! I need the world's best guitarist! It's an emergency!" yelled my Uncle, to get B.B.'s attention. B.B. recognized his voice immediately, but paused a half second to
25 finish his thought before smiling and turning to see us driving up.

"Well, then, let me get in the car and help you look for T-Bone Walker," B.B. said, leaning in through the passenger-side window. Seeing us, he added with a mischievous smile, "So these are the troublemakers?"

30 "Yup. Kathie Mae and Bobby. Kids, this is Mr. King." my uncle warmly, yet formally, announced.

"Aw, they don't gotta call me 'Mister'. I'm B.B." He offered each of us a handshake, which we timidly accepted. His hands were large and calloused, and he wore several gold rings
35 on his fingers.

Sis and I sat silently in the back, peering nervously at this strange new arrival who was filling the car with his large frame, his guitar, and his Sunday-best cologne. His pockmarked face was worn but jubilant. He seemed like a man who had seen
40 all the hardships of the road, but whose youthful, joyous spirit still remained.

My uncle was chatting with B.B., asking him about his recent performances, and about all the money he must be making, but B.B. seemed reluctant to boast. "Ah, you know. We just
45 make enough money to get to the next town and get a meal in us. Maybe sometimes a little extra to bring home."

My sister burst out, inquisitively, "Where's home?" B.B. was seated in front of Sis, but wanting to acknowledge her, he turned his head halfway and said, "Itta Bena." She asked back,
50 "Itta Whatta?" The adults laughed. Uncle Randy clarified that it was a town in Mississippi, near Indianola, where we had come to visit him before he moved to Iowa. Feeling particularly fearless for a ten year old, Sis asked B.B. why he likes playing sad music. B.B. gave a rich chuckle and decided he had to look
55 Kathy Mae in the eyes for this one. He shifted his guitar to the side and turned his husky frame as far as he could, until his marbled, twinkling brown eyes could look straight into hers.

"Honey, the music isn't sad. Life is sad ... sometimes. And the Blues is just how you get through it. It's hard for a young
60 'un to hear the Blues right because you haven't been through enough pain of livin' yet." My Uncle was smiling, looking in the rear-view mirror at Sis, trying to judge her reaction. She seemed to be partly insulted by the implication that she would not be able to "get" the Blues.

65 "Have you ever cried yourself to sleep?" B.B. asked. Sis tightened her lips in resentment. "Don't be shy. We all have. Didn't you feel better when you woke up?" Sis tentatively agreed.

B.B. explained, "it's because the pain is distant when you wake up. The Blues is how I cry myself to sleep. It puts a dream
70 in between me and the pain, just like a thick frosted window pane that muffles it and makes it fuzzy to see." Sis and I turned to each other, finding this pearl of wisdom difficult to digest and resigning to the fact that some things were not meant for kids.

75 Years later, I would find a deep appreciation for B.B.'s music. Whenever I hear him play, I can't help but to imagine a waterfall—the pressure of the falling water was the weight of the pain. The mournful verses he sung made me think of the space behind the waterfall, a calm place of imprisonment,
80 where a thundering curtain of water is all you see in front of you. And when he started his guitar solo, it was like I turned into a bird that flew out through the waterfall. The heavy water pounded my light, buoyant frame down as I passed through it, but, once through, I was able to feel the freedom of lift, the
85 droplets of water rolling off my wings as I soared up towards the clouds, and the waterfall was only something beautiful to behold in the distance.

21. According to the passage, which of the following events occurred last chronologically?

  A. The narrator meets B.B. in the hotel parking lot.
  B. The narrator develops a strong fondness for B.B.'s music.
  C. The narrator helps his uncle perform chores for parishioners.
  D. The narrator helps clean his uncle's car.

22. Based on the passage, how old was the narrator's sister when she met King?

  F. Six
  G. Ten
  H. Twelve
  J. Fifteen

23. As it is used in line 72, the word *digest* most nearly means:

  A. understand.
  B. stomach.
  C. memorize.
  D. study.

24. The point of view from which the passage is told is best described as that of someone:

  F. trying to learn more about Mississippi culture.
  G. vacationing with his sister and his Uncle Randy.
  H. recounting how he learned to play blues guitar.
  J. remembering fondly an encounter with B.B. King.

25. Through his description of his meeting with B.B. King, the narrator portrays King most nearly as:

  A. flashy.
  B. morose.
  C. undignified.
  D. modest.

26. King uses the simile in lines 70–71 to convey the ability of the Blues to:

  F. get the most emotion out of a musical instrument.
  G. dull the sharpness of suffering.
  H. transform complex feelings into simple ones.
  J. help people relax and get to sleep.

27. Based on the passage, the narrator's and his sister's initial reaction to meeting King is one of:

  A. warmth and informality.
  B. caution and anxiety.
  C. amazement and confusion.
  D. skepticism and disappointment.

28. The narrator compares the feeling created by King's guitar solos to the feeling of:

  F. "a thick frosted window pane" (lines 70–71)
  G. "the space behind the waterfall" (line 79)
  H. "a thundering curtain of water" (line 80)
  J. "a bird that flew out through the waterfall" (line 82)

29. It is most reasonable to infer from the passage that King believes a true appreciation of the Blues comes primarily from:

  A. an upbringing similar to King's in Mississippi.
  B. watching it performed live by musicians.
  C. recognizing the struggles of life.
  D. having deeply held religious beliefs.

30. It is reasonable to infer that, following King's explanation of the Blues to Kathy Mae, the narrator and his sister:

  F. resolved to listen to Blues music more in order to understand the meaning behind King's words.
  G. decided they would ask Uncle Randy more about the Blues once King was no longer in their company.
  H. accepted that the point King was attempting to communicate was beyond their level of comprehension.
  J. gained the newfound impression that Blues music is a response to, not a cause of, sadness.

Passage IV

NATURAL SCIENCE: The following is adapted from the article "Seeking an Intelligent Definition of Intelligence" by Clark Matthews (© 2010 by Clark Matthews).

Cognitive psychologists who study humans and other animals are perpetually attempting to understand the type and extent of intelligence possessed by their subjects. Hindering their efforts is the ongoing debate about how we should define
5 such a nebulous concept as 'intelligence' in the first place. A scatter-hoarder species of squirrel would probably define intelligence as the ability to remember and re-locate the thousands of caches of food it has burrowed in hiding places throughout its environment. A dog, on the other hand, may emphasize its
10 ability to trace the source of objects in its environment based on the direction of the air current containing that smell.

There is a risk of bias in how we define intelligence because each species has evolved very specialized abilities based on its unique environmental niche and the techniques and strategies
15 that niche requires for survival. If we use our concepts of human capacities to define intelligence, we may be creating a standard that other animals couldn't hope to meet. Conversely, if we only mean by intelligence "the most highly refined capacities of that species" we make intelligence something that can only
20 be compared within a species, not across species.

One definition of intelligence holds that it is "a wide range of abilities relating to learning from one's environment and experience, and combining that learning with abstract reasoning to solve problems." Scientists frequently begin assessing
25 an animal's intelligence based on its susceptibility to classical or operant conditioning. Both methods involve pairing either a stimuli or a behavior with certain consequences, and waiting to see if a subject learns to associate the two and act accordingly. The faster the animal appears to absorb and act on the
30 association, the faster we believe it has 'learned' it. This gives us one supposedly objective means of comparing intelligent behavior across species.

The other primary evidence of an animal's intelligence is its ability to solve novel and/or complex problems. A spider
35 that spins a web to solve the problem of trapping insects for food is not considered to be displaying intelligence because the problem (food gathering) and behavior (spinning webs) are both embedded in the evolutionary history of a spider's habitat. An elephant that picks a lock at the zoo is thought to be acting
40 intelligently, since elephants do not pick locks in their native habitat and hence have no instinctive knowledge of how do undo them. The veined octopus is seen as a tool-user, scouring the ocean for coconut shells, which it proceeds to bring back to its homestead for the sake of building shelter. Although many
45 other animals, such as crabs and ants will take shelter using nearby objects, animal psychologists consider the long-term planning involved in the veined octopus's behavior as better evidence that it can conceptualize a goal and then act on it.

As if defining intelligence weren't tricky enough, measur-
50 ing intelligence is also a tenuous task. Ultimately, scientists can only observe an animal's behavior. So how can they ascertain if the animal is just behaving instinctively or if it is actually conceptualizing, thinking abstractly, and aware of its problem solving process? Because understanding is a private experience,
55 observing an animal's external behavior and hoping to infer its level of understanding is always a guessing game.

Both "intelligent" behavior and "unintelligent" behavior can be deceiving. Irene Pepperberg's famous subject, the parrot Alex, showcased a variety of impressive problem solving and
60 communication abilities that suggested an internal awareness and capacity for intelligence was present. For instance, Alex correctly called a "key" a "key," no matter what size, color, or orientation a certain key was. This suggests Alex had grouped the individual keys used to train him into a general category that
65 could be applied to novel stimuli. However, sometimes Alex gave wrong answers to a task he had completed successfully many times before. This was interpreted as Alex's boredom and frustration at repeating a task he had already mastered. Although the behavior looked unintelligent, experimenters
70 believed it was not due to a lack of understanding. Conversely, there is also the perpetual concern of the Clever Hans Effect, in which seemingly intelligent behavior is not believed to be the result of genuine understanding. The name comes from a horse named Clever Hans who was paraded around Europe in
75 the early 20th century, supposedly a marvel of animal intelligence. Hans could indicate the correct solution to arithmetic problems by tapping his hoof the appropriate number of times. Ultimately, though, scientists realized that Hans was getting the answer by reading nonverbal clues from his trainer. The trainer
80 would unknowingly tense up as the correct number of taps was getting nearer, which signaled to Hans when it was time to stop tapping. So although Hans exhibited behavior that seemed indicative of underlying intelligence, scientists do not believe he was actually solving the problems conceptually in his mind.

31. The main function of the second paragraph (lines 12–20) in relation to the passage as a whole is to:

   A. explain the human bias that is the focus of the rest of the passage.
   B. advance the argument that intelligence should be defined in human terms.
   C. showing how certain types of definitions have undesirable consequences.
   D. provide background information about the evolutionary niches of species.

32. According to the passage, what is the primary problem with defining intelligence as "the most highly refined capacities" of a given species?

   F. It would be a standard that no species could hope to meet.
   G. It would not take into account each species' unique environmental niche.
   H. It would too closely mimic our concepts of human intelligence.
   J. It would not be a standard we could use to compare one species to another.

33. According to the passage, all of the following behaviors seem to be intelligent EXCEPT:

   A. a spider solving the problem of trapping insects by spinning a web.
   B. an elephant picking a lock at the zoo.
   C. a veined octopus finding coconut shells for its shelter.
   D. a parrot identifying keys of various shapes and sizes.

34. According to the passage, scientists often start their assessment of animal's intelligence by:

   F. analyzing its ability to solve new and complex problems.
   G. identifying the most highly refined capacities of that species.
   H. stimulating the animal and observing its behavior.
   J. seeing how much information the animal can absorb.

35. Suppose beavers typically gather sticks from the forest floor and bring them to a stream to construct a dam. One beaver that cannot find enough sticks on the ground begins to strip bark from dying trees. Based on the passage, the author would most likely describe the behavior of this gopher as:

   A. intelligent if the lack of sticks is a novel problem.
   B. unintelligent if there was long-term planning.
   C. impressive and the result of operant conditioning.
   D. deceptive and illustrating the Clever Hans effect.

36. The passage indicates that the shelters of the veined octopus differ from those of crabs and ants in that the octopus shelters:

   F. are more likely to be constructed from nearby objects.
   G. are made of much sturdier materials than are crab and ant shelters.
   H. have more architectural interest than those of the crabs and ants.
   J. seem more to be the result of a long-term plan.

37. The primary purpose of the passage is to:

   A. define intelligence as it applies to non-human species.
   B. explore some of the challenges, both conceptual and practical, involved in assessing intelligence.
   C. identify the criteria used to discriminate between intelligent and unintelligent behavior.
   D. compare and contrast how intelligence appears within human species versus how it appears in non-human species.

38. The author mentions the behavior of the parrot Alex in the last paragraph primarily to:

   F. demonstrate that poor performance does not necessarily indicate poor comprehension.
   G. illustrate the meaning of intelligent behavior as applied to parrots.
   H. highlight an animal believed to be unintelligent which nonetheless acted intelligently.
   J. supply proof that animals can indeed learn the meaning of a concept.

39. As it is used in line 54, the word private most nearly means

   A. internal
   B. secretive
   C. subtle
   D. shy

40. In the context of the passage, the phrase "can be deceiving" (line 58) most nearly suggests that an animal's behavior:

   F. often is intended to trick other animals in its environment.
   G. is the hardest thing about an animal to measure in a scientific way.
   H. will fool observers who are not trained to know better.
   J. does not always serve as a reliable indicator of that animal's mental activities.

Chapter 7
Reading Practice Drills for the ACT Answers and Explanations

ACT READING DRILL 1 ANSWERS

1. D
2. H
3. B
4. F
5. D
6. G
7. B
8. J
9. C
10. F
11. A
12. H
13. D
14. F
15. B
16. H
17. D
18. H
19. B
20. F
21. A
22. H
23. C
24. F
25. A
26. J
27. C
28. J
29. A
30. J
31. D
32. F
33. B
34. J
35. A
36. F
37. B
38. H
39. D
40. G

ACT READING DRILL 1 EXPLANATIONS

Passage I

1. **D**   By saying that air travel is *bittersweet magic* (line 2) and that it is *cheating time*, the author is describing it as unnatural. Choice (A) is incorrect because no comparison is being made, and the author mentions some uncomfortable aspects of his flight. Choice (B) is incorrect, since the author describes air travel as *magic*. Choice (C) is incorrect because, while the author does mention uncomfortable aspects of flying, he is still taking the flight for the convenience of getting from the west coast to the east coast in the course of a *long nap*.

2. **H**   The narrator is looking for Denver when he thinks the flight is a third of the way through, which means he did not depart from Denver. Choices (F) and (G) are revealed in the very first sentence. Choice (J) is supported by numerous references to estimating city size by the grid of light seen from above.

3. **B**   The passage involves the experiences of someone who has moved out of his parents' house, returns to visit them, and becomes a bit depressed by the changes that have taken place. Choice (A) is incorrect since the passage never mentions a vacation and suggests the narrator has been absent for some time (he doesn't remember what car his father drives). Choice (C) is incorrect because the coma was only involved in an in-flight movie the narrator watches. Choice (D) is incorrect—the narrator's new home is in Southern California.

4. **F**   In line 54 the author states he doesn't recognize the trinkets on the wall—they have been added during his absence. (G), (H), and (J) can all be eliminated: although the *fridge* (line 56), the *brown Lexus* (line 35), and the *bird-feeders* (line 60), are all mentioned, they are not described as "new."

5. **D**   Although a dance studio is mentioned, there is no mention of dancing. Choices (A) and (C) are both mentioned once in the first and once in the second paragraph. Choice (B) is mentioned in the third and eighth paragraph.

6. **G**   The narrator uses the phrase *most depressingly* to describe the way his parents *often fall asleep in front of the television, mouths gaping* (lines 64–65). Choice (F) is incorrect because, though a new car is mentioned, no habit of buying new cars is ever described. Choice (H) is incorrect because it is not described as the *most* depressing habit. Choice (J) is never discussed as a habit that upsets the narrator.

7. **B**   The passage states that *as a physicist*, the coma victim *knew that time is a relative phenomenon* (line 75), implying a connection between the two ideas. Choices (A), (C), and (D) are not supported by any details in the passage.

8. **J**   The narrator explains that a *cluster of shops famously burned to the ground* (lines 49–50), in the past, but that presently it is back up and running with customers filtering in and out. Choices (F), (G), and (H) are all mentioned in the sixth paragraph as present-day changes to his hometown that the narrator notices.

9. **C**   The narrator says that as soon as he sees *dense stands of oak*, he knows he's home. Choices (A), (B), and (D) are details which describe Southern California, which is not the author's hometown.

10. **F**   The narrator refers to science as *that rock of immutable truths* as a way to emphasize the physicist's sense of bewilderment—before his coma he had believed scientific truth to be unchanging, but awoke to find his life's work obsolete. Choice (G) is incorrect because there is no support for the physicist's inability to comprehend the scientific advances, Choices (H) and (J) can be eliminated, since both refer to the time he spent in a coma, not before.

Passage II

11. **A** The men felt suspicious because, as stated in the previous paragraph, the traditional roles for women in these villages were food preparation and child care. Choice (B) is incorrect because no mention is made of how the representatives introduced themselves or why the men would doubt such an introduction. Choice (C) is incorrect because the passage does not suggest that the strangeness of the MayaWorks representatives was due to their language, but more that it was due to their intention of partnering with the village women. Choice (D) is unsupported by anything in the passage relating to men's estimation of the women's artistic abilities.

12. **H** The content of the second paragraph depicts the problems facing Mayan villagers as well as the *irreplaceable* nature of their heritage, foreshadowing the way in which MayaWorks hopes to modernize and sustain these communities. Choice (F) is unsupported since *legal rights* are never mentioned in the passage. Choice (G) is incorrect because, although the size of Mayan villages is mentioned in this paragraph, it is too narrow a fact to be considered the purpose of the paragraph in relation to the rest of the passage. Choice (J) is incorrect because the passage does not indicate that Berhorst is based in Guatemala, nor is Berhorst an important part of the paragraph in relation to how it functions in the passage.

13. **D** In the third paragraph, it says that the artisans used local materials for the hanging rods. Choice (A) is supported by information in the fifth paragraph as the artisans worked on kippahs. Choice (B) is supported by information in the seventh paragraph about the complications of not speaking Spanish in a Spanish-speaking marketplace. Choice (C) is supported by information in the sixth paragraph about a 36-inch treadle loom that allowed the artisans to now sell fabric by the yard.

14. **F** While the author writes in a relatively neutral voice, she provides nothing but positive affirmations of what MayaWorks intends to do and what its partnerships have accomplished. Choice (G) is unsupported because the author doesn't discuss whether people in other countries will join MayaWorks. Choice (H) is unsupported, because the author never questions the quality of the Mayan commodities. In fact, she mentions at one point that the artisans use the finest yarn they can find. Choice (J) is incorrect because, although MayaWorks has several objectives in mind, they are never indicated to be in conflict with each other.

15. **B** The fourth paragraph describes the more confident demeanor shown by the Mayan artisans when they were through with their work and getting paid for it. More generally, the author discusses the positive effects these art partnerships have had on the morale and self-sufficiency of the Mayan communities. Choice (A) is incorrect because, although the author points out the advantages of having some Spanish literacy, the author portrays the efforts of MayaWorks as being directed at helping the women grow with the times while retaining their invaluable heritage. She would not want *full* assimilation. Choice (C) is incorrect because the author mentions the success of the Mayan women learning to make Jewish kippahs. Choice (D) is incorrect because the final paragraph indicates that Mayan villagers would be typically excluded from *traditional banks*, hence the need for innovative micro-loans.

16. **H**   The passage states that *each of eight women was to weave a dozen* (line 28). Eight times twelve is 96, leaving (H) as the only possible answer choice—the others are far too big or small.

17. **D**   The last sentence of the fifth paragraph says the effect of being told of the kippah's symbolic meaning was becoming *even more devoted and loving in their craft* (line 51). Choice (A) is incorrect because the confusion regarding the shape had no relation to the kippah's religious significance. Choices (B) and (C) are unsupported by anything in the passage.

18. **H**   Although the passage indicates that MayaWorks artists make fabrics that are sold side-by-side with mass-manufactured textiles, it does not imply that the Mayan artists are mass-manufacturing textiles. Choices (F) and (J) are supported in the fifth paragraph. Choice (G) is supported by the third paragraph.

19. **B**   The paragraph relates another way that MayaWorks seeks to improve these communities, via coordinating loans that allow Mayans to improve their quality of living and sustainability. Choice (A) is incorrect because the terms of the loans are not explicitly discussed or focused upon. Choice (C) is incorrect because the money in the final paragraph comes from loans, not from money the artisans have earned selling their wares. Choice (D) is incorrect because the function of this paragraph is not to convince the reader that Mayans are trustworthy, but rather inform the reader of another way in which MayaWorks provides a benefit to these communities.

20. **F**   The passage states that the success of MayaWorks *has more to do with the economic initiatives…than its literacy campaigns* (lines 76–77); eliminate choice (J). While the rules of the marketplace are certainly mentioned, there is no indication that the Guatemalan women had to learn them from the people at MayaWorks—eliminate choice (G). Choice (H) is unsupported and goes against the goal of helping the Mayans preserve their culture.

Passage III

21. **A** The discussion of the author's infatuation with cars is prefaced by the explanation that it came before his interest in music. The end of the discussion (lines 59–67) of cars states that *Eventually, my fixation on cars was to take a "back seat" to a new, greater, and this time lasting, passion*, (music). Choice (B) is incorrect because the author indicates that his infatuation with cars was ultimately overtaken by his interest in music. Choice (C) is incorrect because the passage never describes the author's playing style, so there is no support for calling it "mechanical." Choice (D) is incorrect because the author explains his love of cars came before his love of music; this answer makes it seem as though they were in competition and his love of cars was winning.

22. **H** The author says *rewarding as this existence was* (lines 7–8) it did not fulfill him; he needed *greater pursuits to occupy* (line 10) his imagination. Choice (F) is wrong because the passage does not support that the author usually worked with his brother. Choice (G) is incorrect because the passage makes it seem like the author's upbringing made *the thought of embarking on a music career* beyond his *wildest imagination*. Choice (J) is incorrect because the passage does not support invariably resulting in parental approval. It even contains the phrase *much to my parents' dismay* (line 9).

23. **C** The third paragraph (lines 44–67) explains the author's previous obsession (*years before I began to pursue music*) with cars. The end of that paragraph refers to his *previous infatuations* (before cars) of *archery, and before that dinosaurs.* This means that dinosaurs is the earliest. Choices (A), (B), and (D) are incorrect because the passage clearly indicates that some other passion predated each of them.

24. **F** The context of the statement is the author summarizing his impressed delight with how effectively the music replicates the sensory and emotional experience of a thunderstorm. Choice (G) is incorrect because the passage does not suggest movies mislead the audience, only that they often do not replicate the experience of the thunderstorm as well as this music does. Choice (H) is incorrect because the author is not concerned with changing the character of news reports. He is only pointing out how well music can communicate. Choice (J) is incorrect because the author does not comment on whether thunderstorms are "among the hardest." Though it is suggested that it is not easy to replicate a thunderstorm, since *few, if any*, movies or television programs can do it, the context of this statement is not trying to make a point about thunderstorms but rather a point about music's ability to convey a rich experience.

25. **A** In the second paragraph, the author is recounting the early experiences in his youth that led him to have an interest in music. He describes the thrill he took in learning Latin, Greek, Yiddish, German, Spanish, and Italian and compares the eagerness with which he learned them to *the energy of a lepidopterist netting butterflies* (lines 22–23). Eliminate both (B) and (D) because the comparison being made is between collecting butterflies and learning foreign phrases, not anything music-related. Choice (C) is incorrect because Ms. Fenchurch does not have anything to do with this paragraph or what it is describing.

26. **J**   There is chaos described in the thunder and lightning stage, resolution when *the music eases, hope and reason are restored* (line 37), and relaxation in *soothing notes*. Choice (F) is incorrect because jealousy and resentment do not match up with anything. Although there is a violent thunderstorm described, violence is different from jealousy and resentment. Choice (G) is incorrect because "hate" and "disbelief" do not match up very well with the storm being described. Although storms are sometimes described as "angry," they are not described as "hateful." Also, *disbelief* is not a strong match for anything in the sentence. Choice (H) is incorrect because love is not a strong match for anything described in the sentence.

27. **C**   The lesson Ms. Fenchurch imparts to the author is that music is more than just the notes on the page, *it's about expression, and perhaps more important, communication* (lines 82–83). Since language involves conveying meaning, choice (C) is supportable. Choice (A) is incorrect because the speed of notes is not discussed. Choice (B) is incorrect because it does not provide an accurate summary of the "argument" being made by Ms. Fenchurch in the last paragraph. Choice (D) is incorrect because Ms. Fenchurch places greater emphasis on communication.

28. **J**   These two lines portray a calm lightness darkening into a cloudy apprehension and ultimately becoming a howling, thrilling, and frightening sensory overload. Choice (J) describes the transition in reverse. Choices (F), (G), and (H) all match up with something in these two sentences and are in correct chronological order.

29. **A**   The last paragraph begins with the author's rhetorical question *So what made the difference?* The author reveals that what made his love for music *continue to burn where other passions had fizzled* (line 69) was a "who," Ms. Fenchurch. Choice (B) is incorrect because an anecdote means a specific story, which the author does not provide, and there are no details relating to Ms. Fenchurch's "conducting style." Choice (C) is incorrect because, although there are some character traits mentioned about Ms. Fenchurch, there is little "detailed background information," and even if there were, the purpose of the paragraph is to explain how influential Ms. Fenchurch was on the author's musical development. Choice (D) is incorrect because the paragraph does not mention the effect music has on Ms. Fenchurch. Rather, the paragraph mentions the influence Ms. Fenchurch had on the author's love of music.

30. **J**   Phrases such as *sense of wonder* and *unforeseen path*, support that the author is surprised by his career choice, and several paragraphs deal with people, events, and subject matter that influenced the author's interest in music. Choice (F) is incorrect because the passage is not linear. It moves back and forth in time. Also, the passage does not list momentous events in the author's career, but more momentous influences on why the author has such a career. Choice (G) is incorrect because the passage does not delve into any specifics regarding Mozart and Handel, and the description of *The Tempest* is presented without comparison to any other piece of music. Choice (H) is incorrect because the passage as a whole is not persuasive in nature. The author is relating personal reflections, not advocating a certain course of action.

Passage IV

31. **D** The end of the second paragraph (lines 29–30) indicates that *courtship typically lasts about two weeks, during which the female and her potential mate will meet once a day*. Choice (A) is incorrect because the males snap their heads at other males to try gain the attention of females. Choice (B) is incorrect because during courtship, the seahorses *dress up* their body coloring, whereas it is normally camouflaged. Choice (C) is incorrect because it relates to mating/birth, not courtship.

32. **F** The third sentence of the first paragraph (lines 7–9) states that the seahorse's *tapered body shape is a great disadvantage* when it comes to *swimming ability*. Choice (G) is incorrect because the seahorse *lacks* a caudal fin. Choice (H) is incorrect because the dorsal fin is what gives the seahorse what little swimming ability it has. Choice (J) is incorrect because the passage does not link the seahorse's lack of teeth to swimming ability.

33. **B** The confusion relates to Bateman's principle, which holds that whichever sex expends less energy in the reproductive process should be the sex that spends more energy competing for a mate. It may then seem confusing to scientists that males both compete for mates and give birth. However, Robinson's research shows that females do in fact expend more energy in the reproductive process than do males, which means that males should be the ones competing for mates after all. Choice (A) is incorrect because, although it is a detail involved in the mechanics of males giving birth, it does not resolve the confusion surrounding why the males also compete for mates. Choice (C) is incorrect because it provides no illumination as to why males give birth yet compete for mates. The monogamy of seahorses is explained by efficient birthing cycles, but it does not itself explain anything. Choice (D) is incorrect because the length of time spent competing for mates still does not explain why males, who give birth, are the ones who compete for mates.

34. **J** The very first sentence of the passage foreshadows that the seahorse's *unusual mating habits* will be addressed. The last paragraph also begins by explaining that seahorses *have the distinction of being one of a very small number of monogamous species* (lines 73–75). Choice (F) is contradicted by information in the first paragraph. Although the passage explains that the seahorse manages some mobility, it still portrays the seahorse as a poor swimmer. Choice (G) is contradicted by information provided in the second to last paragraph. Pierre Robinson's research would potentially provides a coherent explanation for why male seahorses are responsible for birth. Choice (H) is incorrect because, although true, it can hardly be said to be a main idea of the passage.

35. **A** The first paragraph mentions the seahorse's *remarkable appearance* and *distinctive equine head*. This mention of its *signature* prehensile tail is another indication that this feature is associated primarily with seahorses. Choice (B) is incorrect because, although the tail is useful, that is not what *signature* conveys. Choice (C) is a trap answer based on the equivalent meanings of "autograph" and "signature." Choice (D) is incorrect because it makes no sense to call a seahorse's tail legally obligated. This choice is also tempting because of the association to one's signature.

36. **F**   Because the paragraph begins with fertilization, ends with hatching, and contains sequential details in between those two events, choice (F) is well supported. Choices (G) and (H) may be eliminated since both capillaries and the number of fry are only mentioned in passing. Choice (J) is incorrect since the amount of tolerable salinity is never specified. Also, salinity does not relate to the whole paragraph, which means this could not be the main purpose of the paragraph.

37. **B**   The last paragraph explains that *a stable monogamous couple can develop an efficient birthing cycle in which* (lines 81–82) the male is incubating eggs at the same time that the female is generating eggs. Therefore, when the males give birth to one clutch of eggs, the females are almost ready with the next clutch. Choices (A) and (C) are incorrect because the transition from low to high salinity and the transition from fertilization to incubation both take place in and only relate to the gestation stage within the male's brood pouch. Choice (D) is incorrect because the initial transition from courtship to mating is when a female would actually select her mate. Monogamy only has meaning once a mate has been selected.

38. **H**   If the female can't find a male to receive her eggs, she expels them into the ocean, which is essentially throwing them away. The months she spent growing the eggs are wasted, or *squandered*. Choices (F), (G), and (J) are synonyms for *lost*, but none make sense in the context of the passage.

39. **D**   The second to last paragraph (lines 56–72) explains the paradox scientists see in the seahorse species, which is that males both give birth and compete for mates. According to Bateman's Principle, the sex that expends more energy in the reproductive process should NOT be the sex that competes for mates. Pierre Robinson found that male seahorses' increased oxygen intake during pregnancy does not qualify males as the sex that expends more energy in the reproductive process. Hence, seahorses conform to Bateman's Principle. Choices (A), (B), and (C) are incorrect because, although they refer to aspects of the seahorse's reproductive process, they do not relate to Bateman's Principle, which focuses on energy expenditure.

40. **G**   The fourth paragraph (lines 46–55) states that the brood pouch regulates a low-salinity environment initially, but the salinity increases *to help acclimate* the eggs to the salt-water of the ocean that awaits them. Choice (F) is incorrect because nothing suggests or supports the idea of premature hatching. Choice (H) is incorrect because nothing suggests that the capillary network extracts salt. Choice (J) is incorrect because the passage does not suggest other mammals have exposure to salt.

ACT READING DRILL 2 ANSWERS

1. D
2. J
3. B
4. F
5. C
6. G
7. D
8. H
9. C
10. H
11. D
12. G
13. B
14. J
15. A
16. G
17. C
18. J
19. C
20. F
21. C
22. G
23. C
24. F
25. D
26. G
27. A
28. G
29. D
30. F
31. D
32. G
33. D
34. F
35. A
36. G
37. C
38. J
39. D
40. G

ACT READING DRILL 2 EXPLANATIONS

Passage I

1. **D** The passage states that the bright sky color was something *Clara picked*, and it suggests that Grandpa *wanted to do* the narrator's father *a favor* and *wanted the painted room to be a surprise*. There is no support for Clara's reluctance, which eliminates choice (A). There is no support for Garth coming up with the idea, which eliminates choice (B). There is no support for Garth providing any of the supplies, which eliminates choice (C).

2. **J** The passage explains that the narrator and his sister feel *reluctance* about sitting up front. The narrator reminds her with his *eyes* that it is her turn to accept that *fate*. Choice (F) is unsupported by the passage because nothing ever suggests that Garth shows up late. Choice (G) is unsupported because the narrator does not suggest confusion, and their exchange is purely about who is riding in front. Choice (H) is off the mark because the context does not portray the front seat as an *honor*, nor is their taking turns much of a *game*.

3. **B** Posture is only mentioned while describing Garth. Since Garth offers painting advice (lines 31–38), and Grandpa wears *paint-covered overalls* (lines 44–45), (A) is supported. Because they have both picked up the narrator and his sister before, (C) is supported. Because the passage mentions their *jovial back-and-forth*, (D) is supported.

4. **F** The context leading up to this quote involves Clara mentioning a talent her mother had for swirling icing that Clara does not possess. Once Garth explains how to achieve that effect, Clara remains skeptical about her own ability to perform the feat. Choice (G) lacks support because Clara's sigh and her skepticism do not indicate "excitement." Choice (H) is incorrect because there is no context to indicate Clara's confusion. Choice (J) is incorrect because Clara is not self-conscious of her intelligence. Her use of the adjective *smarter* applies only to her wrists and is in response to Garth's phrase *clever twist*.

5. **C** Since the context is Grandpa watching the kids getting started painting, and his following comment is making sure they're having fun, we can infer that he is feeling good about the situation. There is nothing in the context to support "intense" relaxation, as choice (B) implies. There is also nothing in the context to support "irony" or "disapproval" as choices (A) and (D) imply.

6. **G** The narrator describes both the car and Garth's personality as *boring but reliable* (lines 14–15). This agrees with choice (B). The narrator is not critiquing Garth's choice in cars as choice (A) indicates, rather the narrator says Garth's car is a very fitting choice. There is no comparison between Garth and other Oldsmobile drivers in the passage to support choice (C). There is no also no support for choice (D), that Garth is concerned about how he is seen by others.

7. **D**   Garth's painting and icing advice consists of starting with a large dollop and then *cleverly* swooshing it on. Because the context emphasizes applying a healthy quantity of paint in a single motion, choice (D) is supported. Choices (A), (B), and (C) seems to go against the idea of large dollop of paint and one swift but effective motion. They all suggest a more tentative process.

8. **H**   The paragraph describes Garth's habitual planning and Grandpa's assessment of the motivation for Garth's behavior. When he says *I believe him* (line 12), the narrator concludes that Grandpa is correct about the idea that Garth uses his routine to distract himself from his wife's death. Choices (F) and (G) mention traits resembling the paragraph's description of Garth, but neither are the main conclusion the narrator reaches. Similarly, choice (J) says something seemingly true about Grandpa, but it does not address the conclusion the narrator reaches.

9. **C**   In the last paragraph (lines 63–66), the passage implies that the narrator's mom has died and reveals the reluctance the narrator feels to move on without her. Although the narrator's sadness about painting over the old color of the wall may imply some degree of guilt, choice (A) is incorrect because the paragraph is not focused solely on that one negative emotion and the answer implies that the last paragraph *adds* to the portrayal of the narrator's guilt, when such an emotion is never discussed before this paragraph. Choice (B) is close, but the paragraph does not provide any details explaining their relationship. It provides details about the narrator's reaction to covering up a memory of his mother. Choice (D) is unsupported because there is no context in the passage that portrays a strained relationship between the narrator and Grandpa.

10. **H**   Since in lines 61–62 the narrator asks about his father, it makes sense to think that Grandpa's response is referring to the narrator's father by name. There is no context to suggest it's Grandpa's friend as choice (F) states. Grandpa is responding to the narrator about a third person, so there is no context for choice (G). And there is no discussion of the ladder belonging to a neighbor to support choice (J).

Passage II

11. **D**   In the sixth paragraph, the author states that the monthly lease payment *skewed demand towards a more affluent customer base* (lines 54–55). Choice (A) is incorrect because, though unusual, the body shape is not mentioned as undesirable. Choices (B) and (C) are mentioned in the passage, but there is no indication of consumers' negative reactions to them.

12. **G**   CARB would not have required automakers to offer electric vehicles if it thought that they would lose money in doing so. Choice (F) is incorrect because the passage indicates that the EV1 was designed with the expectation that it would fail. Choice (H) is incorrect because the passage suggests that automakers considered the CARB mandate to be bad news that would potentially be very costly. Choice (J) is incorrect because Dr. Train's study suggested that consumers would only buy electric vehicles if they cost much less than gas-powered cars.

13. **B**   The sixth paragraph states the *initial fleet* (line 49) was 288 EV1s. Choice (A) refers to the distance in miles an EV1 got on one battery charge. Choice (C) refers to the average monthly payment of lease holders. Choice (D) refers to the CETC's estimate.

14. **J**   At the end of the third paragraph, the author says that GM planned to show CARB an electric car was not viable by bringing one to the market and letting everyone *watch it fail*. Choice (F) is incorrect because GM was pessimistic about the market for electric cars. Choice (G) is incorrect because, if anything, GM was more concerned about building a working car and less concerned about helping it succeed in the marketplace. Choice (H) is incorrect because the passage never mentions a competitive motivation. Rather, it suggests the motivation was to demonstrate that CARB's mandate was ill-advised.

15. **A**   The author states that the EV1 was *designed from the start as electric*, while the previous prototypes were just converted from gasoline models. He also mentions that *lightness and efficiency were incorporated into the design* (lines 28–29). Choice (B) is incorrect because the electric prototypes were converted, not the EV1. Choice (C) is incorrect because the author points out a distinct difference in the design process of EV1s and lists several details that resulted. Choice (D) is incorrect because the prototypes were described as expensive conversions and the light materials were only mentioned in relation to the EV1.

16. **G**   If most car buyers would not even consider buying a car over $25,000, then there would be few buyers who would consider an electric vehicle, which carries a price tag of $34,000. Choice (F) is incorrect because the study did not address environmental concerns of customers. Choice (H) is incorrect because the study did not address the motivation of car companies to comply with other states' regulations. Choice (J) is incorrect because the study did not address a psychological connection between car buyers and famous wealthy people.

17. **C**   The passage explains that aluminum was used for the car's body unlike the typical choice of steel. Choice (A) is incorrect because that describes the role of the magnesium alloy. Choice (B) is incorrect because that describes the role of the body shape. Choice (D) is incorrect because the aluminum replaced what would have otherwise been steel.

18. **J**   The author presents the two explanations offered in the eighth paragraph (lines 67–74) as *alleged* and something *others pointed to*. The author treats these theories with some degree of legitimacy but does not fully endorse either. Choice (F) is incorrect because the author does not use language supporting "definitive, real answers." Choice (G) is incorrect because the author does not mention an undiscovered influence from CARB. Choice (H) is incorrect because the author is not unsure about the motives— he goes on to talk about what they may have been.

19. **C**   The passage states that *GM was currently making billions per year on the spare parts market* (lines 71–72) that would be threatened by an expanded electric vehicle market. Choice (A) is incorrect because the owners were willing to do anything to keep their vehicles, including renew their leases. Choice (B) is incorrect because the passage only mentions CARB repealing its mandate, not changing its terms. Choice (D) is incorrect because the suggested retail price of the car was $34,000, not $28,000.

20. **F**   The last paragraph discusses the *political, economic, and social obstacles* new technologies face. None of these are technological problems. Choices (G) and (H) are incorrect because the author states that whether the electric car can transcend the obstacles of consumer skepticism and automaker reluctance is *unknown*. Choice (J) is incorrect because, even though the passage discusses the price of electric cars as a disincentive for consumers, the author never says anything strong enough to justify choice (J)'s prediction.

Passage III

21. **C**   The author credits Torres as *the father of the modern classical guitar* and Tarrega as the *singular authority on classical guitar playing techniques* (lines 76–77). Choice (A) is unsupported because there is nothing in the passage that relates to being appreciated more after death. Choice (B) is unsupported because there is nothing in the passage that restricts the influence of either man to a certain geographical area. Choice (D) is incorrect because Tarrega was famous for playing guitar, not making guitars.

22. **G**   The fifth paragraph (lines 51–63) describes the genius of Torres's design is the way he re-engineered the *internal structure* of the guitar. Choice (G) refers to the fan-bracing layout that Torres *perfected* (line 60). Choice (F) is incorrect because nothing in this paragraph relates to the idea of the guitar as a showcased instrument. That guitars became a more featured instrument is an effect of Torres's ingenious restructuring, but it isn't referring to Torres's design. The passage does not say that Torres invented the arched neck, nor does it say that he widened it to fit a sixth string—eliminate choices (H) and (J).

23. **C**   Although the first paragraph establishes that the passage will focus on how Torres paved the way for the modern guitar, the second paragraph (lines 11–22) begins providing background info on the emergence of early guitar forms. Choice (A) is unsupported because there is no mention that Torres was involved in adding a fifth string. Choice (B) is incorrect because the second paragraph does not mention the modern guitar and, thus, did not compare it to anything. Choice (D) is incorrect because there is nothing in the second paragraph that mentions or compares advantages of early guitars versus later ones.

24. **F**   Since Tarrega went from composing music on a piano, as did most people, to composing on guitar, he would be searching for the songwriting possibilities on the guitar. This agrees with (F). Choice (G) is too literal, and it is a trap answer based on similarity between colors and palettes. Volume output and structural limitations are mentioned as a consideration for performing music (lines 36–37 and 40–41), not composing it—eliminate choices (H) and (J).

25. **D**   The passage states that Spanish guitarists *rekindled the public's respect and admiration for guitar music* (lines 32–33). There is nothing supporting their reluctance to consider new designs as choice (A) says; in fact, the passage explains the limitations of the traditional design that frustrated them. There is no support for choice (B), that they had contact with Torres during his design process. They are guitar players, not lute players, as choice (C) suggests.

26. **G**   Specific dates for the Renaissance are never given. Choice (F) is answered in the fourth paragraph. Choice (H) is answered in the first paragraph. Choice (J) is answered in the second paragraph.

27. **A** The passage states that the *guitarra latina became the national preference and rendered the vihuela obsolete* (lines 21–22). Choice (B) is incorrect because the passage does not indicate that the *vihuela* was intended to be a substitute for the lute. Choice (C) is incorrect because there is no mention that Ferdinand Sor played or popularized the *vihuela*. Choice (D) is incorrect because the passage never mentions Torres as having any involvement with the *vihuela*.

28. **G** The first paragraph explains that Torres's innovations allowed the guitar to go from being a *supporting* instrument to a *featured solo* instrument. Choice (F) is unsupported because the passage never discusses the demands placed on a guitarist in playing Beethoven's works. Choice (H) is incorrect because Torres did not work with five string guitars. Choice (J) is incorrect because it is the opposite of what Torres guitars accomplished: they brought the guitar out of its folk context and into the spotlight of formal concerts.

29. **D** The passage states that as more *"prestigious"* (line 28) instruments rose in popularity, the guitar was *relegated* (line 30) back to being a folk instrument. Choice (A) is incorrect because it describes what happened in the 17th century. Choice (B) is incorrect because the passage states that the growing popularity of other instruments hurt the guitar's popularity. Choice (C) is unsupported as the passage never discusses whether common folk could master playing techniques.

30. **F** The passage indicates that Torres originally planned to sell Tarrega a stock guitar until Torres heard him play. *Deeply impressed* (line 73), Torres instead sold him a more sentimentally valuable guitar. Choice (G) is incorrect because this is something Tarrega did himself, not something someone did for Tarrega out of respect. Choice (H) is incorrect because the passage attributes this to the fifth string added to the *guitarra latina*. Choice (J) is incorrect because the passage attributes this to the popularity of Spanish guitarists such as Ferdinand Sor.

Passage IV

31. **D**   From the outset, the author introduces the fish as the two biggest of their kind, explains that their size puts them near the top of their local food chain, and goes on to describe their behaviors. Choice (A) is incorrect because, although the author mentions each species potentially being harmed by proximity to humans, these dangers are not described as species-threatening. Choice (B) is incorrect because nowhere is the author's tone or language resentful. Choice (C) is incorrect because the author suggests in the first paragraph that the mola and whale shark have much less to worry about in terms of predators than do other fish.

32. **G**   The passage states that *molas have a beaked mouth that does not totally close, so they chew their food in several stages* (lines 34–36). Choice (F) is unsupported, since the passage does not discuss eating habits as a function of being bony or cartilaginous. Choice (H) is unsupported, since the passage does not indicate that the mola eats only at the surface. Choice (J) is unsupported, since the passage indicates the mola floats on its side to warm up, not to eat.

33. **D**   The passage indicates that the whale shark has *no natural predators* (line 58), while smaller molas are *sometimes subject to attack by sea lions* (line 76). Choice (A) is unsupported since neither species is subject to consistent predation, and there is no discussion of a predator's food source. Choice (B) is incorrect because the passage indicates that both species are sometimes adversely affected by contact with humans. Choice (C) is incorrect because the passage only speaks of molas being bothered by parasites.

34. **F**   The passage states that the *mola, like the whale shark, often runs the risk of being hit by boats* (lines 74–75). Choices (G) and (J) are unsupported by any details in the passage. Choice (H) is incorrect because, although nautical debris is said to be a hazard for whale shark's filter feeding, it is not identified as a threat to both species, and the threat is not from debris landing on the fish.

35. **A**   The first paragraph states that molas and whale sharks *must focus on finding enough food to sustain the massive amounts of nutrients needed to support their bulky bodies* (lines 9–11). Choice (B) is incorrect because the passage never connects ocean depth and food requirements. Choice (C) is incorrect because it only relates to how the whale shark eats, not the quantity that any fish eats. Choice (D) is incorrect because the passage doesn't connect teeth or mouth size with dietary needs.

36. **G**   Choices (F), (H), and (J) are all mentioned as part of the mola's diet in the third paragraph (lines 27–38). Zooplankton are specifically described as part of the whale shark's diet (line 47).

37. **C**   The transition into the last two paragraphs begins with a mention of how these big fish are rarely picked on (lines 55–57). The paragraphs then go on to detail the types of dangers each fish faces, which are not very numerous or threatening in nature. Choice (A) is incorrect because, although some details in these paragraphs reinforce the large size of the two species, the purpose of the paragraphs is to discuss potential threats. Choice (B) is incorrect because it would only relate to the mola and conveying irony is not the main purpose of these paragraphs. Choice (D) is incorrect because the whale shark *has no natural predators*, so this answer couldn't apply to the second to last paragraph.

38. **J**   The passage indicates that the gill rakers function by *separating the tiny* (line 52) bits of food from the mouthful of water. Choice (F) is incorrect because the mola, not the whale shark, spits out partially chewed food. Choice (G) is incorrect because the whale shark does not rip apart prey. Choice (H) is incorrect because the gill rakers are not mentioned in connection with the whale shark's teeth.

39. **D**   The passage explains that *these fish live up to their name* (line 25) and proceeds to discuss the mola's impressive size. Choices (A), (B), and (C) are details mentioned about the mola but not connected to the explanation of the Latin name presented in the passage.

40. **G**   The tone of the passage is mostly objective and informative. Choice (F) is incorrect because the two fish are rarely compared and never on the level of their hunting abilities. Choice (H) is incorrect because, though he does discuss what threats are present in their environment, the author does not specifically mention that either species is threatened. Choice (J) is incorrect because although the author refers to evolution in one passing remark, his discussion of the two fish is not based on how they evolved.

ACT READING DRILL 3 ANSWERS

1. A
2. F
3. B
4. G
5. A
6. H
7. B
8. F
9. C
10. J
11. A
12. G
13. C
14. F
15. C
16. J
17. A
18. J
19. D
20. G
21. B
22. G
23. A
24. J
25. D
26. G
27. B
28. J
29. C
30. H
31. C
32. J
33. A
34. H
35. A
36. J
37. B
38. F
39. A
40. J

ACT READING DRILL 3 EXPLANATIONS

Passage I

1. **A** Choice (A) refers to a detail that comes from the description of Jacob's job working for his uncle. During the tour guide job, Jacob pointed out completed buildings, not works in progress. Choice (B) is supported by the script the tour guide had him read. Choice (C) is supported by the fact that the tour mostly attracted *Civil War enthusiasts*. Choice (D) is supported by the phrase *fancying himself as cutting quite a figure in his clean, pressed uniform* (lines 33–34).

2. **F** The first few sentences of the second paragraph establish that Gettysburg is a town that is stuck in the past, or at least doing very little to modernize. *This lack of innovation* affects Jacob and gives him the impression that *there was little of interest to be discovered outside Gettysburg* (lines 26–27). Choice (G) is incorrect because the passage never offers Jacob's ideas for improving old buildings. Choice (H) is incorrect because the passage never discusses Jacob having difficulty finding a job. Choice (J) is incorrect because the passage does not suggest Jacob planned to work for the railroad.

3. **B** The passage is essentially narrating Jacob's thoughts the majority of the time, and otherwise providing exposition on Jacob's life. Choices (A) and (C) are incorrect because there is nothing in the passage that provides an inner thought from Erin. Choice (D) is incorrect because there is no dialogue in the passage.

4. **G** The passage refers to a fantasy Jacob had about being called to Erin's house and impressing her parents, but the passage never indicates that it happened. Choice (F) is supported in the second sentence of the fifth paragraph. Choice (H) is supported in the last sentence of the fifth paragraph. Choice (J) is supported in the second to last sentence of the fifth paragraph.

5. **A** The last sentence of the first paragraph says that Jacob's *ambition towards ascending in the field* (lines 12–13) was basically to be able to impress a *fetching girl on his arm* (line 14) by describing architectural features of their environment. Choice (B) is incorrect because the passage never mentions Jacob devising a new approach to plumbing. Choice (C) is incorrect because the passage never mentions a desire to redesign the Dobbin House. Choice (D) is contradicted by details in the first paragraph which state that Jacob went to Mount St. Mary's, *not because it had a renowned architectural program* (lines 6–7).

6. **H** Although Jacob's high school is mentioned as being small in comparison to Mount St. Mary's College, the number of students is never provided. Choice (F) is answered in the first paragraph—Jacob's tennis scholarship and yearning for Erin are the main factors. Choice (G) is answered in the third paragraph. *As each tour began*, Jacob was disappointed to not see Erin, so she never came to his tour. Choice (J) is answered in the second paragraph—*this lack of innovation deepened Jacob's disinterest in personal or academic enterprise* (lines 25–26).

7. **B** The last sentence of the fourth paragraph (lines 48–52) indicates that it wasn't *until he left the job* that Jacob started thinking more about the buildings. Choice (A) is incorrect because it is the opposite of what the passage indicates. Choices (C) and (D) are incorrect because the passage provides no comparison between how historically noteworthy Jacob thought the buildings were during and after his job as a tour guide.

8. **F** The paragraph begins with Jacob's frustration regarding his inability to run into Erin at college. It ends with Jacob, *With a resigned sigh* (line 76), recounting a memory of his one date with Erin. His final thought is that they were on two different tracks, hers a fearless stride toward the future and his an attempt to get used to the present. These sad details support choice (F)'s notion that he and Erin had grown apart. Choice (G) is incorrect because, although Jacob was frustrated by the campus size in his efforts to run into Erin, there is not support for something so strong as anger. Also, this would only relate to the beginning of the paragraph and not address the rest of it. Choice (H) is incorrect because there is no attitude mentioned or suggested towards Jacob's marriage to Martha. Also, this answer would not address the majority of the paragraph. Choice (J) is incorrect because, although you would assume Jacob was happy to get the date, the details in the paragraph are largely relating to why a relationship with Erin failed. There is no wording in the passage that indicates Jacob's contentment.

9. **C** The wording *an indelible streak of humility* is used in the second sentence of the first paragraph (lines 2–5), attributed to Jacob's grandmother telling him that the rest of the world was under no obligation to think he was special. Choice (A) is incorrect because humility is never suggested by the passage to be a trait of working class communities. Choice (B) is incorrect because Jacob's humility is more the cause of his feeling that he won't be famous than it is a consequence. Choice (D) is incorrect because the passage never links humility to Jacob's pursuit of Erin.

10. **J** This statement is from the last sentence of the passage, which begins *With a resigned sigh, he remembered...* Hence, all the details in the sentence are things Jacob remembers about his first date with Erin. Choice (F) is incorrect because this is Jacob's impression, not the author's. Choice (G) is incorrect because this detail is presented as part of Jacob's memory of his date with Erin, not as part of his struggle to find her at college. Choice (H) is incorrect because this is part of Jacob's reminiscence, not Erin's.

Passage II

11. **A** The statement from Jergensen compares the way in which Wells looked out for her siblings to the way in which she looked out for the rights of any humans suffering from racial inequality. Choice (B) is incorrect because the passage does not suggest that any of her family members *persuaded* her to be an activist. Choice (C) is incorrect because the passage does not suggest she learned any *lessons of equality* via taking care of her siblings. Choice (D) is incorrect because the passage doesn't suggest any family metaphor used by Wells in her speeches.

12. **G** The passage relays Aunt Georgine's comment that Ida wanted to be the grown up she knew her brothers and sisters needed. Ida mourned privately in order to keep a strong appearance. Choice (F) is incorrect because *frightened* goes against the portrayal of Ida stepping into the caretaking role. Choice (H) is incorrect because *relieved* goes against the sadness Ida felt over her parents' passing. Choice (J) is incorrect because *hopeless* is too strong to be supported by anything in the passage.

13. **C** The passage states that *domestic life didn't spell the end of Wells's struggle against inequality* (lines 60–61), and the passage proceeds to describe Wells's activism after she was married. Choice (A) is contradicted by the aforementioned excerpt from the passage as well as by the general sense of Wells's lifelong commitment to the struggle depicted by the author. Choice (B) is incorrect because Wells met her husband in Chicago, not England. Choice (D) is incorrect because there is no implied connection between her husband and the book club, and, additionally, she didn't start the club with that name.

14. **F** The passage calls Wells a *"hushed voice in the race debate"* (lines 7–8) since she was saying things people didn't want to hear and people were unaccustomed in those times to hearing such things from a woman. Choice (G) is incorrect because the word *hushed* is not literally referring to her volume, and otherwise this answer is unsupported. Choice (H) is the opposite of the impression given by the passage, which is that Wells *did* recognize her gender and race as an obstacle to getting her message across. Choice (J) is incorrect because although the passage mentions her writing under a pseudonym (line 12), it was to protect her identity and it certainly wasn't for a "mainstream" newspaper.

15. **C** The passage indicates that following the publishing of Wells's article, she became *a despised figure in Memphis* (line 21). Choices (A), (B), and (D) are all incorrect because the passage states and/or implies that these parties would be sympathetic to Wells's public outcry.

16. **J** The passage provides a positive treatment of Wells, discussing her bold outrage in the first few paragraphs and her techniques of persuasion in the fifth paragraph. All these details correspond well with this account. Choice (F) is incorrect because the passage never calls into question the *fairness* of Wells's objectives. Choice (G) is incorrect because the passage *does* mention, in the first few paragraphs, the danger Wells put herself in. Choice (H) is incorrect because there is nothing to support the author's *unflattering* portrayal of Wells.

17. **A** Two sentences prior to this one, the author mentions Wells's long toil with only occasional rewards, and then mentions women's suffrage in 1920 as one of these "rewards." The sense of change on a societal level that the sentence in question refers to is women achieving suffrage in 1920, so it supports choice (A). Choice (B) is unsupported by the passage, which never says that family motivated Wells's struggle. Choice (C) is unsupported by the passage, which does not ever suggest each generation brings significant changes to society.

18. **J** The passage states that Wells baited *her opposition into admitting certain core principles before challenging them* (lines 48–49) to apply those principles to racial inequality. Choice (F) is incorrect because, though Wells certainly must have had strong philosophical convictions and Socrates sought to weaken the strong convictions of his opponents, a shared sense of certainty is not part of the comparison Jergensen makes to Socrates. Choice (G) goes against the passage since Wells definitely has an agenda to promote racial and gender equality. Choice (H) is incorrect because the passage never discusses Wells's thoughts on the limits of what oration can accomplish.

19. **D** The passage states in the last sentence of the sixth paragraph (lines 66–69) that the book motivated an audience of *progressive thinkers*, while the practical and statistical measures of the problem it addressed did not improve. Choice (A) is incorrect because "philosophical inconsistencies" are not mentioned or suggested. There is no support for calling the book "unusually" radical as choice (B) does. The author does not praise the "scope" of the book, mentioning only its purpose of documenting racially influenced lynchings.

20. **G** The last paragraph states that Wells *nobly walks a self-chosen path of monumental toil, with rewards few and far between* (lines 80–81). This agrees best with choice (G). Choice (F) is too pessimistic for the passage's overall heroic portrayal of Wells. Choice (H) is incorrect since the idea that Wells's steadfast struggle to attain equality was *confusing* is not justified. Choice (J) is incorrect because it goes against the passage's portrayal of Wells's life as being filled with challenge and strife.

Passage III

21. **B** The last paragraph begins *years later*, indicating that the narrator's explanation of his love for B.B.'s music developed years after the summer of 1953 trip. Choices (A) and (D) took place during the summer of 1953 trip. Choice (C) is suggested to have taken place before the summer of 1953 trip.

22. **G** In the eleventh paragraph (lines 47–57), the passage says *feeling particularly fearless for a ten year old, Sis asked ...* Choices (F), (H), and (J) are incorrect because they contradict the age given for the narrator's sister.

23. **A** Saying King's words are difficult to process is akin to saying they are difficult to understand. Choice (B) is a trap answer due to its similarity to the normal meaning of *digest*. Saying something is difficult to stomach means one is reluctant to accept its meaning, not that one does not understand its meaning. Choices (C) and (D) relate to the process of learning and understanding, but neither one itself is a good substitute for the concept of understanding.

24. **J** The narrator is retelling events from the summer of 1953 that involve him meeting B.B. King, and describes the effect B.B.'s music came to have on him. This best supports choice (J). Choice (F) is incorrect because, other than the fact that B.B. and Uncle Randy both lived in Mississippi, there is nothing in the passage about trying to learn that state's culture. Choice (G) is incorrect because, although some of the passage's events take place during a vacation the narrator took with his sister to see his Uncle Randy, the narrator is describing those events in the past tense, not currently on vacation with them. Choice (H) is incorrect because it is never implied that the narrator plays guitar or learned to from B.B. King.

25. **D** B.B. is very polite with the narrator and his sister, having them address him informally by his first name. B.B. refuses to be acknowledged as *the world's best guitarist*, substituting instead the name of *T-Bone Walker*. And, in talking to the narrator's uncle about life on the road, he seemed *reluctant to boast* (line 44). These details all support choice (D). Choice (A) is not supported, other than by the fact that B.B. wore gold rings and his Sunday-best cologne. These are not necessarily flashy things, though, as any adult might wear such things. Choice (B) is not supported because, although B.B. plays the Blues and discusses times in his life where he is sad, the narrator describes him having a *youthful, joyous spirit* (line 40). Choice (C) is not supported by anything in the passage.

26. **G** King explains that the Blues helps him put some distance between himself and his pain, like a *frosted window* that *muffles it and makes it fuzzy* (lines 70–71). This supports the idea of dulling one's suffering in choice (G). Choice (F) is incorrect because King is not referring to any particular instrument Choice (H) is close, but too broad—King is speaking about one particular feeling, not multiple ones. Choice (J) is too literal. Although sleep is mentioned in the extended metaphor/simile King describes, he is primarily discussing the way the Blues softens the feeling of pain.

27. **B** The passage states that the narrator and his sister *timidly accepted* (line 33) B.B.'s handshake. They *sat silently* (line 36) and peered *nervously*. These details support the adjectives used in choice (B). Choice (A) is incorrect because the kids were not warmly greeting him if they were timidly accepting his handshake. Choice (C) is incorrect because amazement and confusion both are more extreme than the general sense of curiosity and strangeness described in the passage. Choice (D) is incorrect because there is no support for either skepticism or disappointment in the passage.

28. **J** The author says when B.B. *started his guitar solo, it was like I turned into a bird that flew out through the waterfall* (lines 81–82). Choice (F) refers to how King compared the effect the Blues has on making pain feel more distant. Choice (G) refers to how the narrator compared the verses of King's music. Choice (J) refers to how the narrator compared the pain felt by the musician or listener.

29. **C** As King explains the Blues to Kathy Mae, he says she wouldn't *hear the Blues right* because she hasn't had enough *pain of livin' yet* (lines 60–61). Choices (A), (B), and (D) are incorrect because King never stresses his hometown, one's childhood upbringing, live versus recorded music, or one's degree of religious commitment.

30. **H** The passage indicates that the narrator and his sister had trouble digesting King's wisdom and resigned themselves to the idea that it was beyond a child's understanding. Choice (F) is incorrect because by resigning themselves to the fact that King's words were beyond them, they are giving up on understanding it, not resolving to expend more effort to understand it. Choice (G) is incorrect because the passage does not suggest any intent to speak with Uncle Randy about it. Choice (J) is incorrect because this answer sums up King's main message, which the children did not seem to absorb.

Passage IV

31. C The paragraph explains that if we define intelligence in human terms, other species might be hopeless to meet human criteria. However, if we define intelligence relative to a given species, we can't compare intelligence between animals of different species. These are suggested to be undesirable consequences. Choice (A) is incorrect because "human bias" is not the focus of the rest of the passage. Choice (B) is incorrect because the author does not endorse any specific definition of intelligence, and in this paragraph he explains a problem that would result from defining intelligence this way. Choice (D) is incorrect because the paragraph only mentions a general statement that every species has an evolutionary niche. This is not really background information, nor is that the focus of this paragraph.

32. J The last line of the second paragraph states that if we adopted this definition, we make intelligence something that cannot be compared *across species*. Choice (F) is incorrect because animals of the "given species" could definitely meet the standard as defined for their species. Choice (G) is incorrect because this definition, in being defined in terms of a given species, would take into account that species unique traits. Choice (H) is incorrect because this definition would not use human intelligence as a measurement, but rather the unique capacities of each species.

33. A The passage specifically states that a spider that spins a web *is not considered to be displaying intelligence* (lines 35–36). Choices (B) and (C) are presented in the fourth paragraph as intelligent, and choice (D) is presented in the fifth paragraph as indicative of some intelligence.

34. H The passage states that *scientists frequently begin assessing an animal's intelligence* (lines 24–26) by analyzing the animal's *susceptibility to classical or operant conditioning*, which involves providing a stimulus and observing the animal's behavior. Choice (F) is incorrect because this is identified by the passage as the *other primary evidence* (line 33) of intelligence. Although this is an important form of evidence, it doesn't address the wording in the question stem, which specifically asks about where scientists *start* their assessments. Choice (G) is given (lines 18–19) as an example of something problematic in determining intelligence. Choice (J) is incorrect because the passage never mentions testing an animal's capacity to absorb information.

35. A The beginning of the fourth paragraph states that one of the primary sources of evidence for intelligence mentioned in the passage is the ability to solve novel problems. So if the lack of sticks is a new problem and the beaver devises a solution to address it, the author would call that intelligent behavior. Choice (B) is incorrect because *long-term planning* (lines 46–47) is described in the passage as evidence of intelligent behavior. Choice (C) is incorrect because there is no reason to think the beaver's behavior is the result of *operant conditiong*. Choice (D) is incorrect because there is no reason to assume the Clever Hans Effect is involved.

36. **J**   The passage makes a contrast between crab and ant shelters and octopus shelters, saying the latter's *long-term planning* is better evidence of some intelligence. Choice (F) is incorrect because this would apply to crab and ant shelters. The veined octopus scours the ocean floor for coconut shells, which indicates a more extended search for materials. Choices (G) and (H) are incorrect because the passage mentions nothing about *sturdiness* and *architectural interest*, respectively.

37. **B**   The passage spends the first four paragraphs (lines 1–48) discussing the conceptual difficulties involved in creating a definition of intelligence that would be applicable across a range of species. The rest of the passage describes the practical challenges involved in trying to measure intelligent behavior. Choice (A) is incorrect because the passage does not offer one clear definition for intelligence, but rather seeks a definition that would apply to human and non-human species alike. Choice (C) is incorrect because, although the passage describes some behavior as intelligent and other behavior as unintelligent, it does not identify specific criteria. Also, this answer is too narrow in terms of the passage's overall subject matter. Choice (D) is incorrect because the passage is not organized around a comparison between humans and non-humans. It is organized around the search for an understanding of intelligence that would relate to all animals.

38. **F**   The author begins the paragraph by explaining that intelligent and unintelligent behavior isn't always what it seems. The example with Alex getting problems wrong is intended to demonstrate that *although the behavior looked unintelligent, experimenters believed it was not due to a lack of understanding* (lines 69–70). Choice (G) is incorrect because the author has no clear definition of intelligence, so he couldn't possibly be applying it to parrots. Choice (H) is incorrect because the parrot example mainly illustrated the opposite of this answer. Even though the parrot is described having seemingly intelligent behavior, the passage never says that parrots are believed to be unintelligent. Choice (J) is incorrect because the word *proof* is too strong. The author said that Alex's behavior *suggests* that it learned a concept, not that it *proves* it did.

39. **A**   The sentence is making a contrast between the animal's private experience, which scientists can't observe, and the *external* behavior that scientists can observe. Choice (B) is incorrect because, although secrets are things that are hidden from some people, the adjective *secretive* implies an intention of hiding something, which is not present in the use of *private experience*. Choice (C) is incorrect because a private experience could be subtle or strong—either way it is something outsiders cannot perceive. Choice (D) is incorrect because *shy* implies being nervous or uncomfortable in the presence of others, and that is not what the passage implies about an animal's *private experience*.

40. **J**   This topic sentence (lines 57–58) for the last paragraph foreshadows a discussion of a parrot who behaved unintelligently despite researchers believing it knew how to behave intelligently, and a horse who behaved intelligently but ultimately seemed to not have an intelligent grasp of its behavior. Choice (F) is incorrect because the examples provided do not suggest the animals intended to trick others; this is a trap answer based on the normal meaning of "deceive." Choice (G) is incorrect because the question asks about animal behavior, and that would not be the *hardest thing* to measure. The passage does not state what is the *hardest*, but it is suggested that the mental state of the animal is *harder* to measure than is the animal's behavior (lines 49–56). Choice (H) is incorrect because the passage maintains that even trained researchers still can only hazard a guess as to the thought processes that exist behind an animal's behavior. This answer implies that one can be trained enough to not be fooled.

Part IV
The SAT:
Strategies

Chapter 8
SAT Strategies

THE ART OF ELIMINATION

Take a look at the following sentence completion—in an unusual format that you will never see on the SAT:

> 7. Bien qu'il soit trés vieux, il parait
>   toujours -------.

You may think the unusual thing about this question is that it's in French, (okay, we admit that's pretty unusual), but the *really* unusual thing about this question—the thing that makes it different from every question on the Critical Reading and Writing parts of SAT—is that it's not in a multiple-choice format.

You might be saying, "Who cares? Multiple-choice or fill-in—I can't answer it anyway. It's in *French*."

As it stands right now, unless you speak French, you have no idea what word goes in the blank (and by the way, there are no questions in French on the SAT). But let's turn this question into a multiple-choice question and see if you can figure out the answer now:

> 7. Bien qu'il soit trés vieux, il parait
>   toujours -------.
>
>   (A) earnest
>   (B) timid
>   (C) exhausted
>   (D) jeune
>   (E) elated

Cross out all of the answers you know must not fit the sentence. All of a sudden, this problem doesn't seem so hard, does it? Multiple-choice tests (in *any* language) always give test takers an inherent advantage: There are only a finite number of possible choices. And while you might not know the correct answer to this problem, you know that four choices are probably wrong. (The correct answer is choice D.)

Eliminating Wrong Answers

There will be many problems on the SAT for which you will be able to identify the correct answer (particularly if you learn the Hit Parade words). However, there will be others about which you will not be sure. Should you simply skip these problems? Not if you can eliminate wrong answers. Wrong answers are often easier to spot than right answers. Sometimes they just sound wrong in the context of the sentence. Other times they are logically impossible. While you will rarely be able to eliminate all the incorrect answer choices on an SAT question, it is often possible to eliminate two or three. And each time you eliminate an answer choice, your odds of guessing correctly get better.

Guessing Is Good

Every time you get a question right, ETS gives you one raw point. To discourage you from guessing at random, ETS deducts a quarter of a raw point from your score for each incorrect answer you choose. ETS calls this a guessing penalty, but in fact, it is not a penalty at all. Let's say you guess at random on five questions. The laws of probability say that you will get one of these questions right (so ETS gives you 1 raw point) and the other four wrong (so ETS takes away 4 quarter points). In other words, you will come out dead even. This means that guessing completely at random on the SAT won't help your score, and it won't hurt your score.

Ah, but who said anything about guessing at random?

Let's look at the same question again, but with slightly different answers:

> 7. Bien qu'il soit trés vieux, il parait
>   toujours -------.
>
>   (A) earnest
>   (B) timid
>   (C) sérieux
>   (D) jeune
>   (E) elated

This time, even without knowing French, you can eliminate three of the answer choices. This gives you a fifty-fifty guess—much better than random guessing. It turns out that if you can eliminate even one answer choice, then it is in your interest to guess. You will find that our techniques for sentence completions will help you eliminate answer choices, even when you don't know the words.

ORDER OF DIFFICULTY

Sentence completion questions on the SAT are arranged in order of difficulty. There will be five sentence completions in one of the two 25-minute Critical Reading sections and eight in the other. The 20-minute section has six sentence completions. Within each section, these questions are arranged so that the easiest question comes first, the most difficult question comes last, and the others are arranged in ascending order of difficulty in between.

The critical reading questions are *not* arranged in order of difficulty. Instead, these questions appear in the order in which the information that is required to answer them is found in the passage.

The difficulty level of a question reflects the percentage of test takers who usually get that question correct. Depending on which words you happen to know, a question that is considered "hard" might be easy for you, while you might find an "easy" question to be difficult if it contains unfamiliar words. Nevertheless, it is a good idea to think of each group of questions in sentence completions as being in thirds. The first third is relatively easy. The second third is medium. The last third contains the questions that most people find difficult.

Easy Questions Have Easy Answers— Hard Questions Have Hard Answers

The order of difficulty is important because it will prevent you from overthinking. An easy question is supposed to have an easy answer. A difficult problem will have a difficult answer. If you find yourself wrestling with the first sentence completion, you are probably looking for subtlety that isn't there. If you find yourself picking the first choice that comes into your head on the last sentence completion, you may want to think it through again.

Distractors

The ETS test writers think constantly about the order of difficulty because they are obsessed with making sure that students correctly answer only the questions that they "deserve to get right." The average test taker is supposed to get all of the easy questions right, some of the medium questions right, and all of the difficult questions wrong.

There's only one potential problem here: What if the average test taker were to guess correctly on a difficult question? The ETS test writers hate this idea so much that in the difficult third of a group of questions they sometimes include distractor answers that are designed to trick the average test taker.

JOE BLOGGS

Joe Bloggs is our name for the average test taker. He's the guy who always writes down the first answer that comes into his head. Because the first answer that comes into his head is correct on easy questions, he gets all the easy questions correct. And because the first answer that comes into his head is *sometimes* correct on medium questions, he gets *some* of the medium questions correct. But the first answer that enters Joe's mind is always wrong on difficult questions, so Joe Bloggs gets all of the difficult questions wrong.

To make sure this remains true, the ETS test writers will occasionally help Joe to make the *wrong* decision. Let's see how this works. Here's a sentence completion from the last and hardest third of a group of sentence completions:

8. Despite the ------- of evidence against the suspect, the jury found him guilty on all counts.

   (A) preponderance
   (B) weight
   (C) paucity
   (D) deliberation
   (E) objection

Don't Be Like Joe

We're going to talk about how to approach sentence completions later in the book, so don't worry if you're not sure how to get the correct answer. For now, let's discuss how Joe tries to tackle this problem (and if Joe's method is similar to yours, that's okay; there's a little of Joe Bloggs in each of us). When Joe reads a sentence completion, he likes to pick an answer that sounds good in the sentence. Usually the word that sounds good to Joe reminds him of the other words in the sentence. Do any of the answers seem like something he'd like?

If you said choice D or E, you've got the idea. When Joe isn't entirely sure of what the sentence is saying, he's likely to pick a choice that feels right to him. Because this sentence has a courtroom theme, Joe might go with "objection" or "deliberation," two words he's probably heard on popular TV court shows. Of course, ETS knows this, and both of those choices are wrong. The best answer is choice C.

Remember, though, that the only time you need to look out for distractor answers is in the last third of a group of questions (the hardest questions in the set).

PACING

Each of the 25-minute Critical Reading sections will contain three types of questions: sentence completions, short reading, and critical reading. The 20-minute section has only sentence completion and long-passage critical reading questions. In general, the reading questions take longer to do than the sentence completions. If you have a good vocabulary, tackle the sentence completions first and then move on to the reading questions. If vocabulary isn't your strong point, spend more time with the reading questions (but be sure to study the vocabulary in Chapter 7; the better your vocabulary, the better your reading level—and your score). Use whatever time you have left to deal with the sentence completions.

The 35-question Writing section will contain questions broken down into three types: error identification, improving sentences, and improving paragraphs. As with sentence completions, error identification and improving sentences questions are arranged roughly in order of difficulty. The error identification questions generally take the least amount of time and should be done first. After you've finished them, or if the last third of error identifications gets tough, move on to the improving sentences. The order of difficulty starts over with easy questions at the beginning of both question types. Save the improving paragraphs questions for last. There is no order of difficulty for improving paragraphs—most are of medium difficulty.

The 10-minute Writing section is always Section 10. It has only 14 questions, all of which are improving sentences questions.

You don't have to answer every question on the test to get a good score; it's okay if you skip questions as you work. However, as you learn the strategies in this book, you'll see that on most questions you will be able to eliminate at least one answer. In that case, it pays to be aggressive and guess. The higher you aim to score, the more questions you'll need to attempt.

Pace Yourself

While the following pacing charts for Critical Reading and Writing give you an idea of how many questions to do, they don't tell you *which* questions to do. If the chart tells you to do 16 questions in a particular section, that doesn't necessarily mean you should do the *first* 16. Focus on doing the medium and easy questions first; then work on the more difficult ones if you need more questions to reach your target score.

In Critical Reading, only the arrangements of sentence completion questions follow an order of difficulty.

In Writing, the improving sentences have an order of difficulty, and the error identifications start with easy questions and a fresh order of difficulty even though they start at question 12. There is no order of difficulty for improving passages.

These pacing charts are only an approximate guide. ETS has a way of changing things at the last minute, so don't worry if there are slightly more or fewer questions in each section when you take the test. Just hold your pacing to your score level, and you'll do fine.

Critical Reading Pacing Chart

To get: (scaled score)	You Need: (raw points)	Answer this many questions			
		24 question section	24 question section	19 question section	Total # of questions to attempt
300	5	6	6	3	15
350	9	8	8	4	20
400	14	11	11	8	30
450	21	14	14	10	38
500	29	16	16	11	43
550	38	19	19	13	51
600	46	22	22	16	60
650	53	23	23	17	63
700	59	23	23	18	64
750	63	all	all	all	67
800	67	all	all	all	67

Writing

The scaled Writing section score (200–800) is derived from two components: the essay score and the multiple-choice grammar score (which is scaled from 20–80). Two different people grade your essay, and each gives it a score on a scale of 1–6. The sum of these two scores is weighted to make the essay score worth approximately 30 percent of the total score; then the result is added to your grammar raw score to get your final writing score.

Writing Scores

If your scaled grammar score is ...	Depending on your essay score, your writing score will range from
20	200–320
25	200–370
30	250–420
35	280–460
40	330–500
45	360–540
50	410–590
55	450–630
60	490–670
65	530–710
70	570–750
75	620–800
80	680–800

The following pacing chart will help you decide how many multiple-choice grammar questions to do.

Grammar Pacing Chart

To get: (scaled score)	You Need: (raw points)	Answer this many questions		
		35 question section	14 question section	Total # of questions to attempt
35	5	10	5	15
40	11	13	7	20
45	17	18	8	26
50	22	22	9	31
55	27	26	10	36
60	31	27	11	38
65	36	31	all	45
70	40	all	all	49
75	44	all	all	49
80	49	all	all	49

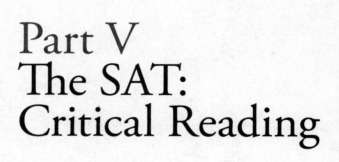

Part V
The SAT:
Critical Reading

Chapter 9
SAT Sentence Completions

Every Critical Reading section of the SAT begins with a group of sentence completion questions. There are five or eight sentence completions in the 25-minute sections and six in the 20-minute section for a total of 19 sentence completions per test. The questions within each section are arranged in order of difficulty. Because of the terrific elimination techniques we will show you below, you will probably be able to take a good guess on all of the sentence completions—even when you don't know the definitions of some of the words.

Let's begin by looking at an example of a sentence completion that unfortunately you will *never* see on the SAT:

1. Jane ------- the DVD player.

   (A) installed
   (B) dropped
   (C) programmed
   (D) stole
   (E) shot

Why won't you ever see this question on the SAT? Because the way this sentence is written, all of the answer choices would be correct. What? You didn't think choice E could be right? Well, how about this:

2. After trying unsuccessfully to program it for three hours,
   Jane ------- the DVD player.

   (A) installed
   (B) dropped
   (C) programmed
   (D) stole
   (E) shot

To make sure that only one answer choice is correct per question, ETS always provides you with a clue (such as the one you just saw above) within the sentence itself. The clause "after trying unsuccessfully to program it for three hours..." gives away Jane's state of mind, and helps us to choose the correct answer. Let's look at the same sentence written several different ways. See if you can supply the missing word:

3. While trying to lift the DVD player, Jane ------- it.

   (A) installed
   (B) dropped
   (C) programmed
   (D) stole
   (E) shot

4. Because she wanted to tape a program when she wasn't home, Jane ------- the DVD player.

(A) installed
(B) dropped
(C) programmed
(D) stole
(E) shot

5. After breaking into the house through the window, Jane ------- the DVD player.

(A) installed
(B) dropped
(C) programmed
(D) stole
(E) shot

(Answers: 2. E, 3. B, 4. C, 5. D)

Each of these sentences contained a clue that led you to the correct answer. While the real SAT sentence completion questions are a bit more difficult, the same principle always applies. The way to answer a sentence completion question is to look for the clue that must be there, in order for the question to have one answer that is better than the others.

THE CLUE

Take a look at the following two questions.

1. The woman told the man, "You're very -------."

(A) handsome
(B) sick
(C) smart
(D) foolish
(E) good

2. The doctor told the man, "You're very -------."

(A) handsome
(B) sick
(C) happy
(D) foolish
(E) good

Which of these two questions actually has a single correct answer, question 1 or 2?

If you said question 2, you're right. In question 2, there's only one possible answer: choice B. The words are the clue. Every sentence completion has a the clue: a key word or phrase that tells you what kind of word you need to fill in the blank.

> Always be on the lookout for the clue: the word or phrase that ETS gives you to help anticipate the word that will best fit in the blank.

Here's an example.

5. So ------- was the young boy's behavior that his teachers decided to give him a gold star.

   (A) exemplary
   (B) unruly
   (C) arrogant
   (D) radical
   (E) imaginative

THE PRINCETON REVIEW METHOD

Step One   Cover up the answer choices. ETS wants several of these choices to appear likely if you haven't found the clue. For example, if you were to look straight at the answer choices in this question, your eye might be caught by choice B, "unruly," or choice C, "arrogant"—just because those are often words a teacher might use to describe a student's behavior.

> Cover up the answer choices until you have found the clue in the sentence.

Step Two   Look for the clue. Have you spotted it? In this case, the clue was in the very last words of the sentence: "gold star." If these teachers want to give a student a "gold star," what word would you use to describe his behavior? Try making up your own word to fit the blank. If you chose a word like "good" or "excellent" or "flawless," you were right on track.

Step Three	Look at the answer choices and see which one comes closest to the word you think should go in the blank. Eliminate any that are definitely wrong. In this case, eliminate choices B and C because they are almost exactly the opposite of the word you are looking for. *Physically cross off these two choices.* Would "radical" behavior necessarily lead to a gold star? Not really, so cross off choice D as well.
Step Four	If you still have choices left, guess among the remaining possibilities. In this example, you are down to choice A, "exemplary," and choice E, "imaginative." If you know the meaning of the word "exemplary" (one of the words on the Hit Parade), then your choice is easy. But let's say for a moment that you aren't sure. The first thing to do in this situation is not to panic—you are down to a fifty-fifty guess, which is already pretty good. Now, if you don't know the meaning of the word, of course you can't cross it off. So look instead at the other word. Do teachers reward imagination? They might. But do they reward imaginative *behavior*? What exactly would imaginative behavior look like? Mostly, teachers like imagination only when it is in a composition or a finger painting. It might be a little threatening if it exhibited itself in *behavior*.

You're down to choices A and E. Guess. If you picked choice A, you are 10 points ahead. Exemplary means "ideal," or "worthy of imitation."

QUICK QUIZ #1

Begin by covering up the answer choices. Try to spot the clue, and come up with your own idea of what the missing word might be. Then go to the answer choices and eliminate wrong answers. Finally, pick the answer you think is correct.

1. By means of her ------- demeanor, Lucy Ortiz calmly worked her way up to the position of head salesperson at the chaotic brokerage house.

   (A) cunning
   (B) serene
   (C) frenzied
   (D) gullible
   (E) unstable

2. Large facial features have often been the mark of successful people; many of our recent presidents have had ------- noses.

   (A) insignificant
   (B) typical
   (C) unusual
   (D) prominent
   (E) subtle

3. Sightings of the tern, a small marsh bird once considered endangered, are becoming almost -------.

   (A) commonplace
   (B) erratic
   (C) precarious
   (D) virtuous
   (E) uniform

4. Glaucoma, a serious eye ailment that can lead to blindness, is almost always ------- if it is caught in its early stages.

   (A) fatal
   (B) congenital
   (C) unethical
   (D) verifiable
   (E) treatable

5. The consummate opera singer Kathleen Battle has long had the reputation for being a difficult, even -------, personality.

(A) entertaining
(B) malleable
(C) contentious
(D) deliberate
(E) bland

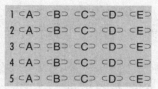

Answers and Explanations: Quick Quiz #1

1. **B** The clue here is the word "calmly." You might be thrown off by the "chaotic" atmosphere at the brokerage house and think that Lucy must be pretty chaotic herself in order to fit in. However, the sentence makes clear that it is her calmness that allows her to succeed in the hectic business. If you came up with a word like "evenness" or "placid" or "tranquil," you were right on the money. Looking at the answer choices, you can eliminate everything but choice B, "serene."

2. **D** The clue in this sentence is the word "large" referring to the facial features of successful people. What kind of noses, then, according to this sentence, would you expect to find on recent presidents? If you chose words like "huge" or "big" or "gigantic," you were right on the money. Choice C is tempting, because a really large nose would be kind of unusual, but choice D is better because it clearly signifies "large."

3. **A** The clue here is the phrase "once considered endangered." If the bird was *once* considered endangered, then it isn't *now*. What word would describe sightings of this bird, which is no longer in danger of becoming extinct? If you chose a word like "mundane" or "everyday" or "routine," then you are doing just fine. Both choices B and C would be good possibilities if the bird were still endangered, but because it is not, eliminate them. Choice E might seem tempting at first, but the secondary definition of uniform (not what a boy scout wears) is "identical or alike." The best answer is "commonplace."

4. **E** Both choices A, "fatal," and B, "congenital" (meaning "from birth"), are often used to describe diseases, but neither is the right answer this time. The clue in this sentence is the phrase "if it is caught in its early stages." What word would you use to describe a disease discovered in its early stages? If you came up with "curable" or "correctable" or "relievable," you were right on track. The best answer here is choice E, "treatable."

5. **C** The clue in this sentence is the phrase "a difficult, even ------- personality." Whenever you see this format, (a -------, even -------), the second word is almost always a more extreme version of the first word. (For example, "The weather was gray, even gloomy.") Therefore, what you are looking for in this sentence is a more extreme version of the word "difficult." If you came up with words like "troublesome" or "argumentative," you were right on the money. The best answer is choice C, "contentious" (meaning "quarrelsome").

TRIGGER WORDS

Certain words reveal a lot about the structure of a sentence. We call these words "trigger words." Trigger words work with the clue to help you figure out the meaning of the word in the blank. Take a look at the following sentence:

> You're beautiful, *but* you're . . .

What kind of word would go in the blank? Something negative, such as "rude" or "unpleasant."

The word "but" in the sentence above tells you all you have to know: Whatever has been expressed in the first half of the sentence is about to be contradicted in the second half. Words like "but" are structural clues to the meaning of the sentence.

Here's a list of the trigger words that signal a contradiction:

but	however
although	even though
despite	though
rather	on the contrary
yet	in contrast

On the other hand, there are other words that signal that the second half of the sentence will continue in the same general direction as the first half. Here's an example:

> You're beautiful, *and* you're very. . .

What kind of word go in this blank? Something positive, such as "smart" or "sweet."

The word "and" in the sentence above tells you what kind of word will go in the blank: Whatever thought has been expressed in the first half of the sentence (something positive) will be continued or amplified in the second half (something positive). Words like "and," when they appear in a sentence completion problem, are also structural clues to the meaning of the sentence.

Here's a list of the words that signal a continuation or an amplification of the direction in a sentence:

and	in fact
not only	but also
because	indeed, even

Always circle these trigger words whenever you see them. These words, along with the clue, will help you to figure out the meaning of the blank.

QUICK QUIZ #2

Begin by covering up the answer choices. Try to come up with the missing word using trigger words and the clue. Then go to the answer choices and eliminate wrong answers. Finally, pick the answer you think is correct.

1. Despite government efforts at population control, the number of people in China continues to ------- rapidly.

   (A) decline
   (B) increase
   (C) fluctuate
   (D) stabilize
   (E) deploy

2. Archeologists believed until recently that the ancient Mayans lived exclusively in permanent settlements, but new evidence suggests that some of the Mayans made seasonal -------.

   (A) migrations
   (B) resolutions
   (C) renunciations
   (D) sanctions
   (E) speculations

3. During the height of the civil war, the diplomatic efforts by Sweden to enforce a cease-fire were regarded by both sides not only with ------- but also with derision.

   (A) delight
   (B) reverence
   (C) scorn
   (D) vigor
   (E) yearning

4. The museum has many fine paintings by van Gogh, including his ------- and haunted self-portrait with the bandaged ear.

   (A) tranquil
   (B) haughty
   (C) colorful
   (D) repetitive
   (E) anguished

5. Although many of the people at the party accepted John's account of the evening's events, Jason believed it to be -------.

(A) generous
(B) credible
(C) unusual
(D) inferior
(E) apocryphal

```
1 ⊂A⊃ ⊂B⊃ ⊂C⊃ ⊂D⊃ ⊂E⊃
2 ⊂A⊃ ⊂B⊃ ⊂C⊃ ⊂D⊃ ⊂E⊃
3 ⊂A⊃ ⊂B⊃ ⊂C⊃ ⊂D⊃ ⊂E⊃
4 ⊂A⊃ ⊂B⊃ ⊂C⊃ ⊂D⊃ ⊂E⊃
5 ⊂A⊃ ⊂B⊃ ⊂C⊃ ⊂D⊃ ⊂E⊃
```

Answers and Explanations: Quick Quiz #2

1. **B** The trigger word in this sentence ("despite") signifies that the second half of the sentence is going to contradict the first. Because the first half refers to population *control*, what do you think the number of people is going to continue to do? If you said "multiply" or "grow" you were right. The correct answer is choice B.

2. **A** The trigger word ("but") signifies that the new evidence is going to contradict what archeologists believed until recently. The missing word should mean something like "trips" or "movements." The best answer is choice A.

3. **C** The construction "not only...but also..." means that the word in front of the "but also" must be similar to the word after the "but also." Thus, the missing word must resemble the word "derision." If you know the meaning of "derision" then the choice is fairly clear. However, let's say for a moment that you aren't sure. Have you at least got a feeling about the word? Does it sound positive or negative? If you said "negative," you were right. Which of the answer choices also sounds negative? The word that is most similar to "derision" (meaning "mockery") is choice C, "scorn."

4. **E** An "and" injected in between two adjectives usually means the two adjectives must be somewhat similar. In this case, you don't know the first word describing a painting by van Gogh, but it must be similar to the second word, "haunted." Which choices can you eliminate? It's pretty easy to eliminate choices A, C, and D. "Haughty" (meaning "arrogant or condescending") doesn't exactly seem similar to "haunted." The correct answer is choice E.

5. **E** The trigger in this sentence is the word "although," which signals that the second half of the sentence will contradict the first. In the first half, you are told that many people accepted John's story as true. In the second half, you are supposed to learn that Jason did not. If you chose a word like "a lie" then you were right on track. Go through the answer choices. If Jason believed John's story was choice A, "generous," would that contradict the general belief that his story was true? Not really. If Jason believed John's story was choice B, "credible" (meaning "believable"), would that contradict the general belief? Actually, just the reverse. If Jason believed John's story was choice C, "unusual," would that contradict the general belief? Maybe. Hold on to that one and look at the other two. If Jason believed

John's story was choice D, "inferior," would that contradict the general belief? Maybe. Hold on to that one as well. If Jason believed John's story was choice E, "apocryphal" (meaning "fictional or made up"), would that contradict the general belief? You bet. The best answer to this fairly difficult problem is choice E.

DEGREE OF DIFFICULTY

Because all sentence completions are arranged in order of difficulty, you can frequently learn important things about a missing word simply by the question number, which tells you how hard the question is. The first two or three sentence completions in a group are supposed to be relatively easy. This means that the correct answer to one of these questions should be a relatively easy vocabulary word as well. The middle three or four sentence completions are supposed to be of medium difficulty. The correct answers to these questions will be words of medium difficulty. The last two or three sentence completions are supposed to be quite difficult. The correct answers to these questions will be quite tough vocabulary words, or medium words that have secondary meanings.

If you don't know some of the words in a difficult sentence completion question, you might think that you would have to leave it blank—but that is not necessarily the case. Let's see how you could use order of difficulty to eliminate answer choices on the last three sentence completions. What follows are only the answer choices from one of the last three sentence completion questions of an actual SAT. Based on the fact that tough questions tend to have tough answers, which of these choices are *unlikely* to be the correct answer?

      (A) cosmopolitan
      (B) wavering
      (C) plucky
      (D) vindictive
      (E) bellicose

Put it this way: Which of these words would be familiar to just about anyone? "Cosmopolitan" is a fairly common word, as are "wavering" and "plucky." Therefore, if you were simply to guess the answer to this difficult sentence completion without the benefit of the sentence itself, you would be tempted to pick either choice D, "vindictive," or choice E, "bellicose." The correct answer to this real ETS question turns out to be choice E. Will this work every time? Of course not. This is merely a last-ditch guessing strategy if you don't understand enough of the sentence to be able to search for contextual clues.

Remember that the answers to difficult sentence completions tend to use difficult vocabulary words.

The real value of this strategy comes when you have already eliminated several answer choices by other means: You're down to two, and you can't figure out which one is the answer. If the question is one of the last three sentence completions, you should pick the answer choice containing the more difficult word.

QUICK QUIZ #3

Pretend that the following are answer choices for the last, and therefore hardest, sentence completions in a set of eight. As a last-ditch guessing strategy, eliminate answer choices that seem too easy to be the correct answers to difficult problems.

1. (A) supplied
   (B) tainted
   (C) betrayed
   (D) corrected
   (E) increased

2. (A) complexity
   (B) uniqueness
   (C) exorbitance
   (D) paucity
   (E) fragility

3. (A) already eliminated
   (B) indifference .. legitimate
   (C) already eliminated
   (D) immunity .. hyperbolic
   (E) already eliminated

```
1 ⊂A⊃ ⊂B⊃ ⊂C⊃ ⊂D⊃ ⊂E⊃
2 ⊂A⊃ ⊂B⊃ ⊂C⊃ ⊂D⊃ ⊂E⊃
3 ⊂A⊃ ⊂B⊃ ⊂C⊃ ⊂D⊃ ⊂E⊃
```

Answers and Explanations: Quick Quiz #3

1. **B** Eliminate choices A, D, and E. The correct answer to this real ETS question is choice B.

2. **D** Eliminate choices A and B. The correct answer to this real ETS question is choice D.

3. **D** Imagine that you have already eliminated A, C, and E through context clues, but you can't decide between choices B and D. Do either of them seem too easy to be the answer to a tough question? Eliminate choice B. The correct answer to this real ETS question is choice D.

IS A MISSING WORD POSITIVE OR NEGATIVE?

While sometimes you may not be sure *exactly* what word would fit the blank, you may be able to get a feeling for whether the missing word should be generally positive or generally negative.

> **6.** When Lattitia Douglas was ------- by the railroad company in 1903, it represented a personal victory for her.

While you may not know exactly what word ETS chose for this blank, you can be pretty sure it was a positive word based on the clue ("a victory").

Just as important, when you look at the answer choices, you may not know the meaning of every word, but you may have a "feeling" about certain words even without knowing their exact definitions. Here are the answer choices to this question:

> (A) censured
> (B) lauded
> (C) rebuked
> (D) rebutted
> (E) undermined

As you go through the Vocabulary section of this book, you will probably be amazed at how often the words you've just learned come up on real SAT practice sections. Because we show you only words that appear again and again on the test, this is really not all that amazing. However, for every new word that you learn, there will be several whose meanings you haven't quite memorized yet—but that you have seen several times before.

NOTE: You can decide that a word is negative or positive only if you have seen it before.

These are the words you may be able to identify as positive or negative. By the way, we don't mean to suggest that you should try this technique with words you've never encountered before. Looking at a mystery word and saying, "Hmm, I don't like the look of that word," doesn't count. You have to have seen it before and have a vague sense of what it means.

You may not know the exact meaning of each of the words above (remember to look them up when you're done with this example—several are from the Hit Parade), but you may have a *feeling* about whether each is positive or negative.

As it turns out, "censured," "rebuked," "rebutted," and "undermined" are all negative words. Because you are looking for a generally positive word to fill the blank, you can eliminate all four of them—or as many of them as you have a negative feeling about. The correct answer is "lauded," which means "praised."

TWO-BLANK SENTENCE COMPLETION

About half of the sentence completions on the SAT contain two blanks instead of one. The same clues we've already discussed above are vital in answering these questions, but to use these clues effectively, it helps to concentrate on one blank at a time. Think about it this way: When you go to buy a new pair of shoes, you can eliminate pairs that don't fit after trying on just one. If the left shoe doesn't fit, you don't bother trying on the right shoe. So try one blank at a time. If the answer choice doesn't fit for that one blank, you can eliminate it. Which blank should you start with? Whichever you think is easiest. Try the following sentence:

5. Although the food at the restaurant was usually -------, the main course was ------- by an overabundance of salt.

   (A) bland . . enhanced
   (B) indifferent . . supplanted
   (C) delectable . . marred
   (D) distinguished . . elevated
   (E) diverse . . superb

THE PRINCETON REVIEW METHOD

Step One Cover the answer choices and read the entire sentence. Decide which blank you think would be easier for you to fill in with your own word. In this case, the first clause of the sentence, which contains the first blank ("Although the food at the restaurant was usually -------"), is not very helpful. The food might be delicious, or it might be terrible. You just don't know yet. Concentrate instead on the second clause of the sentence: "The main course was ------- by an overabundance of salt." How would you describe food to which much too much salt has been added? If you chose words like "ruined" or "spoiled" or "flawed," you were right on track.

In two-blank sentence completions, attack the blanks one at a time.

Step Two Completely ignoring the first word in each answer choice, take a look at the *second* word in each answer choice. You are looking for a word like "ruined." Clearly, choices A, "enhanced," D, "elevated," and E, "superb," are all wrong. Physically cross them off. Before you've even looked at the first blank, you're down to two possible choices!

Step Three Look at the first blank to decide between the two remaining choices. You've figured out that the second half of the sentence is saying that the food was bad. Did you notice that the first half of the sentence began with a trigger word? The word "although" told you that the second half of the sentence would contradict the first half. Let's summarize what you know about the sentence so far:

Although the food at the restaurant was usually -------,
tonight it was (something negative).

What kind of word are you looking for in the first blank? If you suggested "delicious" or "good" or "tasty," you were right on track. Look at the answer choices.

    (A) already eliminated
    (B) indifferent . . supplanted
    (C) delectable . . marred
    (D) already eliminated
    (E) already eliminated

Remember that you have already crossed off three choices just by looking at the second blank. You're down to two remaining choices. Looking only at the first word in each, which do you think is closest to "delicious"? If you said choice C, you are 10 points ahead. "Delectable" means "highly pleasing." "Marred" (meaning "flawed") was much better than "supplanted" (meaning "to take the place of").

TWO-BLANK POSITIVE/NEGATIVE

On two-blank problems, you will sometimes need to watch out for the relationship between the two blanks. For instance, the blanks will often have a generally positive/generally negative relationship. Take a look at the question below:

> Although he was ------- by nature, his duties as a prison
> guard forced him to be more -------.

As always, try to supply your own words before you look at the answer choices, but sometimes (as in this case) the sentence is a little too vague to supply precise words. Work with what you have. Did you notice the trigger word "although" at the beginning of the sentence? Because of this, you know that the first half of the sentence will contradict the second half. What kind of clues do you have in this sentence? In the second phrase, the sentence discusses how he must behave as a prison guard.

If you had to guess, do you think the second blank is going to be a generally positive word or a generally negative word? Even though you don't know exactly what the word will be, the second blank is likely to be negative. And that means that the first blank is likely to be positive.

Now look at the answer choices. It sometimes helps to actually write into the blanks the directions you think the words will go in, as shown:

6. Although he was (<u>positive word</u>) by nature, his duties as
   a prison guard forced him to be more (<u>negative word</u>).

   (A) hermetic . . lonely
   (B) lenient . . strict
   (C) unhappy . . stylized
   (D) gentle . . witty
   (E) trite . . tactful

Even though you have a general idea of both blanks, it still makes sense to work on one at a time. You are looking for a generally negative word for the second blank. So eliminate any choices whose second words are positive. That gets rid of choices D, "witty," and E, "tactful." Cross them off with your pencil. Now look at the first blank in the answer choices that remain. The first blank should be generally positive, which means you can get rid of choices A, "hermetic," and C, "unhappy," as well. There's only one answer left: It must be choice B. Read the sentence again with "lenient" and "strict," just to make sure. Does one word contradict the other? Yes. Does the sentence make sense? You bet!

NEGATIVE/POSITIVE? POSITIVE/NEGATIVE? WHO KNOWS?

The most difficult sentence completions are probably the ones in which all you know is the relationship between the blanks. Take a look at the following, and note the trigger word:

> Although he was ------- by nature, he has recently become more -------.

All that you really know about the missing two words in this sentence is that they must be opposites. Fortunately, problems like this appear infrequently on the SAT. When they do show up, you will be forced to go to the answer choices in search of opposites.

(A) generous . . frugal
(B) liberal . . dependable
(C) insensitive . . indifferent
(D) practical . . cooperative
(E) knowledgeable . . casual

Which pair of words above are opposites? The correct answer is choice A.

QUICK QUIZ #4

In each of the following sentences, try to decide whether the blanks should be positive or negative, or whether it is impossible to tell.

1. The new law will be very unpopular with the citizens of New Mexico because it ------- many ------- beliefs.

2. Despite the ------- of the men and women in the rescue team, their effort was -------.

3. The team had looked forward to the semifinal match with great -------, but the event proved to be -------.

4. Unlike their ------- ancestors, the whales of today are -------.

5. For all their apparent -------, the rich are just as ------- as the poor when it comes to an earthquake.

Answers and Explanations: Quick Quiz #4

1. – then +. The two words were "debunks" and "popular."

2. + then –. The two words were "courage" and "useless."

3. + then –. The two words were "enthusiasm" and "a debacle."

4. + then – or – then +. While you can't tell exactly what the values of the blanks are, you know they must be opposites. The two words were "solitary" and "gregarious."

5. + then –. The two words were "advantages" and "vulnerable."

GUESSING AND PACING

Even if you don't know some of the vocabulary words in a sentence completion, it is difficult to imagine a case in which you won't be able to eliminate at least one answer choice using the techniques we've just shown you. And if you eliminate one answer choice or more, then you *must* guess on the problem.

How long should you spend on each group of sentence completions? About four to six minutes, if you plan to finish the Critical Reading section. This works out to 40–45 seconds per problem. Of course, in the real world, you won't spend exactly the same amount of time on each question; some will take 10 seconds, others will take much longer. Use the practice sections that follow to work on your pacing.

SENTENCE COMPLETION CHECKLIST

1. As you read the sentences, cover up the answer choices and look for
    *   The clue (meaning from the context of the sentence)
    *   Trigger words (------- and -------: two words are usually similar; ------- but ------- : two words are usually opposed)
    *   Degree of difficulty clues (easy questions have easy answers; hard questions have hard answers)
2. When there are two blanks, do them one at a time.
3. If you're having trouble with the meaning of the sentence or the individual words in the answer choices, think + or –.
4. Remember that it's often easier to eliminate wrong answer choices than to pick the right choice.

SENTENCE COMPLETIONS: PROBLEM SET 1

Directions: For each question in this section, select the best answer from among the choices given and fill in the corresponding circle on the answer sheet.

Each sentence below has one or two blanks, each blank indicating that something has been omitted. Beneath the sentence are five words or sets of words labeled A through E. Choose the word or set of words that, when inserted in the sentence, <u>best</u> fits the meaning of the sentence as a whole.

Example:

Medieval kingdoms did not become constitutional republics overnight; on the contrary, the change was ------- .

(A) unpopular (B) unexpected (C) advantageous
   (D) sufficient (E) gradual

Ⓐ Ⓑ Ⓒ Ⓓ ●

Recommended time: 4 to 5 minutes

1. The shark possesses ------- sense of smell; in experiments, a small quantity of blood released into the ocean has ------- sharks from as far away as three quarters of a mile.

   (A) a cautious . . maimed
   (B) a keen . . attracted
   (C) a deficient . . enticed
   (D) a negligent . . repelled
   (E) a foul . . frightened

2. When the computer chip first became available, many companies were quick to ------- it, hoping to ------- this technological innovation.

   (A) reject . . benefit from
   (B) deflate . . succeed with
   (C) deny . . participate in
   (D) embrace . . profit from
   (E) accept . . escape from

3. The witness accused the young man of breaking the window, but later ------- the accusation.

   (A) recanted
   (B) recounted
   (C) predicted
   (D) arranged
   (E) supported

4. In his extraordinary ------- of the daily life of the early colonists, the historian captured the ------- hardships of the first winter.

   (A) revelation . . tranquil
   (B) evocation . . bleak
   (C) premonition . . dreary
   (D) exacerbation . . tacit
   (E) celebration . . blithe

5. Character traits that are quickly learned in social settings can often be altered just as quickly; by contrast, ------- characteristics are more difficult to -------.

   (A) credible . . respect
   (B) trivial . . protect
   (C) abrupt . . supply
   (D) tasteless . . believe
   (E) innate . . modify

6. Although the number of opening moves in the game of chess is not -------, there are more than enough to confuse the beginner.

   (A) circumscribed
   (B) measurable
   (C) estimable
   (D) familiar
   (E) infinite

7. The Big Bang theory is regarded as the most likely explanation for the beginning of the universe, but a few scientists, who regard the theory as -------, continue to search for an -------.

   (A) practical . . estimate
   (B) proven . . objective
   (C) implausible . . alternative
   (D) controversial . . agenda
   (E) comprehensive . . answer

8. The composer saw his latest composition not as ------- the music he had traditionally composed but rather as a ------- progression.

   (A) a continuation of . . lurid
   (B) an alternative to . . contradictory
   (C) an affront to . . despotic
   (D) a departure from . . logical
   (E) an interpretation of . . reasonable

1 ⊂A⊃ ⊂B⊃ ⊂C⊃ ⊂D⊃ ⊂E⊃
2 ⊂A⊃ ⊂B⊃ ⊂C⊃ ⊂D⊃ ⊂E⊃
3 ⊂A⊃ ⊂B⊃ ⊂C⊃ ⊂D⊃ ⊂E⊃
4 ⊂A⊃ ⊂B⊃ ⊂C⊃ ⊂D⊃ ⊂E⊃
5 ⊂A⊃ ⊂B⊃ ⊂C⊃ ⊂D⊃ ⊂E⊃
6 ⊂A⊃ ⊂B⊃ ⊂C⊃ ⊂D⊃ ⊂E⊃
7 ⊂A⊃ ⊂B⊃ ⊂C⊃ ⊂D⊃ ⊂E⊃
8 ⊂A⊃ ⊂B⊃ ⊂C⊃ ⊂D⊃ ⊂E⊃

WORDS YOU DIDN'T KNOW FROM PROBLEM SET 1

Before you check your answers below, take a minute to write down the words you didn't know from the previous questions. Look them up and review them tomorrow.

Word   Definition

_____   _____

_____   _____

_____   _____

_____   _____

_____   _____

Answers and Explanations: Problem Set 1

There are 8 sentence completions in this section, so you know that the first two or three will be relatively easy, the second three or four will be medium, and the last two or three will be relatively difficult. Did you remember not to skip any questions?

1. **B**   Attack the first blank first. If the shark has no sense of smell to speak of, then it would be neither attracted to nor repelled by the blood in the water; the shark simply wouldn't know the blood was there. Thus, you want a word that indicates the shark has a "good" sense of smell. Looking at the answer choices, you can eliminate choices C, "a deficient," and D, "a negligent." Can anyone have a "cautious" sense of smell? Not really. And just to check, even if the shark did have a cautious sense of smell, how would the smell of blood "maim" the shark? Eliminate choice A. A "foul" smell is an expression you have probably heard, but a foul sense of smell? Not too likely. To check, would a shark be frightened by the smell of blood? Not the sharks we knew and loved in *Jaws I* and *II*. Eliminate choice E. If the shark's sense of smell were "keen," then it would be attracted to the blood. The correct answer is choice B.

2. **D**   This is one of the infrequent sentence completions in which the sentence itself does not completely clue you in as to which words will best answer the question. For example, the sentence could use two positive words to read,

   ...many

   companies were quick to utilize it, hoping to succeed with this technological innovation. Or it could use two negative words to read,

   ...many

   companies were quick to dismiss it, hoping to ignore this technological innovation.

   Either of these would be fine. So what you have to do here is look at the answer choices for either two positive words or two negative words. Choice A is – then + , choice B is – then + , choice C is – then + , choice D is + then + , and choice E is + then –. The correct answer is choice D.

3. **A**   The trigger word ("but") signifies that the witness does something in the second half of the sentence that is somewhat contradictory to what he or she does in the first half of the sentence—and the only thing the witness does in the first half is to accuse the young man. What would be contradictory to making an accusation? The correct answer is choice A.

4. **B**   In this question, the second blank is probably easier to start with. "Hardships" is a negative sort of word, so you can expect that the adjective used to describe it will be negative as well. This allows you to eliminate choices A, "tranquil," D, "tacit" (meaning "implied, or not stated outright"), and E, "blithe" (meaning "joyous").

   Choices B and C remain, so look now at the first blank.

Choice C, "premonition" (meaning "a feeling that something is about to happen"), is unlikely. How could a historian have a premonition about something that happened 200 years ago? The correct answer is choice B. An "evocation" means "a bringing forth."

5. **E** The trigger words ("by contrast") signify that the first blank describes character traits that contradict the "quickly learned" character traits described at the beginning of the sentence. Which of the first words in the answer choices is a rough opposite of "quickly learned"? Choice E, "innate" (meaning "existing in a person since birth"), is the only one.

Suppose for a minute that you aren't sure of the meaning of "innate." You would now have to tackle the second blank. The first half of the sentence talks about traits that "can be altered...quickly." The second half, by contrast, talks about traits "that are harder to -------." What word do you think might fit in this blank? If you said "change" or "altered," you are right on the money. The correct answer is choice E.

6. **E** Here's a summary of this sentence using the trigger word:

Although -------, there's more than enough.

If we were talking about money, we might say, "Although we don't have all the money in the world, there's more than enough for us." If we were talking about a Thanksgiving turkey, we might say, "It isn't the biggest turkey in the world, but it's more than enough for us."

If we are talking about the number of opening chess moves, we would say, "The number of moves isn't infinite, but it's more than enough to confuse us."

7. **C** The trigger word ("but") signifies that the "few scientists" don't completely agree with the Big Bang theory. Tackle the first blank. Which of the answer choices implies doubt about the theory? Both choices C and D imply doubt. Thus, eliminate choices A, B, and E. If you don't buy one theory, do you search for an alternative or an agenda? The correct answer is choice C.

8. **D** The trigger word here is "not as [one thing] but rather as [something else]." Thus, the second half of the sentence is likely to contradict the first half.

If you check the answer choices for the different possible first words, you will notice that they are all nouns: "a continuation," "an alternative." The construction "not as [one thing] but rather as [something else]" must always compare two nouns. The possible second words are all adjectives describing the noun "progression."

This means the first blank must be a noun that contradicts the noun "progression." Rule out choice A, "a continuation," because it is almost a synonym. Choices C and E have nothing to do with contradicting a progression, so eliminate them as well. Choices B and D contradict the notion of a progression, so hold onto them. Now look at the second blank in the two remaining choices. The second blank is an adjective describing "progression." Which makes more sense? A "logical" progression or a "contradictory" progression? The best answer is choice D.

SENTENCE COMPLETIONS: PROBLEM SET 2

Directions: For each question in this section, select the best answer from among the choices given and fill in the corresponding circle on the answer sheet.

Each sentence below has one or two blanks, each blank indicating that something has been omitted. Beneath the sentence are five words or sets of words labeled A through E. Choose the word or set of words that, when inserted in the sentence, <u>best</u> fits the meaning of the sentence as a whole.

Example:

Medieval kingdoms did not become constitutional republics overnight; on the contrary, the change was ------- .

(A) unpopular   (B) unexpected   (C) advantageous
    (D) sufficient   (E) gradual

Recommended time: 4 to 5 minutes

1. Though he claimed that the computer he had just purchased contained the latest features, in fact it was already -------.

 (A) expensive
 (B) obsolete
 (C) technical
 (D) unreliable
 (E) impressive

2. For most film audiences, the ------- of a scary event is more ------- than the event itself.

 (A) anticipation . . frightening
 (B) expectation . . skeptical
 (C) experience . . mundane
 (D) application . . interesting
 (E) unfolding . . formal

3. Although Laura's uncle was ------- by nature, he was always ------- for his luncheon dates with his niece.

 (A) predictable . . on time
 (B) tardy . . punctual
 (C) generous . . late
 (D) unstable . . tardy
 (E) hostile . . unprepared

4. In their efforts to ------- the existence of a new strain of bacteria, scientists may be ------- by the lack of a suitable microscope.

 (A) establish . . hampered
 (B) eradicate . . aided
 (C) disprove . . defined
 (D) justify . . hindered
 (E) substantiate . . unmoved

5. The doctor not only had ------- for the new treatment, but he also found it -------.

 (A) a contempt . . necessary
 (B) an esteem . . contagious
 (C) a fondness . . irredeemable
 (D) a disgust . . repugnant
 (E) a weakness . . irrational

1	⊂A⊃	⊂B⊃	⊂C⊃	⊂D⊃	⊂E⊃
2	⊂A⊃	⊂B⊃	⊂C⊃	⊂D⊃	⊂E⊃
3	⊂A⊃	⊂B⊃	⊂C⊃	⊂D⊃	⊂E⊃
4	⊂A⊃	⊂B⊃	⊂C⊃	⊂D⊃	⊂E⊃
5	⊂A⊃	⊂B⊃	⊂C⊃	⊂D⊃	⊂E⊃

WORDS YOU DIDN'T KNOW FROM PROBLEM SET 2

Before you check your answers below, take a minute to write down the words you didn't know from the previous questions. Look them up and review them tomorrow.

Word	Definition
_____	_____
_____	_____
_____	_____
_____	_____
_____	_____

Answers and Explanations: Problem Set 2

There are 5 sentence completions in this section, so you know that the first one or two will be relatively easy, the middle one will be medium, and the last one or two will be relatively difficult. Did you remember not to skip any questions?

1. **B** While most of the adjectives in the answer choices could describe a computer, the structure of the sentence provides a clue. The clue in this sentence is the phrase "the latest features." However, the trigger word that begins the sentence ("though") tells you that the second half of the sentence is in opposition to the first. What would be the opposite of something that has all the latest features? That's right: obsolete.

2. **A** The construction "...of a scary event is more ------- than the event itself," makes it likely that the second blank will just be another word for "scary."

3. **B** The trigger word ("although") signifies that the second word is going to be in opposition to the first word. In choices A and D, the two pairs of words are not in opposition to each other—rather the reverse. In choices C and E the two pairs of words are unrelated to each other. Only choice B provides opposites: a "tardy" person is unlikely to be "punctual."

4. **A** The best clues in this sentence are the three words "the lack of." It seems like "the lack of" a suitable microscope would be a problem for a scientist. Thus, the second blank needs to be filled by a word like "hampered" or "hindered." To fill in the first blank, consider what a bunch of scientists would want to do about the existence of a new strain of bacteria. Well, they might want to eradicate (or destroy) the bacteria, but they wouldn't want to eradicate the existence of the bacteria. Also, scientists wouldn't be "aided" by the lack of a microscope. They might want to do things like "disprove" or "substantiate" but they wouldn't be "defined" or "unmoved" by the lack of a microscope.

5. **D** Unlike a simple trigger word, the construction "not only...but also..." implies two thoughts that are quite similar. Thus you are looking for either two positive words or two negative words.

    This is a difficult question (number 5 out of 5) so be on the lookout for Joe Bloggs answers. Choice B, containing the word "contagious," might be very tempting to Joe because the stem sentence is about a doctor. Eliminate it simply because Joe wants to pick it. Each of the other answer choices mixes a negative word with a positive word except for choice D.

SENTENCE COMPLETION: PROBLEM SET 3

Directions: For each question in this section, select the best answer from among the choices given and fill in the corresponding circle on the answer sheet.

Each sentence below has one or two blanks, each blank indicating that something has been omitted. Beneath the sentence are five words or sets of words labeled A through E. Choose the word or set of words that, when inserted in the sentence, <u>best</u> fits the meaning of the sentence as a whole.

Example:

Medieval kingdoms did not become constitutional republics overnight; on the contrary, the change was ------- .

(A) unpopular   (B) unexpected   (C) advantageous
   (D) sufficient   (E) gradual

Ⓐ Ⓑ Ⓒ Ⓓ ●

Recommended time: 4 to 5 minutes

1. The city planner argued that the proposed convention center would create new traffic patterns, some of them benign, but others potentially ------- .

   (A) unexpected
   (B) productive
   (C) older
   (D) harmful
   (E) conventional

2. It is unclear whether the new treatment will be approved for general use because its ------- has not yet been ------- .

   (A) usefulness . . denied
   (B) diversity . . proven
   (C) effectiveness . . established
   (D) performance . . preserved
   (E) integrity . . lampooned

3. Henrietta behaves in such ------- manner that no one expects her to accomplish anything.

   (A) an intelligent
   (B) a zealous
   (C) a slothful
   (D) an imperious
   (E) an efficient

4. The young children, who willingly stood in line for hours to get the basketball star's autograph, referred to him only in the most ------- terms.

   (A) cynical
   (B) detrimental
   (C) neutral
   (D) objective
   (E) reverential

5. When choosing works of art, museum curators should base their selections not on the artists' current ------- but rather on the artists' ------- qualities, for the public can be very fickle.

   (A) tableaus . . trivial
   (B) standing . . capricious
   (C) renown . . enduring
   (D) aesthetics . . impudent
   (E) philanthropy . . innocuous

6. In her later paintings, the artist exchanged her wild brush strokes and chaotic layerings of paint for ------- attention to detail that verged on fussiness.

   (A) a bohemian
   (B) a fastidious
   (C) an unconventional
   (D) an indelible
   (E) an opaque

1 ⊂A⊃ ⊂B⊃ ⊂C⊃ ⊂D⊃ ⊂E⊃
2 ⊂A⊃ ⊂B⊃ ⊂C⊃ ⊂D⊃ ⊂E⊃
3 ⊂A⊃ ⊂B⊃ ⊂C⊃ ⊂D⊃ ⊂E⊃
4 ⊂A⊃ ⊂B⊃ ⊂C⊃ ⊂D⊃ ⊂E⊃
5 ⊂A⊃ ⊂B⊃ ⊂C⊃ ⊂D⊃ ⊂E⊃
6 ⊂A⊃ ⊂B⊃ ⊂C⊃ ⊂D⊃ ⊂E⊃

WORDS YOU DIDN'T KNOW FROM PROBLEM SET 3

Before you check your answers below, take a minute to write down the words you didn't know from the previous questions. Look them up and review them tomorrow.

Word   **Definition**

_____   _____

_____   _____

_____   _____

_____   _____

_____   _____

Answers and Explanations: Problem Set 3

There are six sentence completions in this section, so you know that the first two will be relatively easy, the second two will be medium, and the last two will be relatively difficult. Did you remember not to skip any questions?

1. **D** Again, the trigger word ("but") signifies that you are looking for a word that is in opposition to something that comes before—but which something? If you picked choice C, you thought the missing word should oppose the "new" traffic patterns. However, in this sentence, the clue is the word "benign" and the "but" is contrasting two types of traffic patterns: "some of them benign... but others -------." Thus, you need a word that means the opposite of "benign."

2. **C** In order for the treatment to be approved, it will have to be shown to be effective. Therefore, the first blank has to be a positive word such as "effectiveness," and the second word should also be a positive word, such as "proven." In choice A, "usefulness" is positive, but "denied" is negative. In choice B, "diversity" is positive but it doesn't seem like a word that describes a positive attribute for a treatment. Choice C gives you two positive words. In choice D, "performance" might be okay, but would "preserving" a treatment help to get it approved? Choice E also gives you a positive first word, but the second word, "lampooned," is negative.

3. **C** Because no one expects Henrietta to accomplish anything, you have to assume that she is putting out some kind of negative attitude. Which answer choices are negative? Both choices C and D are possibilities. If she "imperious," Henrietta would arrogantly order people around, and she might actually get a lot done, so eliminate choice D. "Slothful" means lazy and sluggish.

4. **E** If the children willingly stood in line for hours to get the star's autograph, that implies that they think well of him. Thus, look for a positive word to fill in the blank. "Objective" might be considered a positive word, but it doesn't have the connotation of respect that the children seemed to be showing. The best answer is choice E.

5. **C** In this tough question, the trigger word ("but") is helpful, but only up to a point, because the vocabulary is difficult. The second blank is probably the best place to start. What kinds of qualities do you think ETS would want museum curators to look for in an artist? If you said "good" qualities, you were exactly right. Looking at the second words in the answer choices, can you eliminate any because they were not good? Yes, if you know what they mean. Choice A, "trivial," choice B, "capricious" (meaning "impulsive, whimsical") and choice D, "impudent" (meaning "disrespectful or rude"), can all be crossed off. Choice C, "enduring," is good, so hold onto that. Choice E, "innocuous" (meaning "causing or intending little harm"), is mildly good, so do not eliminate it either.

Now look at the first words in the two remaining choices. The word "renown" means "fame." The word "philanthropy" means "the practice of giving money or support to worthy causes." A philanthropic artist might be of help to a museum, but this sentence suggests the curator ignores philanthropy in favor of an artist who causes little harm. That doesn't sound right. The correct answer is choice C.

6.   **B**   The clues here are that the artist "exchanged" wild and chaotic stuff for something else, presumably quite different. What would be an adjective very different from "wild" and "chaotic" that would describe "...attention to detail that verged on fussiness"? If you are thinking words like "conservative" or "careful" you are right on track.

Look at the answer choices. "Bohemian" (meaning "setting social conventions aside") is clearly wrong, as is "unconventional." "Fastidious" (meaning "careful with details") seems pretty good. "Indelible" (meaning "incapable of being erased") and "opaque" (meaning "not transparent") are both artsy words and so might seem tempting in this sentence about an artist, but neither means "careful." The correct answer is choice B.

SENTENCE COMPLETION: PROBLEM SET 4

Directions: For each question in this section, select the best answer from among the choices given and fill in the corresponding circle on the answer sheet.

Each sentence below has one or two blanks, each blank indicating that something has been omitted. Beneath the sentence are five words or sets of words labeled A through E. Choose the word or set of words that, when inserted in the sentence, best fits the meaning of the sentence as a whole.

Example:

Medieval kingdoms did not become constitutional republics overnight; on the contrary, the change was ------- .

(A) unpopular　(B) unexpected　(C) advantageous
　(D) sufficient　　(E) gradual

Ⓐ Ⓑ Ⓒ Ⓓ ●

Recommended time: 4 to 5 minutes

1. The orator was so ------- that even those who were not interested in the subject matter found themselves staying awake.

   (A) tactful
   (B) listless
   (C) pious
   (D) intriguing
   (E) sullen

2. To make sure their ------- would be heard, the coal workers went on strike to protest the ------- lack of safety precautions in the mines.

   (A) voices . . generous
   (B) demands . . deplorable
   (C) complaints . . uneventful
   (D) neighbors . . dangerous
   (E) case . . immaculate

3. In his review, Greenburg argues that the ------- nature of this artist's paintings ------- the artist's conviction that the twentieth century has spun wildly out of control.

   (A) chaotic . . reflects
   (B) controlled . . demonstrates
   (C) disordered . . belies
   (D) symmetrical . . interprets
   (E) dangerous . . saps

4. A recent barrage of media reports on the health benefits of physical activity has fostered a national ------- exercise, but new studies show surprisingly little ------- in the life expectancy of people who exercise.

   (A) preoccupation with . . improvement
   (B) revulsion toward . . increase
   (C) obsession with . . decline
   (D) conception of . . speculation
   (E) solution to . . reduction

5. Previous to the discovery of one intact ancient burial site in Central America, it had been thought that all of the Mayan tombs had been ------- by thieves.

   (A) eradicated
   (B) exacerbated
   (C) prevaricated
   (D) subordinated
   (E) desecrated

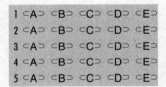

WORDS YOU DIDN'T KNOW FROM PROBLEM SET 4

Before you check your answers below, take a minute to write down the words you didn't know from the previous questions. Look them up and review them tomorrow.

Word

_____

_____

_____

_____

_____

Definition

_____

_____

_____

_____

_____

Answers and Explanations: Problem Set 4

There are 5 sentence completions in this section, so you know that the first one or two will be relatively easy, the middle one will be medium, and the last one or two will be relatively difficult. Did you remember not to skip any questions?

1. **D** What kind of speaker would make people stay awake even when they were not interested in what he was talking about? An *intriguing* speaker.

2. **B** Most people might choose to tackle the first blank first, and they would probably guess that the first word would be something like "demands." Unfortunately, a quick look at the answer choices shows you that four of the five alternatives sound possible. Oh well. Try the second blank. Do you think the lack of safety precautions in a coal mine would be a good thing or a bad thing? Obviously, the adjective describing this lack is going to be a negative word. So eliminate everything but choices B and D. Looking now at the first word in the two choices that remain, it is easy to see that "neighbors" makes no real sense.

3. **A** It seems likely that the artist's conviction (that things are out of control) might have something to do with the art he or she produces. Choice A works on this level. Choice B does not, for a "controlled" painting style doesn't demonstrate a world gone out of control. Choice C doesn't either, for a "disordered" style would not "belie" (meaning "expose as false") a world gone out of control. In choice D, a "symmetrical" style would not "interpret" a world gone out of control. Why would a painter's style of painting "sap" (meaning "to drain away") his or her convictions? The best answer is choice A.

4. **A** The trigger word "but" signifies that the second part of the sentence is likely to somehow contradict the supposed health benefits of exercise. Attack the second blank first: ". . . new studies show surprisingly little ------- in the life expectancy of people who exercise." Considering that the result is surprising, what do you think the word should be? If you said "rise" or "increase" you were right on target.

   Look at the answer choices. Choices C and E can be ruled out right away, because they are headed in the opposite direction. Choice D doesn't make a lot of sense.

   Now look at the first words in the two remaining answer choices. Choice A, "preoccupation with," seems right. Choice B, "revulsion toward," might be all right if the structural clue "but" had not been there. The correct answer is choice A.

5. **E** It's pretty clear from the context that you are looking for a word like "destroyed" here. Unfortunately, because this was the fifth question out of five, the vocabulary is very tough. Even the positive/negative technique is not helpful here, because *all* the words are negative. The only real way to get this is to know the meaning of the correct word. "Desecrate" means "to abuse something sacred." "Exacerbate" means "to make something worse." "Prevaricate" means "to lie." "Subordinate" means "to place in a lower order." "Eradicate" means "to root out," which might have seemed tempting, but didn't give the sense of destruction of something sacred. The best answer is choice E.

SENTENCE COMPLETION: PROBLEM SET 5

Directions: For each question in this section, select the best answer from among the choices given and fill in the corresponding circle on the answer sheet.

Each sentence below has one or two blanks, each blank indicating that something has been omitted. Beneath the sentence are five words or sets of words labeled A through E. Choose the word or set of words that, when inserted in the sentence, best fits the meaning of the sentence as a whole.

Example:

Medieval kingdoms did not become constitutional republics overnight; on the contrary, the change was ------- .

(A) unpopular (B) unexpected (C) advantageous
   (D) sufficient (E) gradual

Ⓐ Ⓑ Ⓒ Ⓓ ●

Recommended time: 4 to 5 minutes

---

1. The association agreed to ------- one of its members when she was discovered to have ------- an infraction of the association rules.

   (A) discipline . . prevented
   (B) denounce . . impeded
   (C) censure . . committed
   (D) honor . . supported
   (E) promote . . aided

2. While old books are often considered ------- by modern readers, librarians see them as historic documents that allow us to look back through time.

   (A) reclusive
   (B) fascinating
   (C) detrimental
   (D) relevant
   (E) obsolete

3. The robin, a bird common to the Northeast, is neither rare nor reclusive, but is as ------- and ------- a bird as you can find.

   (A) wily . . tolerant
   (B) amicable . . wary
   (C) commonplace . . amiable
   (D) vulnerable . . capable
   (E) powerful . . fragile

4. The professor's lecturing style was certainly -------, but he told his students that in teaching such a complicated subject, clarity was more important than levity.

   (A) scintillating
   (B) unbiased
   (C) monotonous
   (D) arrogant
   (E) stimulating

5. During a ten-year period, Napoleon conquered most of the Baltic States and ------- Spain as well.

   (A) vanquished
   (B) forfeited
   (C) reiterated
   (D) transcended
   (E) refuted

6. Unlike the unequivocal accounts provided by eyewitnesses, the evidence provided by the flight recorder was more -------, leading to the development of several different theories to explain the crash.

   (A) indisputable
   (B) ambiguous
   (C) lucid
   (D) infallible
   (E) theoretical

7. Engineers attribute the building's ------- during the earthquake, which destroyed more rigid structures, to the surprising ------- of its steel girders.

   (A) obliteration . . strength
   (B) damage . . weakness
   (C) survival . . inadequacy
   (D) endurance . . suppleness
   (E) devastation . . inflexibility

8. By nature he was -------, generally limiting his comments to ------- remarks.

   (A) reticent . . terse
   (B) stoic . . superfluous
   (C) trite . . concise
   (D) verbose . . succinct
   (E) arrogant . . self-effacing

1 ⊂A⊃ ⊂B⊃ ⊂C⊃ ⊂D⊃ ⊂E⊃
2 ⊂A⊃ ⊂B⊃ ⊂C⊃ ⊂D⊃ ⊂E⊃
3 ⊂A⊃ ⊂B⊃ ⊂C⊃ ⊂D⊃ ⊂E⊃
4 ⊂A⊃ ⊂B⊃ ⊂C⊃ ⊂D⊃ ⊂E⊃
5 ⊂A⊃ ⊂B⊃ ⊂C⊃ ⊂D⊃ ⊂E⊃
6 ⊂A⊃ ⊂B⊃ ⊂C⊃ ⊂D⊃ ⊂E⊃
7 ⊂A⊃ ⊂B⊃ ⊂C⊃ ⊂D⊃ ⊂E⊃
8 ⊂A⊃ ⊂B⊃ ⊂C⊃ ⊂D⊃ ⊂E⊃

WORDS YOU DIDN'T KNOW FROM PROBLEM SET 5

Before you check your answers below, take a minute to write down the words you didn't know from the previous questions. Look them up and review them tomorrow.

Word

_____

_____

_____

_____

_____

Definition

_____

_____

_____

_____

_____

Answers and Explanations: Problem Set 5

There are 8 sentence completions in this section, so you know that the first two or three will be relatively easy, the second three or four will be medium, and the last two or three will be relatively difficult. Did you remember not to skip any questions?

1. **C** If the association member took part in the infraction, then it seems almost certain that the association will punish her. While it was just possible that the sentence was going to go the other way— i.e., they were going to reward her for discovering the infraction—the first possibility was more likely. Look through the answer choices and pick the one that works. The answer is choice C.

2. **E** The trigger word "while" opposes librarians' views of old books and those of modern readers. How do you think librarians are likely to feel about old books? If you said "positive," you are right on track. That means the modern readers will feel negative. This gets us down to choices A, C, or E. Choice E is the best answer.

3. **C** When ETS sets up pairs of words in opposition (trigger word: "but") as it does here, it helps to deal with the pairs in the correct order: The robin is not "rare" but -------; not "reclusive" but -------. Thus, for the first blank you want a word that means "not rare." For the second blank you want a word that means "not reclusive." The correct answer is choice C.

4. **C** The second half of the sentence following the trigger word "but" tells you that the professor is clearer than he is funny. So his style is "not funny." Which of the answer choices is closest to "not funny"? That's right, the answer is choice C.

5. **A** The trigger word "and" signifies that the two verbs of the sentence are going to be similar. Napoleon conquered the Baltic states and conquered Spain as well. So you need a word like "conquered." The correct answer is choice A.

6. **B** The trigger word "unlike" signifies that the recorder's evidence is the opposite of "unequivocal." If you know what "unequivocal" means, this is a great clue. But if you don't, there is another clue later in the sentence: The evidence of the flight recorder led to several different theories. What kind of evidence would lead to several different theories? "Indisputable" evidence? Not likely. "Ambiguous" evidence? That sounds correct! "Lucid" (meaning "clear") evidence? No. "Infallible" (meaning "unable to be proven wrong") evidence? No. "Theoretical" evidence? Maybe, but "ambiguous" is better. The correct answer is choice B. "Unequivocal" means "certain, not open to interpretation."

7. **D** The clue here is the phrase ". . .which destroyed more rigid structures." Obviously, unlike other buildings that were more rigid, this building didn't fall down. Attack the first blank first. What word would you pick to describe this building's performance during the earthquake? If you were thinking of words like "survival" or "strength," then you were right on track.

Eliminate any answers that suggest the building was destroyed: choices A, B, and E. You are left with choices C and D. Now look at the second blank. Do you think the building's survival hinged on the "inadequacy" of its girders or the "suppleness" (meaning "the ability to bend easily") of its girders? "Inadequacy" is certainly wrong, but at first, you might think "suppleness" sounded wrong too. The two contextual clues here were "...more rigid structures," and ". . .the surprising _____." Steel girders are not usually thought of as being "supple," which is why the word "surprising" is appropriate.

8.   A   What makes this a difficult question is its lack of clues. Really, there is only one small clue: the word "limiting." And one small trigger word: The second half of the sentence is not going to contradict the first half—it is going to continue in the same direction. With these two clues noted, take a look at the answer choices.

If he were "reticent" (meaning "untalkative, shy"), would this person limit himself to "terse" (meaning "brief, free of extra words") remarks? Sure. Just check the other answer choices. If he were "stoic" (meaning "having great emotional control"), would he limit himself to "superfluous" (meaning "unnecessary") remarks? No. If he were "trite" (meaning "overused, lacking freshness"), would he limit himself to "concise" remarks? No. If he were "verbose" (meaning "talkative"), would he limit himself to "succinct" (meaning "concise") remarks? No. If he were "arrogant" (meaning "overconfident"), would he limit himself to "self-effacing" (meaning "putting yourself last") remarks? No way! The answer is choice A.

SENTENCE COMPLETION: PROBLEM SET 6

Directions: For each question in this section, select the best answer from among the choices given and fill in the corresponding circle on the answer sheet.

Each sentence below has one or two blanks, each blank indicating that something has been omitted. Beneath the sentence are five words or sets of words labeled A through E. Choose the word or set of words that, when inserted in the sentence, <u>best</u> fits the meaning of the sentence as a whole.

Example:

Medieval kingdoms did not become constitutional republics overnight; on the contrary, the change was -------.

(A) unpopular   (B) unexpected   (C) advantageous
   (D) sufficient   (E) gradual

Ⓐ Ⓑ Ⓒ Ⓓ ●

Recommended time: 4 to 5 minutes

---

1. It was obvious from the concerned look on David's face that his spendthrift habits had placed him in a ------- financial situation.

   (A) solvent
   (B) solid
   (C) global
   (D) precarious
   (E) benign

2. Some crops do not need to be replanted every spring; a grape arbor, while initially requiring intensive -------, can produce ------- harvests for many years afterward without much work.

   (A) suffering . . barren
   (B) negotiation . . rich
   (C) labor . . cooperative
   (D) inertia . . forgotten
   (E) toil . . abundant

3. Henry Kissinger argued that a successful diplomat must always remain something of a -------, which is why he counseled President Nixon, known for his tough stance on communism, to normalize relations with communist China.

   (A) novice
   (B) pioneer
   (C) paradox
   (D) raconteur
   (E) sluggard

4. Although the playwright Ben Johnson was not highly regarded by most Elizabethans of his day, a few scholars of that time ------- his work and ------- many of his plays.

   (A) championed . . obliterated
   (B) disparaged . . legitimized
   (C) abetted . . destroyed
   (D) revered . . preserved
   (E) invoked . . undermined

5. Despite ------- training, the new paratroopers awaited their first jump from an airplane with -------.

   (A) paltry . . alarm
   (B) comprehensive . . assurance
   (C) extraneous . . indifference
   (D) methodical . . presumptuousness
   (E) extensive . . trepidation

6. Unfortunately, during the process of making a motion picture it sometimes happens that ------- revisions, poor casting decisions, and hasty compromises can be ------- the original intention of the authors.

   (A) well-planned . . essential to
   (B) ill-conceived . . detrimental to
   (C) uncompromising . . divergent from
   (D) meticulous . . injurious to
   (E) distorted . . fundamental to

1 ⊂A⊃ ⊂B⊃ ⊂C⊃ ⊂D⊃ ⊂E⊃
2 ⊂A⊃ ⊂B⊃ ⊂C⊃ ⊂D⊃ ⊂E⊃
3 ⊂A⊃ ⊂B⊃ ⊂C⊃ ⊂D⊃ ⊂E⊃
4 ⊂A⊃ ⊂B⊃ ⊂C⊃ ⊂D⊃ ⊂E⊃
5 ⊂A⊃ ⊂B⊃ ⊂C⊃ ⊂D⊃ ⊂E⊃
6 ⊂A⊃ ⊂B⊃ ⊂C⊃ ⊂D⊃ ⊂E⊃

WORDS YOU DIDN'T KNOW FROM PROBLEM SET 6

Before you check your answers below, take a minute to write down the words you didn't know from the previous questions. Look them up and review them tomorrow.

Word

_____

_____

_____

_____

_____

Definition

_____

_____

_____

_____

_____

Answers and Explanations: Problem Set 6

There are six sentence completions in this section, so you know that the first two will be relatively easy, the second two will be medium, and the last two will be relatively difficult. Did you remember not to skip any questions?

1. **D** The clues here are the "concerned" look on David's face and the word "spendthrift" (meaning "one who spends extravagantly"). Clearly his financial position is not too good. Choice A, "solvent," in this case means "able to pay all debts," so that's wrong. Choice E, "benign," means "harmless." The correct answer is choice D, "precarious" (meaning "unstable, insecure").

2. **E** The trigger word "while" combines with the clue ("without much work") to signify that although at first a grape arbor requires -------, later it's rather easy. If the word you are thinking of is "work" or "labor," you are on just the right track. Looking at the first words in the answer choices, there are two that seem possible: choices C and E. Now, look at the second blank. Do you think the harvests are going to be described with a positive adjective or a negative adjective? You got it! You are looking for a good adjective. "Abundant" fits the bill. "Cooperative" is neither good nor bad, and makes no real sense. The correct answer is choice E.

3. **C** Kissinger advises the President to do something that seems to contradict Nixon's normal behavior. Which of these words describes contradictory behavior? Choice C, "paradox" (meaning "something that seems to contradict itself"), is the best answer. A "raconteur" is a "skilled storyteller," and a sluggard is a "person lacking energy."

4. **D** The trigger word "although" signifies that, contrary to most Elizabethans, the scholars mentioned in the second half of the sentence did like Ben Johnson. In this sentence, either blank is fine to start with, and your choice will probably be determined by whether you knew more of the vocabulary words for the first blank or for the second.

   What if you don't know the meaning of a number of the possible words for either blank in the answer choices. Why not try the +/– technique? Here are the correct symbols for the missing words in the sentence and the answer choices:

   ...a few scholars of that time + his work and + many of his plays.

   (A) + . . –

   (B) – . . +

   (C) + . . –

   (D) + . . +

   (E) ? . . –

Choice D was the only one in which both words were positive. "Revered" means "regarded with awe," "disparaged" means "spoke disrespectfully about," "abetted" means "acted as an accomplice or aided," and "championed" means "defended or supported."

5. **E** This sentence could have gone one of two ways:

1) Despite [good] training, they awaited their jump with [fear], or 2) Despite [bad] training, they awaited their jump with [confidence].

Given the way most people feel about jumping out of an airplane, the first alternative seems more likely, and in fact, choice E gives you a clear version of that alternative. "Trepidation" means "fear." All of the other choices mix up their meanings. For example, choice A says, roughly speaking, "Despite [bad] training, they awaited their jump with [fear]," and choice B says, roughly speaking, "Despite [good] training, they awaited their jump with [confidence]."

6. **B** The first word of the sentence lets you know that the writer is not pleased with what is to follow. There is also a structural clue in the way the list of three things is presented in the middle of the sentence: ------- revisions, poor casting, and hasty compromises. What type of word do you think belongs in the blank? That's right: something negative. Only two of the answer choices begin with negative words: choices B and E.

Now, look at the second blank. How do you think all these compromises and bad casting are going to affect the "original intention" of the authors? That's right—badly. Do you want "detrimental to" or "fundamental to?" The best answer is choice B.

SENTENCE COMPLETION: PROBLEM SET 7

Directions: For each question in this section, select the best answer from among the choices given and fill in the corresponding circle on the answer sheet.

Each sentence below has one or two blanks, each blank indicating that something has been omitted. Beneath the sentence are five words or sets of words labeled A through E. Choose the word or set of words that, when inserted in the sentence, <u>best</u> fits the meaning of the sentence as a whole.

Example:

Medieval kingdoms did not become constitutional republics overnight; on the contrary, the change was ------- .

(A) unpopular   (B) unexpected   (C) advantageous
    (D) sufficient   (E) gradual

Ⓐ Ⓑ Ⓒ Ⓓ ●

Recommended time: 4 to 5 minutes

1. The sculptor avoided the sharp angles and geometric shapes of abstract art, instead creating ------- shapes that seemed to expand or contract as one looked at them.

    (A) static
    (B) infallible
    (C) fluid
    (D) methodical
    (E) residual

2. The initial ------- of many of the first-year law students ------- when they discover how many hours per week are necessary just to complete the course reading.

    (A) apprehensiveness . . subsides
    (B) torpor . . increases
    (C) courage . . rebounds
    (D) enthusiasm . . wanes
    (E) satisfaction . . continues

3. The graduate student's radical theories were ------- by the elder scientist because they did not ------- the elder scientist's own findings.

    (A) accepted . . confirm
    (B) discounted . . corroborate
    (C) confounded . . disprove
    (D) praised . . prove
    (E) tolerated . . support

4. Because the course was only an introduction to the fundamentals of biology, the students were surprised to be asked for such ------- information on the exam.

    (A) irrelevant
    (B) mundane
    (C) redundant
    (D) superficial
    (E) esoteric

5. Torn between a vacation in Florida and a vacation in Wyoming, Lisa ------- for several weeks.

    (A) vacillated
    (B) mitigated
    (C) terminated
    (D) speculated
    (E) repudiated

6. The lemur, a small, monkey-like animal native to Madagascar, is not, as was once mistakenly thought, a direct ------- of man; new discoveries reveal that the lemur and man once shared a common ancestor but then proceeded on ------- evolutionary paths.

    (A) relative . . converging
    (B) ancestor . . divergent
    (C) descendant . . synchronous
    (D) terrestrial . . parallel
    (E) subordinate . . similar

7. Although many believed that the problems of the community were -------, the members of the governing council refused to give in and came up with several ------- solutions.

    (A) indomitable . . ingenious
    (B) intractable . . inconsequential
    (C) exorbitant . . promising
    (D) irrelevant . . lofty
    (E) obscure . . meager

8. No detail is too small for Coach Williams when her little league team is in a playoff game, but some parents find her to be too ------- and wish that she would spend more time ------- qualities such as good sportsmanship in her young charges.

    (A) meticulous . . instilling
    (B) circumstantial . . finding
    (C) ambivalent . . impeding
    (D) conspicuous . . obstructing
    (E) ambidextrous . . thwarting

1 ⊂A⊃ ⊂B⊃ ⊂C⊃ ⊂D⊃ ⊂E⊃
2 ⊂A⊃ ⊂B⊃ ⊂C⊃ ⊂D⊃ ⊂E⊃
3 ⊂A⊃ ⊂B⊃ ⊂C⊃ ⊂D⊃ ⊂E⊃
4 ⊂A⊃ ⊂B⊃ ⊂C⊃ ⊂D⊃ ⊂E⊃
5 ⊂A⊃ ⊂B⊃ ⊂C⊃ ⊂D⊃ ⊂E⊃
6 ⊂A⊃ ⊂B⊃ ⊂C⊃ ⊂D⊃ ⊂E⊃
7 ⊂A⊃ ⊂B⊃ ⊂C⊃ ⊂D⊃ ⊂E⊃
8 ⊂A⊃ ⊂B⊃ ⊂C⊃ ⊂D⊃ ⊂E⊃

WORDS YOU DIDN'T KNOW FROM PROBLEM SET 7

Before you check your answers below, take a minute to write down the words you didn't know from the previous questions. Look them up and review them tomorrow.

Word   **Definition**

_____   _____
_____   _____
_____   _____
_____   _____
_____   _____

Answers and Explanations: Problem Set 7

There are 8 sentence completions in this section, so you know that the first two or three will be relatively easy, the second three or four will be medium, and the last two or three will be relatively difficult. Did you remember not to skip any questions?

1. **C** This question would be more difficult if the wrong answer choices matched the level of difficulty of the right one. "Fluid" (meaning "capable of changing") is on the Hit Parade, and it's an important word to commit to memory.

2. **D** How would you feel if you had just gotten into law school—and you had really wanted to go there? Probably pretty good. Now, how would you feel if you found out that once you were there you were going to have to put in 50 hours per week just to keep up with the reading? Probably pretty bad. That is all you need to know to answer this question.

   Initially they feel pretty [good], and then that good feeling [goes away]. Starting with the first blank, you can eliminate choices A, "apprehensiveness," and B, "torpor" (meaning "lack of energy").

   Now look at the second words in the answer choices that remain. The only one that means "goes away" is choice D, "wanes" (meaning "to decrease in size").

3. **B** The elder scientist is either going to accept or reject the student's radical theories—so which one is it going to be? The clue here is ". . . the scientist's own findings." The scientist is only human; if the student agrees with the scientist, the scientist will be more likely to accept the student's findings. If the student disagrees with the scientist, the scientist will be more likely to throw out the student's wild theories.

   Look at the answer choices. Choices A, D, and E make no sense because why should the scientist "accept," "praise," or "tolerate" theories that do not "confirm," "prove," or "support" his own? Choice B seems very likely because the scientist is "discounting" (meaning "to put a reduced value on, or to ignore") theories that don't corroborate his own. (By the way, if you got this one wrong, make a note to yourself to remember secondary meanings—"discounting" does not always have to take place in a store.) Choice C implies that the scientist disliked the ideas because they agreed with his own, which doesn't make sense. "Confound" means "to confuse or perplex."

4. **E** The trigger word "because" helps a little, but the key words here are "only" and "fundamentals." Here is a slightly simplified version of the sentence: "Because the course was really basic, the students freaked out at the [hard] questions on the test." You are looking for a word like "hard." The best answer is choice E, "esoteric" (meaning "known only by a select few").

5. **A** Basically, Lisa can't make up her mind. Which of these answer choices means that? Choice A, "vacillated," means "to go back and forth," and is the correct answer. To "mitigate" means "to make milder." To "repudiate" means "to disown, or refuse to acknowledge."

6. **B** Tackle the second blank first. The lemur and man once shared a common ancestor BUT (trigger word) they then did something else. The "but" tells you that the sentence is going off in a different direction, just as apparently did the lemur and man. Which of the second words in the answer choices would indicate a new direction? There's really only one: choice B, "divergent." Just to check, look at the first blank now. In choice A, "relative" was possible, but "converging" (meaning "coming together") is the opposite of what you need. In choice C, "descendant" is wrong, because the monkey didn't evolve from man. Choice D doesn't make sense either because "terrestrial" simply means "living on the earth." In choice E, "subordinate," meaning "placed in a lower order," might be okay, but the two paths are not similar. The best answer is choice B.

7. **A** The first blank describes the community's problems, and the second blank describes the solutions. If you had to guess, the first word is going to be negative, and the second word is going to be positive. Tackle the first blank first. You need a negative word to describe problems. "Indomitable" (meaning "unable to be overcome") fits the bill, as does "intractable" (which means "not easily managed"). The other words don't really describe problems that the community refuses to give in about.

    Now look at the second words in the answer choices that remain. "Ingenious" seems just right to describe solutions. "Inconsequential" (meaning "of little consequence, or importance") does not. The best answer is choice A.

8. **A** Look at the second blank. Parents think that qualities like good sportsmanship are important. Would they want the coach to "teach" these qualities in their children or "ignore" these qualities in their children? You want a word like "teach." Choices A and B provide words closest to "teach" for the second word. "Impeding," "obstructing," and "thwarting" are all negative words meaning "to prevent."

    Now look at the first blank. The clue here is "No detail is too small" for the coach. However, note the trigger word "but" that follows. The parents think she is too detail-oriented. Which answer choice gives you a word like "detail-oriented" for the first blank? The best answer is choice A. "Meticulous" means "attentive to details." "Circumstantial" means "consisting only of details." "Ambidextrous" means "able to use either the right hand or the left hand equally well."

Chapter 10
SAT Short Reading

Each short reading passage will consist of a brief paragraph—usually fewer than 100 words—followed by two questions. You might also see a pair of short passages followed by three or four questions. By using the approach we will show you in this chapter, you'll learn not only the best way to tackle this type of problem but also some effective strategies for eliminating wrong answers.

Let's take a look at a sample short reading passage:

Questions 1-2 are based on the following passage.

Line In 1782, philosopher J. Hector St. John de Crèvecoeur became the first to apply the word "melting" to a population of immigrants: "Here individuals of all nations are melted into a new race of men." Crèvecoeur idealized a nation built
5 from individuals who had transcended their origins and embraced a common American ethos: "From involuntary idleness, servile dependence, penury, and useless labour, he has passed to toils of a very different nature, rewarded by ample subsistence. This is an American." While debate
10 raged as to what exactly "melting" meant—diverse peoples coexisting peacefully while maintaining their differences or refashioning themselves to blend indistinguishably into a new, common substance—Crèvecoeur's term was here to stay: America, settled by immigrants, was to have a unified
15 populace.

Fascinating, right? Now let's figure out the best way to approach a short reading passage.

THE PRINCETON REVIEW METHOD

Step One   Read the questions first. Before you dive into the passage, take a moment to read the questions first and figure out what type of information ETS is going to ask you about. Each passage contains a huge number of facts—most of which are completely irrelevant. Don't read the passage without knowing what you're looking for.

Step Two   Read what you need. The answer to the question is contained somewhere in the passage. Read only enough of the passage to answer the question ETS asks you.

THE QUESTION TYPES

Information Retrieval Questions

Many of the questions on short reading passages will require you to find specific information contained within the paragraph. Use the line references or lead words that are found in the question to jump right to the appropriate part of the passage to find the answer.

Let's return to the sample passage and take a look at question number one:

1. According to the passage, "debate raged" (line 11) over whether immigrant groups

    (A) had the ability to put their differences aside and coexist peacefully.
    (B) understood what Crèvecoeur originally meant by the term "melting."
    (C) would ultimately reject America's open immigration policy.
    (D) needed to change their identity to match an American identity.
    (E) transcended their humble origins merely by moving to America.

ETS will not always provide a line reference. If this occurs, look for a lead word—a name, a date, or a term that will stand out as you skim about the passage.

For example:

1. According to the passage, ongoing debate over Crèvecoeur's term centered primarily on whether

If ETS had asked the above question, you would use "debate" as your lead word.

In either case, your plan is the same: Locate the appropriate line reference or lead word in the passage and read a few lines before and a few lines after it. Keep reading until you find the answer to the question.

Let's go back to the passage and re-read the last sentence. Were you able to find the answer? If you said that the debate over "melting" was whether different ethnic groups would preserve their unique cultural identities and respectfully accommodate each other or whether they would create a new, common American identity, you're on the right track. Now find this paraphrase in the answer choices. The best answer is choice D.

Inference Questions

The key to success on inference questions is to first understand what an inference is. An inference is a statement that must be true based on the information provided in the passage. In other words, you should never actually try to infer something in an inference question. Stick to the facts. Let's try one:

2. It can be most reasonably inferred from the passage that

   (A) debate continues to this day over whether the American ethos has changed.
   (B) people did not refer to immigrants melting into a new populace in the seventeenth century.
   (C) Crèvecoeur believed his aristocratic upbringing was a humble origin.
   (D) all Americans were able to find ample subsistence in 1782.
   (E) many immigrants moved to America because they felt useless in their country of origin.

Where should you look to find the answer to this question? While it appears that there is no line reference or lead word, there actually is. On inference questions, it's usually a good strategy to use lead words in the answer choices to help guide you to the right answers. Start with answer choice A and check the passage to see if debate *continues to this day* over the American ethos. Can you prove that answer to be true with information from the passage? If not, it cannot be the correct answer. Check the other choices. Which one is supported by the passage? The correct answer is choice B because the first sentence says that Crèvecoeur was "the first" to use the term "melting" in reference to immigrant groups. If you selected choices C, D, or E, you assumed something that wasn't stated in the passage.

Main Idea Questions

Main idea questions ask you to find the point of the entire paragraph. If possible, do a main idea question after doing any inference or information retrieval questions. On main idea questions, eliminate answers that are too broad or too specific. Here's another passage and question:

Question 3 is based on the following passage.

Line   Perhaps the scientists most excited about reigniting the
lunar program are not lunar specialists, but astronomers
studying a wide range of subjects. Such scientists would like
new missions to install a huge telescope with a diameter
5 of 30 meters on the far side of the moon. Two things that
a telescope needs for optimum operation are extreme cold
and very little vibration. Temperatures on the moon can be
as frigid as 200 C below zero in craters on the dark side.
Because there is no seismic activity, the moon is a steady
10 base. Permanent darkness means the telescope can be in
constant use. Proponents claim that under these conditions a
lunar-based telescope could accomplish as much in seventeen
days as the replacement for the Hubble telescope will in ten
years of operation.

3. The main idea of the above passage is most accurately
described by which of the following statements?

(A) Most astronomers are in favor of re-igniting the
lunar program.

(B) New lunar missions could discover important new
features of the moon.

(C) The new lunar telescope will replace the defunct
Hubble telescope.

(D) Recent discoveries have been made about weather
on the dark side of the moon.

(E) Some scientists believe the moon is an ideal
location for an interplanetary telescope.

A good way to tackle a main idea question is to read the first and last lines of the paragraph. From those two lines, you know that some scientists are excited about restarting the lunar program and that a lunar telescope would be very effective. Start eliminating answers right away. Choices B and D should go because they don't even mention a lunar telescope. If you're leaning towards answer choice E right now, you're on to something. You should be wary of choice A because it says "most" astronomers. Does the passage support that statement? Nope, get rid of it. Choice C makes it sound as if the telescope is already being built. But the passage doesn't state that the telescope is definitely going to be built. Thus, choice E is best.

QUICK QUIZ #1

Questions 1-2 are based on the following passage.

Line Some historians believe that the English Reformation
actually began when Edward VI succeeded Henry VIII.
By creating the Church of England in the 1530s, Henry
VIII not only annulled his marriage, but was also able to
5 improve his bankrupt kingdom's fortunes. By 1540, more
than 500 Catholic monasteries were closed and their wealth
was transferred to the Crown. By the time of Edward VI's
succession, the fundamental changes had been made, so the
new king began a campaign against iconography. Starting
10 in 1547, the order to remove religious icons from places of
worship was carried out. Zealous followers of the Protestant
monarch destroyed wall paintings, statues, and shrines,
effectively divesting the country of most of its decorative
religious art.

1. The passage most strongly implies that

   (A) by 1540, there were no monasteries left in
        England
   (B) Henry VIII was primarily interested in reforming
        the Church
   (C) Edward VI was not interested in the financial
        aspects of the Reformation
   (D) Henry VIII had secular reasons for creating the
        Church of England
   (E) Henry VIII and Edward VI shared the same views
        on marriage

2. The reference to "zealous followers" (lines 12-13) serves
    primarily to indicate that

   (A) some of Edward's subjects willingly obeyed the
        King's edict
   (B) Edward's followers were apathetic about this
        campaign
   (C) the English hated decorative art at that time
   (D) Protestants are passionate about their beliefs
   (E) the Church of England condoned iconography

Answers and Explanations: Quick Quiz #1

1. **D** The word "implies" indicates an inference question. Choice D is correct because at least one secular reason is stated in the passage. Choice A is not supported in the passage. Watch out for choices that make extreme statements. Choices B, C, and E are incorrect because they are not mentioned in the passage.

2. **A** The passage states that the "zealous followers...destroyed" the religious art following the order to remove the icons. Choice B is the opposite of what is stated. Choice C is wrong because it generalizes that all decorative art was hated. Choice D is also a generalization; it makes a statement about present day Protestants ("are") even though the passage is about the sixteenth century. Choice E is contradicted in the passage.

OTHER QUESTION TYPES

Now let's look at some other question types that may appear. These question types don't show up as frequently as do information retrieval, inference, and main idea questions, but it is important to know how to approach them.

Structure Questions

Structure questions ask you how a particular sentence functions in the paragraph. Read the sentence in question and a sentence or two before and after it. Ask yourself "What does this sentence do?"

Questions 1-2 are based on the following passage.

> *Line*   An infant's lack of sparkling dialogue may obscure the
>   fact that we are all born with an ability to communicate. A
>   capacity for language exists in our tiny, screaming bodies in
>   the delivery room, along with our eyes, ears, arms, legs, and
> 5   vital organs. Our language instincts must be stimulated—
>   we need to hear people talk in order to form words—but
>   we are born eager to speak. The newborn baby is patiently
>   waiting for answers to questions: "What will I call the objects
>   that surround me? How will I form positive and negative
> 10   sentences? How can I express feelings about objects and
>   people?" The child's brain instinctively searches for answers
>   to these questions and then, like a sponge, soaks them up.

1. The author asks a series of questions in order to show that newborn babies

    (A) are eager to communicate
    (B) can speak certain questions
    (C) are ignorant about language
    (D) are curious about their futures
    (E) are able to teach themselves to speak

Scan the passage for question marks; then read the third, fourth, and fifth sentences. What's the point of the questions in the fourth sentence? According to the third sentence, the baby is eager to speak and is waiting for answers to questions; in the fifth sentence, the author states that the baby searches for the answers to these questions. The fourth sentence seems to be examples of questions a baby might want to ask and have answered. Which answer choice states this? Choice A is best. If you fell for choice D, be careful. All the lines mention communication, but none of them mention the future. Remember: The right answer is always stated in the passage.

Vocabulary in Context

These questions test your vocabulary. Luckily, you have some context to help you figure out the word. Always go back to the passage and look for clues and triggers, just as you would do for a sentence completion. Beware of Joe Bloggs trap answers!

2. In line 6, the word "stimulated" most nearly means

   (A) created
   (B) touched
   (C) aroused
   (D) encouraged
   (E) quickened

Did you pick choice C? Sorry, Joe, it's a trap. While "aroused" is one meaning of "stimulated," it's not the *right* meaning in this context. Go back to the passage and find the right answer. The clue in the third sentence is "we need to hear people talk in order to form words"—which word most closely matches this idea? "Encouraged" in choice D is best.

Argument Questions

An argument question requires you to strengthen or weaken one of the author's points. Argument questions can be tough and are good questions to skip if you can afford to.

Question 4 is based on the following passage.

Line   The goal of plants, or any living organism, is to propagate as much as possible. To this end, many plants in the wild, including wheat's ancestor, have mechanisms that scatter seeds as widely as possible. However, this adaptation makes
5   it difficult to cultivate some plants; it is impossible to farm productively if a crop is spread hither and thither! Wild wheat had a number of other mechanisms that supported its existence in nature but lessened its usefulness in the field. A number of mutations had to take place before wild wheat
10   was a suitable candidate for agriculture. Humans encouraged these mutations by providing a stable environment that favored and nurtured the mutations that would have proven deleterious in the wild.

4. Which of the following would most strengthen the author's claim about the development of wheat?

   (A) Scientists are now able to manipulate a plant's genes to achieve desired traits.
   (B) There are presently 18 different strains of wheat being cultivated in different parts of the world.
   (C) In the wild, an occasional wheat plant develops that does not spread its seeds.
   (D) Wheat has an unusually stable genome, which rarely manifests any change.
   (E) Wild wheat varies from domestic wheat only in an insignificant manner.

First, go back to the passage and figure out exactly which claim the question is referring to. What claim is the author making about the development of wheat? The author concludes that "humans encouraged" the mutations that would be favorable to agriculture. Now find an answer choice that would support this claim. Choice A is the best answer; it says that humans can in fact change a plant's characteristics.

Before you move on, take a look at choice D. Some argument questions ask you to weaken the author's point. If so, pick the answer that counters the author's conclusion. This author wants us to believe that humans changed the characteristics of wheat by encouraging mutations. But choice D states that, in fact, the genome of wheat doesn't change much. If this question had asked you to weaken the author's conclusion, the best answer would have been choice D.

QUICK QUIZ #2

Questions 1-2 are based on the following passage.

Line   The Avon lady is getting a makeover. In an effort to improve sales in the teen and young adult market, Avon has launched a new line of cosmetics sold by young sales representatives. For example, female college students across
5 the country are now coordinating makeup parties in their dorm rooms to peddle Avon's wares. Winning the loyalty and name recognition of women between the ages of 16 and 24 is imperative for beauty companies who hope that these now-youthful customers will continue buying cosmetic
10 products throughout their adult lives. One challenge faced by Avon's new campaign, however, is the fickle nature of this demographic group and the need to keep products fresh and enticing.

1. The primary purpose of this passage is to

    (A) describe a successful marketing strategy employed by Avon

    (B) provide a convincing argument for other companies to emulate Avon

    (C) explain why more cosmetics have recently been bought by teens and young adults

    (D) understand the challenging aspects of marketing cosmetics to young women

    (E) discuss Avon's approach for securing a new base of customers

2. Which of the following statements would most *weaken* the author's explanation for the targeting of young women by cosmetics companies?

    (A) Cosmetic sales for this demographic group are already on the rise.

    (B) Previous marketing campaigns aimed at young women have failed.

    (C) Avon's strategy has not been tested enough on the teen and young adult market.

    (D) There is little correlation between what women buy early in their lives and later in their lives.

    (E) Marketing aimed at younger customers will alienate older customers.

Answers and Explanations: Quick Quiz #2

1. **E**   Choice E is the best answer. The first sentence doesn't tell you much, so take a look at the second. Now read the last sentence. It appears that Avon has a campaign to reach a new market. Choices A and C are incorrect because the passage does not mention if Avon's strategy has been successful in increasing sales among young women. Choice B is wrong because the passage is not trying to persuade other companies to do something. Choice D is incorrect since the passage mentions only one challenge.

2. **D**   The author concludes that "Winning the loyalty and name recognition of women between the ages of 16 and 24 is imperative for beauty companies who hope that these now-youthful customers will continue buying cosmetic products throughout their adult lives." However, if there were little correlation between what women buy in their youth and what they buy later in life, there would be no need to target young women. The other answer choices are incorrect because they would not weaken this argument.

GUESSING AND PACING STRATEGIES FOR SHORT READING QUESTIONS

Try to do all information retrieval, inference, and main idea questions. Remember to support your answers with information from the passage. If you can't point to particular parts of the passages that makes your answers correct, don't pick them.

Process of elimination is a powerful tool on short reading passages. You should be able to eliminate at least one answer on every question. Be aggressive; the odds are in your favor if you can get rid of an answer or two. Eliminate answers that aren't mentioned in the passage or use extreme language such as "all," "always," "never," "impossible," and "only."

No matter how strange the question seems, keep in mind that the answer must be in the passage somewhere. Find it!

SHORT READING: PROBLEM SET 1

Directions: Each passage below is followed by questions based on its content. Answer the questions on the basis of what is <u>stated</u> or <u>implied</u> in each passage and in any introductory material that may be provided.

Questions 1-2 are based on the following passage.

Line
Ben Jonson, a well-known playwright and seventeenth-century contemporary of John Donne, wrote that while "the first poet in the world in some things," Donne nevertheless "for not keeping of an
5 accent, deserved hanging." Donne's generation admired the depth of his feeling, but was puzzled by his often irregular rhythm and obscure references. It was not until the twentieth century and modern movements that celebrated emotion and allusion that Donne really began
10 to be appreciated. Writers such as T. S. Eliot and W. B. Yeats admired the psychological intricacies of a poet who could one moment flaunt his earthly dalliances with his mistress and the next, wretched, implore God to "bend your force, to break, blow, burn, and make me new."

1. The main idea of the passage is that

   (A) poetry is judged by different standards at different times
   (B) Jonson misjudged Donne's worth
   (C) the value of Donne's poetry was not really recognized until the twentieth century
   (D) Donne was a deeply conflicted and complex man
   (E) Donne's rough meter prevented him from being understood in his own time

2. It can be inferred from the passage that W. B. Yeats was

   (A) uninterested in meter and rhythm
   (B) a modern writer
   (C) close to T. S. Eliot
   (D) interested in imitating Donne's technique
   (E) suspicious of solely religious poets

Questions 3-4 are based on the following passage.

Line
Astronauts have the opportunity to take photographs from unprecedented perspectives. However, the fairly easy task of taking a photograph on Earth is much more arduous in space. Zero gravity makes it difficult to stand
5 still, but at least it makes it easy to move heavy camera equipment. The spacesuits and other accessories worn by astronauts prove to be very cumbersome when trying to snap the shutter. Other technicalities also make space photography less than straightforward. For example,
10 photos could be blurred by dirt on windows, and there is always the risk of damaging film due to exposure to just a small amount of radiation.

3. According to the passage, all of the following would affect space photography except

   (A) bulky clothing and gloves
   (B) moving heavy equipment
   (C) dirty windows
   (D) film exposed to radiation
   (E) floating in zero gravity

4. It can be inferred from the passage that

   (A) experience taking photographs on Earth is not as helpful when in space
   (B) it is better to have film exposed to radiation than to have dirt on a window
   (C) the absence of gravity is the greatest challenge faced by astronauts
   (D) astronauts are envious of photographers who take photographs on Earth
   (E) opportunities to take photographs in space are more abundant than on Earth

Answers and Explanations: Problem Set 1

1. **C**   The passage states that it was not until the twentieth century "that Donne really began to be appreciated." Choice A is too broad; it doesn't even mention Donne. Choice B is too narrow; the passage is not primarily about Jonson and his opinions. The passage is about Donne's poetry, not his psyche; thus choice D is incorrect. Choice E is too narrow; the passage states that several factors hindered Donne's contemporaries from fully appreciating him.

2. **B**   Yeats is referenced as an example of the "modern movement" who appreciated Donne. Choice A is too extreme; while the passage suggests Yeats had other interests, it does not imply that he was uninterested in rhythm. Nothing in the passage supports any personal relation between Yeats and Eliot, so eliminate choice C. Choice D is not correct; while Yeats admired Donne, the passage does not suggest that he wished to imitate him. There is nothing in the passage to support choice E.

3. **B**   Choice B is the correct answer because of the phrase "but at least it makes it easy to move heavy camera equipment." The other answer choices are all listed as challenges affecting space photography.

4. **A**   The passage contrasts what is easy about taking photographs on Earth with what's difficult in space. Choice B is wrong because the passage does not say which situation is worse. Choice C is incorrect because it is too broad (it's not specific to space photography), and the passage mentions that zero gravity makes moving heavy equipment easy. Choice D is wrong because there's nothing in the passage that talks about astronauts being envious. Choice E is wrong because the passage does not compare the number of opportunities on Earth with those in space.

SHORT READING: PROBLEM SET 2

Directions: Each passage below is followed by questions based on its content. Answer the questions on the basis of what is <u>stated</u> or <u>implied</u> in each passage and in any introductory material that may be provided.

Questions 1-2 are based on the following passage.

Line
February 9, 1964 marks an important date in American pop culture history: the Beatles performed live on *The Ed Sullivan Show*. Although the British rock group had appeared on American television twice
5   before, this particular performance was unlike any other. With more than 73 million viewers watching that night, it is not hard to understand how less than an hour of on-air time helped propel the Beatles to unprecedented international superstardom. Several decades later, the
10 audience remains one of the largest ever to watch a television program. And the inimitable band, as well as the historic date, is still commemorated for changing the music scene in America.

1. Lines 9-11 ("Several decades...television program") serve primarily to

(A) further describe the demographic nature of the audience

(B) emphasize the historic nature of the event

(C) explain the popularity of *The Ed Sullivan Show*

(D) compare the Beatles' popularity in 1964 with that of today

(E) show the effect of television on American popular culture

2. It can be inferred from the passage that

(A) the Beatles would have achieved great fame even without a television appearance

(B) more than 73 million new viewers tuned in to watch the Beatles' performance

(C) *The Ed Sullivan Show* provided a venue for musical performances in the 1960s

(D) the Beatles are the most celebrated rock band to have achieved international fame

(E) the Beatles' two earlier American television appearances are now forgotten

Questions 3-4 are based on the following passage.

Line
Robert Schuman's orchestral music has been under-appreciated and misunderstood for many years by critics and audiences alike. The nineteenth-century virtuoso's works for the piano are acknowledged as
5   brilliant masterworks. However, his large scale orchestral works have always suffered by comparison to those of contemporaries such as Mendelsohn and Brahms. Perhaps this is because Schuman's works should be measured with a different yardstick. His works are often
10 considered poorly orchestrated, but they actually have an unusual aesthetic. He treats the orchestra as he does the piano: one grand instrument with a uniform sound. This is so different from the approach of most composers that, to many, it has seemed like a failing rather than a
15 conscious artistic choice.

3. The author's primary purpose is to

(A) praise Schuman for his innovative approach

(B) re-evaluate the standing of Mendelsohn and Brahms

(C) reassess a portion of Schuman's portfolio

(D) reaffirm the value of the piano

(E) examine the influence of Schuman's performances

4. The author's argument would be most weakened if it were true that

(A) Schuman's piano music was overrated

(B) Mendelsohn and Brahms wrote exceptional piano music

(C) Mendelsohn's music was strongly influenced by that of Schuman

(D) audiences find orchestral music easier to appreciate than piano music

(E) most of Schuman's critics did not evaluate music based on comparisons with other composers

Answers and Explanations: Problem Set 2

1. **B** The referenced sentence mentions that the audience is still one of the largest in history. Choice A is incorrect because the passage does not describe who comprised the audience. Choice C is incorrect because the passage does not explain the general popularity of *The Ed Sullivan Show*. The passage does not compare the Beatles' popularity then and now (choice D), nor does it mention what effects television generally has on American pop culture (choice E).

2. **C** The passage mentions that at least one musical group (the Beatles) appeared on *The Ed Sullivan Show*. Choice A is wrong because you cannot come to that conclusion solely based on this passage. Choice B is incorrect because you do not know if all the viewers were new to watching the show. Choice D is too extreme ("most celebrated"). Choice E is wrong; because the earlier performances are mentioned in the passage, they aren't entirely forgotten.

3. **C** While Schuman is praised in the passage as stated in choice A, the primary purpose is to re-evaluate his orchestral works. Choices B, D, and E are not mentioned in the passage.

4. **E** Choice E is correct because the passage states that "his large scale orchestral works have always suffered by comparison to those of contemporaries such as Mendelsohn and Brahms" and that is one reason the music is "under-appreciated and misunderstood." Choices A, B, C, and E are not relevant to the author's argument; if any of them were true, they would have no bearing on critical or popular opinions of his orchestral music.

SHORT READING: PROBLEM SET 3

Directions: Each passage below is followed by questions based on its content. Answer the questions on the basis of what is <u>stated</u> or <u>implied</u> in each passage and in any introductory material that may be provided.

Questions 1-2 are based on the following passage.

Line
Modern warfare is defined by the use of high-tech communications systems that allow military leaders to manage their forces instantaneously from thousands of miles away. In contrast, because of slow-moving
5 communications systems, the greatest victory for U.S. forces during the War of 1812 actually occurred two weeks after a treaty was signed that officially ended the war. On January 8, 1815, the British, hoping to take control of Louisiana, attacked American militiamen
10 in New Orleans. In the failed attack, British casualties numbered approximately 2,000. Even though they were grossly outnumbered at the onset, only eight Americans died in the short battle. Unbeknownst to the commanders in New Orleans, the leaders of both countries had
15 already signed a peace agreement in Ghent, Belgium, on December 24, 1814.

1. According to the passage, American forces in New Orleans

   (A) turned the tide of the war and helped secure an American victory
   (B) did not abide by the Treaty of Ghent
   (C) outnumbered the British at the end of the battle
   (D) lacked communications systems
   (E) defended the city against a larger contingent of British troops

2. Which of the following best describes the structure of the passage?

   (A) A generalization is stated and then is followed by a specific example that undermines the generalization.
   (B) A present-day reality is stated and then is highlighted using a historical event as a contrasting example.
   (C) A historical era is described in terms of a significant battle.
   (D) An argument is outlined, and counterarguments are mentioned.
   (E) A diplomatic error is discussed and its implications are explained.

Questions 3-4 are based on the following passage.

Line
Originally formed to protect Christian pilgrims on the roads to Jerusalem, the Knights Templar quickly gained significant political and financial power. The Knights became early moneylenders and advisors to
5 monarchs in both Europe and the Middle East. Some historians say that the Knights' rapidly expanding power was in fact the cause of their demise. Regents, jealous of the Knights' hold over medieval politics, pressured the Pope to brand the Knights as heretics. Orders to
10 confiscate the property of the Knights and execute them arrived on October 13, a date that to this day is considered unlucky. Many historians maintain this order was the end of the Knights Templar. Some conspiracy theorists, however, say the Knights survived in Scotland
15 and constitute a secret society that is still alive today.

3. It can be inferred from the passage that

   (A) the Knights Templar were interested in preventing crime, not practicing religion
   (B) the Knights' actions conflicted with the Pope's politics
   (C) monarchs had a financial motive in pressing for the Knights' execution
   (D) the Knights are a powerful force in Scottish politics
   (E) the Knights were executed to protect Christian theology

4. The tone of the passage is best described as

   (A) insincere
   (B) indifferent
   (C) antithetical
   (D) diffident
   (E) objective

Answers and Explanations: Problem Set 3

1. **E**   Choice E is the only choice that is clearly stated in the passage ("Even though they were grossly outnumbered..."). Choice A does not work because the war was officially over when the battle occurred and the passage does not state that the Americans won the war. Be careful with choice B; the American forces were unaware of the treaty at the time of the battle. Choice C is not stated in the passage—remember, don't assume anything. Choice D does not work because the Americans at New Orleans did not totally lack communications systems, just high-tech ones.

2. **B**   Choice B works because the reality of modern warfare is stated and the Battle of New Orleans is used as an example of warfare that lacks real-time command. Nothing is undermined in the passage, therefore choice A is incorrect. Choice C is wrong because no era is described. Choice D does not work because the author is not making an argument—he's stating facts neutrally. Choice E is incorrect because there was no error in diplomacy; it just took too long for the word to spread.

3. **C**   Choice C is correct; the monarchs pressured the pope to "confiscate the property of the Knights," which points to a financial motive. Choice A is extreme and unsupported by the passage. Choice B is incorrect because the Knights' power conflicted with the monarchs, not with the Pope's. Choice D uses the present tense; despite the claims of conspiracy theorists, there is no evidence that the Knights are a political force today. Choice E is wrong because the Knights were executed for political, not religious, reasons.

4. **E**   For tone questions, look for support in the passage. Choice E is correct; the passage does not display particular bias for or against the Knights Templar. The author also gives balanced attention to a couple of different viewpoints on the topic, showing objectivity. Choice A is unsupported; the author never demonstrates other motives for his discussion. Choice B is too extreme—an ETS author will never be indifferent about his topic. Choice C is incorrect because the author is not making a statement that contrasts anything. It is unlikely that the author would be shy, so eliminate choice D.

SHORT READING: PROBLEM SET 4

Directions: Each passage below is followed by questions based on its content. Answer the questions on the basis of what is <u>stated</u> or <u>implied</u> in each passage and in any introductory material that may be provided.

Questions 1-2 are based on the following passage.

Line
The term "genetic modification" refers to technology that is used to alter the genes of living organisms. Genetically modified organisms are called "transgenic" if genes from different organisms are combined. The
5 most common transgenic organisms are crops of common fruits and vegetables, which are now grown in more than fifty countries. These crops are typically developed for resistance to herbicides, pesticides, and disease, as well as to increase nutritional value. Some
10 of these transgenic crops currently under development might even yield human vaccines. Along with improving nutrition and alleviating hunger, genetic modification of crops may also help to conserve natural resources and improve waste management.

1. The primary purpose of the passage is to

   (A) establish that transgenic crops are safe
   (B) provide information about transgenic crops
   (C) critique the process of genetic modification
   (D) praise the virtues of genetically modified foods
   (E) overcome opposition to genetically modified foods

2. In line 11, the word "yield" most nearly means to

   (A) surrender
   (B) drive slowly
   (C) replace
   (D) back down
   (E) produce

Questions 3-4 are based on the following passage.

Line
Climatologists find it hard to determine if dramatic changes in weather are the result of pollution or part of a natural series of events. Modern weather records don't extend far enough back in time to map out definitive
5 cycles. Recently climatologists have begun digging up data where historians usually tread—in ships' logs from the golden age of seafaring. England required its navy to keep records of each journey, a practice that became universal. Recording wind speed and other climatic
10 details was essential for navigation. On the open sea this was the only way for the crew to determine its location, so readings were taken every six hours. A vast amount of weather data from around the world dating back to the mid-eighteenth century can now be compared with
15 measurements derived from ice core samples, sunspot activity, and tree ring patterns.

3. The phrase "where historians usually tread" is used in the passage to indicate that

   (A) a centuries-old rivalry exists between climatologists and historians
   (B) climatologists have been taking ships' logs out of the historians' office
   (C) climatologists find valuable books alongside the historians' walking path
   (D) scientists are utilizing resources typically regarded as historical rather than scientific
   (E) scientists are more intrepid than historians have been in the past

4. It can be most reasonably inferred from lines 15-16 ("measurements . . . patterns.") that

   (A) meteorological data of the past can be deduced from ice samples, sunspot activity, and tree rings
   (B) eighteenth-century ship captains collected samples of ice and wood from around the world
   (C) the yearly accumulation of ice and snow can be determined by the patterns left in tree rings
   (D) only these items can give modern meteorologist clues to eighteenth-century weather
   (E) scientists no longer need to use this information now that the ships' logs have been found

Answers and Explanations: Problem Set 4

1. **B**   Choice B is correct because there is a lot of information with very little analysis or interpretation. Choice A is wrong because the safety of the foods is not discussed. Choice C is wrong because the process is not critiqued. Choice D is too strong when compared to choice B. Choice E is wrong because an opposing perspective is not mentioned in the passage.

2. **E**   Look for the clue. The sentence before says the crops are "developed" for different purposes. Choice E is correct because "produce" is the best definition of "yield" as it used in the passage. Choices A, B, and D are valid definitions of "yield," but not appropriate in the context of the passage. Choice C is not a definition of "yield."

3. **D**   Choice D is correct because the passage indicates scientists "have begun" to use this information, while historians "usually tread" among the material, indicating the information has typically been used by historians rather than by scientists. There is no evidence for any of the other answer choices.

4. **A**   Choice A is correct because the newly discovered weather data is going to be compared to measurements from these three sources, implying that all the data measure the same thing. There is no evidence in the passage for choices B and C. Choice D is contradicted by the passage; the ships' logs show eighteenth-century weather. There is no evidence for choice E in the passage.

SHORT READING: PROBLEM SET 5

Directions: Each passage below is followed by questions based on its content. Answer the questions on the basis of what is <u>stated</u> or <u>implied</u> in each passage and in any introductory material that may be provided.

Questions 1-2 are based on the following passage.

Line
If you could take a picture of the soul, it might look something like the black and white photos of certain slaves and soldiers during the Civil War. They are men and women who didn't have time to look at themselves
5 or worry about their appearance, and it shows. Their faces transmit their passions and experiences and never betray their character. One photo shows a large man with a hard stare and a spiky beard that conveys fierceness. In another, a mother's wisdom can be seen in the dark
10 circles under her eyes. A child's skepticism is visible in his small, taut mouth. Somehow, their situations allowed their spirits to develop in their faces, untainted by luxury and self-examination.

1. The author argues that pictures taken during the Civil War are significant primarily because they

    (A) display people who were unaware they were being photographed

    (B) show people who were not self-conscious in front of the camera

    (C) portray unkempt, unattractive men and women

    (D) convey people who tried to express emotions for the camera

    (E) reveal that the soul is tangible and photographable

2. In line 7, the word "betray" most nearly means

    (A) contradict
    (B) reveal
    (C) compromise
    (D) attack
    (E) debase

Questions 3-4 are based on the following passage.

Line
The emotional reaction of disgust is often associated with the obdurate refusal of young children to consume certain vegetables. While such disgust may seem absurd to parents determined to supply their children with
5 nutritious foods, scientists interested in hygienic behavior have a rational explanation. This theory contends that people have developed disgust as a protective mechanism against unfamiliar and possibly harmful objects. A recent study shows that disgust not only deters the ingestion of
10 dangerous substances, but also dissuades people from entering potentially contagious situations. For instance, subjects of the study declared crowded railcars to be more disgusting than empty ones and lice more disgusting than wasps.

3. The primary purpose of the passage is to

    (A) develop a general theory from a specific case
    (B) utilize scientific evidence to prove a theory
    (C) supply a logical reason for an apparently irrational action
    (D) suggest a method for developing a defensive mechanism
    (E) describe two functions served by the same reaction

4. According to the passage, the purpose of disgust is to

    (A) prevent the ingestion of all dangerous substances

    (B) protect people from wasps and other stinging insects

    (C) limit overcrowding in railcars and other modes of public transportation

    (D) encourage the avoidance of detrimental materials and situations

    (E) give children a reason for refusing to eat nutritious foods

Answers and Explanations: Problem Set 5

1. **B** The author admires the subjects of the photos for being "untainted by luxury and self-examination." The other choices do not express this significance.

2. **B** Use the clue. The author uses the word "transmit" in the sentence. Pick the word that's closest in meaning to this word. The other choices do not reflect this meaning.

3. **C** Choice C is correct because the passage explains why children's disgust is not necessarily absurd. The passage isn't long enough to develop choice A, or prove any theories in choice B. Additionally, it doesn't talk about how to develop anything in choice D, and it isn't primarily concerned with the two very similar functions of disgust, as in choice E.

4. **D** Choice D is correct, as it is supported in the fourth sentence. Choice A is extreme, because disgust doesn't *prevent* the ingestion of *all* dangerous substances. Choice B contradicts the passage because people are more disgusted by lice than wasps. Choices C and E aren't supported by the passage.

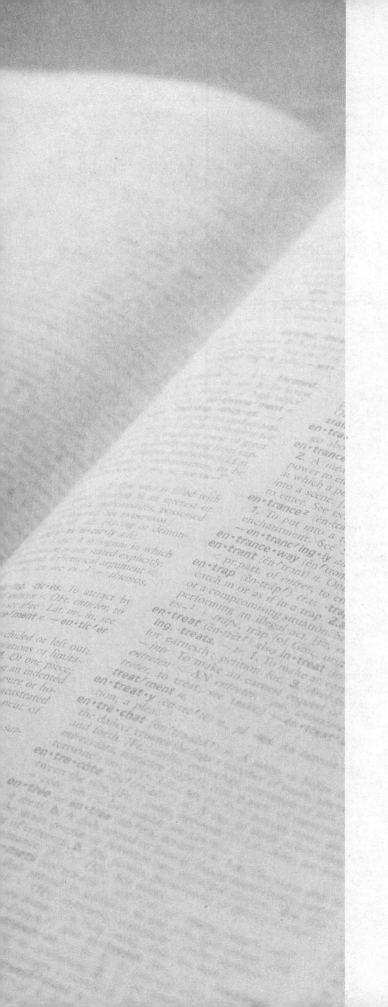

Chapter 11
SAT Critical
Reading

All three Critical Reading sections on the SAT will contain critical reading passages. One of the sections will contain dual passages: two separate passages giving contrasting viewpoints on one topic. Critical reading questions are not arranged in order of difficulty like sentence completions, but are instead arranged in a rough chronological order. Usually the earlier questions refer to the beginning of the passage, and the answers to the later questions will be found toward the end of the passage.

The critical reading passages are simply longer versions of the short reading passages; everything you learned in the last chapter is applicable to these questions as well.

Try answering the two questions below, using what you've learned from the last chapter.

5. In line 14, "blotted out" most nearly means

(A) stained
(B) blemished
(C) obscured
(D) extinguished
(E) removed

6. The author mentions Sweden and Brazil in order to emphasize which point about the Krakatoa eruption?

(A) Although the eruption was devastating in Krakatoa, there were no effects felt in other parts of the word.
(B) The volcanic eruption was so powerful that it affected the climate of countries thousands of miles away.
(C) Local destruction in Krakatoa was enormous, but the destruction in Europe and South America was, if anything, greater.
(D) Brazil and Sweden had higher safety preparedness and thus escaped serious damage.
(E) The explosion would have been even more destructive had it happened today.

The eruption of Krakatoa sent clouds of ash and dust into Earth's atmosphere to a height of 50 miles. The Sun was blotted out entirely for two days within a 100-mile radius of the volcano, and Earth temperatures as far away as Sweden and Brazil were several degrees lower than average that year.

What do you notice? The answers to the above questions were located in specific places in the passage, and you didn't have to read the entire passage to get them right.

Your Goal Is to Answer Questions

No matter how much you read, the proctor will not be walking around the examination room, saying, "Ah, Jessica! Excellent reading form. I'm giving you 20 extra points on your Critical Reading score." The only way you get points in SAT Critical Reading is by correctly answering questions.

The sooner you get to the questions, the sooner you start earning points. For example, both of the questions on the previous page could be answered without reading the rest of the passage (which we didn't show you). In question 5, you needed to supply a word that would fit in place of the quoted words "blotted out." The best answer was choice C, "obscured," because the volcanic ash filled the sky to the point that the sun's rays couldn't get through. Even if you had read the entire passage several times and made extensive notes, the answer to this question was based on only one thing: your understanding of this sentence in this paragraph.

The best answer to question 6, which asked us why the author brought up Sweden and Brazil, was choice B. In the context of this paragraph, the two countries were mentioned to show just how powerful the eruption had been. Again, even if you had memorized the entire passage, the only place to find the answer to this question was right here in this paragraph.

These questions are pretty typical of the SAT in that they include either a line reference or an identification of the paragraph in which the answer can be found. Most of the questions in critical reading tell you where in the passage to look for the answer. You can find the answers to the other questions because the questions are arranged in chronological order. The answer to question number 3 will come between the answers to questions 2 and 4.

They're Too Long!

Many students look at a passage of 70 to 90 lines and feel defeated at the thought of trying to keep track of a passage this long—but the situation is much better than they think. Critical reading passages are actually a series of small paragraphs like the one you just read. Each of these paragraphs has a couple of very specific questions based on it. And when you answer these questions, all you have to think about is the paragraph in question. Think of these longer critical reading passages as just a series of short reading passages, and you'll do fine.

THE PASSAGE TYPES

The Social Science Passage

This passage will be about a topic involving history, politics, economics, or sociology.

The Humanities Passage

This might range from an excerpt about an artist to an essay about literature, music, or philosophy.

The Science Passage

Usually not too dry, the science passage frequently involves a discussion of a scientific discovery, a new scientific theory, or a controversy in any of the scientific fields.

The Narrative Passage

Often an excerpt from a novel or short story, this type of passage frequently has actual dialogue and is often the most fun to read.

The Dual Passage

One of the passages on your SAT will actually be two shorter passages giving two perspectives on one topic, followed by up to 13 questions. Recent dual passages have given two views of architecture in cities, two views on the jazz saxophonist Miles Davis, and two views on whether controversial books should be banned. Although the double passage is generally located in the 15-minute section of the SAT, it doesn't have to be. Wherever it is, you should tackle it in the following way:

1) Answer the questions based on the first passage.

2) Answer the questions based on the second passage.

3) Finally, answer the questions that refer to both passages.

THE PRINCETON REVIEW METHOD

Step One   Read the "blurb" (the introductory sentence which describes the passage).

Step Two   Go to the questions and figure out what parts of the passage you need to read.

Step Three   Read just what you need to find the answer and get your points. Almost every question will give you a line number or a lead word that will tell you where to look in the passage for your answer. Read just those parts, and if ETS does ask the question, it will include a line number so that you can go back and read about it as carefully as you like

> NOTE: Remember that the only way to get points in critical reading is by correctly answering questions.

THE QUESTION TYPES

Line Reference and Lead Word Questions

The majority of the critical reading questions will be line reference or lead word questions. In each case, the question will tell you where in the passage to look for the answer.

Line reference questions ask you about a part of the passage and tell you to which lines the question refers. These questions will look like one of the following:

> In paragraph 4, why does the author mention Harry McCallan?

> The author cites "many interesting creatures" in lines 34-36 in order to . . .

Sometimes, instead of a line or paragraph number, you will be asked about a proper name or important word that will be pretty easy to find in the passage by running your finger down the passage until you come across it.

In either case, you should look back to the passage and find the lines indicated by the question or the lines in which the lead word can be found. It's important to read a little above and a little below the line number mentioned or the line on which the lead word is, to make sure you understand the line in context. Then you need to pick the answer that best restates what the passage itself says on those lines.

From time to time, you will see a question that seems specific, even though it has neither a line reference nor a colorful word to help you find the reference in the passage. It's not a bad idea to skip a question like this until after you've answered the rest of the questions and have a better understanding of the passage. Remember, however, that the questions are arranged chronologically. If this is question 3, then the information you need to answer it will probably be found right after the information needed to answer question 2 and right before the information needed to answer question 4.

Vocabulary-In-Context Questions

Vocabulary-in-context questions always include line numbers and ask you to pick alternate words for the quoted word or phrase. Here's what they look like:

In line 44, "objective" most nearly means. . .

The thing to bear in mind in these questions is that ETS often picks words that have more than one meaning, and the words are generally not being used in their primary sense. For example, ETS's answer to the question above about the meaning of the word "objective" was the word "material"—certainly not the first meaning anyone would think of picking.

If you find yourself running out of time as you get to a critical reading passage then these are the questions to answer first. Not only do they take the least amount of time but they also require the smallest amount of overall knowledge of the passage.

General Questions

Usually there will be one general question per passage. It will probably look like one of the following:

The main idea of this passage is to

The primary purpose of the passage is to

The passage is best described as

The passage serves primarily to

The author uses the example of the [Krakatoa eruption] primarily to

Save the general questions for last. By the time you have answered all of the line reference and lead word questions, you will have read enough of the passage that you will probably have a good idea of the main point. If not, try going back and re-reading the opening line of each paragraph. It's a good bet that these lines will be a good paraphrase of the main idea.

PACING STRATEGIES FOR CRITICAL READING

Critical reading questions account for about half of the Critical Reading section on the SAT. But not all critical reading questions are created equally. Spend your time on the questions that you find to be the easiest. Usually, this will be the line reference and lead word questions. Skip any oddball questions or any questions that are difficult to understand.

If you're shooting for a top score, you should attempt all the critical reading questions. By using process of elimination, you should be able to always eliminate an answer choice or two. Once you've done that, you can and should guess. Remember that the answer to even the weirdest question is still somewhere in the passage. If you have time left over at the end of the test, go back to any questions you've skipped and comb the passage for the correct answer.

CRITICAL READING CHECKLIST

1. Read the beginning blurb.
2. Answer the line reference and lead word questions. Remember to read above and below the specified lines to understand their context. For other specific questions that don't have a line reference, use chronology to figure out where the answer will be found in the passage.
3. Answer the vocabulary-in-context questions.
4. Answer any general questions.
5. With dual passages, read the first passage first, and answer all questions relating to that passage. Then read the second passage and answer all questions related to that passage. Finally, do the questions related to both passages. These are always at the end.

CRITICAL READING: PRACTICE PASSAGE 1

Each passage below is followed by questions based on its content. Answer the questions on the basis of what is <u>stated</u> or <u>implied</u> in the passage and in any introductory material that may be provided.

Questions 1-7 are based on the following passage.

The following passage gives a critical overview of the work of Frank Lloyd Wright, one of America's most famous architects.

Line   It is 30 years since Frank Lloyd Wright died at 91, and it is no exaggeration to say that the United States has had no architect even roughly comparable to him since. His extraordinary 72-year career spanned the shingled
5 Hillside Home School in Wisconsin in 1887 to the Guggenheim Museum built in New York in 1959.

    His great early work, the prairie houses of the Midwest in which he developed his style of open, flowing space, great horizontal panes, and integrated structure of
10 wood, stone, glass, and stucco were mostly built before 1910. Philip Johnson once insulted Wright by calling him "America's greatest nineteenth-century architect." But Mr. Johnson was then a partisan of the sleek, austere International Style which Wright abhorred. Now, the
15 International Style is in disarray, and what is significant here is that Wright's reputation has not suffered much at all in the current antimodernist upheaval.

    One of the reasons that Wright's reputation has not suffered too severely in the current turmoil in
20 architectural thinking is that he spoke a tremendous amount of common sense. He was full of ideas that seemed daring, almost absurd, but which now in retrospect were clearly right. Back in the 1920s, for example, he alone among architects and planners
25 perceived the great effect the automobile would have on the American landscape. He foresaw "the great highway becoming, and rapidly, the horizontal line of a new freedom extending from ocean to ocean," as he wrote in his autobiography of 1932. Wright wrote approvingly of
30 the trend toward decentralization, which hardly endears him to today's center-city-minded planners—but if his calls toward suburban planning had been realized, the chaotic sprawl of the American landscape might today have some rational order to it.
35   Wright was obsessed with the problem of the affordable house for the middle-class American. It may be that no other prominent architect has ever designed as many prototypes of inexpensive houses that could be mass-produced; unlike most current high stylists, who
40 ignore the boredom of suburban tract houses and design expensive custom residences in the hope of establishing a distance between themselves and mass culture, Wright tried hard to close the gap between the architectural profession and the general public.
45   In his modest houses or his grand ones, Wright emphasized appropriate materials, which might well be considered to prefigure both the growing preoccupation today with energy-saving design and the surge of interest in regional architecture. Wright, unlike the architects of
50 the International Style, would not build the same house in Massachusetts that he would build in California; he was concerned about local traditions, regional climates, and so forth. It is perhaps no accident that at Wright's Scottsdale, Arizona home and studio that continues to
55 function, many of the younger architects have begun doing solar designs as a logical step from Wright's work.

1. The phrase "comparable to" (line 4) most nearly means

   (A) as good as
   (B) similar to
   (C) like
   (D) related to
   (E) associated with

2. According to the passage, Wright's typical style included all of the following EXCEPT

   (A) the integrated use of different types of building materials
   (B) open flowing spaces
   (C) large horizontal panes
   (D) solar-powered heating systems
   (E) regional architectural elements

3. Philip Johnson's quotation about Wright (line 14) was an insult because

   (A) Wright did not respect Johnson's opinion
   (B) Johnson was a rival architect who wanted the title for himself
   (C) it ignored the many famous buildings that Wright built in the twentieth century
   (D) Johnson's International Style has since fallen out of favor
   (E) Wright was an elderly man and deserved to be treated with more respect

4. In the third paragraph, the author mentions Wright's thoughts about the importance of the automobile primarily to illustrate

(A) the general mood of the times
(B) Wright's ability to correctly predict the future
(C) the absurdity of Wright's ideas
(D) the need for centralization in America
(E) Wright's somewhat egotistical demeanor

5. According to the passage, Wright foresaw that "the great effect" of the automobile (lines 28-30) would be to

(A) increase the number of highways in America
(B) enhance the need for solar-powered designs
(C) create decentralized suburban communities
(D) reduce the number of city planners
(E) weaken the International Style, an architectural movement of which Wright disapproved

6. In lines 45-46, the phrase "who ignore the boredom of suburban tract houses" most closely means the architects

(A) find these houses to be in bad taste
(B) are sympathetic to the plight of the poor
(C) are willing to overlook the financial limitations of designing houses that could be mass-produced
(D) design expensive, stylized homes for the masses
(E) do not want to be bothered with designing inexpensive homes

7. Wright's refusal to build an identical house in both Massachusetts and California (lines 56-58) came out of his conviction that

(A) each house should be a unique design, never to be duplicated
(B) only International Style homes could be duplicated anywhere
(C) each design should reflect features of regional architecture and climate concerns
(D) he would design only for midwestern locations
(E) although he designed homes for mass production, he felt others should do the actual duplication

1 ⊂A⊃ ⊂B⊃ ⊂C⊃ ⊂D⊃ ⊂E⊃
2 ⊂A⊃ ⊂B⊃ ⊂C⊃ ⊂D⊃ ⊂E⊃
3 ⊂A⊃ ⊂B⊃ ⊂C⊃ ⊂D⊃ ⊂E⊃
4 ⊂A⊃ ⊂B⊃ ⊂C⊃ ⊂D⊃ ⊂E⊃
5 ⊂A⊃ ⊂B⊃ ⊂C⊃ ⊂D⊃ ⊂E⊃
6 ⊂A⊃ ⊂B⊃ ⊂C⊃ ⊂D⊃ ⊂E⊃
7 ⊂A⊃ ⊂B⊃ ⊂C⊃ ⊂D⊃ ⊂E⊃

Answers and Explanations: Practice Passage 1

As you read the passage, you looked for the main idea of the passage and a general sense of what goes on in the individual paragraphs. The italicized introductory material told you this would be an overview of the work of a famous architect, but it was not until you read the first paragraph that you knew how the author felt about Wright: The first paragraph could be summarized as "Wright is great!" The second paragraph is devoted to his early work. The third paragraph is about his common sense and his foresight. The fourth paragraph concerns his attempts to design affordable homes for the middle class. The fifth paragraph speaks of how his designs prefigured today's concerns with regional architecture and energy-saving design.

Now, attack the questions.

1. **A**   From the blurb, you know that this passage is basically about the famous architect. Reading the entire sentence in which the quoted word appears, it's clear the author says that no other architect has come close to being as good as Wright. Thus, it is not enough to use the words in choices B or C. You need something stronger. Choices D and E, which merely say there have been no architects connected to Wright, seem both factually incorrect (based on what you learn later in the passage) and inconsistent with the intended meaning of the sentence. The best answer is choice A.

2. **D**   You may have initially skipped this question because it did not contain a line reference, while many of the other questions did. However, this being the second question, you can assume that the answer will be found somewhere near the beginning of the passage. In this case, the answers (correct and incorrect) can be found in lines 8-12 at the beginning of the second paragraph.

    Remember that this is an EXCEPT question, so look for the one answer that is NOT true. Choices A, B, and C were easy to find in the lines just mentioned. Choices D and E seem less obvious. Did Wright's homes use solar power? Much later in the passage, the author says that his later disciples used solar power in their designs as a kind of logical extension of Wright's principles, but nowhere is it stated that Wright himself used solar heating. Wright's taste for regional elements is spoken of later as well, but you get a good hint of this in the lines already cited, where the author speaks of Wright's "prairie houses of the Midwest." The best answer is choice D.

3. **C**   This question is a little tough because the answer is not completely spelled out. In the previous paragraph you had been told that Wright designed buildings from the 1880s through at least 1959 when he designed the famous Guggenheim Museum. Obviously, most of his designs were done during the twentieth century. Thus, Johnson put Wright down by implying that his only important work had taken place very early in his career.

    Because this was a subtle point, you may have been better off eliminating incorrect answer choices.

    (A)   If Wright really didn't respect Johnson's opinion, then he wouldn't have been very insulted by Johnson's comment.

    (B)   The fact that Johnson was a jealous rival would not explain why his seeming compliment was in fact an insult.

(D) Why would what later happened to Johnson's movement have anything to do with his statement being an insult?

(E) This is a possible answer, but you actually have no way of knowing when Johnson made the statement—Wright might still have been a relatively young man when it was made.

> **Read a few lines above and below the quoted lines to understand the context.**

4. **B** As always, you should read the paragraph not only for the sentences related to the automobile, but for the context in which those sentences are presented. A bit earlier in the paragraph, the author says, "He was full of ideas that seemed daring, almost absurd, but (*trigger word*) which now in retrospect were clearly right." The automobile sentences are presented as an example of Wright's foresight. The correct answer is choice B. Choice A is a little too vague. If you selected choice C, you missed the trigger word. Choice D gets the meaning wrong: Wright favored decentralization. If you selected choice E, you might well have been correct about his demeanor, but you didn't get it from this passage. Be careful about outside information.

5. **C** It's always great when two questions refer to the same patch of passage—you've just been reading and thinking about these sentences in order to answer question 4. The beginning of the sentence that contained the quote stated, "…he alone among architects and planners perceived…." Thus, he thought about these issues as an architect. What relevance could the expansion away from cities have on an architect? This expansion would lead to an expansion of suburban communities. This is spelled out further toward the end of the paragraph. Choice A would have little effect on an architect. Choice B speaks of a design that was not possible during Wright's lifetime. Choices D and E might both be true, but neither was stated in the passage. The correct answer is choice C.

6. **E** In this paragraph, Wright is set in opposition to most current architects. Note the trigger word in the following sentence: "Unlike (*trigger word*) most current high stylists, who ignore the boredom of suburban tract houses…, Wright tried hard to close the gap between the architectural profession and the general public." Wright designed for the common person; most current architects do not. Thus choices B, C, and D can be eliminated—D because the masses can't afford expensive homes. Choice A got these architects' distaste right, but didn't catch the intention of the passage to portray them as not wishing to get involved in the business of mass-produced homes. The best answer is choice E.

7. **C** The answer to this question came from the sentences immediately before and immediately after the quoted lines. "Local traditions and regional climates" were Wright's reasons for not duplicating houses in different parts of the country.

CRITICAL READING: PRACTICE PASSAGE 2

Each passage below is followed by questions based on its content. Answer the questions on the basis of what is stated or implied in the passage and in any introductory material that may be provided.

Questions 1-7 are based on the following passage.

Many articles and books have been written proposing a major revamping of the nation's school system. In this excerpt, the author presents his own views on this subject.

Line   When nearly everybody agrees on something, it probably isn't so. Nearly everybody agrees: It's going to take a revolution to fix America's public schools. From the great national think tanks to the
5 neighborhood PTA, the call to the barricades is being trumpeted. Louis V. Gerstner Jr., head of RJR Nabisco and one of the business leaders in education reform, proclaims the Noah Principle: "No more prizes for predicting rain. Prizes only for building arks. We've got
10 to change whole schools and the whole school system."
        But it isn't so; most of that is just rhetoric. In the first place, nobody really wants a revolution. Revolution would mean junking the whole present structure of education overnight and inventing a new one from
15 scratch, in the giddy conviction that anything must be an improvement—no matter what it costs in terms of untaught kids, wrecked careers, and doomed experiments. What these folks really want isn't revolution but major reform, changing the system radically but in an
20 orderly fashion. The changes are supposed to be tested in large-scale pilot programs—Gertner's "arks"—and then installed nationally.
        But even that is just a distant gleam in the eye and a dubious proposition too. There's nothing like a
25 consensus even on designing those arks, let alone where they are supposed to come to ground. And anyone who has watched radical reforms in the real world has to be wary of them: Invariably, they take a long time and cost a great deal, and even so they fail more often than they
30 succeed. In organizations as in organisms, evolution works best a step at a time. The best and most natural changes come not in wholesale gulps, but in small bites.
        What the think-big reformers fail to acknowledge is that schools all over the country are changing all the
35 time. From head-start programs to after-school big brother/big sister projects to self-esteem workshops, it's precisely these small-scale innovations and demonstration programs that are doing the job, in literally thousands of schools. Some of these efforts

40 are only partly successful; some fail; some work small miracles. They focus varyingly on children, teacher, and parents, on methods of administration and techniques of teaching, on efforts to motivate kids and to teach values and to mobilize community support. Some are relatively
45 expensive; others cost almost nothing. But all of them can be done—and have been done.
        The important thing is that local schools aren't waiting for a revolution, or for gurus to decree the new model classroom from sea to shining sea. They
50 are working out their own problems and making their own schools better. And anyone—teachers, parents, principals, school board members—anyone who cares enough and works hard enough can do the same.

1. The primary purpose of the passage is to

    (A) present an alternative view on a widely-held belief
    (B) refute the notion that change of any kind is needed
    (C) describe several plans to implement an educational revolution
    (D) uncover and analyze new flaws in an old system
    (E) relate the historical events that have shaped a situation

2. The quotation in lines 8-10 ("No more prizes... arks.") can best be interpreted to mean that Gerstner believes

    (A) the present school system is functioning adequately
    (B) rather than focus on describing problems, the emphasis should be shifted to finding solutions
    (C) the author of the passage is a religious person
    (D) school curriculum should include more classes on topics such as shipbuilding, and fewer classes on meteorology
    (E) in the value of monetary prizes to outstanding students

3. The author views the pilot programs mentioned in lines 21-35 as which of the following?

    I. Costly and time-consuming
    II. A product of consensus
    III. Uncertain to succeed

  (A) I only
  (B) II only
  (C) III only
  (D) I and III only
  (E) I, II, and III

4. In line 35, "wholesale" most nearly means

  (A) cheap
  (B) fair
  (C) large
  (D) valuable
  (E) intensive

5. Which best summarizes the idea of "small bites" (line 35)?

  (A) Changing the system radically but in an orderly fashion
  (B) Making the system gradually look more like it did in the past
  (C) Allowing children to choose from a variety of programs
  (D) Teaching the theory of evolution in the classroom
  (E) Using modest innovations to improve schools

6. According to the author, the "small-scale innovations" referred to in lines 40-41

  (A) are largely theoretical so far
  (B) are producing a revolution in education
  (C) have in many cases been shown to work
  (D) do not work on a large scale
  (E) are unavailable in many areas

7. Judging from the author's discussion, he believes that local schools

  (A) should embrace sweeping plans for national educational reform
  (B) are relatively expensive
  (C) can be only as good as their curricula
  (D) are producing small but useful innovations all the time
  (E) will fall victim to doomed experiments

```
1  ⊂A⊃  ⊂B⊃  ⊂C⊃  ⊂D⊃  ⊂E⊃
2  ⊂A⊃  ⊂B⊃  ⊂C⊃  ⊂D⊃  ⊂E⊃
3  ⊂A⊃  ⊂B⊃  ⊂C⊃  ⊂D⊃  ⊂E⊃
4  ⊂A⊃  ⊂B⊃  ⊂C⊃  ⊂D⊃  ⊂E⊃
5  ⊂A⊃  ⊂B⊃  ⊂C⊃  ⊂D⊃  ⊂E⊃
6  ⊂A⊃  ⊂B⊃  ⊂C⊃  ⊂D⊃  ⊂E⊃
7  ⊂A⊃  ⊂B⊃  ⊂C⊃  ⊂D⊃  ⊂E⊃
```

Answers and Explanations: Practice Passage 2

1. **A** This general question asks you for the main idea of the passage—which you probably figured out while answering the other questions. In this case, the blurb tells you everything you need to know: You are told that the author presents an alternate view. To confirm this, look at the first paragraph; it tells you what "everybody agrees about." Then, in the second paragraph, after the trigger word "but," you find out what the author thinks instead. Choice B is contrary to the passage itself. No large-scale programs are described in the passage, so choice C can be eliminated. Choices D and E are also somewhat contrary to the intent of the passage. The best answer is choice A.

2. **B** As always, when ETS gives you specific lines to look at, you should remember to read above and below the quote to get a sense of the purpose of the entire paragraph. The paragraph as a whole describes what "everybody" thinks they want: a revolution in the way children are taught. Gerstner is quoted as representing this feeling. Thus choice A can be eliminated immediately; Gerstner wants radical change. It is unclear whether Gerstner is even aware of the author's existence, thus choice C is impossible. Choices D and E take the quotation too literally. Gerstner is making a metaphorical point. The best answer is choice B.

3. **D** While the pilot programs are mentioned at the end of paragraph 2, the answer to this question comes at the beginning of paragraph 3. In lines 30–32, the author says, ". . .they take a long time and cost a great deal, and even so they fail more often than they succeed." A bit earlier in the paragraph, she says, "there's nothing like a consensus even on designing those arks, let alone . . ."

    Look at the choices. Roman numeral I was definitely said, so eliminate any answer choice that does not include I. Choices B and C bite the dust. Roman numeral II gets the author's thoughts backward, so eliminate any choice that includes II; choice E can be crossed off. Roman numeral III was also definitely stated, so the best answer is choice D.

4. **C** Specific line vocabulary questions are normally quick to do, but as always, beware of secondary and far-fetched definitions. In other contexts, "wholesale" might mean cheap or fair, but in this case, the best answer is choice C. You can get this from the context of the rest of the sentence: "Not in ------- gulps, but in *small* bites."

5. **E** The answer to this question can be found in paragraph 4, lines 40–42:   ". . . it's precisely these small-scale innovations. . .that are doing the job. . . ." You might not have realized where you needed to look to find this answer, but you could have eliminated several of the answer choices anyway. Because the author does not favor revolution, you can eliminate choice A. Because the author proposes small changes, you can eliminate choice B. Choice C is not mentioned in the passage at all. Choice D is a trap answer for anyone who noticed the word evolution right in front of the quoted lines. However, the author writes of the "evolution" of the school system, not evolution as it is taught (or not taught) in the schools. The best answer is choice E.

6. **C** You may have noticed that questions 5, 6, and 7 all referred to the same paragraph, which is great! By now, you must be an expert on paragraph 4. Reading from the beginning of the paragraph in which the quoted words appear, you see that "schools. . . are changing all the time." Then a bit later, you see that "it's precisely these small-scale innovations. . . that are doing the job in . . . thousands of schools. . . ." Thus, the innovations are not theoretical (cross off choice A), revolutionary (cross off choice B), or unavailable in many areas (cross off choice E). You don't have any information on whether they will work on a large scale, so the best answer is choice C.

7. **D** Because this question did not have a specific line number, you may have initially skipped it. However, if you had looked toward the end of the passage for the lead words, "local schools," the answer was to be found at the beginning of the fourth paragraph. "Schools all over the country are changing all the time." Choice A is clearly against the author's stated preference. Choices B and C are not mentioned in the passage. Choice E is a trap answer based on language in paragraph 2. The best answer is choice D.

CRITICAL READING: PRACTICE PASSAGE 3

Each passage below is followed by questions based on its content. Answer the questions on the basis of what is <u>stated</u> or <u>implied</u> in the passage and in any introductory material that may be provided.

Questions 1-7 are based on the following passage.

Scientists, theologians, and lay persons have debated the origins of life on Earth for hundreds of years. The following passage presents one scientist's explanation.

Line
How did the earliest, most primitive, forms of life begin? Let's start with the formation of Earth 4.5 billion years ago. We can allow the first few hundred million years to pass while Earth settles down to more or less its
5 present state. It cools down and squeezes out an ocean and an atmosphere. The surrounding hydrogen is swept away by the solar wind, and the rain of meteors out of which Earth was formed dwindles and virtually ceases.

Then, perhaps 4,000 million years ago, Earth is
10 reasonably quiet and the period of "chemical evolution" begins. The first live molecules are small ones made up of two to five atoms each—the simplest form of life we can imagine—a single-strand RNA molecule.

Different scientific theories have been proposed as
15 to how this molecule first came into being. In 1908 the Swedish chemist Svante August Arrhenius theorized that life on Earth began when spores (living, but capable of very long periods of suspended animation) drifted across space for millions of years, perhaps until some landed
20 on our planet and were brought back to active life by its gentle environment.

This is highly dramatic, but even if we imagine that Earth was seeded from another world, which, long, long before, had been seeded from still another world, we
25 must still come back to some period when life began on some world through spontaneous generation—and we may as well assume that this generation began on Earth.

Why not? Even if spontaneous generation does not (or, possibly, cannot) take place on Earth now, conditions
30 on the primordial Earth were so different that what seems a firm rule now may not have been so firm then.

What won't happen spontaneously may well happen if energy is supplied. In the primordial Earth, there were energy sources—volcanic heat, lightning, and most of
35 all, sunshine. At that time, Earth's atmosphere did not contain oxygen, or its derivative, ozone, and the Sun's energetic ultraviolet rays would reach Earth's surface undiluted.

In 1954 a chemistry student, Stanley Lloyd Miller,
40 made a fascinating discovery that shed light on the

passage from a substance that is definitely unliving to one that is, in however simple a fashion, alive. He began with a mixture of water, ammonia, methane, and hydrogen (materials he believed to have been present
45 on Earth at its beginning). He made sure his mixture was sterile and had no life of any kind in it. He then circulated it past an electric discharge (to mimic the energy sources roiling the planet at that time.) At the end of a week, he analyzed his solution and found that some
50 of its small molecules had been built up to larger ones. Among these larger molecules were glycine and alanine, the two simplest of the twenty amino acids. This was the first proof that organic material could have been formed from the inanimate substances that existed on Earth so
55 long ago.

1. In the first paragraph, the author discusses the "first few hundred million years" after Earth was formed in order to

   (A) illustrate two theories as to how Earth was created
   (B) demonstrate how hardy living organisms had to be to survive this initial period
   (C) describe Earth as it was before life began
   (D) discredit the theory that life had an extra-terrestrial origin
   (E) explain the concept of spontaneous generation

2. The author most likely views the theories of Svante August Arrhenius as

   (A) innovative and daring
   (B) dramatic but logical
   (C) interesting but unlikely
   (D) impossible and illogical
   (E) lunatic and unscientific

3. The word "generation" in line 30 most nearly means

   (A) descendants
   (B) development
   (C) offspring
   (D) designation
   (E) period

4. According to the passage, the "energy" mentioned in lines 37-43 may have been important for which of the following reasons?

(A) Sources of energy found at that time produced the oxygen in Earth's atmosphere.
(B) This energy may have helped to promote spontaneous generation.
(C) It was more powerful than volcanic heat and ultraviolet rays at that time.
(D) Ultraviolet energy converted oxygen into ozone.
(E) It mimicked exactly the energy of electric discharge.

5. In line 43, the word "undiluted" most nearly means

(A) purified
(B) condensed
(C) watered down
(D) unweakened
(E) untested

6. The author uses the example of Stanley Miller's experiment primarily to suggest

(A) a laboratory confirmation of the theoretical possibility of spontaneous generation
(B) the need for further research in this field
(C) a discovery of the list of materials that were present when Earth was first created
(D) that amino acids are not, in fact, building blocks of organic materials
(E) the possibility of an extraterrestrial source for the first organic matter on Earth

7. The author's conclusion at the end of the last paragraph would be most directly supported by additional information concerning

(A) what other chemical materials were present on Earth 4 billion years ago
(B) why life did not begin during the first few hundred million years after Earth formed
(C) whether other chemistry professors were able to re-create the same results attained by Miller
(D) how Arrhenius went about his search for spores in meteorites
(E) why hydrogen in Earth's atmosphere was removed by solar wind

1 ⊂A⊃ ⊂B⊃ ⊂C⊃ ⊂D⊃ ⊂E⊃
2 ⊂A⊃ ⊂B⊃ ⊂C⊃ ⊂D⊃ ⊂E⊃
3 ⊂A⊃ ⊂B⊃ ⊂C⊃ ⊂D⊃ ⊂E⊃
4 ⊂A⊃ ⊂B⊃ ⊂C⊃ ⊂D⊃ ⊂E⊃
5 ⊂A⊃ ⊂B⊃ ⊂C⊃ ⊂D⊃ ⊂E⊃
6 ⊂A⊃ ⊂B⊃ ⊂C⊃ ⊂D⊃ ⊂E⊃
7 ⊂A⊃ ⊂B⊃ ⊂C⊃ ⊂D⊃ ⊂E⊃

Answers and Explanations: Practice Passage 3

1. **C** You know from the introductory blurb that the passage will be about a theory that explains the origin of life on Earth, not the origin of the Earth itself. Certainly there were not two theories presented. Thus eliminate choice A. Choice B, while seemingly plausible, is wrong because even the beginnings of primitive life on Earth do not start until later, according to the second paragraph. Choice C correctly describes the purpose of this description: to set the scene for the "chemical evolution" that was about to begin. Extraterrestrial origins were not brought up until the third paragraph, so eliminate choice D. If you selected choice E, you were thinking too much. Ultimately, the entire passage is helping to explain spontaneous generation, but the specific purpose of paragraph 1 is best described by choice C.

2. **C** Where do you find Arrhenius? Paragraph 3—but the author's reaction to Arrhenius is in paragraph 4. The trigger word ("but") in the middle of the first sentence tells us that the author does not totally buy Arrhenius's theory, which gets rid of choices A and B. On the other hand, does the author think he's a crackpot? No, so get rid of choices D and E. The best answer is choice C.

3. **B** Specific line vocabulary questions are easy in that you know right where to look, and you don't have to read much beyond the sentence before and after the quoted word. But they're tough in that the definitions are not always exactly what you'd expect and often entail secondary meanings. For example, here the word "generation" can mean descendants or offspring or even possibly period—but none of these is right in this case. The "generation" that's being talked about is "spontaneous generation" as it is discussed in this passage: the starting spark of primitive life where none existed before. Choice B is the best answer.

4. **B** The entire passage is about the origin of primitive life on Earth. The paragraph in question describes how this spontaneous generation might happen—by the application of various kinds of energy. If you didn't notice this while you were doing the question, you still could have eliminated a few of the other answer choices:

   (A) It was the lack of oxygen at that time that helped to let one form of energy (ultraviolet rays from sunlight) through to the surface of the planet. Eliminate.

   (C) The energy referred to in the question included volcanic heat and ultraviolet rays. Cross it off.

   (D) The paragraph didn't say this. Cross it off.

   (E) Just the opposite—the electric discharge described in the next paragraph was used by Miller to mimic the primordial energy. Eliminate.

   The best answer is choice B.

5. **D** Oxygen and ozone in Earth's atmosphere dilute the sun's rays so that they are less powerful. Four billion years ago, there was no oxygen or ozone, and so these rays were not weakened. The best answer is choice D.

6.   A   There is no line number here, but by scanning for the lead words "Stanley Miller" you will find the answer in the last paragraph. The topic sentence of the paragraph gives it all away: " . . . Miller made a fascinating discovery that shed light on the passage from a substance that is definitely unliving to one that is, in however simple a fashion, alive." His experiment helped to confirm the explanation of the origins of primitive life (spontaneous generation) that the author describes·in this passage. The best answer is choice A. You could eliminate choice B because, while there is always a need for further research, this need was not mentioned at all in the passage. Miller's choice of materials may have been based on a new discovery, but again this was not the central point of the passage, so cross off choice C. Choice D contradicts the author. Miller's experiment tends to contradict choice E: Miller tried to recreate the chemicals and the energy that existed on Earth at that time.

7.   C   Miller's results wouldn't be worth much unless they could be corroborated, and this was why choice C is best. Choices B, D, and E addressed issues that were brought up in earlier paragraphs, and had little bearing on spontaneous generation. It might be interesting to know what other chemicals were present, but as long as these chemicals were present, then the experiment is valid. The best answer is choice C.

CRITICAL READING: PRACTICE PASSAGE 4

Each passage below is followed by questions based on its content. Answer the questions on the basis of what is stated or implied in the passage and in any introductory material that may be provided.

Questions 1-6 are based on the following passage.

The following passage is an excerpt from a memoir written by writer John Burke, about the novelist Joseph Heller.

Line   I became a fan of Joseph Heller's writing while I was a student in high school in the 1970s. His most famous book, Catch-22, was practically an anthem for my friends and me. We had dissected it, sitting in the park
5 outside school, reciting certain key passages aloud and proclaiming to anyone who would listen that this was quite possibly the best book ever written. Nearly twenty years later I am not sure that we were wrong.

Heller created a modern-day anti-hero who was a
10 soldier trying to stay sane in the midst of a war in which he no longer believed. This spoke to my generation, growing up as we did during the turmoil of Vietnam, and—however you felt about the issue—his ideas were considered important.

15 I had spent many hours imagining what the man who had created the savage wit and brilliant imagery of that book would be like in person. I was soon to find out. To this day, I have no idea how it was arranged, but somehow an invitation to speak at my high school was
20 extended and duly accepted.

On the day, I made sure to be near the gate of the school to see him arrive. I was looking for a limousine, or perhaps an entourage of reporters surrounding the man whose dust-jacket picture I had scrutinized so
25 often. But suddenly, there he was, completely alone, walking hesitantly toward the school like just a normal person. He walked by me, and I was amazed to see that he was wearing rather tattered sneakers, down at the heel.

30 When he began speaking in the auditorium, I was dumbfounded, for he had a very heavy speech impediment.

"That can't be him," I whispered loudly to a friend. "He sounds like a dork."

35 My notions of a brilliant man at that time did not extend to a speech impediment—or any handicap whatsoever. Ordinary people were handicapped, but not men of brilliance. There was, in fact, a fair amount of whispering going on in the auditorium.

40 And then somehow, we began to listen to what he was saying. He was completely brilliant. He seemed to know just what we were thinking and articulated feelings that I had only barely known that I had. He spoke for forty

minutes and held us all spell-bound. I would not have
45 left my seat even if I could.

As I listened, I began to feel awaken in me the possibility of being more than I had supposed that I could be. With some difficulty I managed to get to the school gate again and waited for twenty minutes while I suppose
50 he signed autographs and fielded questions inside the auditorium. Eventually, he came out, as he had come in, alone.

I screwed up all my courage and called to him, "Mr. Heller."
55 He almost didn't stop but then he turned around and came over to me.

"I just wanted to say how much I enjoyed your book." He looked down at me in my wheelchair, smiled as if it was the most normal thing in the world and shook my
60 hand. I think that day may have been very important in the future direction of my life.

1. To the author, Joseph Heller's novel, *Catch-22* was

    (A) an important but little-known work
    (B) unusual in its frank portrayal of high school students and their problems
    (C) too traditional for most readers
    (D) inspiring and thought-provoking
    (E) more suited to an older generation

2. The major purpose of the passage is to

    (A) describe an event that may have changed the author's perception of himself
    (B) profile a famous novelist
    (C) relate in dramatic form the author's early childhood memories
    (D) suggest the sense of disappointment the author felt at encountering his hero in person
    (E) discuss the literary significance of Heller's most famous novel

3. The description of Heller's sneakers in lines 28-30 provides all of the following EXCEPT

(A) a contrast between the actual appearance of Heller and the author's image of him
(B) a telling detail about Joseph Heller
(C) a revealing insight into the mind of the author at that time
(D) a suggestion that Heller may have been dressing down deliberately to put his young audience at ease
(E) information to suggest that Heller had owned the sneakers for some time

4. The author describes Heller's speech (lines 31-46), primarily in order to

(A) illustrate the wit and imagery of the novelist's ideas
(B) describe the disappointment of the high school kids at the inarticulateness of the speaker
(C) respond to charges that Heller's work is overrated
(D) show that the students' initial skepticism was overcome by their interest in what he was saying
(E) demonstrate the lack of respect that was shown to the novelist because of his speech impediment

5. In line 51, "fielded" most nearly means

(A) evaded
(B) asked
(C) responded to
(D) delved into
(E) caught

6. The author most likely remembers his handshake with Heller because

(A) Heller almost didn't stop to shake his hand
(B) it was a form of recognition from someone who had overcome his own obstacles
(C) the author was a genuine fan of Heller's most famous book
(D) the author had been so unimpressed by Heller's speech at his high school
(E) Heller had taken the time to come to visit a high school, even though he was a celebrity

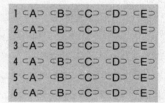

1 ⊂A⊃ ⊂B⊃ ⊂C⊃ ⊂D⊃ ⊂E⊃
2 ⊂A⊃ ⊂B⊃ ⊂C⊃ ⊂D⊃ ⊂E⊃
3 ⊂A⊃ ⊂B⊃ ⊂C⊃ ⊂D⊃ ⊂E⊃
4 ⊂A⊃ ⊂B⊃ ⊂C⊃ ⊂D⊃ ⊂E⊃
5 ⊂A⊃ ⊂B⊃ ⊂C⊃ ⊂D⊃ ⊂E⊃
6 ⊂A⊃ ⊂B⊃ ⊂C⊃ ⊂D⊃ ⊂E⊃

Answers and Explanations: Practice Passage 4

1. **D** This is the first question—which makes it likely that you will find the answer in the first paragraph. Was the book "little-known" as choice A says? No, according to the author it was famous and "an anthem" for the author and his friends. Was the book about high school students, as choice B suggests? No, according to the author it was about a soldier (it was actually during World War II). Was the book too traditional, as choice C suggests? From the description offered in paragraph 2, this was not a traditional book. Traditional books have heroes, not anti-heroes. Inspiring and thoughtful as choice D suggests? Yes, and note that the answer came from the first paragraph. Hold onto this one. Was the book more suited to an older generation as choice E suggests? These kids seemed to like it just fine. The best answer is choice D.

2. **A** You probably had a good idea of the answer to this general question by the time you'd finished your fast read. Was this a profile of Joseph Heller? Of course not. It was mostly about one incident in which the writer of this passage saw and met Heller. Scratch choice B. Choice C might have been tempting but for the word "early" and the "s" on the end of "memories." This passage concerned one memory, and it did not concern the author's early childhood. Choice D reflected a momentary disappointment the author felt, but by the end of the passage he was clearly over it. While the passage does fleetingly describe *Catch-22*, it is mostly devoted to describing the day of Heller's appearance at the school. The best answer is choice A.

3. **D** To answer this EXCEPT question, you have to read a little above the quoted lines, to find out how this sentence fits the context of the entire paragraph. The writer had expected Heller to make the big entrance of a famous person, but instead he just walked up by himself. This tells us something about: choice A, the difference between the writer's picture of Heller and the reality; choice B, the normal way that Heller chose to live his life; choice C, how the writer of the passage was thinking; and choice E, the age of the sneakers themselves. However it does not suggest that Heller had dressed like this just to make an impression on his audience. The best answer is choice D.

4. **D** Choice A is tempting here because clearly by the end of the speech, the wit and imagery of the novelist had captured his audience. However, the purpose of the paragraph was to illustrate the fact that the audience was captured, which makes choice D the best answer. Likewise, choices B and E accurately describe how the students first reacted to Heller, but by the end of the speech, they had changed their minds. Choice C says this paragraph was to respond to charges against Heller's works, but no such charges are made in the passage.

5. **C** The expression, "to field a question" probably has its roots in baseball, where you "field" a hit, but the sense of the word in this case was simply "responded to." There was no reason to suppose that Heller was on the defensive and had to "evade" questions, or that he was so caught up in the questions that he had to "delve" (meaning "go deeper") into them. The best answer is choice C.

6. **B** Get rid of the impossible answer choices. Choice A does not seem like enough of a reason to remember a handshake. Choice D is wrong because the author of the passage ended up being very impressed by Heller. Choice E seems a bit too generic to be the reason the author would remember a handshake from someone he clearly admired a lot. You're down to choices B and C. Was it just because he liked Heller's work, or had he been somehow touched by something deeper? The best answer is choice B.

CRITICAL READING: PRACTICE PASSAGE 5

Each passage below is followed by questions based on its content. Answer the questions on the basis of what is stated or implied in the passage and in any introductory material that may be provided.

Questions 1-9 are based on the following passage.

This passage describes the first detailed observations of the surface of the planet Mars—observations that indirectly led some to the mistaken belief that intelligent life existed there.

Line   The summer of 1877 had been an exceptional time for observing Mars. Every 26 months the slower-moving Mars comes especially close to Earth, creating the most favorable opportunity for observations—or, in
5 the space age, for travel to the planet. Sometimes these opportunities are better than others. Because of the large ellipticy* of the Martian orbit, the distance between Mars and Earth at the closest approach of opposition (when Mars is on the opposite side of Earth from the
10 Sun) varies from as near as 35 million miles to as far as 63 million. The closest of these oppositions occurs approximately every 15 years, and 1877 was one of those choice viewing times.

     Among the astronomers taking advantage of
15 the opportunity was Giovani Virginio Schiaparelli, director of the Milan Observatory and a scientist highly esteemed, particularly for his research concerning meteors and comets. While examining Mars with a relatively small 8-inch telescope, Schiaparelli saw faint
20 linear markings across the disc. Earlier observers had glimpsed some such streaks, but nothing as prominent and widespread as those Schiaparelli described seeing. His drawings of Mars showed the dark areas, which some took to be seas, connected by an extensive network
25 of long straight lines. Schiaparelli called the lines canali.

     In Italian, the primary meaning of canali is "channels" or "grooves," which is presumably what Schiaparelli intended in the initial announcement of his
30 discovery. He said that they "may be designated as canali although we do not yet know what they are." But the word can also mean "canal," which is how it usually was translated. The difference in meanings had tremendous theoretical implications.
35   "The whole hypothesis was right there in the translation," science writer Carl Sagan has said. "Somebody saw canals on Mars. Well, what does that mean? Well, canal—everybody knows what a canal is. How do you get a canal? Somebody builds it. Well, then
40 there are builders of canals on Mars."

     It may be no coincidence that the Martian canals inspired extravagant speculation at a time when canal building on Earth was a reigning symbol of the Age of Progress. The Suez Canal was completed in 1869, and the first efforts to breach Central America at Nicaragua
45 or Panama were being promoted. To cut through miles of land and join two seas, to mold imperfect nature to suit man—in the nineteenth-century way of thinking, this was surely how intelligent beings met challenges, whether on Earth or on Mars.
50   Schiaparelli seemed to be of two minds about the markings. Of the canal-builders' interpretation he once remarked, "I am careful not to combat this suggestion, which contains nothing impossible." But he would not encourage speculation. At another time, Schiaparelli
55 elaborated on observations suggesting to him that the snows and ice of the Martian north pole were associated with the canals. When snows are melting with the change of season, the breadth of the canals increases and temporary seas appear, he noted, and in the winter
60 the canals diminish and some of the seas disappear. But he saw a thoroughly natural explanation for the canals. "It is not necessary to suppose them to be the work of intelligent beings," he wrote in 1893, "and notwithstanding the almost geometrical appearance of
65 all of their system, we are now inclined to believe them to be produced by the evolution of the planet, just as on Earth we have the English Channel."

     His cautionary words had little effect. Those who wanted to believe in a system of water canals on Mars,
70 built by intelligent beings, were not to be discouraged—or proven wrong—for another 70 years.

     * *Ellipticy* refers to an oval (rather than a perfectly round) orbit around the sun.

1. Which of the following dates was likely to be the best for viewing Mars?

    (A) 6 months prior to the summer of 1877
    (B) 26 months after the summer of 1877
    (C) 15 years after the summer of 1877
    (D) 26 months before the summer of 1877
    (E) 1 month prior to the summer of 1877

2. In line 13, "choice" most nearly means

(A) accepted
(B) optional
(C) exclusive
(D) preferred
(E) selected

3. According to the author, which best indicates the definition of "canali" (line 26) that Schiaparelli most likely originally intended?

(A) extensive networks
(B) dark sea-like areas
(C) channels or grooves
(D) long canals
(E) moon-like deserts

4. The author quotes Carl Sagan in lines 35-40, primarily to

(A) introduce another modern writer's views into his discussion
(B) illustrate the thought process that led to a misunderstanding
(C) discuss the feasibility of building canals on Mars
(D) discount the theories of Schiaparelli
(E) reveal that the sightings of the canali were unsubstantiated and incorrect

5. Which statement best summarizes the point made in the fifth paragraph?

(A) The sightings of the Mars canals in 1877 led to a surge of canal building on Earth.
(B) The readiness to believe that the canali were constructed by intelligent beings may have come from a general fascination with canal building at the time.
(C) The Suez Canal's completion in 1869 set in motion another canal-building project that ultimately became the Panama Canal.
(D) Canal building is one important way to measure the relative intelligence and development of civilizations.
(E) Differences in the meaning of the word "canali" caused imperfections in the efforts to join two seas in Central America.

6. The author's tone in using the words, "surely how... on Mars." (lines 49-51) is meant to express

(A) irony
(B) despair
(C) uncertainty
(D) rage
(E) apathy

7. In line 52, "of two minds" means

(A) undecided
(B) tentative
(C) changeable
(D) vague
(E) skeptical

8. To what did Schiaparelli attribute the periodic changes in the appearance of the Martian canals described in the sixth paragraph?

(A) The ellipticy of the Martian orbit exerts a tidal pull on the water in the canals.
(B) The visual distortion of Schiaparelli's relatively small telescope caused the image to change.
(C) Changes in the distance between Earth and Mars make objects appear to get smaller or larger.
(D) The canals get inundated by temporary seas.
(E) Melted ice from the north pole flows into the canals during some seasons, enlarging them.

9. According to the author, what did Schiaparelli ultimately decide about the *canali* he had discovered?

(A) The *canali* showed that life on Mars is not impossible.
(B) Their geometrical appearance was misstated: the canals did not exist as straight lines, but as curves.
(C) They were most likely a phenomena created by nature.
(D) The canals evolved from less intelligent life.
(E) They were constructed to provide irrigation to lands far away from the seas.

1 ⊂A⊃ ⊂B⊃ ⊂C⊃ ⊂D⊃ ⊂E⊃
2 ⊂A⊃ ⊂B⊃ ⊂C⊃ ⊂D⊃ ⊂E⊃
3 ⊂A⊃ ⊂B⊃ ⊂C⊃ ⊂D⊃ ⊂E⊃
4 ⊂A⊃ ⊂B⊃ ⊂C⊃ ⊂D⊃ ⊂E⊃
5 ⊂A⊃ ⊂B⊃ ⊂C⊃ ⊂D⊃ ⊂E⊃
6 ⊂A⊃ ⊂B⊃ ⊂C⊃ ⊂D⊃ ⊂E⊃
7 ⊂A⊃ ⊂B⊃ ⊂C⊃ ⊂D⊃ ⊂E⊃
8 ⊂A⊃ ⊂B⊃ ⊂C⊃ ⊂D⊃ ⊂E⊃
9 ⊂A⊃ ⊂B⊃ ⊂C⊃ ⊂D⊃ ⊂E⊃

Answers and Explanations: Practice Passage 5

1. **C** The answer to this first question is, as you might imagine, in the first paragraph. The summer of 1877 had been one of the best times for viewing Mars. According to the passage, every 26 months there was another good opportunity to view Mars, but the best time to observe the planet was every 15 years. Thus, the best answer is in some increment of 15 years before or after the summer of 1877. The best answer is choice C.

2. **D** The "choice viewing time" the author is talking about in the quoted line is one of the occasions referred to in the explanation to question 1, when Earth and Mars are closest and can be most easily viewed with a telescope. In this context, the best definition offered is choice D, "preferred."

3. **C** Re-reading from the beginning of the third paragraph, "...the primary meaning of canali is 'channels' or 'grooves,' which is presumably what Schiaparelli intended..." Well, that's enough for us! The best answer is choice C.

4. **B** Sagan does not discuss whether or not the hypothesis was true, or the feasibility of building canals on Mars, nor does he make fun of Schaparelli, or discredit the sightings of the canali. He merely illustrates how the people at that time reached the conclusion that there might be intelligent life on Mars. The best answer is choice B. Choice A is just kind of odd; would the author mention a modern writer just for the heck of it?

5. **B** Choice A gets the chain of events backward. The Suez canal was finished in 1869—well before the canali were spotted on Mars. The canal across Panama was mentioned in the passage, but it certainly wasn't the main idea of the paragraph—so rule out both choices C and E. It may be that at the time people thought canal-building represented higher intelligence, but once again this was not the main idea of the paragraph, so eliminate choice D.

    The best answer is choice B. Because canal building was trendy at the time on Earth, it made people more interested—and more willing to believe—in the so-called canals on Mars.

6. **A** This part of the passage gently mocks the nineteenth-century people who thought canal building was the highest possible pinnacle of intellectual progress. The best answer is choice A, "irony." If you weren't sure about the correct answer, you could still have eliminated a few choices because they were almost ridiculous. Reading this paragraph, did you think the tone was that of despair, rage, or apathy? These were easy eliminations.

7. **A** In the context of this sentence, Schiaparelli's being "of two minds" did not mean he was changing his mind every five minutes ("changeable"), that he didn't believe in either of the two theories ("skeptical"), that he was indistinct or blurred ("vague"), or that he was feeling experimental ("tentative"). The best answer here is choice A, that he was "undecided."

8. E   Where did Schiaparelli describe the changes in the canals? That's right: the second to last paragraph. In lines 57–61, he spoke of "observations suggesting to him that the snows and ice of the Martian north pole were associated with the canals. When snows are melting...the breadth of the canals increases." Choice D might have seemed tempting because the temporary seas are mentioned here, but the passage does not say that the seas swallow up the canals. The best answer is choice E.

9. C   This is the last question, so the answer will probably be found toward the end of the passage. In lines 63–64, the author writes, "But he saw a thoroughly natural explanation for the canals," and then the author quotes Schiaparelli saying, "...we are now inclined to believe [the canals] to be produced by the evolution of the planet...." The best answer is choice C.

CRITICAL READING: PRACTICE PASSAGE 6

Each passage below is followed by questions based on its content. Answer the questions on the basis of what is <u>stated</u> or <u>implied</u> in the passage and in any introductory material that may be provided.

Questions 1-6 are based on the following passage.

In the following excerpt from a novel, Pearl, an elderly woman, is speaking to her son.

Line
Pearl opened her eyes when Ezra turned a page of his magazine. "Ezra," she said. She felt him grow still. He had this habit—he had always had it—of becoming totally motionless when people spoke to him. It was
5 endearing but also in some ways a strain, for then whatever she said to him ("I feel a draft," or "the paper boy is late again") was bound to disappoint him, wasn't it? How could she live up to Ezra's expectations? She plucked at her quilt. "If I could just have some water,"
10 she told him.
   He poured it from the pitcher on the bureau. She heard no ice cubes clinking; they must have melted. Yet it seemed just minutes ago that he'd brought in a whole new supply. He raised her head, rested it on his shoulder, and
15 tipped the glass to her lips. Yes, lukewarm—not that she minded. She drank gratefully, keeping her eyes closed. His shoulder felt steady and comforting. He laid her back down on the pillow.
   "Dr. Vincent's coming at ten," he told her.
20 "What time is it now?"
   "Eight-thirty."
   "Eight-thirty in the morning?"
   "Yes."
   "Have you been here all night?" she asked.
25 "I slept a little."
   "Sleep now. I won't be needing you."
   "Well, maybe after the doctor comes."
   It was important to Pearl that she deceive the doctor. She didn't want to go to the hospital. Her illness was
30 pneumonia, she was almost certain; she guessed it from a past experience. She recognized the way it settled into her back. If Dr. Vincent found out he would take her out of her own bed, her own house, and send her off to Union Memorial, tent her over with plastic. "Maybe you should
35 cancel the doctor altogether," she told Ezra. "I'm very much improved, I believe."
   "Let him decide that."
   "Well, I know how my own self feels, Ezra."
   "We won't argue about it just now," he said.

40 He could surprise you, Ezra could. He'd let a person walk all over him but then display, at odd moments, a deep and rock-hard stubbornness. She sighed and smoothed her quilt. Wasn't it supposed to be the daughter who came and nursed you? She knew she should send
45 him away but she couldn't make herself do it. "I guess you want to get back to that restaurant," she told him.
   "No, no."
   "You're like a mother hen about that place," she said. She sniffed. Then she said, "Ezra, do you smell smoke?"
50 "Why do you ask?" he said (cautious as ever).
   "I dreamed the house burned down."
   "It didn't really."
   "Ah."
   She waited, holding herself in. Her muscles were so
55 tense, she ached all over. Finally she said, "Ezra?"
   "Yes, Mother?"
   "Maybe you could just check."
   "Check what?"
   "The house, of course. Check if it it's on fire."

1. How does the author reveal the passage of time in the second paragraph?

   (A) The sun has just come up.
   (B) The ice cubes in the pitcher have melted.
   (C) Ezra has finally arrived.
   (D) Pearl closes her eyes and dreams.
   (E) The water in the pitcher is cold.

2. It can be inferred from the dialogue in lines 20-28 that Pearl has spent the night

   (A) talking to Ezra about the past
   (B) making plans to go to the hospital
   (C) talking on the telephone to her friends
   (D) sleeping in her bed
   (E) worrying about the future

3. If Ezra knew that Pearl had pneumonia, he would most probably

(A) agree to let her stay where she is
(B) insist that she go to the hospital
(C) make sure that she gets more rest and drinks fluids
(D) agree to lie to the doctor about her illness in order to help his mother stay out of the hospital
(E) ask another doctor for a second opinion

4. The passage suggests that in this scene Pearl is

(A) in the hospital
(B) staying with Ezra at his house
(C) living at home
(D) living in a hotel
(E) at a health clinic

5. The author writes, " She sighed and smoothed her quilt," (lines 44-45) in order to convey that Pearl

(A) is exasperated with her son and wishes he would leave her alone
(B) is tired and wishes to sleep
(C) has given up trying to persuade Ezra to cancel the doctor
(D) is a fastidious person who dislikes wrinkled things
(E) is no longer completely in touch with reality

6. The passage suggests that Pearl's fears that the house is on fire

(A) are likely to turn out to be true
(B) have no basis whatsoever
(C) came as a result of a dream she had
(D) are just a way to get her son to leave her alone for a moment
(E) are the result of a sleepless night

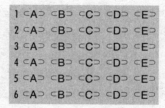

Answers and Explanations: Practice Passage 6

1. **B**   Go back to the second paragraph and read it again. How do you know from this paragraph that time has gone by? Go through the answer choices and do a little elimination. The second paragraph doesn't mention that the sun has come up. Later in the passage, Ezra tells Pearl it is already morning, but he hasn't told her this by the second paragraph. Eliminate choice A. Choice B seems very possible. If Pearl feels that Ezra brought ice only a few minutes ago, and yet the ice has melted, that implies that she has missed some time. Hold on to that one. Choice C is wrong because Ezra has been present all night. Eliminate choice C. Pearl does close her eyes in this passage, but only while she is drinking. It's hard to see the passage of time in a sip of water, so choice D bites the dust. Choice E directly contradicts the passage: the water is not cold—it is now lukewarm. The correct answer must be choice B.

2. **D**   At no time in this passage is the answer to this question stated directly. However there are a series of clues. First, Pearl opens her eyes at the beginning. Second, the ice cubes that Ezra had brought "it seemed just minutes ago" were already melted. And third, she doesn't know whether it is day or night. What has she been doing? That's right: getting some z's. The best answer is choice D.

3. **B**   This question has no line number, but it's easy to find the lead word "pneumonia" in line 31.

   If Ezra knew Pearl had pneumonia, what would he do about it? This is a hypothetical question. To answer it, you must think about what you know of Ezra. He stayed with Pearl all night. When she drank some water, he propped her up with his own shoulder. And he refused to go to sleep until after he'd heard what the doctor had to say. Given all this, what do you think he would do if he knew she had pneumonia? The best answer is choice B.

4. **C**   Again, there is no line number, but the answer to question 4 is likely to come right after the answer to question 3.

   When you first started the passage, you may have leapt to the conclusion that she was in the hospital already. However, there is one key place in the passage where you find out exactly where she is: lines 33–36. Here, directly stated, is her intention to try to avoid going to the hospital (meaning she isn't there now) and her intention to stay in "her own bed, her own house." The only possible answer is choice C.

5. **C**   As always, you should read a little bit above and below the cited line to understand the context of the quoted words. Pearl has been trying to persuade Ezra not to let the doctor come, but he has been stubborn and without actually saying no, has indicated he will not cancel the doctor's visit. Choices B, D, and E do not seem to have anything to do with what has just happened. Both choices A and C could be legitimate reactions to Ezra's refusal to let her have her way. But "sighing" seems more a sign of resignation than of anger. The best answer is choice C.

6. **C** There is no real indication that the house is actually on fire, so eliminate choice A, but Pearl's fears are not based on nothing—she has had a dream. Thus, eliminate choice B, and the best answer is choice C. Choice D is theoretically possible, but not supported by the text. Choice E is contradicted by the fact that Pearl has been dreaming.

CRITICAL READING: PRACTICE PASSAGE 7

Each passage below is followed by questions based on its content. Answer the questions on the basis of what is stated or implied in the passage and in any introductory material that may be provided.

Questions 1-12 are based on the following passage.

The following two passages present two views of the funeral industry in the United States. The first passage is an excerpt from a book written in 1963 by a journalist and takes a hard look at funeral practices at the time. The second passage was written in the 1980s by a member of the funeral business and looks at the changes in the industry since the first book appeared.

Passage 1

Line
Oh death, where is thy sting? O grave, where is thy victory? Where, indeed. Many a badly stung survivor faced with the aftermath of some relative's funeral has ruefully concluded that the victory has been won
5 hands down by a funeral establishment—in disastrously unequal battle.

Much has been written of late about the affluent society in which we live, and much fun poked at some of the irrational "status symbols" set out like golden
10 snares to trap the unwary consumer at every turn. Until recently, little has been said about the most irrational and weirdest of the lot, lying in ambush for all of us at the end of the road—the modern American funeral.

If the dismal traders (as an eighteenth-century
15 English writer calls them) have traditionally been cast in a comic role in literature, a universally recognized symbol of humor from Shakespeare to Dickens to Evelyn Waugh, they have successfully turned the tables in recent years to perpetrate a huge, macabre,
20 and expensive practical joke on the American public. It is not consciously conceived of as a joke, of course; on the contrary, it is hedged with admirably contrived rationalizations.

Gradually, almost imperceptibly, over the years, the
25 funeral men have constructed their own grotesque cloud-cuckoo-land where the trappings of Gracious Living are transformed, as in a nightmare, into the trappings of Gracious Dying. The same familiar Madison Avenue language has seeped into the funeral industry.
30 So that this too, too solid flesh might not melt, we are offered "solid copper—a quality casket which offers superb value to the client seeking long-lasting protection," or the "colonial Classic Beauty—18 gauge lead-coated steel, seamless top, lap-jointed welded
35 body construction." Some caskets are equipped with foam rubber, some with innerspring mattresses. One company actually offers "the revolutionary Perfect-Posture bed."

Passage 2

In the past 20 years, many of the questionable
40 excesses of the funeral trade have been curbed: legislation and self-policing by funeral home associations have brought some measure of regulation to an industry that was at one time sadly deficient. And yet, if the sharp practices of shoddy morticians are no longer cause
45 for customers to "whirl in their urns," as Jessica Mitford once put it so trenchantly, I fear that we may have somehow tilted too far in the other direction.

True, the costs of funerals in the 1960s were escalating out of all proportion to real value, but I am
50 convinced that in our search for economy and avoidance of discomfort we have weakened a very important family rite. Consider the case of one funeral "park" in Southern California that has instituted "drive-in" funerals. Believe it or not, you can view the remains, attend the chapel
55 service, and witness the interment—all without leaving your car.

To the extent that measures such as these have cut costs, I would applaud, but in my opinion these measures have also produced a disconnection from the real
60 purposes of a funeral. The process of spending time mourning the dead fills a real need for the bereaved. There is a purpose to each of the steps of a funeral, and if there is a commensurate cost to those steps, then so be it. These days it is possible to have a funeral without
65 a service for friends and family to gather, without a graveside interment, even without a casket. More frequently now, families will ask that contributions to charity be made in lieu of flowers and wreaths—without recognizing that buying flowers provides a chance for
70 friends and relatives to show their concern in a more tangible way than a gift to charity.

Let us not forget that feelings are as important as economy.

1. Why does the author of the first passage use the quote "O, death, where is thy sting?" (line 1)

   (A) To introduce the subject of death in a literary fashion
   (B) As a quick way to get people's attention
   (C) To suggest that the sting of death can also affect the living who must pay for the funeral
   (D) To illustrate that funeral directors are caring members of a sensitive profession
   (E) To suggest that death has no affect on the author of this passage

2. According to the passage, the "dismal traders" mentioned in line 15 are

   (A) undertakers
   (B) shopkeepers
   (C) writers such as Shakespeare and Dickens
   (D) practical jokers
   (E) stock and bond salesmen

3. According to the fourth and fifth paragraphs of the first passage, to sell their new products, funeral directors are using

   (A) free consultation and advice sessions
   (B) incentive plans designed to get customers to purchase funerals while they are still alive
   (C) the language of advertising
   (D) family specials
   (E) young spokespersons who are skilled at sales tactics

4. The tone of the first passage's author could best be described as

   (A) nostalgic
   (B) ironic
   (C) happy
   (D) indifferent
   (E) lyrical

5. If the author of the first passage were to plan her funeral in advance, which of the following would she most likely try to do?

   (A) Buy an expensive casket with a Perfect Posture mattress inside
   (B) Invite her friends to a service at a funeral home
   (C) Buy a burial plot overlooking a river
   (D) Prepay her funeral so that it could be as elaborate as possible
   (E) Leave instructions for a simple, inexpensive funeral

6. In line 42, "curbed" most nearly means

   (A) brought under control
   (B) kept under wraps
   (C) led aside
   (D) established
   (E) kept at a constant level

7. According to the second passage, the excesses of the funeral trade have been changed for the better as a result of

   (A) the passage of time
   (B) the institution of services such as drive-in funerals
   (C) the elimination of flowers and wreaths at services
   (D) new government laws and trade association rules
   (E) the practices of shoddy morticians

8. The author cites the example of the "drive-in funerals" (line 57) in order to

   (A) illustrate the point that such practices take away from the real purposes of a funeral
   (B) condemn the people who consent to mourn in this way
   (C) demonstrate the ways in which the funeral industry has changed for the better
   (D) respond to charges that the industry is still sadly deficient
   (E) rebut claims that the industry has failed to change in the past twenty years

9. The phrase "in lieu of" (line 72) most nearly means

   (A) as well as
   (B) because of
   (C) instead of
   (D) in addition to
   (E) on the side of

10. The contrast between the two descriptions of the funeral industry is essentially one between

    (A) rank pessimism and new-found dread
    (B) greedy opportunism and mature professionalism
    (C) uncertain pride and unsure self-esteem
    (D) jealous warnings and alert alarms
    (E) lawless exhaustion and tireless energy

11. Both authors indicate that the funeral industry

    (A) continues to engage in shoddy practices
    (B) fulfills a real need in the community
    (C) can police itself
    (D) preys on the suffering of the bereaved
    (E) was in a troubled state in the 1960s

12. The contrast between the two passages reflects primarily the biases of

    (A) an older woman and a younger man
    (B) a native of the United States and a native of Europe
    (C) an optimist and a pessimist
    (D) an investigative journalist and a member of the funeral industry
    (E) a person from the east coast, and a person from the west coast

```
1  ⊂A⊃ ⊂B⊃ ⊂C⊃ ⊂D⊃ ⊂E⊃
2  ⊂A⊃ ⊂B⊃ ⊂C⊃ ⊂D⊃ ⊂E⊃
3  ⊂A⊃ ⊂B⊃ ⊂C⊃ ⊂D⊃ ⊂E⊃
4  ⊂A⊃ ⊂B⊃ ⊂C⊃ ⊂D⊃ ⊂E⊃
5  ⊂A⊃ ⊂B⊃ ⊂C⊃. ⊂D⊃ ⊂E⊃
6  ⊂A⊃ ⊂B⊃ ⊂C⊃ ⊂D⊃ ⊂E⊃
7  ⊂A⊃ ⊂B⊃ ⊂C⊃ ⊂D⊃ ⊂E⊃
8  ⊂A⊃ ⊂B⊃ ⊂C⊃ ⊂D⊃ ⊂E⊃
9  ⊂A⊃ ⊂B⊃ ⊂C⊃ ⊂D⊃ ⊂E⊃
10 ⊂A⊃ ⊂B⊃ ⊂C⊃ ⊂D⊃ ⊂E⊃
11 ⊂A⊃ ⊂B⊃ ⊂C⊃ ⊂D⊃ ⊂E⊃
12 ⊂A⊃ ⊂B⊃ ⊂C⊃ ⊂D⊃ ⊂E⊃
```

Answers and Explanations: Practice Passage 7

1. **C** Reading just a little further past the cited line, it becomes clear that the author thinks that one of death's stings these days is the bill relatives have to pay for the funeral. While you could make an argument for both choices A and B, choice C is the best answer.

2. **A** This question is a bit difficult. The author does not spell out her meaning here, but the entire passage is about the funeral industry, so it is a logical inference that the "dismal traders" are, in fact, undertakers. While Dickens and Shakespeare are mentioned in the paragraph, it is fairly clear from the context that they are not the "dismal traders." Similarly, while the passage says the dismal traders have perpetrated a practical joke, it also says that this joke is not "consciously conceived of as a joke," and thus it seems incorrect to call them practical jokers. The best answer is choice A.

3. **C** It is in the fourth and fifth paragraphs that the author talks about new funeral products. In those paragraphs she says that the funeral industry uses the vocabulary of "Madison Avenue"—a common reference to the advertising industry. She also quotes the industry's jargon to describe its products, and the jargon sounds just like the phrases you would read in an advertisement for a new car.

4. **B** The author is certainly making fun of the funeral industry, mocking its language and its practices. Her tone is not nostalgic, happy, indifferent, or lyrical. It is ironic, choice B.

5. **E** After reading the passage it is clear that the author detests expensive, overblown funerals. The best answer is choice E.

6. **A** The key to this vocabulary question came in the same sentence as the key to question 6: "The excesses...have been curbed" by legislation, etc., that "have brought some measure of regulation... to the industry." Effectively, "curbed" means to bring excesses under regulation. Which answer choices are close to this meaning? The only two possibilities are choices A and E. Now, does the author mean that the "questionable excesses" of the funeral industry have been brought under control or kept at a constant level? Because it's clear she believes the situation has improved, the best answer choice is A.

7. **D** The answer to this question can be found in the first paragraph of the second passage, right after the colon in the first sentence: "...legislation and self-policing by funeral home associations have brought some measure of regulation...." Thus the best answer is choice D. Choices B and C, while economies that might help customers, are not broad enough to stop the excesses of an entire industry.

8. **A** The example of the "drive-in" is introduced with the words "Consider the case of..." Obviously this is meant to be an example to illustrate a point that was just made: "...that in our search for economy and avoidance of discomfort, we have weakened a very important family rite." Which answer choice resembles this sentiment? If you said choice A, you were right. Choice B is tempting because the author does seem to be condemning drive-in funerals, but the point of the example is

not to make fun of the people who attend, but to point out an important feature that these funerals lack.

9. **C** If you weren't sure what "in lieu of" meant, the second half of the sentence might help. Here, the author makes it clear that if a contribution has been made "in lieu of" flowers, then the contributors have not bought the flowers. Get rid of choices A, D, and E. Substituting "because of" for "in lieu of" does not produce an understandable sentence. Hence, the best answer is choice C.

10. **B** The first passage paints a bleak view of an industry run amok—overcharging customers left and right. The second passage portrays a more mature, self-policing industry. The best answer is choice B. Because you know from the introductory material that the two passages are presenting at least slightly differing opinions on the same subject, it is easy to eliminate choices A and C, which do not offer contrasting visions of the industry.

11. **E** The second passage maintains that the funeral industry is much better than it used to be, so eliminate choices A and D. The first passage would disagree with choices B and C, allowing us to eliminate them as well.

The introductory material was crucial to understanding the answer to this question. The first passage was written during the 1960s and detailed the harmful practices of the funeral trade. The second passage was written during the 1980s and looked back 20 years to the same harmful practices. The best answer is choice E.

12. **D** The answer to this question is also found in the introductory material. The ages, nationalities, and regions of the two writers were not discussed, so eliminate choices A, B, and E. While you may have felt the first passage was written by a pessimist and the second by an optimist, choice D is slightly better than choice C.

On the following pages, you will find a practice Reading Comprehension section, similar to what you will find on the SAT. Give yourself exactly 25 minutes to complete this test section. Good luck!

Chapter 12
Practice Section for the SAT

SECTION 2
Time — 25 minutes
24 Questions

Turn to Section 2 of your answer sheet to answer the questions in this section.

Directions: For each question in this section, select the best answer from among the choices given and fill in the corresponding circle on the answer sheet.

Each sentence below has one or two blanks, each blank indicating that something has been omitted. Beneath the sentence are five words or sets of words labeled A through E. Choose the word or set of words that, when inserted in the sentence, <u>best</u> fits the meaning of the sentence as a whole.

Example:

Hoping to ------- the dispute, negotiators proposed a compromise that they felt would be ------- to both labor and management.

(A) enforce . . useful
(B) end . . divisive
(C) overcome . . unattractive
(D) extend . . satisfactory
(E) resolve . . acceptable

Ⓐ Ⓑ Ⓒ Ⓓ ●

1. The work of Max Weber, an early social theorist, was ------- by a student who aided in collecting and organizing a plethora of data.
   (A) prevented (B) compromised (C) limited
   (D) facilitated (E) created

2. However ------- were Marvin Gaye's beginnings as a member of his father's church choir, he became a famous and ------- performer.
   (A) powerful . . wealthy
   (B) popular . . unqualified
   (C) inspiring . . notorious
   (D) humble . . spiritual
   (E) modest . . esteemed

3. Sustainable development is characterized by political -------, with conservationists, oil companies, and public officials each advocating different solutions.
   (A) approval (B) shrewdness (C) distinction
   (D) discord (E) upheaval

4. Although destructive wildfires are often thought to be -------, they are sometimes actually -------, allowing for the growth of new plant and animal species.
   (A) dangerous . . peripheral
   (B) deleterious . . beneficial
   (C) despoiled . . advantageous
   (D) wretched . . exultant
   (E) ruinous . . archaic

5. A painter's ability to render a likeness is both ------- and acquired; the artist blends natural abilities with worldly experience in the creation of his or her art.
   (A) anticipated (B) overt (C) aesthetic
   (D) ubiquitous (E) innate

6. Unlike its counterpart in Manhattan, Brooklyn's Broadway is ------- by an elevated train track that blocks out the sun and casts a gloomy shadow over the street.
   (A) shrouded (B) substantiated (C) perpetuated
   (D) articulated (E) supplanted

7. The interviewer is known for ------- his guests by asking them overly personal questions.
   (A) chronicling (B) disconcerting
   (C) upbraiding (D) mocking (E) distracting

8. Even though their parents were convinced that they were ------- children, the boys were often in trouble at school and on the playground for ------- behavior.
   (A) reprehensible . . pugnacious
   (B) innovative . . compelling
   (C) exemplary . . fractious
   (D) prodigious . . fastidious
   (E) listless . . indolent

GO ON TO THE NEXT PAGE →

Each passage below is followed by questions based on its content. Answer the questions on the basis of what is <u>stated</u> or <u>implied</u> in each passage and in any introductory material that may be provided.

Questions 9-10 are based on the following passage.

Line   Since 1970, national parks have had to double the number
of signs warning visitors of possible hazards. The new signs
have a dual purpose in that they also protect the parks from
unnecessary litigation. In 1972, the National Parks Service

5 in Yellowstone was forced to pay more than $87,000 to the
victim of a bear attack. This ruling prompted Yellowstone
historian Lee Whittlesley to write, "Analogously I could ask,
should New York's Central Park have signs every ten feet
saying, 'Danger! Muggers!' just because a non-streetwise,

10 non-New Yorker might go walking there?"

9.   Which of the following can be inferred from the passage above?

   (A) Before the judge's ruling, Yellowstone contained
no signs warning of bear attacks.

   (B) The only purpose of the new signs is to protect the
National Parks Service from possible lawsuits.

   (C) The National Parks Service can be held
responsible for the safety of its visitors.

   (D) The National Parks Service is more concerned
with lawsuits than the well-being of endangered
animals.

   (E) Visitors to New York's Central Park have the right
to sue the city in the event of a mugging.

10. The author's attitude toward the National Parks Service
in this passage could best be described as

   (A) professional disinterest

   (B) detached curiosity

   (C) mild worry

   (D) bitter scorn

   (E) measured sympathy

GO ON TO THE NEXT PAGE

Questions 11-12 are based on the following passage.

Line   Franz Kafka's stories are so abstruse and his literary style
so unique that a word, "Kafkaesque," was coined to describe
situations that are at once bizarre, illogical, and unfathomable.
Kafka's "The Metamorphosis," for example, has spawned
5 hundreds of possible interpretations, ranging from Freudian
psychoanalytical discussions of the characters' histories to
Marxist readings that focus on the alienation of the worker
from society. At least one literary critic specifically attributes
Kafka's unique style to the stilted relationship between Kafka
10 and his father, Hermann.

11. The author's attitude toward Kafka's literary achieve-
ments is best described as one of

(A) frustration at the inscrutableness of Kafka's work
(B) recognition for the individuality of Kafka's work
(C) indifference toward the range of possible
interpretations of Kafka's work
(D) unabashed appreciation for Kafka's contributions
to literature
(E) disappointment at the lack of meaning found in
Kafka's fiction

12. Which of the following can be inferred from the passage?

(A) The work of Franz Kafka, even though it is mostly
inscrutable, will continue to mystify and delight
readers.
(B) An author's personal history may be relevant to an
analysis of his writing.
(C) Freudian psychoanalytical interpretations, along
with Marxist readings, are particularly useful
approaches to understanding Kafka's works.
(D) Franz Kafka's fiction is so abstruse and so
resistant to interpretation that a new word,
"Kafkaesque," had to be coined to describe it.
(E) "The Metamorphosis" is Kafka's greatest literary
achievement.

GO ON TO THE NEXT PAGE

Questions 13-24 are based on the following passage.

The following passage relates some conclusions the author draws after listening to a seminar speaker denounce some modern conveniences for their negative effects on people's personal lives.

Line   Several weeks ago, when the weather was still fine, I decided to eat my lunch on the upper quad, an expanse of lawn stretching across the north end of campus and hedged in by ancient pine trees on one side and university buildings
5 on the other. Depositing my brown paper lunch bag on the grass beside me, I munched in silence, watching the trees ripple in the wind and musing over the latest in a series of "controversial" symposiums I had attended that morning. The speaker, an antiquated professor in suspenders and a
10 mismatched cardigan, had delivered an earnest diatribe against modern tools of convenience like electronic mail and instant messaging programs. I thought his speech was interesting, but altogether too romantic.

My solitude was broken by two girls, deep in conversation,
15 who approached from behind and sat down on the grass about ten feet to my left. I stared hard at my peanut butter sandwich, trying to not eavesdrop, but their stream of chatter intrigued me. They interrupted each other frequently, paused at the same awkward moments, and responded to each
20 other's statements as if neither one heard what the other said. Confused, I stole a glance at them out of the corner of my eye. I could tell that they were college students by their style of dress and the heavy backpacks sinking into the grass beside them. Their body language and proximity also indicated that
25 they were friends. Instead of talking to each other, however, each one was having a separate dialogue on her cell phone.

As I considered this peculiar scene, this morning's bleary-eyed lecturer again intruded into my thoughts. His point in the symposium was that, aside from the disastrous
30 effects of emails and chatting on the spelling, grammar, and punctuation of the English language, these modern conveniences also considerably affect our personal lives. Before the advent of electronic mail, people wrote letters. Although writing out words by hand posed an inconvenience,
35 it also conferred certain important advantages. The writer had time to think about his message, about how he could best phrase it in order to help his reader understand him, about how he could convey his emotions without the use of dancing and flashing smiley face icons. When he finished
40 his letter, he had created a permanent work of art to which a hurriedly typed email or abbreviated chat room conversation could never compare. The temporary, impersonal nature of computers, Professor Spectacles concluded, is gradually rendering our lives equally temporary and impersonal.
45   And what about cell phones? I thought. I have attended classes where students, instead of turning off their cell phones for the duration of the lecture, leave the classroom to take calls without the slightest hint of embarrassment. I have sat

in movie theaters and ground my teeth in frustration at the
50 person behind me who can't wait until the movie is over to give his colleague a scene-by-scene replay. And then I watched each girl next to me spend her lunch hour talking to someone else instead of her friend. Like the rest of the world, these two pay a significant price for the benefits of
55 convenience and the added safety of being in constant contact with the world. When they have a cell phone, they are never alone, but then again, *they are never alone.*

They may not recognize it, but those girls, like most of us, could use a moment of solitude. Cell phones make it so easy
60 to reach out and touch someone that they have us confused into thinking that being alone is the same thing as being lonely. It's all right to disconnect from the world every once in a while; in fact, I feel certain that our sanity and identity as humans necessitates it. And I'm starting to think that maybe
65 the Whimsical Professor ranting about his "technological opiates" is not so romantic after all.

13. As used in the first paragraph, the word "diatribe" (line 13) most nearly means

(A) excessive praise
(B) vengeful speech
(C) sincere congratulations
(D) harsh criticism
(E) factual explanation

14. The author's reference to "smiley face icons" (line 47) suggests

(A) a desire to return to a time before electronic mail
(B) skepticism that technology is an unequivocal boon
(C) chagrin at the callousness of modern writers
(D) a longing to create a permanent work of art
(E) relief that most modern writers avoid verbosity

15. Which of the following examples, if true, would strengthen the symposium speaker's argument as described in the third paragraph?

(A) A newlywed couple sends copies of a generic thank-you card from an Internet site to wedding guests.
(B) A high school student uses a graphing program for her algebra homework.
(C) A former high school class president uses the Internet to locate and invite all members of the class to a reunion.
(D) A publisher utilizes an editing program to proofread texts before printing.
(E) A hostess uses her computer to design and print nameplates for all her party guests.

GO ON TO THE NEXT PAGE

16. The author mentions all of the following examples of the negative effects of modern technology EXCEPT

    (A) a student leaves class to take a cell phone call
    (B) two friends spend their lunch hour talking on their respective cell phones
    (C) a cell phone user disturbs other patrons at a movie theater
    (D) email writers compose and send messages without regard to spelling and grammar
    (E) a professor delivers a polemic against "technological opiates"

17. As used in lines 16 and 79, the word "romantic" most nearly means

    (A) charming and debonair
    (B) given to expressions of love
    (C) a follower of Romanticism
    (D) demonstrating absurd behavior
    (E) imaginative but impractical

18. The main idea of the passage is that

    (A) modern forms of communication encourage users to disregard conventions of written English
    (B) the instruments of modern technology may have a negative impact on our personal and social lives
    (C) computers and cell phones destroy the romantic aspect of relationships
    (D) the devices used by modern societies to communicate are temporary and impersonal
    (E) one teacher's opinion about a controversial subject does not constitute fact

19. According to the passage, writing out words by hand

    I. offers time to think about how best to express ideas and feelings
    II. allows people to grow closer
    III. can be tiresome

    (A) I only
    (B) III only
    (C) I and II only
    (D) I and III only
    (E) II and III only

20. The purpose of the third paragraph is to

    (A) contradict the symposium speaker's argument
    (B) continue the story begun in the previous paragraph
    (C) elucidate the mystery of the girls' conversations
    (D) justify the author's belief that cell phones are physically harmful
    (E) explain the main points of the symposium speaker's address

21. The speaker at the symposium was most likely in the field of

    (A) psychology
    (B) art history
    (C) literature
    (D) computer science
    (E) mass media

22. In line 69, the author italicizes "they are never alone" primarily to

    (A) emphasize the importance of the phrase
    (B) indicate that the phrase is a translation
    (C) suggest that the phrase is metaphoric
    (D) imply an alternate meaning of the phrase
    (E) denote that the expression is colloquial

23. Which of the following would be the best title for a speech countering the arguments of the "Whimsical Professor" (line 78) ?

    (A) "The Romance of Written Communication"
    (B) "Too Convenient?: Benefits and Costs of Instant Communication"
    (C) "Undoing the Damage of Technological Opiates"
    (D) "Spelling Reform for the Computer Age"
    (E) "Ties That Bind: How Electronic Communication Brings Us Together"

24. The author's attitude toward the symposium speaker can best be described as

    (A) assent tinged with irreverence
    (B) agreement strengthened by admiration
    (C) doubt mixed with scorn
    (D) disbelief bolstered by dislike
    (E) adoration touched by romance

STOP
If you finish before time is called, you may check your work on this section only.
Do not turn to any other section in the test.

Chapter 13
Practice Section for the SAT Answers and Explanations

ANSWERS AND EXPLANATIONS

1. **D**   Choice D is correct because the clue in the sentence is *aided.* A good phrase to use for the blank is "helped out." None of the other answer choices agrees with the clue.

2. **E**   Start with the second blank. You know that Marvin Gaye is *famous,* so the blank is going to mean something close to *famous.* Eliminate Choice B and Choice D. Choice C should also be eliminated because *notorious* means "famous for a bad reason," which is not indicated in the sentence. For the first blank, the word *however* tells you to choose something that is the opposite of famous. *Powerful* is not the opposite of famous, so eliminate Choice A and choose Choice E.

3. **D**   The clue in this sentence is *each advocating different solutions.* This suggests that the blank may mean "disagreement." Choice D means disagreement. Choice E is a sudden, violent disruption, which is too extreme. Choice C is not quite strong enough to indicate disagreement. Choice A and Choice B do not agree with the clue.

4. **B**   The sentence tells you that wildfires are *destructive;* therefore, you are looking for a similar word to fill the first blank. The second blank must be the opposite of the first because of the words *although* and *actually;* a good word for the second blank would be "helpful." Choice B is therefore correct because it comes closest to the right meaning for both blanks. None of the other answer choices agrees with the clues.

5. **E**   The clue for the blank is *the artist blends natural abilities with worldly experience.* A good word to use for the blank would be "inborn." Choice E means just that. None of the other answer choices agrees with the clue.

6. **A**   The clue is *blocks out the sun.* A good word for the blank would be "hidden"; Choice A is closest to this meaning. This would also eliminate Choice B, Choice C, and Choice D. Choice E means "to replace, especially by force," and that is not what is needed here.

7. **B**   Choice B is correct because the clue *asking them overly personal questions* indicates that the interviewer may make the guests feel uneasy, which is what something *disconcerting* does. None of the other answer choices agrees with the clue.

8. **C**   Choice C is correct because the phrase *in trouble* indicates some type of bad behavior for the second blank. This would eliminate Choice B and Choice D. The parents believe the opposite based on the phrase *even though,* so the first word should describe good behavior. This would eliminate Choice A and Choice E.

9. **C**   Choice C is correct because the passage says the judge ruled that the parks had too few warning signs in the case of a bear attack. You don't know that there were no warnings, as Choice A implies, and Choice D doesn't really make sense, considering how politically correct the test is. Choice B is not indicated in the passage and uses extreme language. Choice E is incorrect because the passage draws the analogy of *New York's Central Park* to point out the lack of common sense in the judge's ruling.

10. **E**   Choice E is correct because *unnecessary litigation* is a clue that the author sympathizes with the National Parks Service's legal difficulties. Because of the author's sympathy, Choice B is incorrect. The author is definitely not disinterested (Choice A), worried (Choice C), or scornful (Choice D) toward the National Parks Service.

11. **B**   Choice B is correct because the author twice refers to the *unique* nature of Kafka's work. Choice A is incorrect because the author does not feel Kafka's work is frustrating. Choice C is incorrect because the author refers to *hundreds of possible interpretations*. Choice D and Choice E are not supported in the passage.

12. **B**   Choice B is correct because it is the only choice that encompasses the entire passage. Choice A is too specific and tells the future; you don't know that Kafka's work will *continue to mystify*. Choice C is not supported; the author does not discuss the usefulness of these approaches. Choice D contradicts the passage; *Kafkaesque* describes odd, real-life situations, not Kafka's works. Choice E is not mentioned in the passage.

13. **D**   The word *against* indicates that the professor's speech is negative. This context eliminates Choice A and Choice C. Choice E and Choice B are not indicated in the passage. Choice D correctly defines *diatribe* as it is used in the context of the passage.

14. **B**   The line in question argues that the unavailability of *dancing and flashing smiley face icons* meant that a writer had to think *about how he could convey his emotions* and that being forced to think about this issue was one of the *important advantages* of writing letters by hand (lines 41–51). The development of smiley face icons, therefore, was not entirely a good thing; to use the language in Choice B, the author is indeed skeptical that this particular piece of technology is an unequivocal boon. We can also eliminate Choice E on this basis because the author is arguing that writing letters by hand isn't all bad. However, the author does admit that it isn't all good, either—*writing out words by hand posed an inconvenience* (lines 41–42)—and so you cannot assume that the author wants to return to the past as stated in Choice A. Choice C is too extreme, as the looser standards of modern writers don't mean they are actually unfeeling or callous, and while the author does say that a letter-writer of the past *had created a permanent work of art* (lines 48–49), there's no evidence that the author is longing to do so as stated in Choice D.

15. **A**   Choice A is an example of a couple whose use of technology makes their messages more impersonal than handwritten thank-you cards. None of the other answer choices indicates examples of society being made less personal by technology.

16. **E**   Choice A is mentioned in lines 55–59. Choice B is the subject of the second paragraph and is discussed again in lines 63–65. Choice C appears in lines 59–62. Choice D is strongly hinted at in lines 31–42. But while Choice E is an event related in the passage, it is not a direct effect of modern technology, nor does the author consider it negative: The author calls the speech *interesting* (line 13) and spends much of the passage contemplating it. Therefore, Choice E is the correct answer.

17.   E   Choice A, Choice C, and Choice D are not indicated in the passage. Choice B is one definition of *romantic,* but the passage does not support the definition of *romantic* as love. Choice E is correct because the author indicates that the professor is *antiquated* (which means old or outdated), suggesting his idea is impractical.

18.   B   Choice B correctly states the main idea of the passage without being too specific. Choice A is outside the scope of the passage. Choice C, Choice D, and Choice E do not reflect the passage's central subject.

19.   D   Choice D is the best answer. The passage states that *writing out words by hand posed an inconvenience,* as in III. Therefore, you can eliminate Choice A and Choice C. However, it also gave the writer *time to think about his message and how he could convey his emotions,* as in I. Therefore, you can eliminate Choice B and Choice E. The passage discusses how one can best express oneself through communication, but does not say that that writing by hand *allows people to grow closer* to others, as in II.

20.   E   The third paragraph relates the details of the symposium speaker's idea, as the author remembers them. Choice A is not supported because the author does not contradict the speaker. The paragraph interrupts the story begun previously; therefore, eliminate Choice B. The mystery of the girls' conversation is solved in the last sentence of the second paragraph, so eliminate Choice C. The passage does not indicate that the author believes cell phones are physically harmful; therefore, Choice D is not supported.

21.   C   Choice C is the best answer: The symposium speaker is most concerned with issues such as *spelling, grammar, and punctuation of the English language* and how writers could *best phrase* their words to create a *permanent work of art,* all interests of an English professor. Although aspects of Choice B, Choice D, and Choice E are discussed in his speech, they are not the primary emphasis, nor does the speaker show expertise or enjoyment in them. There is nothing in the passage to support Choice A.

22.   D   Choice D suggests that the author repeats and italicizes the phrase to help the reader reconsider its meaning. *They are never alone* can mean that they never have to feel lonely, but also that they can never get a moment to themselves if they want some solitude. Choice A is close, but too general. Choice B is not supported, as there is nothing in the passage to suggest that the phrase is a translation. Choice C is not supported, as there is no use of metaphor here. The phrase is not more informal than the rest of the passage; therefore, eliminate Choice E.

23.   E   The main point the *Whimsical Professor* (line 78) makes, as described in lines 51–54, is that communication by computer makes people's relationships *temporary and impersonal.* A speech that counters the professor's, therefore, would argue that electronic communication does the opposite: it forges strong relationships. Choice E is a good summary of such a speech. Choice A sounds more

like it would be on the same side as the professor, praising and even arguing for a return to written communication. Choice B is a good summary of the author's even-handed approach but does not answer the question. Choice C suggests that the professor is right in his assessment that electronic communication is damaging. Choice D doesn't address the professor's main point, and it is hard to tell whether the speaker would agree or disagree with the professor's views about spelling in any case. Choice E is therefore the best answer.

24. **A**   The author ends up agreeing with most of the speaker's views, but emphasizes his *whimsical* attributes and *mismatched clothing* and refers to him as *Professor Spectacles,* making Choice A the best answer. Choice B and Choice E are too wholeheartedly positive, while Choice C and Choice D are far more negative than the passage warrants.

Part VI
The SAT:
Writing

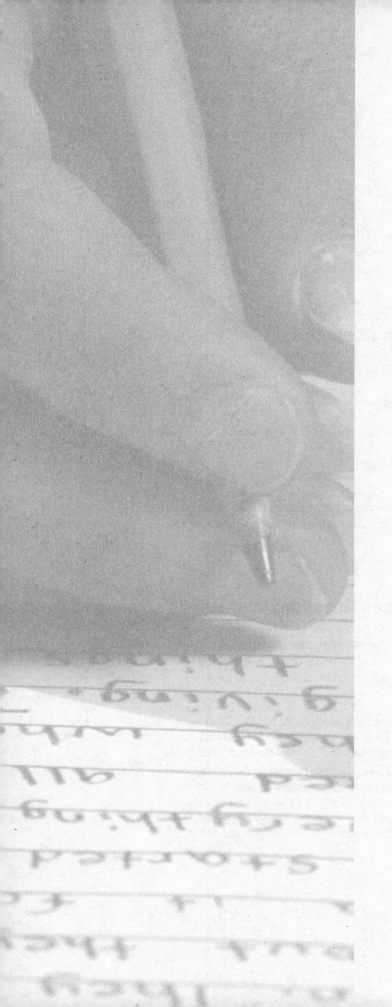

Chapter 14
SAT Grammar

GRAMMAR

Quick—identify the correlative conjunction in the nonrestrictive clause in the following sentence:

1. Just kidding!

Fortunately, the grammar tested on the SAT is not going to be that difficult. Rather, the grammar and writing skills section requires you to know only a few basic rules. ETS will test these rules with three types of questions: error identification, improving sentences, and improving paragraphs.

Error Identification Questions

Error identification questions on the SAT look like this:

1. <u>Most people</u> believe that it is silly <u>to attempt to</u>
         A   B
    test <u>one's</u> writing skills <u>in</u> a multiple-choice
         C   B
    format. <u>No error</u>
                E

Your task is to figure out which part of the sentence is incorrect. Note that about 20 percent of the error identification questions have no error (if you're curious, this sentence is fine as written).

Improving Sentences Questions

A total of 25 questions in the two grammar sections will be of the improving sentences variety. Improving questions make up the first 11 questions in the 25-minute Writing section and all 14 of those in the 10-minute section. These questions require you to not only to identify an error, but also to fix it.

2. The Macaroni Penguin, along with the Erect-Crested,
    Fjordland, Rockhopper, Royal, and Snare Island
    Penguins, <u>have a crest of yellow feathers on their heads</u>.

    (A) have a crest of yellow feathers on their heads
    (B) has a crest of yellow feathers on its head
    (C) having crests of yellow feathers on their heads
    (D) all have a crest of yellow feathers on its head
    (E) each with a crest of yellow feathers on its head

Choice A is always a reproduction of the underlined portion of the sentence as written; again, about one-fifth of improving sentences are correct as written. Unfortunately, this sentence is not. The correct answer here is choice B. Not sure why? Read on.

THE PRINCETON REVIEW METHOD

Step One   Familiarize yourself with the most commonly tested grammatical errors. ETS tests only a handful of errors. Once you learn these rules and become comfortable with them, keep your eyes peeled for them on the test.

Step Two   Make aggressive use of the Process of Elimination. If you're not sure what the right answer is, find and eliminate any answers you know to be wrong. Learn what ETS considers "good" writing.

COMMON GRAMMATICAL ERRORS

Pronoun Errors

Pronouns are one of ETS's favorite grammar subjects to test. When you see a pronoun underlined, check to see if it agrees with the noun it replaces and is in the proper case. Remember, the following pronouns are singular:

anybody	everybody	somebody	nobody	anyone
everyone	someone	no one		
anything	everything	something	nothing	either
neither	each	much		

Also check pronouns for ambiguity. The following sentence is grammatically incorrect:

> Successful athletes pay attention to their coaches because they know the value of experience.

Who does "they" refer to, the coaches or the athletes? If you can't tell, then the pronoun is ambiguous.

QUICK QUIZ #1

1. If it is not raining <u>on Sunday</u>, Sheila and <u>them</u>
                              A   B
   <u>are going</u> on <u>a picnic</u> in Hyde Park. <u>No error</u>
         C   D   E

2. Many photographers are coming to believe

   that color prints are <u>as artistic</u> as black
   <u>A</u>   B
   and white ones because <u>they</u> reveal new
                               C

   definitions <u>of art</u>. <u>No error</u>
               D   E

3. Computers may or <u>may not be</u> <u>superior to</u>
                        A   B
   typewriters; after all, <u>they</u> have a steady
                               C

   power source <u>and</u> extreme flexibility.
                    D

   <u>No error</u>
      E

4. While many cooking experts hold that the only

   <u>proper</u> way to bake a potato is in a conventional
   A
   oven, others contend that <u>cooking</u> <u>them</u> in a
                                 B   C
   microwave is a <u>perfectly</u> acceptable alternative.
                     D

   <u>No error</u>
      E

Answers and Explanations: Quick Quiz #1

1. **B**   The issue here is pronoun case. Always check underlined pronouns for ambiguity, agreement, and case errors. "Sheila and them" are the subject of the sentence, which means that you need the subject pronoun "they" instead of "them." A good way to see this error is to remove the other subject noun, "Sheila," and read the sentence again.

2. **C**   This is a pronoun ambiguity question because "they" could refer to photographers, color prints, or black and white prints.

3. **C**   Ambiguity again. "They" could refer to computers or typewriters. The sentence is additionally confusing because one could argue that both machines have a "steady power source and extreme flexibility."

4. **C**   The pronoun "them" (plural) refers to the noun "potato" (singular). Remember to check pronouns for agreement with the nouns they replace.

Verb Errors

When you see a verb underlined, check to make sure it agrees with its subject. Also, make sure all the verbs in the sentence are in the proper tense.

QUICK QUIZ #2

1. Last year, as in years past, the majority of
            ‾A‾
    candidates are dropping out of the race
               ‾‾‾‾‾‾B‾‾‾‾
    before the actual election because they no

    longer had the funds or the will to campaign.
           ‾C‾   ‾‾‾‾D‾‾‾‾
    No error
    ‾‾E‾

2. Restrictions on one of the committees that

    monitors corporate waste disposal
    ‾‾A‾‾
    were revoked, allowing the committee
    ‾‾‾B‾‾‾   ‾‾‾C‾‾‾
    to levy fines on violators of the disposal laws.
    ‾‾D‾‾
    No error
    ‾‾E‾

3. The Lipizanner stallion, a breed of horses that nearly
    went extinct at the end of World War II, are featured in
    performances at the Hofburg Palace in Vienna.

    (A) stallion, a breed of horses that nearly went extinct
             at the end of World War II, are featured
    (B) stallion, a breed of horses which came very close
             to going extinct at the end of World War II, is
             featured
    (C) stallion, nearly going extinct at the end of World
             War II the breed of horses was, are featured
    (D) stallions, a breed of horses which nearly went
             extinct at the end of World War II, is featured
    (E) stallions, a breed of horses that nearly went extinct
             at the end of World War II, are featured

Answers and Explanations: Quick Quiz #2

1. **B**   The sentence is in the past tense, as indicated by "last year." "Are dropping" is wrong because it's in the present tense.

2. **A**   The verb "monitors" is singular, while "committees," the subject of the verb, is plural.

3. **E**   The subject in the original is "stallion," which takes a singular verb, but here it is paired up with "are." Eliminate choices A and C due to this error. Choice D changes "stallion" to "stallions," while changing the verb to "is," so you still end up with an agreement error. Choice B uses "which" in a restrictive, essential phrase, which requires using "that."

Other Minor Error Types

ETS may also test your knowledge of a few other minor grammar problems. If you don't spot a pronoun or verb error, check for the following:

- **Idioms** are combinations of words that must be used in conjunction. For example, the phrase "responsible for" is an idiom; you wouldn't say "responsible of." If you see a preposition underlined, check to see if it's used idiomatically.
- **Diction** errors are errors in word choice. These are hard to spot, but fortunately don't show up too often. Look for these only after you've determined that there are no grammatical errors.

COMMON IMPROVING-SENTENCES ERRORS

Many of the errors found in the error identification questions will also show up in the improving sentences questions. However, there are a few error types that are more common to the improving sentences question type.

Dangling Modifiers

A dangling modifier has no specific word that it modifies. Take a look at the following sentence:

1. Running down the street, a brick fell on my head.

In this sentence, the modifier is "running down the street," but the noun directly after it is "a brick." It appears that the brick is running down the street, not the person. Make sure your modifiers refer to the correct noun.

This sentence should be rewritten as something like this:

1. As I was running down the street, a brick fell on my head.

Parallel Construction

When making a list of items, make sure all parts of the list are in the same form. The following sentence is incorrect:

1. Ricky wanted to finish his homework, take a walk, and to be in bed by ten o'clock.

The correct form would be the following:

1. Ricky wanted to finish his homework, take a walk, and be in bed by ten o'clock.

If you are making a comparison, make sure the two things being compared are similar.

1. John's drumming style is more explosive than Keith.

This sentence is incorrect because it compares John's *drumming style* to *Keith*. You should compare John's *drumming style* to Keith's *drumming style*.

QUICK QUIZ #3

1. Highly sociable animals living in pods that are fairly fluid, <u>dolphin interactions with other dolphins from other pods is fairly common</u>.

   (A) dolphin interactions with other dolphins from other pods is fairly common
   (B) dolphins commonly interact with other dolphins from other pods
   (C) dolphins interact commonly with other dolphins from other pods
   (D) dolphin interactions with other dolphins from other pods are a common phenomenon
   (E) dolphins can be found commonly interacting with other dolphins from other pods

2. In the 1970s, American youngsters primarily listened to rock music, while in the current decade, <u>anything goes</u>.

   (A) anything goes
   (B) the kids like anything
   (C) they listen to a diverse blend of styles
   (D) many styles appeal to youngsters
   (E) they like almost anything

Answers and Explanations: Quick Quiz #3

1. **B**   The original sentence contains a misplaced modifier; "dolphin inter-actions" are not highly sociable animals, and "interactions" is plural, so the verb "are" (not "is") should be used. Choice D repeats the misplaced modifier error, so eliminate it. In choice C, "interact commonly" describes the way they interact, which is not the intended meaning. In choice E, "commonly interacting" describes the way they interact—not the intended meaning, which is that they interact often.

2. **C**   If a sentence compares two things, verify that it compares apples to apples in a parallel way. This sentence is comparing *what youngsters listened to in the 1970s to what youngsters listen to in the current decade.* Choice C correctly completes the comparison by identifying what "they listen" to in the current decade. In choices B and E, what they *listened to* is compared to what they *like.* Choices A and D are bad comparisons because the subject has become the musical styles, whereas the original subject was the listeners.

How to Eliminate Answers on Improving Sentences

When in doubt, use the following guidelines to help you eliminate answers. These guidelines should be applied only after you're stuck or are down to two or three choices.

Avoid answer choices that

1. contain the word "being" or other "-ing" verbs
2. are wordy or redundant
3. contain unnecessary or ambiguous pronouns
4. change the meaning of the sentence

IMPROVING PARAGRAPH QUESTIONS

For these questions, you will work with a rough draft of an essay. You will be asked not only to fix grammatical errors of the type we've already looked at, but also to revise sentences, add transitions, and add or delete sentences. Just as with critical reading, go right to the questions. You don't get any points for reading the essay. On the test, six questions from 30–35 will follow a passage like the one you see below.

Here's an example.

(1) Clothing can be made from many different types of substances. (2) There are two main groups of fibers: natural and man-made. (3) Some natural fibers are cotton, wool, and linen and some man-made fibers are polyester, rayon, and nylon, and the difference depends on look and feel.

(4) Many people prefer to wear natural fibers because they feel more natural against the skin. (5) You sweat and perspire less because the cloth is organic and breathes. (6) However, it feels good on the body, but cotton and linen can wrinkle more easily.

(7) Artificial fibers tend to make a person sweat more because they are composed of having a plastic base. (8) Plastic does not breathe very much like a plastic rain poncho. (9) But because plastic is man-made, it is easier than natural cloth to get it to do what one wants. (10) Because we don't like wrinkly clothes, we make artificial fabrics that stay and remain wrinkle-free.

(11) So if one wants to look ironed and crisp all day, wear man-made clothes. (12) But if one prefers the comfort and feel of aeration and a perspiration-free feeling, choose natural fibers. (13) Determining whether you're a style or a texture person determines which fabrics you'll prefer. (14) If you cannot decide, try a blend!

1. Which of the following is the best revision of sentence 5 (reproduced below)?

   You sweat and perspire less because the cloth is organic and breathes.

   (A) The wearer perspires less because the organic cloth breathes.
   (B) The cloth ends sweating and perspiring because it is organic and breathes.
   (C) Organic, breathing cloth prevents sweating and perspiring.
   (D) One never sweats while wearing cloth that is organic and breathes.
   (E) Cotton and polyester prevent perspiration.

2. In context, which of the following sentences placed before sentence 7 best connects the second paragraph to the third?

   (A) Unlike natural fabrics, man-made fabrics wrinkle less, but they do not feel as pleasant on the body.
   (B) Cotton and linen are not man-made fibers and, consequently, behave differently.
   (C) Nevertheless, all fibers have their advantages, especially man-made fibers.
   (D) Some fibers encourage perspiration, a healthy, cleansing process of the skin.
   (E) However, appearance is more important than feel, so man-made clothes are preferable.

3. In context, where would sentence 13 (reproduced below) be better placed within the essay?

   Determining whether you're a style or a texture person determines which fabrics you'll prefer.

   (A) Before sentence 12
   (B) Before sentence 11
   (C) Before sentence 2
   (D) After sentence 14
   (E) Before sentence 6

Revision Questions

When revising sentences, first make sure that there are no grammatical errors. Then pick the answer that is concise and does not change the meaning of the sentence. You should also use the Process of Elimination guidelines for improving sentences to aid you.

Let's return to question 1 from the previous page.

1. Which of the following is the best revision of sentence 5 (reproduced below)?

    You sweat and perspire less because the cloth is organic and breathes.

    (A) The wearer perspires less because the organic cloth breathes.
    (B) The cloth ends sweating and perspiring because it is organic and breathes.
    (C) Organic, breathing cloth prevents sweating and perspiring.
    (D) One never sweats while wearing cloth that is organic and breathes.
    (E) Cotton and polyester prevent perspiration

Eliminate choices C, D, and E because they change the meaning of the sentence. Choice B has an ambiguous pronoun. Take it out. You're left with answer choice A, the best answer.

Transition Questions

For transition questions, go back to the passage and read the sentences before and after the one you're going to work with. Determine what direction the sentences are going in—do they maintain the same flow of ideas or do they change the topic? When adding a transition sentence, do not go off the topic or add any new information.

2. In context, which of the following sentences placed before sentence 7 best connects the second paragraph to the third?

    (A) Unlike natural fabrics, man-made fabrics wrinkle less, but they do not feel as pleasant on the body.
    (B) Cotton and linen are not man-made fibers and, consequently, behave differently.
    (C) Nevertheless, all fibers have their advantages, especially man-made fibers.
    (D) Some fibers encourage perspiration, a healthy, cleansing process of the skin.
    (E) However, appearance is more important than feel, so man-made clothes are preferable.

Read sentences 6 and 7. Sentence 6 is about man-made fabrics while sentence seven is about artificial ones. So, we've introduced a new idea. Look for the choice that best expresses this change in topic. Choice A looks like the winner.

Content Questions

Some questions require you to work more with the content of the essay. You may need to rearrange sentences or provide a title for the essay. Read only as much as you need to answer these questions.

> **3.** In context, where would sentence 13 (reproduced below) be better placed within the essay?
>
> *Determining whether you're a style or a texture person determines which fabrics you'll prefer.*
>
> (A) Before sentence 12
> (B) Before sentence 11
> (C) Before sentence 2
> (D) After sentence 14
> (E) Before sentence 6

Take a look at sentence 13. What is it about? Now, read the sentences in the answer choices and use the Process of Elimination to get rid of answers that aren't similar in topic. Putting sentence 13 before 12 makes little sense; it separates the two examples. It certainly shouldn't be placed near sentences 2 or 6, either. How about before sentence 12? That works. Sentence 13 discusses two considerations: style and texture. Sentences 11 and 12 then give example of these two considerations; thus, choice B is best.

GRAMMAR: PROBLEM SET 1

Directions: The following sentences test your knowledge of grammar, usage, word choice, and idiom.

Some sentences are correct. No sentence contains more than one error.
You will find that the error, if there is one, is underlined and lettered. Elements of the sentence that are not underlined will not be changed. In choosing answers, follow the requirements of standard written English.

If there is an error, select the <u>one underlined part</u> that must be changed to make the sentence correct and fill in the corresponding oval on your answer sheet.

If there is no error, fill in oval Ⓔ.

EXAMPLE:

<u>The other</u> delegates and <u>him</u> <u>immediately</u>
    A   B   C

accepted the resolution <u>drafted by</u> the
                       D

neutral states. <u>No error</u>
            E

SAMPLE ANSWER

Ⓐ ● Ⓒ Ⓓ Ⓔ

1. The teacher <u>noted</u> that the inspired writing Joe displayed
          A

  on his <u>homework</u> was <u>incompatible</u> to the prosaic prose
          B   C

  <u>he produced</u> in class. <u>No error</u>
    D   E

2. The well-manicured lawns, the marble columns,

  and the <u>fountains that were impressive</u>
                A

  <u>indicated</u> this <u>was no</u> ordinary <u>summer cottage</u>.
    B   C   D

  <u>No error</u>
    E

3. Considering the blinding snowstorm <u>and</u>
                        A

  ice-covered roads, you and <u>her</u> <u>were</u> lucky
                  B   C

  <u>to arrive</u> here safely. <u>No error</u>
    D   E

4. Although its flavor is <u>derided</u> <u>by connoisseurs</u>,
         <u>A</u>   B   C

  the popularity of milk chocolate is <u>far greater</u>
                            D

  than that of dark chocolate. <u>No error</u>
                       E

5. Eager to reach the widest audience <u>possible</u>,
                           A

  the popular group ABBA recorded songs not

  only in their native Swedish <u>but also</u> in a
              B   C

  number of other languages. <u>No error</u>
    D   E

6. To celebrate the 1976 <u>bicentennial, classes</u>
                    A

  from each local school <u>attended</u> a grand
                 B

  fireworks display and, <u>having</u> never seen such
                C

  a sight, <u>was amazed</u> by the beauty. <u>No error</u>
        D   E

Answers and Explanations: Problem Set 1

1. **C**   Always check prepositions for idioms. The correct idiom is "incompatible with."

2. **A**   This sentence contains a parallelism error. Remember to check that any items in a list are the same part of speech—and if the list contains verbs, then check that those verbs are in the same tense. Because the sentence lists "well-manicured lawns" (an adjective and noun) and "marble columns" (an adjective and noun), the phrase "fountains that were impressive" (noun, verb, and adjective) is not parallel. The phrase correctly written would be "…and the impressive fountains…"

3. **B**   This sentence contains a pronoun case error. The use of the pronoun "her" is incorrect because it is the subject of the sentence and "her" is an object pronoun. A good way to see this error is to remove the other subject noun, "you," and read the sentence again. The correct word is the subject pronoun, "she."

4. **A**   This is a pronoun ambiguity question because "its" could refer to popularity, milk chocolate, or dark chocolate. Because you don't know which is correct, the pronoun is ambiguous.

5. **B**   The pronoun "their" (plural) refers to the collective noun ABBA (singular). Remember to check pronouns for agreement with the noun they replace and, yes, collective nouns are singular.

6. **D**   The verb "was amazed" is singular, but the subject is "classes," which is plural. Ignore the extra information in the middle of the sentence when checking for subject-verb agreement.

GRAMMAR: PROBLEM SET 2

Directions: The following sentences test your knowledge of grammar, usage, word choice, and idiom.

Some sentences are correct. No sentence contains more than one error.

You will find that the error, if there is one, is underlined and lettered. Elements of the sentence that are not underlined will not be changed. In choosing answers, follow the requirements of standard written English.

If there is an error, select the <u>one underlined part</u> that must be changed to make the sentence correct and fill in the corresponding oval on your answer sheet.

If there is no error, fill in oval (E).

EXAMPLE:

<u>The other</u> delegates and <u>him</u> <u>immediately</u>
    A   B   C

accepted the resolution <u>drafted by</u> the
                         D

neutral states. <u>No error</u>
             E

SAMPLE ANSWER

1. Visitors to the zoo have often <u>looked</u> into exhibits
                         A

   designed for lions and <u>saw</u> ducks or crows <u>eating</u> treats or
               B   C

   enjoying water <u>intended</u> for the large cats. <u>No error</u>
           D   E

2. Before the sun <u>rose</u> yesterday, Rebecca <u>has already</u>
              A   B

   awoken and <u>begun</u> her morning <u>regimen</u> of activities.
        C   D

   <u>No error</u>
   E

3. Jill knows that she performs <u>worse</u> on multiple-
                      A

   choice tests <u>than</u> on short answer tests, <u>where she is</u>
         B   C

   required to show <u>her understanding</u> in writing. <u>No error</u>
            D   E

4. Each member of the audience <u>told</u> the director
                  A

   that the thriller was the <u>scariest</u> movie that <u>they</u> <u>had ever</u>
               B   C   D

   seen. <u>No error</u>
      E

Directions: The following sentences test correctness and effectiveness of expression. In choosing answers, follow the requirements of standard written English; that is, pay attention to grammar, choice of words, sentence construction, and punctuation.

In each of the following sentences, part of the sentence or the entire sentence is underlined. Beneath each sentence you will find five ways of phrasing the underlined part. Choice A repeats the original; the other four are different.

Choose the answer that best expresses the meaning of the original sentence. If you think the original is better than any of the alternatives, choose it; otherwise choose one of the others. Your choice should produce the most effective sentence—clear and precise, without awkwardness or ambiguity.

EXAMPLE: SAMPLE ANSWER

Laura Ingalls Wilder published her first book
and she was sixty-five years old then.

(A) and she was sixty-five years old then
(B) when she was sixty-five
(C) at age sixty-five years old
(D) upon the reaching of sixty-five years
(E) at the time when she was sixty-five

---

5. In the summer, the Ruddy Duck <u>male, who lives in marshes, have</u> chestnut colored plumage and its bill is blue, but in the winter, the male is brown with a creamy colored face.

(A) male, who lives in marshes, have
(B) male was living in marshes and has
(C) male that lives in marshes, it has
(D) male lives in marshes with its
(E) male, which lives in marshes, has

6. To be a good psychologist, one must <u>be trustworthy, kind, and a patient listener</u>, or else one's clients will not feel comfortable.

(A) be trustworthy, kind, and a patient listener,
(B) be trusted, kind, and be patiently listening,
(C) be trustworthy, kind, and patient as a listener,
(D) be trusted, have kindness, and also be a patient listener,
(E) have trust, kindness, and be a patient listener,

Answers and Explanations: Problem Set 2

1. **B** "Have...looked" is correct, but "have...saw" is not. Rather, the correct verb tense is "seen."

2. **B** The verb "has already awoken" is in the present perfect tense, but the sentence is referring to something that happened in the past, before yesterday's sunrise. The past perfect tense, "had already awoken," is required.

3. **C** Use the word "where" only to refer to places; in this sentence it incorrectly refers to "short answer tests."

4. **C** The pronoun "they" (plural) incorrectly refers to the noun "member" (singular).

5. **E** Choice A incorrectly uses "who" to refer to an animal and contains a subject-verb error; choice B incorrectly introduces the past tense into the sentence; choice C changes the meaning of the sentence by suggesting that the description applies only to Ruddy Duck males that live in the marshes; choice D makes it sound as if the duck lives with its plumage.

6. **C** In a list of three or more things, always check for parallelism. Choice C is the most consistent and concise, providing a list of three adjectives. Choices A and E have a list that mixes verbs with nouns. Choice B is not consistent because it uses "be" on only the first and third items in the list. Choice D is consistent, but longer and more awkward than is choice C.

GRAMMAR: PROBLEM SET 3

> **Directions:** The following sentences test your knowledge of grammar, usage, word choice, and idiom.
>
> Some sentences are correct. No sentence contains more than one error.
> You will find that the error, if there is one, is underlined and lettered. Elements of the sentence that are not underlined will not be changed. In choosing answers, follow the requirements of standard written English.
>
> If there is an error, select the <u>one underlined part</u> that must be changed to make the sentence correct and fill in the corresponding oval on your answer sheet.
>
> If there is no error, fill in oval Ⓔ.
>
> EXAMPLE:
>
> <u>The other</u> delegates and <u>him</u> <u>immediately</u>
>   A   B   C
>
> accepted the resolution <u>drafted by</u> the
>   D
>
> neutral states. <u>No error</u>
>   E
>
> SAMPLE ANSWER
>
> Ⓐ ● Ⓒ Ⓓ Ⓔ

1. <u>Accept</u> for chocolate <u>desserts</u> in restaurants,
   A   B

   I generally avoid eating <u>sugar, cake, and candy</u>
                                   C

   in order to stay <u>healthy</u>. <u>No error</u>
                          D   E

2. <u>Although</u> pennies seem to be cheap and inconsequential
   A

   donations, charities <u>agree</u> that <u>it</u> adds <u>up</u> to a significant
                              B   C   D

   sum. <u>No error</u>
              E

3. Against the advice of <u>their</u> coach, <u>who</u> <u>has led</u>
                               A   B   C

   many teams to victory, this year's baseball

   team attended more parties than practices and

   <u>had</u> an especially disappointing season. <u>No error</u>
    D   E

4. Neither the ongoing costs associated with <u>feeding</u> so
                                                       A

   many tigers nor the difficulties caused by meddling

   neighbors <u>has been considered</u> prior to <u>purchasing</u> the
                       B   C

   the land and <u>building</u> the sanctuary. <u>No error</u>
                      D   E

5. <u>Impractical for cold climates</u>, Ashley decided against packing her flip-flops for her vacation in Alaska.

(A) Impractical for cold climates,
(B) Because she was impractical for cold climates,
(C) They are impractical, since the climate is cold, so
(D) Because they are impractical for cold climates,
(E) Since the cold climate is impractical for them,

6. Nick's friends enjoyed spending time talking to his mother, unlike <u>spending time with Manny's</u>.

(A) spending time with Manny's
(B) spending time talking to Manny's mother
(C) spending time with Manny's mother
(D) talking to Manny
(E) talking to Manny's household

Answers and Explanations: Problem Set 3

1. **A** Here, the author uses incorrect diction. The word "accept" means "to receive" something offered. The author should have chosen "except," which means "to the exclusion of." If you missed this one, don't sweat it. Diction errors are rare.

2. **C** This pronoun agreement question has the singular word "it" referring to the plural words "pennies" and "donations."

3. **A** Here is another collective noun. The pronoun "their" (plural) incorrectly refers to the collective noun "team" (singular).

4. **B** The verb "has been considered" is singular, but it should agree with "difficulties." When you use "neither…nor" or "either…or," the verb must agree with the noun following "nor" or "or."

5. **D** The sentence intends to say that flip-flops are impractical for cold climates, so Ashley didn't pack hers. Choice D uses the plural pronoun "they," which correctly refers to "flip-flops." Choice A has an introductory phrase with no subject, so it makes "Ashley" the thing that is impractical for cold climates. Choice B also makes Ashley the impractical element. Choice C is awkwardly arranged. Choice E changes the intended meaning of the original sentence.

6. **B** Choice B is correct because the comparison is between talking to either Nick's mother or Manny's. Choices A and D are incorrect because they compare talking to Nick's mother to Manny himself. Although Choice C might be considered correct in that it compares Nick's mother to Manny's mother, it should be eliminated because it changes the meaning. Choice E is eliminated because it compares one person to a group of people.

GRAMMAR: PROBLEM SET 4

Directions: The following sentences test your knowledge of grammar, usage, word choice, and idiom.

Some sentences are correct. No sentence contains more than one error.
You will find that the error, if there is one, is underlined and lettered. Elements of the sentence that are not underlined will not be changed. In choosing answers, follow the requirements of standard written English.

If there is an error, select the <u>one underlined part</u> that must be changed to make the sentence correct and fill in the corresponding oval on your answer sheet.

If there is no error, fill in oval Ⓔ.

EXAMPLE:

<u>The other</u> delegates and <u>him</u> <u>immediately</u>
    A   B   C

accepted the resolution <u>drafted by</u> the
                        D

neutral states. <u>No error</u>
              E

<u>SAMPLE ANSWER</u>
Ⓐ ● Ⓒ Ⓓ Ⓔ

---

1. Either the United States <u>or</u> the Philippines <u>is</u>
                     A   B

the top <u>choice of</u> the State Department
         C

<u>to receive</u> the mining contract. <u>No error</u>
   D   E

2. Anyone <u>seeking to get in shape</u>, <u>regardless of</u> a
          A   B

ge or ability, can benefit from <u>having a</u>
                          C

personal trainer show <u>them</u> the best approach.
                   D

<u>No error</u>
 E

3. <u>Though</u> popular mainly as a device that
   A

played music, Edison's phonograph <u>is</u>
                           B

originally created <u>as</u> an educational tool
              C

to teach spelling and <u>allow</u> deaf people to
                 D

to hear recordings of books. <u>No error</u>
                    E

Directions: The following sentences test correctness and effectiveness of expression. In choosing answers, follow the requirements of standard written English; that is, pay attention to grammar, choice of words, sentence construction, and punctuation.

In each of the following sentences, part of the sentence or the entire sentence is underlined. Beneath each sentence you will find five ways of phrasing the underlined part. Choice A repeats the original; the other four are different.

Choose the answer that best expresses the meaning of the original sentence. If you think the original is better than any of the alternatives, choose it; otherwise choose one of the others. Your choice should produce the most effective sentence—clear and precise, without awkwardness or ambiguity.

EXAMPLE: SAMPLE ANSWER

Laura Ingalls Wilder published her first book
<u>and she was sixty-five years old then</u>.

(A) and she was sixty-five years old then
(B) when she was sixty-five
(C) at age sixty-five years old
(D) upon the reaching of sixty-five years
(E) at the time when she was sixty-five

---

4. <u>Notwithstanding having spent several hours</u> in meetings with each other and with an arbitrator, the parties were unable to reach an agreement.

(A) Notwithstanding having spent several hours
(B) Notwithstanding several hours to be spent
(C) Although the parties spend several hours
(D) Notwithstanding to have spent several hours
(E) Although the spending of several hours

5. Once considered revolutionary and controversial, the movements of impressionism and abstract expressionism <u>have steadily gained popularity; its images can now be found on drugstore postcards</u>.

(A) have steadily gained popularity; its images can now be found on drugstore postcards
(B) have steadily gained popularity; impressionist images can now be found on drugstore postcards
(C) has steadily gained popularity; and so images can now be found on drugstore postcards
(D) has steadily gained popularity, and its images can now be found on drugstore postcards
(E) have steadily gained popularity; their images are now founded on drugstore postcards

6. Alien species piggybacking on human travelers to new <u>countries are wreaking havoc on planet Earth, though they live for only a short time</u>.

(A) wreak havoc on planet Earth, though they live for only a short time
(B) are wreaking havoc on planet Earth, though they are living for only a short time
(C) are wreaking havoc on planet Earth, though the alien species live for only a short time
(D) are wreaking havoc on planet Earth and live for only a short time
(E) are wreaking havoc on planet Earth and though the species live for only a short time

Answers and Explanations: Problem Set 4

1. **E** The subject is "either" and takes the singular verb "is." Countries are collective nouns and thus take a singular verb.

2. **D** The pronoun "them" (plural) does not agree with the pronoun "anyone" (singular). Remember to check pronouns for agreement with the nouns they replace.

3. **B** The error in this sentence occurs at choice B, which is an inappropriate verb form. To match the past tense established and used elsewhere in the sentence ("played," "created"), the past tense "was" is needed.

4. **A** Although "notwithstanding" sounds clumsy, there is no error in the sentence as written. Try not to pick choices just because they sound bad. Look for identifiable errors. Choices B, C, and D are in the wrong tense. Choice E turns "spending" into a noun, so the first phrase lacks a verb and makes no sense.

5. **B** The sentence is ambiguous; "it" could refer to abstract expressionism or impressionism. Choice B clarifies the ambiguity. Choices C and D incorrectly use a singular verb (the subject is "movements"). Choice E is incorrect: one can find the images on postcards, but the images are not founded on (i.e., based on) the postcards.

6. **C** The original sentence contains an ambiguous pronoun; it is unclear who "they" is referring to. Choice B repeats this error; eliminate it. Choice D changes the meaning of the sentence: It no longer contrasts the fact that they wreak havoc with the fact that they live for only a short time. Choice E clears up the ambiguity but in doing so creates a sentence fragment.

GRAMMAR: PROBLEM SET 5

Directions: The following passage is an early draft of an essay. Some parts of the passage need to be rewritten.

Read the passage and answer the questions that follow. Some questions are about particular sentences or parts of the essay or the entire essay and ask you to consider organization and development. In making your decisions, follow the conventions of standard written English. After you have chosen your answer, fill in the corresponding oval on your answer sheet.

Questions 1-6 are based on the following student essay.

(1) In these days of pollution, you must clean one's car with something other than rain. (2) There are many car washing techniques available and they have their pluses and minuses.

(3) First, one type of car wash is the touch-free car wash that a lot of people like because it doesn't scratch the paint on one's car. (4) Basically it's a stream of water at a really high force like a fire hose's pressure. (5) But not everybody likes touch-free because it might not get off really tough dirt and stains. (6) Scrubbing is necessary.

(7) The traditional car wash with the waving strips of cloth touches one's car, it might scratch it, especially if the cloth strips still have attached bits of dirt or gravel from the last car. (8) But the strips can rub the stains out more successfully with friction and water and soap instead of just water and soap.

(9) The best type of car wash is to wash by hand if you have the time. (10) Although this takes up a lot of time, you can get out all the dirt without scratching your car if one is careful and thorough. (11) Car washing by hand is a better idea in the summer or one will freeze.

1. Which of the following is the best version of sentence 3 (reproduced below)?

   First, one type of car wash is the touch-free car wash that a lot of people like because it doesn't scratch the paint on your car.

   (A) The touch-free car wash is a favorite type of car wash among people who do not like their cars' paint scratched.
   (B) Many people prefer the touch-free car wash because it does not scratch car paint.
   (C) Although the touch-free car wash scratches car paint, many prefer it.
   (D) People who do not like scratched car paint will like the touch-free car wash because it does not scratch car paint.
   (E) Many people like the touch-free car wash that is preferred because it does not scratch the paint on cars.

2. In context, which of the following sentences placed before sentence 7 best connects the second paragraph to the third?

   (A) For a scrubbing function, do not use a touch-free car wash.
   (B) Nevertheless, a touch-free car wash has other advantages.
   (C) Therefore, scrub a car to avoid scratching.
   (D) Because a stream of water is never enough to cut through dirt, one should avoid a touch-free car wash.
   (E) For tougher dirt, one should use a car wash that physically scrubs the car.

3. The writer's main rhetorical purpose of the essay is to

   (A) explore the advantages and disadvantages of different car washing methods
   (B) explain how pollution causes dirty cars and thus must be controlled
   (C) establish that touch-free is the best type of car wash because it does not scratch a car's paint
   (D) show how to wash a car quickly and well by hand
   (E) illustrate that hand washing is the superior form of car washing during the winter

4. Which of the following is the best revision of the underlined portion of sentence 8 (reproduced below)?

   But the strips can rub the stains out more successfully <u>with friction and water and soap</u> <u>instead of just water and soap</u>.

   (A) with friction, water, and soap instead of just water and soap
   (B) with friction and soap instead of just water
   (C) with soap added to friction instead of just water
   (D) with friction added to the standard soap and water mixture
   (E) with soap and water instead of just friction

5. In context, which revision would most improve sentence 10 (reproduced below)?

Although this takes up a lot of time, you can get out all the dirt without scratching your car if one is careful and thorough.

(A) Change "Although" to "Because."
(B) Delete "up a lot of."
(C) Change "get out" to "remove."
(D) Change "one is" to "you are."
(E) Add "in one's work" after "thorough."

6. If the essay were to continue after sentence 11, which of the following would be the best content for sentence 12?

(A) However, there are many advantages to each method of car washing.
(B) Depending on the newness of a car, one can determine which car washing method is most effective.
(C) Essentially, car owners have many types of car washing methods to choose from, and their preferences will determine the truly best car wash.
(D) In conclusion, one should choose a sunny, warm day for the cleaning endeavor so that the car being washed will not develop water spots.
(E) Only if a car owner has time is hand washing the best method for cleaning a car.

Answers and Explanations: Problem Set 5

1. **B** Choices A and D perpetuate the original sentence's problem with repetition. Choice C changes the meaning of the original sentence. Choice E is wordy. Choice B is the best choice because it retains the full meaning of the sentence while conveying the thought concisely.

2. **E** Choice C changes the meaning of the paragraphs. Choices A, B, and D focus too much on the touch-free car wash. A sentence added to the beginning of the third paragraph should lead into the topic of that paragraph: the traditional car wash. Because choice E focuses more on the traditional car wash, it is the best choice.

3. **A** Choice B is mentioned but is not the main purpose. Choice C states that the author prefers touch-free car washing; however, the essay refutes this declaration. Choice D is incorrect because the author explains that one cannot hand wash a car well without time. Choice E is disproved by the last sentence. Choice A is the best choice because it encompasses the whole essay.

4. **D** Choices B, C, and E alter the meaning of the original sentence. Choice A looks appealing, but it still has a lot of repetition. Choice D is the best option because it is the most concise without the redundancy problem.

5. **D** This change needs to be made to fix an incorrect switch from the second person pronoun "you" to the third person pronoun "one." Choice A indicates that this sentence would support the prior sentence, but it is intended to be a contrast. Choices B and C make acceptable changes, but the original versions are also acceptable so it isn't much of an improvement. Choice E makes the sentence longer than it needs to be, since the original version is acceptably clear.

6. **C** The last sentence of any essay should draw together all the thoughts presented as a conclusion. Choice A mentions only the positives, not the negatives. Choice B introduces a new idea, the newness of a car, instead of summarizing the essay. Choice D sums up only the last paragraph and brings in the new concept of water spots. Choice E repeats only sentences 9 and 10.

GRAMMAR: PROBLEM SET 6

Directions: The following passage is an early draft of an essay. Some parts of the passage need to be rewritten.

Read the passage and answer the questions that follow. Some questions are about particular sentences or parts of the essay or the entire essay and ask you to consider organization and development. In making your decisions, follow the conventions of standard written English. After you have chosen your answer, fill in the corresponding oval on your answer sheet.

Questions 1-6 are based on the following passage.

(1) I don't think that people living near an active volcano should be forced to move to a safer home. (2) Let me explain why they should be permitted to keep their homes.

(3) First of all, many people think a volcano is a dangerous place to live but there are plenty of active volcanoes in the world with whole cities around them and plenty that haven't exploded in centuries. (4) Sometimes an active volcano just drizzles out lava. (5) Other places have their own potential problems like living on the coast is dangerous for hurricanes, living in the Midwest is dangerous for tornadoes, and living in lower elevated areas is dangerous for flash flooding. (6) People should learn to face their fears because they can never move to a truly safe place.

(7) Secondly, people should be allowed to live where they choose. (8) If someone wants to live on a volcano, maybe they have a good view or a fertile garden. (9) Maybe they live near their families and friends. (10) Maybe they have a house that has been in their family for generations. (11) The government should not force them to move because of the possibility of disaster. (12) They have something precious that is worth sustaining all these scary possibilities for: a home.

1. Which of the following is the best revision of the underlined portion of sentence 3 (reproduced below)?

   First of all, many people think a volcano is a dangerous place <u>to live but there are plenty of active volcanoes in the world with whole cities around them and plenty that haven't exploded</u> in centuries.

   (A) (as it is now)
   (B) to live; accordingly, there are many active volcanoes surrounded by cities that have not exploded in centuries
   (C) to live, although many active volcanoes have remained quiet for centuries in order to encourage cities to grow
   (D) to live, including the quiet, citified ones
   (E) to live. However, many of the world's active volcanoes are surrounded with cities and have remained quiet for centuries

2. In context, which of the following words should be placed at the beginning of sentence 5 (reproduced below)?

   Other places have their own potential problems like living on the coast is dangerous for hurricanes, living in the Midwest is dangerous for tornadoes, and living in lower elevated areas is dangerous for flash flooding.

   (A) Furthermore
   (B) Consequently
   (C) Although
   (D) Subsequently
   (E) However

3. Which of the following words best replaces the underlined word in sentence 6 (reproduced below)?

   People should learn to <u>face</u> their fears because they can never move to a truly safe place.

   (A) View
   (B) Acknowledge
   (C) State
   (D) Address
   (E) Represent

4. The writer's main rhetorical purpose of the essay is to

   (A) advocate for the rights of those who chose to live on volcanoes
   (B) urge the government to instate stricter housing regulations on and around volcanoes
   (C) support the idea that home is a state of mind rather than a geographic location
   (D) offer that daredevils substitute dangerous places to live
   (E) demonstrate how the general populace is composed of cowards

5. In context, which words should be placed at the beginning of sentence 11 (reproduced below)?

The government should not force them to move because of the possibility of disaster.

(A) Despite these realities
(B) For all these reasons
(C) Misunderstanding their excuses
(D) Against these justifications
(E) Escalating these tenets

6. In context, which would be the best place to insert the following sentence?

Slow, predictable lava flow is not much of a hazard.

(A) After sentence 2
(B) After sentence 4
(C) After sentence 6
(D) After sentence 7
(E) After sentence 10

Answers and Explanations: Problem Set 6

1. **E** Choice A is very wordy. Choices B and D say that the second half of the sentence is a continuation of the first half. However, in the original sentence, the second half opposes the first. Choice C may seem appealing, but it personifies the volcano, giving it the ability to choose to let cities grow by not exploding.

2. **A** Choices C and E mean the opposite of "also," the word you need for this transition. Choices B and D mean that this sentence follows the previous one in sequence. However, this sentence does not directly follow the idea of drizzling lava. Instead, it adds another point to the whole argument. Therefore, choice A is the best choice.

3. **D** Choices A, C, and E have different meanings from "face." Choice B seems attractive, but the sentence is looking for people to do more than acknowledge their fears. Therefore, choice D is the best answer.

4. **A** Choices B and C oppose the main point of the essay. Choices D and E make assumptions not stated in the essay. Choice A best summarizes the gist of the essay.

5. **B** Choices A, C, and D incorrectly state that this sentence will be different, rather than include, the previous sentences. Choice E may seem like a good option, but there are no "tenets" mentioned in this paragraph. Therefore, choice B is best.

6. **B** Sentence 4 describes how some active volcanoes merely drizzle out lava, implying that they are therefore not very dangerous. This new sentence would explicitly make that point. Choice A would start the author's rationale too early, since sentence 3 begins *first of all*. Choice C follows a sentence about facing fears, whereas the new sentence is suggesting there is little to fear. Choices D and E relate to why people want to live near a volcano. This new sentence relates to why people do not need to fear living near a volcano, which was discussed in the second paragraph.

On the following pages, you will find a practice Grammar section, similar to what you will find on the SAT. Give yourself exactly 25 minutes to complete this test section. Good luck!

Chapter 15
Practice Section for the SAT

SECTION 6
Time — 25 minutes
35 Questions

Turn to Section 6 of your answer sheet to answer the questions in this section.

Directions: For each question in this section, select the best answer from among the choices given and fill in the corresponding circle on the answer sheet.

The following sentences test correctness and effectiveness of expression. Part of each sentence or the entire sentence is underlined; beneath each sentence are five ways of phrasing the underlined material. Choice A repeats the original phrasing; the other four choices are different. If you think the original phrasing produces a better sentence than any of the alternatives, select choice A; if not, select one of the other choices.

In making your selection, follow the requirements of standard written English; that is, pay attention to grammar, choice of words, sentence construction, and punctuation. Your selection should result in the most effective sentence—clear and precise, without awkwardness or ambiguity.

Example:

Laura Ingalls Wilder published her first book and she was sixty-five years old then.
(A) and she was sixty-five years old then
(B) when she was sixty-five
(C) at age sixty-five years old
(D) upon the reaching of sixty-five years
(E) at the time when she was sixty-five

1. Americans vote for an electoral college, not a president, since such is the case, a candidate can win the popular vote but still lose the election.

    (A) since such is the case, a candidate can win the popular vote but still lose the election
    (B) and a candidate can win the popular vote but still lose the election because of that
    (C) a candidate can win the popular vote but still lose the election as a result
    (D) a candidate can win the popular vote but still lose the election for this reason
    (E) so a candidate can win the popular vote but still lose the election

2. Gabriel García Márquez's novel *One Hundred Years of Solitude* had the same influence as James Joyce's *Ulysses* also did: Both books changed the way we approach literature.

    (A) as James Joyce's *Ulysses* also did
    (B) as that which James Joyce's *Ulysses* also did
    (C) as James Joyce's *Ulysses* did
    (D) like that which James Joyce's *Ulysses* did
    (E) like that of James Joyce's *Ulysses* did

3. The requirements for becoming an astronaut is knowledge of physics and physical fitness rather than simple bravery and a sense of adventure.

    (A) The requirements for becoming an astronaut is
    (B) An astronaut, it requires
    (C) The job of an astronaut requires
    (D) In becoming an astronaut is required
    (E) As for becoming an astronaut

4. The survivor of poverty and child abuse, her show deals with Oprah's recovery as well as the spiritual growth of her viewers.

    (A) her show deals with Oprah's recovery as well as the spiritual growth of her viewers
    (B) Oprah's recovery and the spiritual growth of her viewers is the subject of her show
    (C) the subject of her show is Oprah's recovery as well as the spiritual growth of her viewers
    (D) Oprah deals with her recovery as well as the spiritual growth of her viewers on her show
    (E) Oprah, whose show deals with her recovery as well as the spiritual growth of her viewers, discusses this on her show

GO ON TO THE NEXT PAGE

5. Winning medal after medal at the Olympic Games in 1984, Mary Lou Retton's gymnastic abilities delighted her coaches.

   (A) Winning medal after medal at the Olympic Games in 1984, Mary Lou Retton's gymnastic abilities delighted her coaches.
   (B) Winning medal after medal at the Olympic Games in 1984, Mary Lou Retton delighted her coaches with her gymnastic abilities.
   (C) With winning medal after medal at the Olympic Games in 1984, Mary Lou Retton's gymnastic abilities delighted her coaches.
   (D) Mary Lou Retton, winning medal after medal at the Olympic Games in 1984, her coaches were delighted with her gymnastic abilities.
   (E) The winning of medal after medal at the Olympic Games in 1984 delighting Mary Lou Retton's coaches, thanks to her gymnastic abilities.

6. Wild bears, when surprised in their natural habitats, can be violent, the best course of action is to avoid bears altogether.

   (A) Wild bears, when surprised in their natural habitats, can be violent,
   (B) Wild bears, surprising in their natural habitats, can be violent, therefore
   (C) Wild bears, when surprised in their natural habitats, can be violent, however
   (D) Because wild bears, when surprised in their natural habitats, can be violent,
   (E) When wild bears, surprised in their natural habitats, can be violent,

7. Los Angeles's freeways, usually busier and more crowded than those of other cities, are clogged almost twenty-four hours a day, contributing to the city's pollution problem.

   (A) Los Angeles's freeways, usually busier and more crowded than those of other cities,
   (B) The freeways of Los Angeles, which are usually busier and more crowded with cars than other cities,
   (C) The freeways of Los Angeles, usually busier and more crowded than other cities,
   (D) The freeways of Los Angeles, usually busier and crowding with cars than other cities,
   (E) Usually busier and more crowded than other cities, the freeways of Los Angeles

8. Because the pioneers had to travel across hostile lands, encountering weather, illness, and injury is the reason why many were reluctant to make the journey.

   (A) Because the pioneers had to travel across hostile lands, encountering weather, illness, and injury is the reason why
   (B) Because the pioneers had to travel across hostile lands, encountering weather, illness, and injury,
   (C) Pioneers had to travel across hostile lands, encountering weather, illness, and injury and is the reason why
   (D) As a result of having to travel across hostile lands, encountering weather, illness, and injury
   (E) The fact that the pioneers had to travel across hostile lands, encountering weather, illness, and injury is why

9. Set in the sixteenth century, modern audiences enjoyed the contemporary opera *Galileo, Galilei* written by Philip Glass.

   (A) century, modern audiences enjoyed the contemporary opera *Galileo, Galilei* written by Philip Glass
   (B) century and written by Philip Glass, modern audiences enjoyed the contemporary opera *Galileo, Galilei*
   (C) century, the contemporary opera *Galileo, Galilei* was written by Philip Glass and enjoyed by modern audiences
   (D) century, Philip Glass's contemporary opera *Galileo, Galilei* has enjoyed great success with modern audiences
   (E) century, Philip Glass wrote the contemporary opera *Galileo, Galilei* which enjoyed great success with modern audiences

10. Eating cholesterol-rich foods is one of the leading causes of high cholesterol; another equally damaging is a lack of exercise.

   (A) cholesterol; another
   (B) cholesterol, another one that is
   (C) cholesterol, the other that is
   (D) cholesterol; another one which is being
   (E) cholesterol, another cause that is

GO ON TO THE NEXT PAGE

11. <u>Whenever television is denounced by viewers for its violence, they call</u> on the department of Standards and Practices to take action.

    (A) Whenever television is denounced by viewers for its violence, they call

    (B) Whenever television is denounced by viewers calling on its violence,

    (C) Whenever television is denounced for its violence, viewers call

    (D) Whenever viewers denounce television for its violence, they call

    (E) Whenever a denunciation of television is voiced, they call

GO ON TO THE NEXT PAGE

The following sentences test your ability to recognize grammar and usage errors. Each sentence contains either a single error or no error at all. No sentence contains more than one error. The error, if there is one, is underlined and lettered. If the sentence contains an error, select the one underlined part that must be changed to make the sentence correct. If the sentence is correct, select choice E. In choosing answers, follow the requirements of standard written English.

Example:

The other delegates and him immediately
    A   B   C

accepted the resolution drafted by the
                        D

neutral states. No error
           E

A B C D E

12. The vegetarian movement in this country, which has

   shown increasing growth over the last thirty years,
           A   B

   was begun at a farm in Wheaton, Vermont,
        C

   in the late 1800's. No error
    D   E

13. Although they have radically different career
        A   B

   plans, Luna and Gabriel both hope to be
                   C

   a Michigan State graduate one day. No error
         D   E

14. Ever since his promotion to manager last year, John is the
          A   B

   hardest-working employee of this small and
         C

   highly industrious company. No error
        D   E

15. Even though a promotion might be a
        A

   somewhat easy method for a store to boost sales, they
        B   C   D

   may lead some people to shop irresponsibly. No error
                        E

16. To create a pasta with a richer egg flavor, Martha urged
      A

   her audience to separate the egg whites with the egg
       B   C

   yolks. No error
    D   E

17. Like many other forms of social organization, a commune
             A

   functions smooth only as long as everyone works
      B   C   D

   together. No error
         E

18. Before Homecoming Weekend, Lucia and Kiki took time
                                  A

   to study for the upcoming finals, but as a result of the
                             B

   game and many parties, she needed to study again.
                 C   D

   No error
    E

19. Only infrequently did James laugh at the jokes that the
      A

   comedian has been telling; James simply did not find the
           B

   comedian's punch lines, none of which seemed original,
                       C

   to be funny. No error
      D   E

20. One of the most imminent dangers to the Kemp's ridley
               A

   turtle, the smallest of all sea turtles, is that the female nests
                       B

   only on a small stretch of beach in Mexico that is now the
        C   D

   target of developers. No error
            E

21. Widespread wildfires followed by heavy rains can result
      A   B

   in mudslides, which have harmful affects on the
                   C   D

   environment. No error
         E

GO ON TO THE NEXT PAGE ⟩

22. It is difficult for my friends and I even to contemplate
    _____A_____ _____B_____
    playing chess against someone accused of cheating.
    ___C___   ___D___
    No error
    ___E___

23. The existence of consistent rules are important if a
    _____A_____ ___B___
    teacher wants to run a classroom efficiently.
    _____C___   ___D___
    No error
    ___E___

24. Students in the literature course will explore ways

    in which Medieval authors represented themes of their
    ___A___   _____B_____
    time, and will have read Augustine's *Confessions*,
    _____C_____
    Boccaccio's *Decameron*, and Heloise and Abelard's
                        _____D_____
    Letters. No error
              ___E___

25. When one is sitting in a crowded theater, surrounded by
    ___A___
    an audience that has paid good money to see a play of
                  ___B___
    such historical significance, the least you can do is
                                              ___C___
    refrain from unnecessary conversation. No error
    ___D___   ___E___

26. No matter how many times a person has driven in
                                     ___A___
    inclement weather, they should be especially
                      _____B_____ ___C___
    careful when driving down a road that is covered with wet
                                    ___D___
    snow. No error
         ___E___

27. By the time the composer was considered successful, he
    ___A___   _____B_____
    had already published numerous symphonies.
    ___C___   ___D___
    No error
    ___E___

28. When Dr. Jantos speaks, she does not attempt
    ___A___   ___B___
    to impress her listeners with her speaking.
    ___C___   ___D___
    No error
    ___E___

29. After engaging in a spirited debate, everyone except
          ___A___
    Andrea and I decided to watch the latest action film, even
    ___B___ ___C___
    though the rest of the group had already seen it. No error
                                   ___D___   ___E___

GO ON TO THE NEXT PAGE ⟶

Directions: The following passage is an early draft of an essay. Some parts of the passage need to be rewritten.

Read the passage and select the best answers for the questions that follow. Some questions are about particular sentences or parts of sentences and ask you to improve sentence structure or word choice. Other questions ask you to consider organization and development. In choosing answers, follow the requirements of standard written English.

Questions 30-35 are based on the following passage.

(1) After eating gelato in Italy in Florence, I was amazed that it was not sold in America. (2) Gelato is Italian ice cream, but its smoother and fluffier than ours. (3) Some American cities do have gelato shops also called gelaterias and some ice cream manufacturers produce processed gelato. (4) Neither tastes like Italian gelato. (5) I decided to try to figure out why the flavors and textures differ. (6) I decided to make my own gelato.

(7) I discovered that gelato is very, very hard to make well. (8) First, it needs to have some air by churning it in to make it fluffy, but not too much air because too much air would make it too fluffy. (9) Stores and manufacturers add things like emulsifiers to keep things fluffy long term. (10) Gelato in Italy is made and eaten on the same day so the texture does not need artificial and chemical preservatives.

(11) Flavors of American versions of gelato were bland in comparison in order to mass-produce ice cream of any sort American producers find it easier to use frozen canned or otherwise preserved fruits. (12) By highly processing fruits and other ingredients, they lose a lot of flavor. (13) Italian producers purchase just enough fresh fruit to make the day's batch of gelato.

(14) In conclusion, gelato does not work in America because it's nature prevents it from mass production. (15) Good gelato must be created correctly, in the Italian way, in small batches and using the freshest ingredients.

30. In context, which is the best word to insert before the underlined portion of sentence 4 (reproduced below) to connect this sentence to the rest of the first paragraph effectively?

    Neither tastes like Italian gelato.

    (A) However
    (B) Consequently
    (C) Additionally
    (D) Subsequently
    (E) And

31. In context, which of the following is the best version of sentences 5 and 6 (reproduced below) ?

    I decided to try to figure out why the flavors and textures differ. I decided to make my own gelato.

    (A) In order to make my own gelato, I decided to discern why the flavors and textures differ.
    (B) The flavors and textures differ, so I attempted to create my own gelato.
    (C) In order to determine why the flavors and textures differ, I decided to make my own gelato.
    (D) Since the flavors and textures differ, I decided to find out why.
    (E) My gelato illustrated why the flavors and textures differ.

32. The writer's main rhetorical purpose in the essay is to

    (A) advertise for Florentine ice cream
    (B) describe the process of creating gelato
    (C) explain the narrator's obsession with gelato production
    (D) illustrate why Italians eat gelato on the day of its creation
    (E) show why Italian gelato is superior to American gelato

GO ON TO THE NEXT PAGE

33. In context, which of the following is the best revision of sentence 8 (reproduced below) ?

First, it needs to have some air by churning it in to make it fluffy, but not too much air because too much air would make it too fluffy.

(A) First, one fluffs gelato by churning it carefully to ensure the perfect quantity of air is added.

(B) To make gelato fluffy, one must churn in air and watch the texture so that too much air is not churned in.

(C) By expanding gelato's fluffiness, one is careful to avoid air.

(D) Too much air transforms gelato into ice cream; one can avoid this by churning.

(E) One can churn air into gelato for fluffiness; beware excess air which makes the gelato overly fluffy and incorrect.

34. In sentence 9, "things" is best replaced by

(A) stuff
(B) ingredients
(C) processes
(D) objects
(E) manufacturers

35. In context, which of the following is the best revision of sentence 14 (reproduced below) ?

In conclusion, gelato does not work in America because it's nature prevents it from mass production.

(A) (As it is now)

(B) Since gelato does not work in America because its nature prevents it from mass production.

(C) However, gelato is not possible in America because its nature makes it difficult to mass-produce.

(D) In conclusion, American manufacturers cannot make authentic-tasting gelato because by nature it's difficult to mass-produce.

(E) Being that American manufacturers cannot make authentic-tasting gelato because by nature its difficult to mass-produce.

STOP
If you finish before time is called, you may check your work on this section only.
Do not turn to any other section in the test.

Chapter 16
Practice Section for the SAT Answers and Explanations

ANSWERS AND EXPLANATIONS

1. **E** Choice A, Choice B, and Choice D all have awkward constructions. Choice C is a run-on sentence.

2. **C** Choice A uses the word *also,* which is redundant after *as.* Choice B adds the unnecessary words *that which,* as well as the redundant *also.* Choice D and Choice E use the wrong comparison word *like.*

3. **C** The subject in Choice A, *the requirements,* needs a plural verb. Choice B and Choice D are awkward. Choice E lacks a subject, making it a sentence fragment.

4. **D** Choice A, Choice B, and Choice C do not put the subject of the modifier, *The survivor of poverty and child abuse,* right after the comma where it belongs. Choice E is awkward.

5. **B** Choice A and Choice C say that Retton's abilities were winning the events, not Mary Lou Retton herself. Choice D and Choice E are sentence fragments.

6. **D** Choice D correctly makes the beginning into a clause, so the sentence is no longer a run-on. Choice A, Choice B, and Choice C are run-on sentences. Choice E changes the meaning of the sentence.

7. **A** Choice B, Choice C, and Choice E have a parallelism problem. The freeways of Los Angeles should be compared with the freeways of other cities, not the cities themselves. Choice D incorrectly uses the phrase *crowding with cars.*

8. **B** Choice A, Choice C, and Choice E make the error of using a singular verb *is* to refer to *lands, weather, illness,* and *injury.* Choice D never identifies the subject of the sentence, *pioneers,* and *because* is better construction than *as a result of having to.*

9. **D** Choice A and Choice B are constructed so that the audiences, rather than the opera, are set in the sixteenth century. Choice C employs the passive voice, which is not as strong as the active voice of Choice D. Choice E sets Philip Glass in the sixteenth century.

10. **A** Choice B, Choice C, and Choice E are run-on sentences. Choice D corrects the run-on problem but is awkwardly wordy and uses the *-ing* form of *is.*

11. **D** Choice A, Choice B, Choice C, and Choice E are in the passive voice. Choice D is the only choice that is not passive.

12. **C** If you remove the clause between the commas (*which…years*) you are left with *The vegetarian movement in this country was begun at a farm….* The verb *was begun* is passive and awkward. The movement began once and the action is completed so we should use the simple past tense "began."

13. **D** The subject *Luna and Gabriel* is plural. *A Michigan State* graduate needs to agree with this subject in number but is singular as written. It should be *Michigan State graduates.*

14. **B** Always check that verbs are in the correct tense. The verb *is* is in the simple present tense, yet the context tells us that John was promoted last year and has been a hard worker ever since. To indicate that an action began in the past and continues to the present, use the present perfect tense, "has been."

15. **D** Remember to check that pronouns agree in number with the noun they replace. The pronoun *they* is plural. It replaces the noun *promotion,* which is singular. Therefore, the use of *they* is incorrect.

16. **C** In the correct idiom, the word *separate* should be followed with the preposition *from.* Although *separate* is not right next to its preposition, the rule still applies.

17. **C** *Smooth* is in adjectival form here, but it is modifying the verb *functions,* so it should be an adverb, "smoothly."

18. **C** The sentence includes two singular females (*Lucia and Kiki*). Therefore, the pronoun *she* is ambiguous.

19. **B** The verb *has been telling* (present perfect tense) needs to be the same tense as the verb *did* (past tense). It is therefore incorrect (and should be replaced with "told").

20. **E** There are no errors in the sentence as it is written.

21. **C** *Affects* is usually a verb meaning "to have an influence on," while a noun is needed in the sentence. Therefore, "effects" should be used here to mean "something brought about by a cause or agent; a result."

22. **A** Remember to check that the pronouns are in the correct case. Should the pronoun be *I* or *me*? To see this clearly, remove the other part of the phrase, *my friends and.* Is the correct sentence "It is difficult for I" or "It is difficult for me"? "Me" is correct.

23. **A** Make sure verbs agree with their subjects. The verb is *are,* which is plural. The subject is *existence.* Notice you can take the phrase *of consistent rules* out of the sentence and the sentence still makes sense. This means that *rules* cannot be the subject. Because *existence* is singular and *are* is plural, Choice A is wrong.

24. **C** The verb *will explore* is in the future tense. *Will have read* describes an action that takes place before another action. Because there is no other action that follows, it should be changed to the future tense "will read."

25. **A** The pronoun in the first part of the sentence (*one*) has to be the same as the pronoun in the second part (*you*). Because *you* isn't underlined (and thus can't be changed), our only option is to replace *one is* with "you are."

26. **B** The plural pronoun *they* refers to the singular noun *person* and is therefore incorrect. It should be replaced with "he or she."

27.   **E**   There are no errors in the sentence as it is written.

28.   **D**   The sentence is wordy and redundant. Choice D should simply say "listeners."

29.   **B**   Prepositions like *except* should be followed by the object case; thus, "except Andrea and me" is the correct phrasing.

30.   **A**   Choice B, Choice C, Choice D, and Choice E suggest that sentence 4 stems from the prior sentences as a natural conclusion. However, sentence 4 opposes the previous sentences, so Choice A, *however,* is the best option. Understanding this sentence requires understanding these transition words.

31.   **C**   Choice A is awkward and questionable in meaning. Choice B is close, but leaves out the causal relationship between the sentences, the "why." Choice D, although concise, leaves out the second sentence. Choice E implies the gelato-making experiment was successful, but this is not supported by the text.

32.   **E**   Choice A may have happened inadvertently, but it is not the writer's *main rhetorical purpose.* Choice B is not supported by the text. Choice C is incorrect because *obsession* is extreme and unjustified. Choice D is in the text, but it is not the main purpose of the essay.

33.   **A**   Choice B is still awkward and wordy; it also ends in a preposition. Choice C is incorrect because one is aiming to add air, not avoid it. Choice D is wrong because ice cream is not mentioned. In Choice E, the person speaking changes halfway through the sentence; the first clause is in the third person and the second clause is in the second person command form. Choice E also has unnecessary repetition at the end.

34.   **B**   Choice A is too informal; Choice B is a better choice. Choice C, Choice D, and Choice E aren't things that could be added to the gelato.

35.   **D**   The original sentence is awkward in two places (*gelato does not work in America and prevents it from mass production*) and contains a diction error (*it's,* which means "it is"). Choice B becomes a sentence fragment when *Since,* a word that introduces a dependent clause, replaces *In conclusion.* Also, Choice B corrects only the diction error and does not fix the awkward phrases in the original. The first awkward phrase is replaced by an equally awkward one in Choice C, and the word *However* incorrectly indicates a change of direction in the sentence or a contrast to the previous idea. Both Choice D and Choice E replace both awkward phrases with clearer ones: *gelato does not work in America* becomes *American manufacturers cannot make authentic-tasting gelato,* and *by nature prevents it from mass production* becomes *by nature it's difficult to mass produce.* However, Choice E introduces the sentence with *Being that,* which makes the sentence a fragment, and incorrectly uses *its* to mean "it is." Only Choice D corrects all the errors without adding others.

Chapter 17
The SAT Essay

THE ESSAY

The first section of the SAT will give you 25 minutes to write an essay. ETS will provide you with a brief excerpt, usually no more than about 80 words, often, but not always, from a literary work. This prompt will touch on some issue or perspective, and you will be asked to present your views on the subject.

Your essay will be graded by two readers and will receive a raw score between 2 and 12. This score counts for about 30 percent of your final Writing section score. But don't worry. Writing an essay for a standardized test is a piece of cake, provided you know what qualities are being looked for by ETS.

WRITING THE ETS WAY

Guess how much time is spent reading each essay before assigning a grade. Ten minutes? Nope. Five minutes? Not quite. One to two minutes. And each reader is allowed to read your essay only once. In that amount of time, there's no way the reader can absorb every little detail of your essay. Instead, the reader judges your essay holistically, looking to see if your essay does the following:

1. **Does your essay answer the question?** You have to write your essay on the prompt provided, no matter how dull or uninteresting that topic may be. Make sure you stick to the topic throughout your paper.
2. **Is your essay well-organized?** Make sure your essay contains an introduction paragraph, body paragraphs, and a conclusion. Use nice, clear transitions between topics.
3. **Does your essay make use of specific examples?** Use specific examples to back up your thesis.
4. **Is your essay free of grammatical mistakes?** You don't have to be a top writer to get a great score on the essay. Keep things simple, and avoid the kind of errors found in the grammar section.

PARTS OF THE ESSAY

The Prompt

Here is an example of a typical essay prompt:

Directions: Consider carefully the following excerpt and the assignment below it. Then plan and write an essay that explains your ideas as persuasively as possible. Keep in mind that the support you provide—both reasons and examples—will help make your view convincing to the reader.

> The one constant in human history is change. Whether the change is something as fundamental as the shift from a hunting-and-gathering society to an agricultural society or one as seemingly trivial as the changes in fashion, there is no escaping the mutability of human existence. Clearly, because change is such an inescapable feature of civilization, it must be a good and necessary thing.

Assignment: Do you believe that change is a "good and necessary" thing? In an essay, support your position by discussing an example (or examples) from literature, the arts, science and technology, history, current events, or your own experience or observation.

The essay prompt is designed to be fairly open-ended; you should be able to address the topic in a variety of ways. Most likely, you will

1. agree with the prompt
2. agree, but with certain exceptions
3. disagree with the prompt
4. disagree, but with certain exceptions

Of course, it doesn't matter what angle you take on the prompt—there is no right or wrong answer.

The Introduction

Your goal in the introduction paragraph is to let the reader know what the topic is and then to tell the reader what you will say in your essay about the topic.

If you use the above prompt, your introductory paragraph could look something like this:

> Change is an inevitable fact of life. But is change always for the best? When one considers the potentially dangerous impact of changes such as industrialization and the advent of nuclear technology, it is clear that change, while inescapable, is not always for the best.

That's it. Restate the prompt and then state your thesis.

Body Paragraphs

Each body paragraph should discuss only one example. Your essay will become muddled if you try to do too much in a paragraph. Use a clear transition to begin the body paragraph. Here are some good ones to try.

However	Even though
While	Moreover
Although	Another example
Furthermore	Secondly
In addition	Despite
Therefore	

Your body paragraph should look something like this:

> Although many people might consider industrialization a change for the best, think of all the damage to our culture and environment that industrialization has caused. The proliferation of factories has created serious problems with air and water pollution. Additionally, there has been a human cost. The need for workers has led companies to exploit people and use them as cheap labor. While industrialization does provide us with modern conveniences, it is clear that on the whole this change is not entirely for the best.

Notice how the paragraph stays on topic. The examples support the idea that change is not necessarily good. The sentences are clear and direct.

Try to have two or three body paragraphs. Although it is sad to say, the length of your essay is an important factor. Fill up as many of the available lines as you can.

The Conclusion

Your essay must have a conclusion. All you need to do in the conclusion is restate your thesis, like so:

In light of the above examples, it is clear that change is not always for the best. The examples of industrialization and nuclear technology demonstrate that change, while in some ways beneficial, brings about a number of negative consequences.

PACING ON THE ESSAY

You have 25 minutes for the essay. Spend the first five minutes reading the prompt and brainstorming examples. Try to come up with at least three examples. You may even want to think of general examples before the test. Historical facts, current events, and literature are all good sources of examples for your essay.

Use the next 15 minutes to write your essay. Aim for a five-paragraph essay, with an introduction, three body paragraphs, and a conclusion. Stay focused on the topic, and keep things simple.

Take the last five minutes to proofread your essay. Watch out for grammar mistakes—one or two may be okay, but too many of them will hurt your score. If you're unsure how to spell a word, choose a different one.

The visual appearance of your essay is important, as well. While you should avoid double-spacing or otherwise puffing up your essay, it helps to indent your paragraphs, neatly erase any mistakes, and write as legibly as you can manage. If you make the reader's job easier, you're more likely to get a better score.

ESSAY CHECKLIST

When you are finished with the essay prompts below, check each essay using these criteria. If you want a second opinion, ask a friend, parent, or teacher to grade your essay, as well.

Check your essay for

1. An introduction paragraph. Does your introduction paragraph contain a strong topic sentence, one that lets the reader know what the paper will discuss? Does your introduction paragraph mention what examples your paper will include? Does your introduction paragraph end with a clear thesis statement?

2. Body paragraphs. You should have two to three of these. Does each body paragraph contain a nice clear transition sentence? Does each body paragraph develop one and only one example? Does your example clearly support your thesis statement?

3. A conclusion. Your essay has a conclusion, right? Did you restate your thesis? Did you summarize how your examples support your thesis?

4. Grammar and style. Does your essay contain a minimal amount of grammatical mistakes? Look especially for the types of errors that appear on the error ID and improving sentences questions. Try to avoid

   - subject-verb agreement errors. Remember that words like "everyone," "anyone," and "everybody" are singular.
   - ambiguous pronouns. Your writing will be much clearer if you keep pronouns to a minimum.
   - verb tense errors. Keep all your verbs in the same tense.

5. Now look for stylistic issues. Does your essay contain frequent misspellings? Did you vary the length of your sentences? Are your paragraphs indented? Remember: Neatness counts (somewhat), so strive to write as clearly as possible.

SAMPLE ESSAY PROMPTS

Use the following essay prompts to practice writing under pressure. Give yourself 25 minutes for each prompt.

Prompt #1

Directions: Consider carefully the following excerpt and the assignment below it. Then plan and write an essay that explains your ideas as persuasively as possible. Keep in mind that the support you provide—both reasons and examples—will help make your view convincing to the reader.

> We have strived at every turn to progress, to always push forward. Regression will not be tolerated, nor will stagnation—perseverance our only guiding principle. We will not be satisfied with anything less than progress, for progress is always positive.

Assignment: Do you agree that progress is always positive? In an essay, support your position by discussing an example (or examples) from literature, the arts, science and technology, history, current events, or your own experience or observation.

Prompt #2

Directions: Consider carefully the following excerpt and the assignment below it. Then plan and write an essay that explains your ideas as persuasively as possible. Keep in mind that the support you provide—both reasons and examples—will help make your view convincing to the reader.

> The times that call for immediate action are few and far between. Most situations that arise allow for a prudent analysis of the possible courses of action as well as their consequences. A leader who decides recklessly or in haste is remiss in his or her duties as a leader. A true leader makes decisions only after careful deliberation and consideration.

Assignment: Do you believe it is accurate to say that a true leader makes decisions only after careful consideration? In an essay, support your position by discussing an example (or examples) from literature, the arts, science and technology, history, current events, or your own experience or observation.

Prompt #3

Directions: Consider carefully the following excerpt and the assignment below it. Then plan and write an essay that explains your ideas as persuasively as possible. Keep in mind that the support you provide—both reasons and examples—will help make your view convincing to the reader.

> Up to this point, I had not experienced a challenge of this magnitude. Never before had I felt so assailed from all fronts. It was a test. My character and my will would for the first time be tempered by hardship. I knew at this moment that the quality that would be most instrumental to my success was my sense of patience. Yes, the patience to endure. In moments of strife, there is no more useful quality than patience.

Assignment: Which quality do you believe is the most useful during times of difficulty? In an essay, support your position by discussing an example (or examples) from literature, the arts, science and technology, history, current events, or your own experience or observation.

_____

_____

_____

_____

_____

_____

_____

_____

_____

_____

_____

_____

_____

_____

_____

_____

_____

_____

_____

_____

_____

Prompt #4

Directions: Consider carefully the following excerpt and the assignment below it. Then plan and write an essay that explains your ideas as persuasively as possible. Keep in mind that the support you provide—both reasons and examples—will help make your view convincing to the reader.

> None of this matters...not the money, the job, the house, the car, nothing. What matters is that tree, that flower, that line of ants. What matters is waking up each morning and watching the sunrise. What matters is sitting outside in the rain. Those little things are the ones that matter.

Assignment: Do you agree with the claim that it is the little things in life that matter most? In an essay, support your position by discussing an example (or examples) from literature, the arts, science and technology, history, current events, or your own experience or observation.

_____

_____

_____

_____

Prompt #5

Directions: Consider carefully the following excerpt and the assignment below it. Then plan and write an essay that explains your ideas as persuasively as possible. Keep in mind that the support you provide—both reasons and examples—will help make your view convincing to the reader.

> Philosophers are often concerned with how we know things. One position on knowledge posits that in order to appreciate a concept, we must experience its opposite as well. For example, one cannot know what good is until one has encountered evil.

Assignment: Is this a valid viewpoint? Do you agree with the claim that one cannot know a concept without knowing its opposite? In an essay, support your position by discussing an example (or examples) from literature, the arts, science and technology, history, current events, or your own experience or observation.

_____

_____

_____

_____

_____

_____

_____

_____

_____

_____

_____

_____

_____

_____

_____

_____

_____

_____

_____

_____

Prompt #6

Directions: Consider carefully the following excerpt and the assignment below it. Then plan and write an essay that explains your ideas as persuasively as possible. Keep in mind that the support you provide—both reasons and examples—will help make your view convincing to the reader.

America was founded on a paradox. The founding fathers of this country simultaneously stood for rugged individualism and a government by the people and for the people. This contrast has long made the American spirit, to the extent that there is one, one of the most fascinating to sociologists and political scientists. It seems logical that one cannot stand for both individualism and community.

Assignment: Do you agree with the claim that the needs of the individual and the needs of the community must always be at odds? In an essay, support your position by discussing an example (or examples) from literature, the arts, science and technology, history, current events, or your own experience or observation.

Prompt #7

Directions: Consider carefully the following excerpt and the assignment below it. Then plan and write an essay that explains your ideas as persuasively as possible. Keep in mind that the support you provide—both reasons and examples—will help make your view convincing to the reader.

> These difficult times require sacrifice. They require us to give of ourselves. Each one of us must ask "What is it that I can give?" We all have something that we can contribute, and contribute we must, because there is no more noble act, or more noble calling, than to sacrifice oneself for the good of all.

Assignment: Do you believe that sacrifice is the noblest of acts? In an essay, support your position by discussing an example (or examples) from literature, the arts, science and technology, history, current events, or your own experience or observation.

Prompt #8

Directions: Consider carefully the following excerpt and the assignment below it. Then plan and write an essay that explains your ideas as persuasively as possible. Keep in mind that the support you provide—both reasons and examples—will help make your view convincing to the reader.

1. While secrecy can be destructive, some of it is indispensable in human lives. Some control over secrecy and openness is needed in order to protect identity. Such control may be needed to guard privacy, intimacy, and friendship.

2. Secrecy and a free, democratic government, President Harry Truman once said, don't mix. An open exchange of information is vital to the kind of informed citizenry essential to healthy democracy.

Assignment: Do you agree that people need to keep secrets? In an essay, support your position by discussing an example (or examples) from literature, the arts, science and technology, history, current events, or your own experience or observation.

_____
_____
_____
_____
_____
_____
_____
_____
_____
_____
_____
_____
_____
_____
_____
_____
_____
_____
_____
_____
_____
_____

Chapter 18
SAT Vocabulary

VOCABULARY

From a long-term perspective, the best way to improve your vocabulary is to read. Some teachers and vocabulary books will tell you to read the classics or scholarly journals, but if you aren't interested in these things, then reading will be painful and unpleasant, and you won't end up doing it.

Instead, think of a subject that totally fascinates you. It could be anything: the history of comic books, detective novels, sports, true romances, or biographies of popular movie stars. Believe it or not, there will be at least one book available in your library or bookstore on any subject you can think of.

Your English teacher may be horrified, but reading anything will get you into the habit of reading, as well as expose you to new words.

For more vocab prep, check out The Princeton Review's book, *SAT Power Vocab.*.

Of course, you won't know what those words mean unless you look them up. The test writers at ETS use two dictionaries as they assemble words for the SAT: *The American Heritage Dictionary* and *Webster's New Collegiate Dictionary*. We recommend that you buy one of these; you'll need a good dictionary in college anyway. As you read, get into the habit of looking up words you don't know. It's easy to slide over an unfamiliar word, particularly if you understand the rest of the sentence it's in. However, even if you can figure out the author's meaning, make it a point to look up the word.

Some students like to keep small notebooks and pens next to their dictionaries. Whenever they look up words, they write the words down in the notebooks along with two- or three-word definitions. Later they can quiz themselves on the words.

Using the Words You Know

Research has shown that the most effective way to memorize anything is to use it in some organic way. For example, if you wanted to memorize a recipe for baked chicken, the most effective way to do it would be to cook the recipe several times. If you wanted to memorize your lines for a school play, the best way to do it would be to say your lines out loud a few times with a friend. Probably the least effective way to memorize anything is to stare at it on the printed page.

The best way to remember words is to use them frequently in conversation. You may feel a little self-conscious the first couple of times you try this, but as you get used to it, you will become more brazen. It's actually pretty easy to find an excuse to use new vocabulary words in almost any situation.

For example, here's a word from the Hit Parade, chosen at random: "erratic" (meaning "unpredictably eccentric") and a situation, also chosen at random: You are trying to explain to a parent why you didn't get a good grade on a history test. Here are three ways to use the word:

"Mom, I'm sorry my performance has been a little erratic lately." (Playing for sympathy, but also designed to impress her with an adult-sounding word.)

"My history teacher is just so erratic that I don't know what to study. Last time he tested only material from the class, but this time he tested stuff out of the textbook that we never even talked about." (Don't blame me; it's all the fault of my psychotic history teacher.)

"Dad, I must say I find your concern to be erratic at best. If you wanted me to study for this test, you shouldn't have let me watch television all weekend. (The best defense is a good offense.)

ABOUT THE HIT PARADE

Whether you have a year or a week to prepare for the verbal part of SAT, the best way to start is to learn the words that are most likely to show up on the test. We've taken around 250 of the most often-used words on the SAT and put them together in this chapter. You may be surprised at how many of these words you already know. The SAT does not test esoteric words such as "esurient." Instead, you will find words that a college freshman is likely to need to know (for example: "esoteric." Have you looked it up yet?).

Bearing in mind that the best way to learn words is to use them in conversation, we have organized the words around common situations in which you might find yourself. If you are going to be eating dinner with your family, read the "At the Dinner Table" section first, and then try out a few words on your unsuspecting family. If you are going to a basketball game after school, read the section "At the Game" and then casually drop a few Hit Parade words into your color commentary.

Even if one of these "common" situations does not seem pertinent to you— "On Trial for Your Life" comes to mind—make it a point to learn the words anyway. Time has shown that ETS uses these words frequently.

If you find you can't work all these words into your conversation, there are two other great ways to memorize words.

Mnemonics

Many students find that they remember words best if they come up with images to help them remember. These images are known as mnemonics. For example, one of the students in our SAT course wanted to remember the meaning of hiatus ("a break or lapse in continuity").

So whenever she sees that word, she pretends she's addressing a friend:

"Hi, (long pause) Atus."

Another student in our SAT course wanted to remember the meaning of the word abridge ("to shorten"). Whenever he sees the word, he thinks:

"A short bridge."

It doesn't matter how silly or bizarre your image is, as long as you won't forget it.

Flashcards

Just as running lines will help you to memorize your part in a production of *Death of a Salesman*, going over the words on the Hit Parade again and again will help you to commit them to memory. A good way to accomplish this is to write down the words you want to remember—in a notebook or, even better, on flashcards. Put the word on one side of the card and the definition on the other. By carrying the flashcards around with you, you can quiz yourself in spare moments—riding home from school or waiting for class to begin.

A Final Word

No matter how much you practice the techniques in the other sections of this book, you will not substantially improve your verbal score without learning additional vocabulary. The Hit Parade that follows is hopefully only the beginning.

Almost nothing else that you can do will change people's perception of you as much as using a more erudite vocabulary. It's more effective than plastic surgery and much less expensive.

THE HIT PARADE

At the Dinner Table

I **abhor** lima beans; they taste awful to me.

Would it be **presumptuous** of me to ask for seconds?

Your **subtle** use of seasonings was just right.

Hey! Don't **hoard** the mashed potatoes at your end of the table.

I think this rib roast is **tainted**; don't eat it!

abhor	to loathe or detest
hoard	to accumulate or stash away
presumptuous	bold to the point of rudeness
subtle	hardly noticeable
taint	to affect with something harmful; contaminate

On a Diet

No more for me. I'm being **abstemious**.

I'm totally **satiated**. I couldn't eat another bite.

I'm feeling **replete**. No more mashed potatoes for me.

No thanks, more food would be **superfluous**.

No more brussels sprouts; my plate has reached a **plateau**.

I've already had a **surfeit** of dinner. No more, please.

abstemious	sparing in the use of food or drink
plateau	a condition of neither growth nor decline
replete	gorged with food, sated
satiate	satisfy fully
superfluous	unnecessary
surfeit	excess, overindulgence

"What Do You Want to Do?"
"I Don't Know, What Do You Want to Do?"

(With these words, you can take indecision to new heights.)

I'm **vacillating** between going to a movie or going to the mall. What about you?

I'm completely **apathetic**. I'll do whatever you want to do.

Well I'm **indifferent** too. I'll do whatever you want to do.

Maybe because we're feeling so **ambiguous**, we should just hang out here.

No, my mental state is too **precarious** to just stay here.

If you're **skeptical** about your mental health, then maybe we should just skip it.

ambiguous	unclear, having more than one meaning
apathy	lack of interest or caring
indifference	lack of interest, feeling or opinion
precarious	unstable, insecure
skeptical	showing doubt and disbelief
vacillation	wavering, going back and forth

Shopping

I have a **penchant** for blue suede shoes; I can't have enough!

I have such a **paucity** of clothes that I barely have anything to wear.

Dad, you are such a **philanthropist** with your donations to my shopping funds.

I know you may believe I'm being **prodigal**, but I really need this mp3 player.

Do you think I would be a **spendthrift** if I bought this $100 shirt?

I think this blouse has a lot of **utility**—it goes with everything I own!

This shirt is very **versatile**—you can wear it inside-out too!

paucity	small amount or number
penchant	a strong taste or liking
philanthropist	someone who gives to worthy causes
prodigal	wasteful
spendthrift	a person who spends money wastefully
utility	usefulness
versatile	capable of doing many things well

Strong Words

Kim was known for her honesty and **integrity** and would never **exploit** someone's weaknesses to her advantage.

John knew how hard it was to be a beginner, so he was always ready to teach a **novice**. For this, his friends **revered** him.

Selena had a **yearning** to write a 1,000-page novel, and nothing less would **satiate** her. Sadly, the school newspaper could only print a few hundred words, so she had to **truncate** her story considerably.

Though he tried to resist, Larry **succumbed** to his desire for a triple-chocolate fudge sundae.

After the politician was accused of **slander**, Alexandra decided to **terminate** her work for his campaign.

Even though some people thought it was a laughing matter, James talked about it with extreme **sobriety**.

exemplary	worthy of imitation
exploit	to take advantage of; to use selfishly for one's own ends
integrity	honesty; moral uprightness
novice	a person who is new at something
revere	to regard with awe
satiate	satisfy fully
slander	untruthful spoken attack on someone's reputation
sobriety	being quiet or serious
succumb	to give way to superior force
terminate	bring to an end
truncate	shorten by cutting off
yearning	deep longing

On Trial for Your Life

Your honor, the **defendant** is obviously lying; his nose is getting longer.

I ask that this man's **testimony** about the accident be stricken from the record because it disagrees with mine.

In **rebuttal** of the prosecution's case against me, I would like to call my mother to the stand.

I would like to **debunk** this young woman's claim that I am her mother; I have never seen her before in my life.

He is a known **truant**; last week, he showed up at school only twice.

The governor is going to **repeal** the death penalty, but he wants to wait until after your execution.

If I have steak for my last meal, would that **preclude** my having lobster as well?

The man **swindled** innocent people by persuading them to buy **tracts** of land that were underwater at high tide.

It is **patently** obvious that I won't get a fair trial in this state.

The **tacit** opinion of this court is that you are a crybaby, but of course we wouldn't say that to your face.

It is my **unbiased** and **objective** opinion that you are not good at anything.

The judge has decided to **void** the lower court's decision to set you free and instead send you to jail for 144 years.

My client is basically **innocuous**. He wouldn't harm a fly—unless the fly really provoked him.

We are asking that she be held without bail because she has been **elusive** in the past.

I don't know why you waste your time arguing with me. My reasoning is always **infallible**.

I find your arguments to be **trite**—almost clichés.

I **infer** from your gagging noises that you don't think much of my conclusion.

May I raise one small **quibble**? Your mother wears army boots.

debunk	to expose the falseness of something or someone
defendant	someone who has been accused of committing a crime
elusive	cleverly avoiding or escaping
infallible	unable to be proven wrong
infer	conclude by reasoning
innocuous	causing or intending little or no harm
objective	not affected by personal feelings
quibble	*v*: to make a minor objection *n*: a small objection
patent	obvious, readily visible
preclude	to make impossible
rebuttal	reply to a criticism or challenge
repeal	to take back a law or other decision
swindle	to cheat out of money or property
tacit	implied, not stated outright
testimony	statement in support of something, often under oath
tract	a piece of land
trite	overused, lacking freshness
truant	someone who cuts school or neglects his or her duties
unbiased	without prejudice
void	to invalidate

The "Artsy" Book Report

The **aesthetic** sensibility demonstrated by the writing took my breath away.

I found the book to be so **stylized** that I couldn't empathize with the characters. The central **paradox** of this book is that any publisher would be foolish to print it in the first place.

The author offers a rich **mosaic** of different immigrants' lives all seamlessly bound together.

The meaning of the passage is almost totally **opaque**—we don't understand the character's motivation, or even what happened to her.

Before I comment on the book's themes, I will begin with a long **synopsis** of the plot.

Each **stanza** of the poem contains three lines, none of which rhyme.

My **thesis** is that the author is in search of his inner child; to prove my point I have written this 900-page manuscript.

At the end of the book, the author returns to the scene that began the book, thus giving a pleasing **symmetry** to the work.

The **phenomena** described in the book are less interesting than the unseen forces that produced them.

While it could be said that *Topics in Linguistic Phonetics* is an **esoteric** book, I for one found it to be a good read.

His art was a **synthesis** of ancient Greek and modern styles.

aesthetic	pertaining to beauty
esoteric	known only by a select few
mosaic	a picture made of small pieces of stone or glass
opaque	not transparent, hard to understand
paradox	something that seems to contradict itself
phenomena	occurrences, facts, or observable circumstances
stanza	section of a poem
stylized	in a particular style, often an unrealistic one
symmetry	balanced proportions
synopsis	plot summary
synthesis	the combining of separate parts to form a whole
thesis	unproven theory; long research paper

At the Game

The spirit of the match was **marred** when the home team refused to shake hands with the visitors.

If we are going to win, we have to **obliterate** its defense.

We must **vanquish** the opposing team in the final quarter.

We're behind by 22 points in the fourth quarter; it's looking **ominous**.

The offsetting penalties **nullified** each other.

The personal foul **negated** the touchdown, and the play had to be done over.

I had a **premonition** about this game so I bet my life savings.

The offense is looking **sluggish**—someone had better wake it up.

You know, the cast on his leg has barely affected his **mobility**.

There is **speculation** that he might be traded to the Bulls.

The **supremacy** of our volleyball team was evident as it handily defeated its opponents.

The cheerleaders **synchronized** their movements so that they finished at precisely the same instant.

Lisa was an **unheralded** volleyball player until she won the big game for us; now, of course, we treat her like a star.

The coach was suspended from the NCAA for **unethical** practices.

Its victory over State University was **unprecedented**; in 30 years of competition, State University has always won.

marred	impaired the perfection of
mobility	ability to move or be moved
negate	to destroy the validity of something
nullify	to make invalid or worthless
obliterate	to wipe out, remove all traces
ominous	signaling something evil is about to happen
premonition	a feeling that something is about to happen
sluggish	lacking energy
speculation	the act of thinking about or pondering something
supremacy	the state of being supreme, or having the most power
synchronize	to cause to occur at the same time
unethical	having bad moral principles
unheralded	unnoticed or unappreciated
unprecedented	without parallel
vanquish	overpower an enemy completely

Homework Excuses (My Canine Devoured It)

Do not **condemn** me for not doing my homework, Ms. Cornwell! There are **mitigating** circumstances: I felt it would be **detrimental** to my development if I were to be tied down to the mindless **conformity** of such **conventional** homework.

I also thought that so much typing might **exacerbate** the injury to my wrist.

The book was so **opaque** that I didn't understand a word. Moreover, it was so **soporific** that I couldn't stay awake while reading it.

I know this may sound **implausible**, but as an alternative form of homework I wrote a 50-page paper. I know that it contains a few errors—after all, no one is **infallible**.

Not a single bit of it was **plagiarized**; I wrote it all myself. Although it does contain one paragraph that could be considered a **pastiche**.

condemn	to express strong disapproval of
conformity	the act of becoming similar or identical to
conventional	traditional, mundane
detrimental	causing damage or harm
exacerbate	to make worse
implausible	not possible, not imaginable
infallible	unable to be proven wrong
mitigate	to make less severe
opaque	not transparent, hard to understand
pastiche	piece of music, writing, or art combining several different sources or styles
plagiarist	a person who presents someone else's work as his or her own
soporific	causing sleep

Responses to Parents

But Mom, the music is practically **inaudible** right now.

An 11 o'clock curfew is so **provincial**.

or if you really want to impress them...

This punishment is **tantamount** to **persecution**.

Okay, so I didn't take out the garbage, but don't worry; I'll **rectify** the situation tomorrow.

My room is my **sanctuary**. Please leave.

I'm not active; I'm **slothful**.

Please don't **provoke** me now; I'm feeling very **vulnerable**.

I hereby **renounce** all blood-ties to you.

inaudible	too quiet to be heard
persecution	tormenting a person because of his or her beliefs
provincial	having a narrow scope
provoke	anger, arouse, bring to action
rectify	fix, correct
renounce	to give up or put aside
sanctuary	a safe place or a room for worship
slothful	lazy
tantamount	equivalent in effect or meaning
vulnerable	capable of being hurt

Writing the College Essay

There are many examples that testify to my **indomitable** spirit; for example, when I stubbed my toe before a big test, I went right ahead and took that test, even though I was in tremendous pain. I could have gone to the nurse to get an excuse, but my **innate integrity** would not allow me to take the easy way out.

Although I am only 17 years old, I am considered a **pioneer** in microbiology, having made many important discoveries in the field. Indeed, some colleagues have been tempted to call me **omniscient** because I seem to have an almost encyclopedic grasp of the subject matter. However, my modesty always makes me tell them that they must **temper** their hero-worship. After all, even if my genius makes any modesty **superfluous**, I still **strive** to be a regular guy, who just happens to have the **vitality** of a superhero and the **virtue** of Mother Teresa.

indomitable	unable to be subdued or overcome
innate	existing in a person since birth; part of the character of something
integrity	honesty; moral uprightness
omniscient	having complete knowledge
pioneer	*n.* a leader in a field; *v.* to lead the way in a field
strive	try hard, make a major effort
superfluous	unnecessary
temper	to moderate, to make less extreme
virtue	moral excellence
vitality	energy, liveliness

The Job Interview

My worst attribute? I'm too **meticulous**; no detail is too small for me to keep track of.

My work methods are very **methodical** and **systematic**; I always start with task A and then move to task B.

No task is too **mundane** or **monotonous** for me, and I'll always perform it with a smile.

May I ask how much you paid my **predecessor**?

Give me your biggest problems and I'll solve them. I'm very **resourceful**.

I actually like **subordinate** roles; I don't like responsibility.

I see myself as a **utility** player. I can fit into lots of situations. I'm very **versatile**.

Energy? Are you kidding? I have lots of **vigor**. I'm just full of **zeal**.

So, what's the **prevailing** wage at this Gap outlet?

methodical	orderly; having a set system
meticulous	very careful; attentive to details
mundane	ordinary or commonplace
monotonous	boring; unvarying in tone or content
predecessor	a person who precedes another in an office or a position
prevailing	generally accepted; having superior power
resourceful	able to find solutions
subordinate	placed in a lower order or rank
systematic	regular
utility	usefulness
versatile	capable of doing many things well
vigor	energy, vitality
zeal	enthusiasm and intensity

Alternate Words for "Cool"

"So what do you think of Lisa?"

"She's totally cool."

"Could you be more specific?"

If you think she's clever, "She's **witty**."

If she's clever in a sophisticated sort of way, "She's **urbane**."

If she's clever in a dry sort of way, "She's **wry**."

If she's really lively, "She's **vivid**."

If she's really important, "She's **vital**."

If she's new and different, "She's **novel**."

If her comments are short and to the point, "She's **succinct**."

If she's never ruffled, "She's **serene**."

If she never gives up, "She's **resolute**."

If she can always get out of gym class, "She's **ingenious**."

If she goes beyond all known limits, "She's **transcendent**."

ingenuity	cleverness; originality
novel	original, new, and different
resolute	strongly determined
serene	calm, peaceful
succinct	brief, concise
transcendent	going beyond known limits
urbane	highly sophisticated
vital	full of energy; necessary for life
vivid	sharp, intense; making an impression on the senses
witty	clever or amusing
wry	dryly humorous

You're in Love with Him/Her, So You Have to Try to Explain Him/Her to Your Friends

It's not that he can't talk; he's just **taciturn**.

It's not that he doesn't have an opinion; he's just **reticent**.

She didn't insult you on purpose; it was **unwitting**.

He's not **arrogant**; he's just very confident.

It's not that she hates the entire human race; she's just a little **cynical**.

I'm sure it wasn't **deliberate**. It must have been unintentional.

He's not a **dupe**. He's just very naive.

She's not **gullible**. She's just very innocent.

She's not a **miser**; she's just extremely careful with her money.

She's not **obsessive**. She just happens to like arranging her dolls in exact size order.

He's not a **recluse**. He just enjoys his solitude.

It's not that he isn't passionate. He's **stoic**.

He isn't exactly **strident**; he's just a little grating.

It's not that she's **vengeful**; she just never forgets a slight.

I admit he's a little **vociferous**, but to my knowledge, his **tirades** have never broken anyone's eardrum.

She isn't **verbose**; she just uses a lot of words.

She isn't **sullen**; she's mysterious.

He isn't **torpid** or **slothful**; he's just kind of tranquil.

She isn't a **traitor**; she's just not loyal.

It's not that he's unfaithful. He just likes a lot of **diversity**.

It's not that he's **indecisive**; he just has trouble making up his mind.

She isn't **erratic**; she simply has her own way of doing things.

It's not that she has no personality; she is just **tactful**.

She isn't nosy; she's just very **inquisitive**.

We're a great match; her **tranquility** offsets my nervous personality.

She's not unfocused; she just has **vague** career plans.

arrogance	overconfidence
cynicism	the belief that all human action is motivated by selfishness
deliberate	*adj.* intentional, well thought out; *v.* to consider carefully
diversity	the state of having different elements
dupe	a person easily deceived
erratic	unpredictably eccentric
gullible	easily deceived
indecision	inability to decide
inquisitive	curious
miser	one who saves greedily
obsessive	overly preoccupied
recluse	someone who lives in seclusion
reticent	untalkative, shy, reluctant to speak
slothful	lazy
strident	harsh, grating
stoic	not affected by passion or feeling
sullen	sad, sulky
tactful	saying or doing the proper thing
taciturn	being of few words
tirade	a long, harsh, often abusive speech
torpid	without energy, sluggish

traitor	one who betrays a person, cause, or country
tranquillity	calmness, peacefulness
unwitting	unaware
vague	not precise, unclear
vengeful	wanting or seeking revenge
verbosity	the use of too many words
vociferous	loud

Baby-sitting

Hello, 911? Is there an **antidote** if someone just drank a whole bottle of Maalox?

Young man, your **impudence** is not respectful to someone who is as old as I am.

Young lady, you are **incorrigible**; they are going to lock you up and throw away the key.

Don't write on the wall, Timmy! That magic marker is **indelible**.

You may be your parents' sole **heir**, but if you don't get down from that refrigerator, you won't live to inherit.

Don't **provoke** me, young man.

If you and your sister want to engage in sibling **rivalry**, it's okay with me so long as there are no scars on your bodies.

Jessica screams all night, so I may need something **soporific** to **subdue** my anxiety and get some sleep. . .something strong enough to **stupefy** me.

Don't try to **undermine** my authority!

You **wily** little brat. I can tell you're still awake.

antidote	remedy for a poison
heir	a person who inherits another's belongings
impudence	bold disrespect or rudeness
incorrigible	not capable of being reformed
indelible	incapable of being erased
provoke	anger, arouse, bring to action
rivalry	an ongoing competition
soporific	causing sleep
stupefy	to make less alert
subdued	quiet, controlled, lacking in intensity
undermine	to injure or destroy underhandedly
wily	artful, cunning, deceitful, sly

Alternate Words for "Bogus"

"So what do you think of Dave?"

"He's totally bogus."

"Could you be more specific?"

If he's narrow-minded, he's just very **parochial**.

If he just doesn't matter, he's **irrelevant**.

If he's really ordinary, he's **mediocre** or **mundane**.

If he's got nothing to offer, he's **meager**.

If he's really boring, he's **monotonous**.

If he's gloomy, he's **morose**.

If he's been superseded by someone else, he's **obsolete**.

If he's no longer relevant, he's **extraneous**.

If he has no moral principles, he's **unethical**.

If he makes you nervous, he's **unnerving**.

If he's lacking freshness, he's **trite**.

If he's not in good taste, he's **unseemly**.

If he's not a solid character, he's **unsound**.

If he isn't a serious person, he's **superficial**.

If no one knows who he is, he's **obscure**.

extraneous	not pertinent or relevant
irrelevant	not necessary or important to the matter at hand
meager	lacking in amount or quality; poor
mediocrity	ordinariness; lack of distinction
monotonous	boring; unvarying in tone or content
morose	gloomy; ill-tempered
mundane	ordinary or commonplace
obscure	not known; difficult to understand
obsolete	outdated
parochial	having a narrow scope
superficial	near the surface; slight
trite	overused, lacking freshness
unseemly	unbecoming
unsound	not solid; not well founded; not healthy
unethical	having bad moral principles
unnerving	upsetting; causing nervousness

Meeting Royalty

Well, your highness, it's been a **tumultuous** year what with all the scandals.

Are you planning to disinherit any of your **heirs**?

Do you **sanction** your son's behavior?

Have you considered imposing **sanctions** on your son's behavior?

I hear that to be queen of England you have to be willing to wear **ghastly** clothes.

When a **monarch** has relatives like yours, it must be tough to keep your sense of humor.

The constant **lampoons** in the newspapers must be very hard to laugh at when you are their subject.

With the King's death, I imagine there is very little **levity** in the palace right now.

Tell me, your highness, has anyone tried to **usurp** the throne lately?

I've never met such a **lofty magnate** as yourself. Could I have your autograph?

Actually, I'm very **prominent** in Omaha, Nebraska; everybody knows me there.

Long may you **reign**, but could I have that scepter when you kick the bucket?

Are you thinking of **repudiating** your claim to rule America?

Would you take a picture of me posing with this **sentinel**?

These journalists seem to be **ubiquitous**; can't you get rid of them?

ghastly	shockingly frightful
heir	a person who inherits another's belongings
lampoon	sharp satire
levity	lightness; lacking seriousness
lofty	having great height or a stately manner
magnate	a person of great influence in a particular field
monarch	a ruler; a king, queen, or emperor
prominent	standing out, important
reign	*n.* having supreme power; *v.* to rule
repudiate	to cast off or disown; to refuse to acknowledge
sanction	*v.* to give permission; *n.* a coercive measure designed to make a person or persons comply
sentinel	a guard, a watchman
tumultuous	characterized by a noisy uproar
ubiquitous	being everywhere at the same time
usurp	to seize power by force

Getting Religion

The two religious sects have gone in **divergent** directions, but they still meet twice per year in Rome to try to **reconcile** their differences.

The **tenets** of his faith included turning the other cheek.

The **theologian** had been studying religion for more than 20 years.

She was a **pious** person who spent much time in prayer.

The **fundamental** beliefs of the church have not changed in 500 years.

Having been raised in an agnostic household, he was unfamiliar with religious **jargon**.

There was great **lamentation** when the Buddhist priest died.

In a recent **purgation**, one religious **sect** was invited to leave the main body because of doctrinal differences.

Many religions portray hell as a huge **conflagration** that will burn for all eternity.

conflagration	a widespread fire
divergent	moving in different directions from a common point
fundamental	basic, essential
jargon	words used by people in a particular field of work
lamentation	an expression of sorrow or deep regret
pious	having reverence for a god
purgation	the process of getting rid of impurities
reconcile	to settle a problem
sect	a subgroup of a religion; faction
tenet	idea or belief
theologian	one who studies religion

How to Succeed in Business

Your **proposal** for a new headquarters is too expensive.

Our board of directors voted **unanimously** against the proposal.

We were **uniform** in our hatred of your plan.

Our **agenda** now is to find an alternate proposal.

Using both proposals would be **redundant**.

The **blueprint** for our new building calls for 40 stories.

This is a **comprehensive** plan that covers every eventuality.

We do not want the government to **regulate** our industry. We prefer to police ourselves.

We hope that the **stimulus** of a cash infusion will turn our company profitable.

Our results are **verifiable**; an accounting firm has gone over our books and pronounced them accurate.

Our results are not **theoretical**; they are based on hard evidence.

There may be some **residual** ill-feeling from our workers after we cut their salaries by 40 percent.

agenda	a schedule of a meeting
blueprint	a detailed outline or plan for a building
comprehensive	including everything; complete
proposal	an offer or consideration for acceptance
redundant	characterized by unnecessary repetition of words or ideas
regulate	to control or direct by some particular method
residual	describing the part left over
stimulus	something that causes a reaction
theoretical	not proven true, existing only as an idea
unanimity	complete agreement
uniform	alike, identical
verifiable	able to be proven true

THE HIT PARADE (IN ALPHABETICAL ORDER)

abhor	to loathe or detest
abridge	to shorten
abstemious	sparing in the use of food or drink
aesthetic	pertaining to beauty
agenda	a schedule of a meeting
ambiguous	unclear; having more than one meaning
amorphous	having no shape
antidote	remedy for a poison
apathy	lack of interest or caring
arrogance	overconfidence
blueprint	a detailed outline or plan for a building
comprehensive	including everything, complete
condemn	to express strong disapproval of
conflagration	a widespread fire
conformity	the act of becoming similar or identical to
conventional	traditional, mundane
cynicism	the belief that all human action is motivated by selfishness
debunk	to expose the falseness
defendant	someone who has been accused of committing a crime
deliberate	*adj.* intentional, well thought out; *v.* to consider carefully
detrimental	causing damage or harm
divergent	moving in different directions from a common point
diversity	the state of being different or having different elements
dupe	a person easily deceived
elusive	cleverly avoiding or escaping
erratic	unpredictably eccentric
esoteric	known only by a select few
exacerbate	to make worse
exemplary	serving as an example; commendable
exploit	to take advantage of, to use selfishly for one's own ends
extraneous	not pertinent or relevant

fluid	capable of flowing; changing readily, as a plan
fundamental	basic, essential
ghastly	shockingly frightful
gullible	easily deceived
hiatus	a break or lapse in continuity
heir	a person who inherits another's belongings
hoard	to accumulate or stash away
implausible	not possible, not imaginable
impudence	bold disrespect or rudeness
inaudible	too quiet to be heard
incorrigible	not capable of being reformed
indecision	inability to decide
indelible	incapable of being erased
indifference	lack of interest, feeling, or opinion
indomitable	unable to be subdued or overcome
infallible	unable to be proven wrong
inferred	concluded by reasoning
ingenuity	cleverness; originality
injurious	causing damage or loss
innate	existing in a person since birth; part of the character of something
innocuous	causing or intending little or no harm
inquisitive	curious
integrity	honesty; moral uprightness
irrelevant	not necessary or important to the matter at hand
jargon	words used by people in a particular field of work
lamentation	an expression of sorrow or deep regret
lampoon	sharp satire
levity	lightness; lacking seriousness
lofty	having great height or a stately manner
lurid	gruesome, melodramatic, shocking
magnate	a person of great influence in a particular field
marred	impaired the perfection of
meager	lacking in amount or quality; poor
mediocrity	ordinariness, lack of distinction
methodical	orderly, having a set system
meticulous	very careful, attentive to details
migrate	to move from one place to another
miser	one who saves greedily
mitigate	to make less severe
mobility	ability to move or be moved
monarch	a ruler; a king, queen, or emperor
monotonous	boring; unvarying in tone or content
morose	gloomy; ill-tempered
mosaic	a picture made of small pieces of stone or glass
mundane	ordinary or commonplace
negate	to destroy the validity of something
novel	original, new and different
novice	a person who is new at something

nullify	to make invalid or worthless
obliterate	to wipe out, remove all traces
obscure	not known; difficult to understand
obsessive	overly preoccupied
objective	not affected by personal feelings
obsolete	outdated
ominous	signaling something evil is about to happen
omniscient	having complete knowledge
opaque	not transparent; hard to understand
paradox	something that seems to contradict itself
parochial	having a narrow scope
pastiche	piece of music, writing, or art combining several different sources or styles
patent	obvious, readily visible
paucity	small amount or number
penchant	a strong taste or liking
persecution	tormenting a person because of his or her beliefs
phenomena	occurrences, facts, or observable circumstances
philanthropist	someone who gives to worthy causes
phonetics	the study of sounds in a language
pioneer	*n.* a leader in a field; *v.* to lead the way in a field
pious	having reverence for a god
plagiarist	a person who presents someone else's work as his or her own
plateau	a condition of neither growth nor decline
precarious	unstable, insecure
preclude	to make impossible
predecessor	a person who precedes another in an office or a position
premonition	a feeling that something is about to happen
presumptuous	bold to the point of rudeness
prevailing	generally accepted; having superior power
prevalent	in general use or acceptance
prodigal	wasteful
prominent	standing out, important
promontory	a high point of land projecting into the sea
proposal	an offer or consideration or acceptance
provincial	having a narrow scope
provoke	anger, arouse, bring to action
purgation	the process of getting rid of impurities
quarry	a large open pit from which stone is cut
quibble	*v.* to make a minor objection; *n.* a small objection
raconteur	skilled storyteller
rebuttal	reply to a criticism or challenge
recant	to take back
recluse	someone who lives in seclusion
reconcile	to settle a problem
rectify	fix, correct
redundant	characterized by unnecessary repetition of words or ideas
reminiscence	a story of past experiences
regulate	to control or direct by some particular method

reign	*n.* having supreme power; *v.* to rule
reiteration	saying or doing something repeatedly
renounce	to give up or put aside
repeal	to take back a law or other decision
repertoire	supply of songs, stories, skills, or devices
replete	gorged with food, sated
repudiate	to cast off or disown; to refuse to acknowledge
residual	describing the part that is left over
resourceful	able to find solutions
resolute	strongly determined
reticent	untalkative, shy, reluctant to speak
retort	*v.* to reply sharply; *n.* a sharp reply
revere	to regard with awe
revelation	striking realization
rivalry	an ongoing competition
sanctuary	a safe place or a room for worship
sanction	*v.* to give permission; *n.* a coercive measure designed to make a person or persons comply
satiate	satisfy fully
sect	a subgroup of a religion; faction
sentinel	a guard, a watchman
serene	calm, peaceful
skeptical	showing doubt and disbelief
slander	untruthful spoken attack on someone's reputation
slothful	lazy
sluggish	lacking energy
sobriety	being quiet or serious
solidarity	fellowship between members of a group
solitude	the state of living or being alone
soporific	causing sleep
speculation	the act of thinking about or pondering something
spendthrift	a person who spends money wastefully
stanza	section of a poem
stimulus	something that causes a reaction
strident	harsh, grating
strive	try hard; make a major effort
stylized	in a particular style, often an unrealistic one
stoic	not affected by passion or feeling
stupefy	to make less alert
subdued	quiet, controlled, lacking in intensity
subordinate	placed in a lower order or rank
subtle	hardly noticeable
sullen	sad, sulky
succinct	brief, concise
succumb	to give way to superior force
superficial	near the surface; slight
superfluous	unnecessary
supremacy	the state of being supreme, or having the most power
surfeit	excess, overindulgence

suppleness	ability to bend easily; limberness
swindle	to cheat out of money or property
synopsis	plot summary
synthesis	the combining of separate parts to form a whole
symmetry	balanced proportions
synchronize	to cause to occur at the same time
synthesis	the combining of separate parts to form a whole
systematic	regular
tacit	implied, not stated outright
taciturn	being of few words
tactful	saying or doing the proper thing
taint	to affect with something harmful; contaminate
tantamount	equivalent in effect or meaning
taper	gradually decrease, grow smaller at one end; dwindle
temper	to moderate, to make less extreme
temperament	one's emotional nature
tenet	idea or belief
terminate	bring to an end
terrestrial	having to do with the earth
testimony	statement in support of something, often under oath
theologian	one who studies religion
theoretical	not proven true, existing only as an idea
thesis	unproven theory; long research paper
tirade	a long, harsh, often abusive speech
torpid	without energy, sluggish
tract	a piece of land
traitor	one who betrays a person, cause, or country
tranquillity	calmness, peacefulness
transcendent	going beyond known limits
trite	overused, lacking freshness
truant	someone who cuts school or neglects his or her duties
truncate	shorten by cutting off
tumultuous	characterized by a noisy uproar
unbiased	without prejudice
ubiquitous	being everywhere at the same time
unanimity	complete agreement
undermine	to injure or destroy underhandedly
unethical	having bad moral principles
unheralded	unnoticed or unappreciated
uniform	alike, identical
unnerving	upsetting; causing nervousness
unprecedented	without parallel
unseemly	unbecoming
unsound	not solid; not well founded; not healthy
unwitting	unaware
urbane	highly sophisticated
usurp	to seize power by force
utility	usefulness
vacillation	wavering; going back and forth

vagary	inconsistent or unpredictable action
vague	not precise; unclear
vane	a device that measures wind direction
vanquish	overpower an enemy completely
vegetation	plant life
veiled	covered or concealed
vengeful	wanting or seeking revenge
vent	express with emotion
verbosity	the use of too many words
uniform	alike, identical
verifiable	able to be proven true
versatile	capable of doing many things well
virtue	moral excellence
vigor	energy, vitality
vital	full of energy, necessary for life
vitality	energy, liveliness
vivid	sharp, intense, making an impression on the senses
vociferous	loud
void	to invalidate
vulnerable	capable of being hurt
wallow	to indulge in a particular state of mind
wariness	cautiousness
wharf	a structure built to extend from the land out over the water
whimsical	eccentric; unpredictable
wily	artful, cunning, deceitful, sly
witty	clever or amusing
wry	dryly humorous
yearning	a deep longing
zealous	very enthusiastic and intense

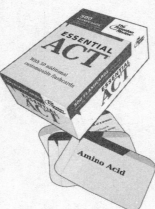

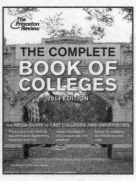